CHILD LANGUAGE

CHILD LANGUAGE:
An Interdisciplinary Guide
to Theory and Research

by
Adele A. Abrahamsen, Ph.D.
NICHD Postdoctoral Research Fellow
Graduate School of Education
University of Pennsylvania

University Park Press
Baltimore • London • Tokyo

UNIVERSITY PARK PRESS
International Publishers in Science and Medicine
Chamber of Commerce Building
Baltimore, Maryland 21202

Typeset by American Graphic Arts Corporation and Alpha Graphics, Inc.
Manufactured in the United States of America by Universal Lithographers,
Inc., and The Optic Bindery Incorporated

Library of Congress Cataloging in Publication Data

Abrahamsen, Adele A.
Child language.

Includes indexes.
1. Children—Language—Bibliography.   2. Psycholinguistics—Bibliography.   I. Title.

Z7004.C45A27   [P118]   016.3726   77-5418
ISBN 0-8391-1128-2

This book is dedicated to Grace Andrus de Laguna, in honor of the 50th anniversary of the publication of her pioneering book, *Speech: Its Function and Development*. A half century later, we are returning to many of her ideas and are enriched by them.

Contents

Preface

Child Language: An Interdisciplinary Guide to Theory and Research is written as a kind of cellulose Excedrin or Cope for academics suffering from the information explosion. The child language literature is spreading exponentially through hundreds of journals and dozens of publishers' book lists. What I have done is to capture the most important literature, organize it, annotate it, and display it in the most useful format I could devise. I hope it helps.

The core of the guide was a modest bibliography written for my graduate course in language development at Rutgers University in the autumn of 1975. However, as my own research emphasis changed from adult to developmental psycholinguistics, I embarked on a systematic attempt to master the literature and incorporated the results into the course bibliography. Also, I found that one of the most difficult aspects of child language research for most people was identifying relevant background material from linguistics, cognitive psychology, and related fields. My original training was in these areas, and so I was frequently called upon to help out with suggestions. I added these to the growing document, along with some introductory comments on the various child language research areas, and the result was the first draft of *Child Language*, completed in the summer of 1976. In January 1977, I revised and updated it through 1976 (limited to about 20 journals and 15 book publishers). Thanks to the efforts of University Park Press to put wings on this project, the guide should be only a few months behind the literature when it reaches its first users.

The prototypical user is someone trying to identify or learn the literature on children's language acquisition or some specific topic in that field. He or she might be a graduate student studying for prelims or taking a language acquisition course, a student or researcher designing an experimental study, or a professional in another field who wants to gain access to material that can be applied to that field. However, *Child Language* is complete enough that child language researchers themselves will find it a time-saving reference book. At the other end of the scale, its topical organization and indices suit it for casual use by people not normally involved with this literature. Because of its subject index, it also serves as a basic bibliography of linguistics, psycholinguistics, cognitive psychology, and cognitive development.

Though there are over 1500 references in these pages, the virtue of this guide is its selectivity. Previously, two major access routes to the child language literature have been available. On the one hand are comprehensive bibliographic sources such as the bibliographies by Leopold and by Slobin (pre-1967) and *Language and Language Behavior Abstracts* (post-1967). These are useful primarily as tools for an intensive literature search. On the other hand are textbooks and review articles, which are helpful for gaining an overview of the field but generally refer only to the most important publications. *Child Language* fills the gap between comprehensive bibliographies and overviews. Entries were selected according to my judgment of what books and articles would be relevant to a person doing or learning child language research in the late 1970's, on the basis of influence, exceptional quality, or recency. Thus, the earliest entry is dated 1894; the number of entries increases with the decades between 1920 and 1970 and with the years between 1970 and 1977; and about 5% of the entries were in press for 1977. Unlike most bibliographies, the organization is topical (supplemented by author and subject indices); basic terminology and issues are explained in introductory material; one-third of the items are relevant publications from adjacent fields; and the annotations are generous. I have made every effort to produce a usable handbook rather than a simple compilation of the literature.

Finally, I have tried to be as nonchauvinistic as possible, reaching out to journals I do not usually read, theories I am inclined not to believe, disciplines on the fringes of my knowledge, and countries I have never visited. There were, however, limits to what I could do. First, I had in mind an English-speaking audience and therefore excluded publications not available in English. Similarly, American journals are best represented (with the important exception of *Journal of Child Language,* published in England). Second, I limited the topics to those usually covered in a course on normal, first-language acquisition. Users will find only scattered references (brought together in the subject index) on topics such as bilingualism and second-language learning, assessment and intervention, language deficiency and retardation, sociolinguistics, and the recently active areas of long-term memory and reasoning. Phonology and speech perception were originally given a cursory treatment but were brought up to the standard of the other sections in response to an anonymous reviewer's indignation. Third, the theoretical orientations with which I am familiar are emphasized, for example, applications of generative grammar, speech act theory, and Piagetian cognitive theory. This reflects predominant current trends. I hope that those who prefer other approaches (e.g., tagmemics) will nevertheless find *Child Language* useful.

The design of the guide makes it well suited for course use as well as individual use. It can help structure a course in which no textbook is used, supplementing assigned reading by helping students to identify important publications and get an overview of the others. It also can be used to supplement an assigned textbook. Finally, the guide can be used to direct students' efforts on research papers.

Acknowledgments

Many people contributed time or thought to the enterprise. In the Rutgers University psychology departments, the students and colleagues with whom I did child language research were my prototypical users, and also suggested references. I would like to thank them by name: Marjorie Arnold, Margaret Carson, Erika Ginsberg, Barbara Landau, Christopher Liuzzo, Jerome Knast, Paula Tinder (who was especially helpful in a variety of ways), and Pamela Webb. I also collectively thank the students in my graduate course on language development. Michael Novey co-taught the course the year that I wrote the core bibliography; I benefited from our interaction and appreciate his many specific suggestions. Other colleagues who offered their personal libraries, suggestions, and encouragement were Ann Bodine, Patricia Di Silvio, Carlton James, and Juliet Vogel. The Rutgers University Research Council provided some of the financial support.

The final version was prepared during my current tenure as a Public Health Service Research Fellow under the auspices of the National Institute of Child Health and Human Development, National Institutes of Health. I am grateful for this support, which was helpful in bringing the project to its conclusion. My fellowship sponsor is Lila Gleitman of the Graduate School of Education, University of Pennsylvania. She and her research group have provided stimulation, moral support, advice, comic relief, and the book's title. I would also like to thank the psychology department for access to its library, and other people at the University for various kinds of help: Suzanne Blanc, Marion Gilbert, Nancy Finkelstein, Douglas Lax, Paul Rozin, and Ivan Sag.

Further advice, assistance, or encouragement were provided by a far-flung group of colleagues, teachers, and friends. I appreciate the contributions of Rita Anderson, Louise Cherry, Allan Collins, David Crystal, Susan Fischer, George Mandler, Susan Goldin-Meadow, Shige-Yuki Kuroda, Donald Norman, David Rumelhart, Marilyn Shatz, Patricia Siple, Robert Springer, Eric Wanner, and also the many others who provided a reference or two. Special thanks go to David Pisoni of Indiana University, who generously suggested improvements to a late version of Section 12 at short notice. The section also benefited from comments by Ivan Sag. Any errors of judgment and fact are, of course, my own responsibility.

The four typists did a great job of transforming scribbled index cards into readable copy. I thank Shirley Saltz, Regina Hill, Patty Potts, and Diane Weinstock.

Finally, many other people were helpful indirectly, particularly in opening to me their research fields and their ways of discovery. I value each of them, but can only thank them collectively in this space.

Introduction

GENERAL ORGANIZATION

Child Language: An Interdisciplinary Guide to Theory and Research has approximately 1500 entries, selected on the basis of importance, quality, or recency. One-third were published during 1971–1974, one-third earlier, and one-third more recently. About 5% predate 1960, and another 5% were in press at the beginning of January 1977.

The primary organization of the guide is topical. There are five parts: General Resources, Syntactic Development, Semantic Development, Beyond Grammar, and Phonology and Orthography. These are further divided into 13 sections (Arabic numerals), with 53 subsections (letters A, B, C, etc.) and further subdivisions where appropriate. Entries are listed chronologically within the lowest level of classification. Chronological order is based on date of first publication, not on date of the English language version. However, a book in a second edition is ordered by that date, not by the first edition date. To review the literature on topics such as children's comprehension of active and passive sentences or the cognitive basis of linguistic universals, you simply turn to the appropriate subsection and start reading.

Furthermore, this interdisciplinary guide lives up to its name. Basic bibliographies on linguistics, cognitive psychology, adult psycholinguistics, Piagetian theory, philosophy of language, and artificial intelligence fill an entire section, and more specific references from these adjacent disciplines are listed with the child language research areas to which they apply. Thus, psycholinguistic experiments on adult processing of active and passive sentences precede the developmental studies, and references on three classes of semantic theories accompany the corresponding references on theories of lexical development. Approximately one-third of the total references are from disciplines adjacent to child language.

As an additional aid, introductory remarks for the sections or subsections define important terms and point out issues and research directions. These are necessarily succinct and do not take the place of a textbook, but they can refresh memory for previously encountered information and can orient attention.

Obviously, alternative organizations of the material would have been possible. A subject index recaptures some of these possibilities. In particular, note the subject index entries for various adjacent disciplines (which combine the Section 2 references with the more specific references found throughout the book); the age period entries; the word-class entries; and the entries for certain topics, such as language deficiency, which are distributed among a number of sections.

There is also an author and publication index, which separately lists each publication by the names of its authors, the date of publication, and the page(s) on which it is listed in the guide. In addition to page references for full, annotated entries, the index notes the pages on which a publication is mentioned within the introductory remarks or in the annotation of some other publication. The order is alphabetical by first author, with cross-references supplied for additional authors. This index should be useful for finding particular items that are only vaguely remembered, and for tracing the thinking of particular researchers through the years. There is also an index of serials (journals and multivolume books).

In addition to the indices, there are a number of cross-references in the introductory remarks and annotations, and many publications are listed under more than one topic. Thus, I have done my part toward introducing lateral as well as hierarchical structure. For users already familiar with the child language area, or for casual users, this should be sufficient. But if you are a newcomer trying to gain initial mastery there is additional work to do. With enough exploration and thought, you can construct an intricate network of ideas and research results which will open unexpected paths. Use my organization as a convenience, not a straight-jacket. In particular, note that the overviews in Section 1 are relevant to all of the research topics; that the indices and cross-references should not be ignored; and that papers on similar issues are often separated by such distinctions as methodology (naturalistic vs. experimental), age period, and theoretical approach. Also, ideas suggested in one context can often put a fresh perspective on other problems. You can make this happen.

NOTE TO USERS IN ADJACENT DISCIPLINES

Most of the publications in *Child Language* fall within the scope of a psycholinguistic approach to child language, the domain in which I feel competent to exercise judgment. However, I hope that the guide will help toward improved communication between psycholinguists and other professionals concerned with language behavior. For example, many therapists are using behavior modification techniques with language-deficient children and adults. In the volume edited by Schiefelbusch & Lloyd (1974), Bricker & Bricker have convincingly argued for the importance of synthesizing behaviorist, cognitive, and psycholinguistic approaches in language therapy programs. Other researchers have reported on such programs in that volume and in Morehead & Morehead (1976). I hope that therapists and researchers who are excited by these integrative approaches will accept my invitation to use *Child Language* as a means of access to the psycholinguistic literature. As a specific example, a therapist wanting to train noun and verb inflections might read the section on morphology in one of the introductory linguistics texts in Section 2-B; get an overview of the developmental literature by scanning Sections 3-A, 3-C, and 4-D; read some of the most relevant papers in full; use the index to find recent references on language intervention; and perhaps consider some of the theoretical views in Sections 10 and 11. A therapy program designed with some of this in mind should itself contribute to the psycholinguistic literature.

I extend a similar invitation to colleagues in speech and hearing, mental retardation, autism, clinical psychology, pediatrics, special education, curriculum development, assessment, reading, sociology, anthropology, artificial intelligence, neurology, ethology, communication, linguistics, cognitive psychology, child development, and other disciplines involved with language behavior. We can learn more together than separately.

KEEPING UP WITH THE LITERATURE

The information explosion mentioned in the preface shows no signs of abating, so *Child Language* should be supplemented by contact with current literature. For the benefit of students and other novices, I suggest some strategies here.

It helps to know where the explosion is occurring. Some of the subsections of this guide deal with approaches that have already peaked. These listings are fairly complete and would be easy to update in a few years. The best examples are Sections 3-A, 3-B, 4-B, 5-A, 8-C, and 8-D. In contrast, Sections 3-D, 5-B, 7-C, 9-A, 10, and 11 cover increasingly active areas. Especially for Section 11, my listings are incomplete and can only point the way to important new approaches to parent-infant interaction, based on theories of pragmatics, speech acts, and discourse. The length of this section increased by 50% in the January 1977 updating, primarily from the addition of 1976 and in-press references.

To keep up with these burgeoning areas, check your library for new issues of the journals listed in Section 1-D, and for new books in the card catalog or *Books in Print*. Some journals print a subject index in the last issue of each volume, and those which publish book reviews usually have a "Books Received" list periodically. See the reports of ongoing research projects in the *Journal of Child Language* and *Papers and Reports in Child Language Development*. Check out the ERIC Clearinghouse. Get on the mailing list of the Indiana University Linguistics Club (310 Lindley Hall, Bloomington, Indiana 47401). Attend conferences like the biennial meeting of the Society for Research in Child Development, the annual Boston University Conference on Language Development, and the winter meeting of the Linguistic Society of America (LSA). See the *American Psychologist,* published monthly by the American Psychological Association, for lists of forthcoming conferences. Also, subscribe to *The Linguistic Reporter* and its Child Language Newsletter. For intensive study in linguistics and related subjects, attend the Linguistic Institute sponsored by LSA each summer. (The 1977 institute is in Honolulu, with a 6-week main session plus presessions, symposia, and the 3-day summer meeting of the LSA.) Book publishers frequently exhibit new and forthcoming books at academic conferences, and also maintain mailing lists. A large number of books on linguistics, psycholinguistics, or child language are published by Academic Press, Cambridge University Press, Indiana University Press, Lawrence Erlbaum Associates, The MIT Press, Mouton, North-Holland, D. Reidel, and University Park Press. Other major academic publishers and university presses also publish books in these fields. There are some helpful periodicals listing abstracts (see Section 1-D), but these tend to be 6 to 18 months behind the literature. You can purchase individualized or standard computer searches through many university libraries. For a more personal approach, ask your teachers or colleagues about new developments, or join groups like the AERA Special Interest Group in Development of Psycholinguistic Processes (contact: Judith Green, Room 330, White Hall, Kent State University, Kent, Ohio 44242) and the New England Child Language Association (contact: Boston University School of Education, 755 Commonwealth Avenue, Boston, Massachusetts 02215). Finally, it is always fun to browse through friends' bookshelves. This group of strategies is not meant to intimidate; most people use only a fraction of them, sporadically.

For exhaustive literature searches including past as well as current work, Slobin's bibliography is extensively indexed, and the abstract and citation services permit systematic search. Don't ignore the reference lists in current books and articles which you like; recurring references tend to be the most influential ones. (*Social Sciences Citation Index* gives more precise information on this point.) Of course, *Child Language* can get you off to a good start.

FORM OF ENTRIES

To indicate what information is provided in each entry, I am supplying a point-by-point description of two fabricated book entries and two actual entries (a journal article and a book chapter). No further explanation should be needed for dissertations, conference papers, and other types of references. Numerals have been added to label the parts of the entries' that are being described.

[1] Spracher, Wilhelm (Ed.). [2] *The Origins of Thought in Infancy* [3] (3 vols.). [4] New York: New Press, [5] 1973. ([6] Also in paperback, Hudson Heights, N.J.: Reynolds, 1974. [7] Originally published in German, 1927.)
[8] These volumes are the best English-language source on the publications of the Structural School in Austria between 1890 and 1925.

[1]   Name of editor. The full name of an editor or author is usually used if known.
[2]   Title (of English version).
[3]   Indicates multi-volume work. If only one volume is referred to, the form is, e.g., "Vol. 1." or "*Vol. 1. Methodological Issues.*" If the work is a current, continuing series, the form is: "Vols. 1–5 and continuing."
[4]   Publisher's location and name.
[5]   Copyright date for the edition noted. In this example, the author and publication index would read "1927/73." If the work is a series, a range of dates may be required: "1973–1975" or "1968–1976 and continuing."
[6]   If there is a paperback as well as a hardcover edition, this is noted. If no publisher and date are included, this generally indicates that the publisher, and usually the date, are the same as the main edition. However, occasionally the paperback publisher or date were simply difficult to obtain and therefore not included.
[7]   If the book was originally published in a language other than English, the language and original copyright date are noted, but not the country, publisher, or original title.

[8] An annotation is usually supplied, indicating the nature of the book and sometimes its importance. Background reading is already highly selected, but particularly good quality is often pointed out. (For the child language books a more comprehensive system of asterisks indicating importance is used.)

  [1] *Learned, Beatrice & Teng, Wen-shun. [2] *Children's First Words* (2nd ed.). [3] San Francisco: Redwood Press, [4] 1974c. ([5] Paperback, $12. [6] First edition published, 1962. [7] Reviewed by T. Coticchio in *Developments in Psychology,* 1975, *19,* 118–120.)

    [8] This classic treatment of single-word speech has a new chapter extending Learned & Teng's analysis to recent data, particularly that of Bunt (1972).

[1] Authors' names, with an asterisk indicating an important publication on child language. A person reading representative publications from Section 1 plus publications with asterisks in Sections 3–13 should obtain a good knowledge of the field. Publications with asterisks are those most likely to be assigned reading in a language acquisition course; they are not necessarily the publications of highest quality by various criteria. For example, an influential study with design flaws would more likely be marked than the better-designed studies which settled the issue it raised. Also, very recent publications are less likely to be marked than those which have had time to become known.

[2] Title and edition. Usually the most recent edition is given as the primary reference.

[3] Publisher's location and name.

[4] Copyright date for the edition noted. The "c" indicates that the authors had two other publications in 1974 (1974a and 1974b).

[5] "Paperback" indicates that there is no hardcover edition. When a paperback edition was known to cost more than $10, the price was added. Even if a price is not indicated, books by Mouton, North-Holland, and Reidel tend to be in paperback editions priced over $10.

[6] The date of a previous edition is usually noted. If the publisher is known to be different, it is included. No attempt has been made to indicate which books or editions are out of print.

[7] If a particular review happened to come to my attention, I included it. In addition, reviews can be found in most linguistics journals, a few psychology journals, *Contemporary Psychology,* and *Journal of Child Language* (see Section 1-D).

[8] Note that the annotations often refer to another publication. In almost every case, these secondary references have full entries elsewhere in the guide which can be accessed through the author and publication index. Also note that the most complete description of a book is often given in its first listing if it appears in more than one section.

  [1] Lenneberg, Eric H. The biological foundations of language. *Hospital Practice,* 1967b, *2,* 59–67. [2] (Reprinted in T. D. Spencer & N. Kass (Eds.), *Perspectives in Child Psychology.* New York: McGraw-Hill, 1970.)

    [3] Short, simple presentation of Lenneberg's main ideas and summary of development.

[1]   Reference in modified APA style.
[2]   Any reprintings known to me are indicated.
[3]   Annotation.

   [1] Smith, Carlota S. [2] An experimental approach to children's linguistic competence. [3] In Hayes, 1970. [4] (Reprinted in Ferguson & Slobin, 1973.)
   [5] In one of two experiments reported, elicited imitation was used to determine the difficulty of complex sentences in grammatical and ungrammatical versions for 3- to 4-year-old children. Smith argues for the importance of surface structure in processing sentences.

[1]   Name of author.
[2]   Title of chapter or article.
[3]   Book in which the chapter or article first appeared. If the complete reference is not given, it can be obtained through the author and publication index. If the book editor had other publications for the year, an identifying letter is added to the date; if the author of the chapter had other publications for the year, an identifying letter is added in parentheses.
[4]   Books in which the chapter or article has been reprinted.
[5]   Annotations for experimental reports always include the task and age of subjects, usually indicate the results, and often note the theoretical significance. In this case, the results were judged too complicated to include. The other experiment mentioned is described in another section (accessible through the name and publication index).

SOURCE OF ENTRIES

It is worth summarizing how the information in the entries was obtained. Several people have asked me, "Did you actually read all these things?" Obviously not; I read what my own interest and time allowed, and the most useful annotations are probably for those publications. Whether or not I read a publication, there were several sources of information I used. Book entries are based on a combination of my skimming the book or using the table of contents; publisher's advertising; references to the book in other publications; and *Books in Print* and other library reference works. Whenever possible I located a copy of the book, since dates of publication are not always reliably reported for recent books, and characterizations of content by publishers or other writers are sometimes incomplete. In the case of books published outside the United States, sometimes I could find reference only to an American edition or distributor. (For example, Humanities Press in New York distributes Mouton's books.) I generally tried to determine the major editions of a book, including paperback editions, but doubtless some were missed.

   In the case of journal articles, I generally supplemented information in the abstract by skimming or reading the article. Sometimes I stayed closer to the data than the author did; for example, if a difference noted in the abstract was found to be nonsignificant and tiny upon checking the results section, I reported what was in the results section. Generally, however, I summarized the author's own statement of the results and theoretical significance, even when I disagreed. Since I did not have time to subject all articles to critical evaluation, I limited my own judgment to deciding which articles to include and which ones to mark with an asterisk for importance. My policy makes it clear what each author believes the results and significance to be, but leaves undecided which authors are right. The user is cautioned to suspend belief until he or she can examine the articles directly.

Relatively few doctoral dissertations, conference papers, and technical reports are included. They are primarily of interest to someone specializing in a particular problem, and are difficult to obtain. The most important ones are usually cited in related published papers and reviews.

ABBREVIATIONS AND SYMBOLS

* Before a bibliographic entry: indicates importance
Before an utterance: indicates ungrammaticality
< The form to the left of the sign develops earlier than (or is easier than) the form to the right
[ ] Used to enclose phones
// Used to enclose phonemes

3;11 Sample notation for children's ages; indicates 3 years, 11 months (some authors use 3:11 or 3-11)
3.5 Sample alternative notation for children's ages; decimal expression indicating age $3\frac{1}{2}$ (3 years, 6 months)

CA Chronological age
CVC Syllable composed of a consonant-vowel-consonant sequence; often refers to a nonsense syllable
(C)CVC Syllable form that begins with one or two consonants
DO Direct object
ed. Edition
Ed(s). Editor(s)
Hz Hertz, or cycles per second; indicates frequency of a tone (related to pitch)
IO Indirect object
MA Mental age
MLU Mean length of utterance, usually measured in morphemes but sometimes in words
N Noun
NP Noun phrase
NVN Noun-verb-noun; often refers to a particular surface-structure order that does not necessarily correspond to subject-verb-object
S Sentence; the topmost node of a phrase-structure tree
SES Socioeconomic status
SVO Subject-verb-object; often refers to a particular deep- or surface-structure order, in contrast to VSO or other orders

V	Verb
Vol(s).	Volume(s)
VOT	Voice onset time
VP	Verb phrase (the predicate of a sentence)
wh-question	Question based on a wh-word (who, what, why, etc.), in contrast to a yes/no question

CHILD LANGUAGE

Part I

GENERAL RESOURCES

Section 1
GENERAL RESOURCES ON LANGUAGE DEVELOPMENT

A Texts and Overviews

CURRENT APPROACHES

The following books present current approaches to child language.

Lenneberg, Eric H. *Biological Foundations of Language.* New York: John Wiley & Sons, 1967b.

Lenneberg views language as a species-specific biological process. Many specific language functions are discussed, with an emphasis on biological constraints, language pathology, and clinical cases. Most suitable for beginning graduate students.

NcNeill, David. *The Acquisition of Language.* New York: Harper & Row, 1970a. (Reviewed by S. Fischer in *Foundations of Language,* 1972, *9,* 288–294.)

A 183-page textbook emphasizing the acquisition of syntax within a transformational grammar framework, though there is also material on phonology, semantics, and biological views. McNeill argues for his own theoretical positions, which have been controversial and influential (for example, linguistic nativism). Most suitable for beginning graduate students.

Menyuk, Paula. *The Acquisition and Development of Language.* Englewood Cliffs, N.J.: Prentice-Hall, 1971.

A 285-page textbook. Transformational linguistics is taken as the main theoretical perspective, but biological and socio-linguistic considerations are included. Most suitable for beginning graduate students.

Eliot, John. *Human Development and Cognitive Processes.* New York: Holt, Rinehart and Winston, 1971.

Collection of new and reprinted essays intended to serve as a resource to students. Part Three has introductory essays on language development by S. Houston, H. G. Furth, E. H. Lenneberg, J. S. Bruner, E. & G. Kaplan, and J. Sachs. Furth and Bruner emphasize the relation to cognitive development. There are also sections on human development, perception, and thinking.

Streng, Alice H. *Syntax, Speech and Hearing: Applied Linguistics for Teachers of Children with Language and Hearing Disabilities.* New York: Grune & Stratton, 1972.

4

Cazden, C. *Child Language and Education.* New York: Holt, Rinehart and Winston, 1972.

> In this introductory textbook, applied topics and nonlinguistic perspectives (e.g., communication, cognition) are considered in addition to the transformational linguistics approach. Most suitable for advanced undergraduates.

McElroy, Colleen Wilkinson. *Speech and Language Development of the Pre-School Child: A Survey.* Springfield, Ill.: Charles C Thomas, 1972.

> Elementary survey for beginning students in speech pathology, audiology, and education.

Brown, Roger. *A First Language: The Early Stages.* Cambridge, Mass.: Harvard University Press, 1973a. (Also in paperback.) (Reviewed by R. A. and B. T. Gardner in *American Journal of Psychology,* 1974b, *87,* 729–757, and by D. Crystal in *Journal of Child Language,* 1974, *1,* 289–306.)

> Brown marshals results of his own studies on child language as well as other recent work relevant to the linguistic description of child language. In contrast to his earlier interpretations, semantics and cognition are considered in addition to syntax. This first volume includes an introduction (touching on Brown's attempt to learn Japanese and a chimpanzee's attempts to learn sign language) and description of the first two (pretransformational) stages of multiword speech: expression of major meanings and acquisition of grammatical morphemes. This is not a general text but is required reading for graduate students and researchers in child language.

Di Vesta, Francis J. *Language, Learning, and Cognitive Processes.* Monterey, Cal.: Brooks/Cole, 1974. (Paperback.)

> A 164-page introductory textbook for undergraduates and education students. Chapters on cognitive development, concept learning, and long-term memory organization provide context for the chapters on language development, reading, and sociolinguistics.

Vogel, Susan A. *Syntactic Abilities in Normal and Dyslexic Children.* Baltimore: University Park Press, 1975.

Crystal, David; Fletcher, Paul; & Garman, Michael. *The Grammatical Analysis of Language Disability.* Amsterdam: North-Holland, 1976. (Also in paperback.)

Describes a program for assessment and treatment (LARSP), based on linguistic analyses.

Dale, Philip S. *Language Development: Structure and Function* (2nd ed.). New York: Holt, Rinehart and Winston, 1976. (Paperback. First edition published, 1972.)
     A 358-page textbook that provides a clear, even-handed survey of the field. It is suitable for advanced undergraduates but can also be used at the graduate level with augmentation.

von Raffler-Engel, Walburga. *Baby Talk and Infant Speech.* New York: Humanities Press, 1976. (Paperback, $30.)

Maratsos, Michael. *Language Development: The Acquisition of Language Structure.* Morristown, N.J.: General Learning Press, 1976b.
     A 20-page module in the University Programs Modular Studies.

Crystal, David. *Child Language, Learning and Linguistics.* London: Edward Arnold, in press.
     Crystal discusses the contributions that linguistics can make to the study of child language.

Oléron, Pierre. *Language and Mental Development.* Hillsdale, N.J.: Lawrence Erlbaum Associates, in press.

Nelson, Katherine. *Learning to Talk.* Cambridge, Mass.: Harvard University Press, forthcoming. (Volume in *The Developing Child* series.)
     Short book aimed toward upper division students and nonpsychologists.

de Villiers, Peter & de Villiers, Jill. *Early Language.* Cambridge, Mass.: Harvard University Press, forthcoming. (Volume in *The Developing Child* series.)
     Short book aimed toward upper division students and nonpsychologists.

Bloom, Lois & Lahey, Margaret. *Language Development and Language Disorders.* New York: John Wiley & Sons, forthcoming. (Publication expected, 1977.)

GESELL

The following three books are representative of work by Gesell and his colleagues at the Yale Clinic of Child Development, mainly in the second quarter of the century. The emphasis on normative description makes for a useful supplement to current work, in which careful age estimates are rarely attempted.

Gesell, A. & Thompson, H. *Infant Behavior: Its Genesis and Growth.* New York: McGraw-Hill, 1934.

> Pages 243–257 summarize normative behavior in standard situations for children 4–56 weeks of age. See also pages 286–291.

Gesell, A.; Halverson, H. M.; Thompson, H.; Ilg, F. L.; Castner, B. M.; Armes, L. B.; & Amatruda, C. S. *The First Five Years of Life: A Guide to the Study of the Preschool Child.* New York: Harper & Row, 1940.

> Chapter 8 by Castner (1) summarizes language behavior for each year to age 5, and (2) describes each test or measure of development used and normative behavior at each age.

Knobloch, Hilda & Pasamanick, Benjamin (Eds.). *Gesell and Amatruda's Developmental Diagnosis* (3rd ed.). New York: Harper & Row, 1974.

> Description of normal and abnormal child development, detailing diagnostic procedure and normative behavior at each age.

PRETRANSFORMATIONAL THEORIES

The following are representative of more theoretically oriented, pretransformational work on child language.

de Laguna, Grace. *Speech: Its Function and Development.* Bloomington: Indiana University Press, 1963. (Also in paperback. Originally published, 1927.)

> In this classic examination of the origin of speech in the species and the individual, de Laguna emphasizes the role of speech function and points out similarities and differences between speech and animal communication systems.

Lewis, M. M. *Infant Speech: A Study of the Beginnings of Language* (2nd ed.). New York: Humanities Press, 1951. (Also published, London: Routledge & Kegan Paul, 1951. First edition published in 1936 and reprinted in New York: Arno Press, 1975.)

Church, Joseph. *Language and the Discovery of Reality.* New York: Random House, 1961. (Also in paperback, New York: Vintage Press.)

Lewis, M. M. *Language, Thought and Personality in Infancy and Childhood.* New York: Basic Books, 1963.

Merleau-Ponty, Maurice. *Consciousness and the Acquisition of Language.* (Hugh J. Silverman, Trans.) Evanston, Ill.: Northwestern University Press, 1973.

Based on lecture notes from a course given by the philosopher at the University of Paris in 1949–1950. Topics include methodology, language at various ages, pathology, and linguistics.

B Review Articles and Summaries

Leopold, Werner F. The study of child language and infant bilingualism. *Word*, 1948a, *4*, 1-17. (Reprinted in Bar-Adon & Leopold, 1971.)
> Concise survey of child language research before 1947, mainly European.

*McCarthy, Dorothea. Language development in children. In L. Carmichael (Ed.), *Manual of Child Psychology* (2nd ed.). New York: John Wiley & Sons, 1954, 492-630. (See also her shorter review, "Language development," reprinted in Bar-Adon & Leopold, 1971.)

Liublinskaya, A. A. The development of children's speech and thought. In B. Simon (Ed.), *Psychology in the Soviet Union*. Stanford: Stanford University Press, 1957. (Also published, London: Routledge & Kegan Paul, 1957.)
> Describes Soviet experiments on the importance of the "second signal system" (language) for perceptual and cognitive development.

Brown, Roger & Berko, Jean. Psycholinguistic research methods. In P. H. Mussen (Ed.), *Handbook of Research Methods in Child Development*. New York: John Wiley & Sons, 1960(a), 517-617.

Carroll, John B. Language development in children. In C. W. Harris (Ed.), *Encyclopedia of Educational Research* (3rd ed.). New York: Macmillan, 1960, 744-752. (Reprinted in Bar-Adon & Leopold, 1971, and in Saporta, 1961.)

Ervin, Susan & Miller, Wick. Language development. In H. W. Stevenson (Ed.), *Child Psychology*, Part I. Chicago: The University of Chicago Press, 1963.

Ervin-Tripp, Susan. Language development. In M. Hoffman & L. Hoffman (Eds.), *Review of Child Development Research*, Vol. 2. Ann Arbor: University of Michigan Press, 1966, 55-105.

McNeill, David. Developmental psycholinguistics. In Smith & Miller, 1966(c), 15-84.

Rebelsky, F.; Starr, R. H.; & Luria, Z. Language development: The first four years. In Y. Brackbill (Ed.), *Infancy and Early Childhood*. New York: The Free Press, 1967.

*Luria. A. R. Speech development and the formation of mental processes. In M. Cole & I. Maltzman (Eds.), *A Handbook of Contemporary Soviet Psychology*. New York: Basic Books, 1969.
    Excellent summary of Soviet research on language development, including relations to classical conditioning, physiological measures, and cognitive and social development.

Palermo, David S. Language acquisition. In H. Reese & L. Lipsitt (Eds.), *Experimental Child Psychology*. New York: Academic Press, 1970.

*McNeill, David. The development of language. In P. H. Mussen (Ed.), *Carmichael's Manual of Child Psychology* (3rd ed.), Vol. 1. New York: John Wiley & Sons, 1970(b), 1061–1161.

Braine, Martin D. S. The acquisition of language in infant and child. In Carroll Reed (Ed.), *The Learning of Language*. New York: Appleton-Century-Crofts, 1971 (b).

Slobin, Dan I. Developmental psycholinguistics. In W. O. Dingwall (Ed.), *A Survey of Linguistic Science*. College Park, Md.: University of Maryland Press, 1971 (d).

Palermo, David S. & Molfese, D. L. Language acquisition from age five onward. *Psychological Bulletin,* 1972, *78,* 409–428.

Ryan, Joanna. Early language development. In M. P. M. Richards (Ed.), *The Integration of the Child into a Social World*. London: Cambridge University Press, 1974.

Bellugi, Ursula. Some aspects of language acquisition. In T. A. Sebeok (Ed.), *Current Trends in Linguistics,* Vol. 12. The Hague: Mouton, 1974.
    Introductory article, based primarily on the Harvard studies of Adam, Eve, and Sarah at stages I, III, and V, and Bellugi's more recent study of a deaf child, Pola, at stage I.

Brown, Roger. Development of the first language in the human species. In Haugan & Bloomfield, 1974(a).
    Summarizes parts of Brown (1973a).

Brown, Roger. The development of the human child's native language. In A. Silverstein (Ed.), *Human Communications: Theoretical Explorations*. Hillsdale, N.J.: Lawrence Erlbaum Associates, 1974(b).

Cazden, Courtney B. & Brown, Roger. The early development of the mother tongue. In Lenneberg & Lenneberg, Vol. 1, 1975.

*Bloom, Lois. Language development. In F. Horowitz (Ed.), *Review of Child Development Research,* Vol. 4. Chicago: The University of Chicago Press, 1975.

Sachs, Jacqueline S. Development of speech. In Carterette & Friedman, Vol. 7, 1976.

Carton, Aaron S. & Castiglione, Lawrence V. Psycholinguistics and education: Directions and divergences. *Journal of Psycholinguistic Research,* 1976, *5,* 233–244.
    Considers the relationship between psycholinguistics and educational psycholinguistics on a variety of dimensions.

C Collections

The following books either have selections of previously published papers or are collections of new papers written especially for the volume. Books with older papers are listed before books with newer papers. See also the developmental selections in Saporta (1961) and Jakobovits & Miron (1967).

Bar-Adon, Aaron and Leopold, Werner F. (Eds.). *Child Language: A Book of Readings.* Englewood Cliffs, N.J.: Prentice-Hall, 1971.
> Sixty selections, from the 18th to 20th centuries. Less than half the book is oriented toward the transformational grammar approach.

Ferguson, Charles A. & Slobin, Dan I. (Eds.). *Studies of Child Language Development.* New York: Holt, Rinehart and Winston, 1973. (Reviewed by R. F. Cromer in *Journal of Child Language,* 1974c, *1,* 144–148.)
> An excellent selection of readings, emphasizing data from many languages rather than theory. Most selections are on phonology and syntax; many have never been published before in English.

Reed, Carroll (Ed.). *The Learning of Language.* New York: Appleton-Century-Crofts, 1971.
> Selected readings.

Bellugi, Ursula & Brown, Roger (Eds.). *The Acquisition of Language.* Chicago: The University of Chicago Press, 1964. (Paperback. Originally published in *Monographs of the SRCD,* 1964.)
> From a 1961 conference; includes formal and open discussion of seven papers. Reflects a transitional period in language study, with a few papers that are still widely read.

Lenneberg, Eric H. (Ed.). *New Directions in the Study of Language.* Cambridge, Mass.: The MIT Press, 1964b. (Also in paperback.)
> From a 1962 conference; seven papers on a variety of topics, primarily in child language.

Smith, Frank & Miller, George A. (Eds.). *The Genesis of Language.* Cambridge, Mass.: The MIT Press, 1966. (Also in paperback.)
> From a 1965 conference. Eleven papers cover a variety of topics; summary of the open discussion is included.

Brown, Roger. *Psycholinguistics: Selected Papers by Roger Brown.*
New York: The Free Press, 1970a. (Also in paperback.)
The first half of the book has Brown's best-known papers on
grammatical descriptions of early speech.

Adams, Parveen (Ed.). *Language in Thinking.* Baltimore: Penguin
Books, 1972. (Paperback.)
Selection of papers (first published 1927–1970) on sign language and deafness, language acquisition, the Whorfian
hypothesis, concept formation, and other topics on the relation
of language and thought. Includes excerpts from Piaget,
Vygotsky, and Chomsky.

Ervin-Tripp, Susan. *Language Acquisition and Communicative
Choice. Essays Selected and Introduced by Anwar S. Dil.* Stanford:
Stanford University Press, 1973a. (Reviewed by E. Oksaar in
Journal of Child Language, 1974, *1,* 307–317.)
A collection of 17 papers on bilingualism, language acquisition,
and sociolinguistics, written over a 20-year period.

Slobin, Dan I. (Ed.). *The Ontogenesis of Grammar.* New York:
Academic Press, 1971a.
From a 1965 conference; includes discussion of pivot grammar
and theories of how language is learned.

Lyons, John & Wales, R. J. (Eds.) *Psycholinguistic Papers: The
Proceedings of the 1966 Edinburgh Conference.* Edinburgh:
Edinburgh University Press, 1966.
Five papers on adult and child psycholinguistics.

Huxley, Renira & Ingram, Elisabeth (Eds.). *Language Acquisition:
Models and Methods.* New York: Academic Press, 1971.
From a 1968 conference; sections on sociolinguistics, gram-
mar, cognition and language, and clinical application.

Hayes, John R. (Ed.). *Cognition and the Development of Language.*
New York: John Wiley & Sons, 1970. (Reviewed by L. Bloom in
Language, 1974b, 398–412.)
From a 1968 conference. In addition to papers taking a pri-
marily linguistic approach, some of the earliest papers reflect-
ing the new interest in cognition and language appear here.

Flores d'Arcais, G. B. & Levelt, W. J. M. (Eds.). *Advances in
Psycholinguistics.* Amsterdam: North-Holland, 1970. (Distributed
by American Elsevier Publishing Company, New York. Also in
paperback, $13.75.)

From a 1969 conference; includes a number of good developmental papers.

Moore, Timothy E. (Ed.). *Cognitive Development and the Acquisition of Language*. New York: Academic Press, 1973. (Reviewed by C. Smith in *Journal of Child Language*, 1975, *2*, 303–318.)
From a 1971 conference; transformational grammar is in the background, but the emphasis is on semantics and cognition.

Longhurst, T. M. (Ed.). *Linguistic Analysis of Children's Speech: Readings*. New York: MSS Information Corporation, 1974.

Schiefelbusch, Richard L. & Lloyd, Lyle L. (Eds.). *Language Perspectives—Acquisition, Retardation, and Intervention*. Baltimore: University Park Press, 1974.
From a 1973 conference; includes summary and background articles on normal language development as well as recent views on language pathology.

Lenneberg, Eric H. & Lenneberg, Elizabeth (Eds.). *Foundations of Language Development*, Vol. 1. New York: Academic Press, 1975.
Includes general articles, biological views, general characterizations of phonological, syntactic, and semantic development, and cognitive basis for language, written for this volume.

Lenneberg, Eric H. & Lenneberg, Elizabeth (Eds.). *Foundations of Language Development*, Vol. 2. New York: Academic Press, 1975.
Includes articles on normal language development, aphasiology, deafness and blindness, speech disorders, reading, and writing, written for this volume. Many are theoretical or general.

Morehead, Donald M. & Morehead, Ann E. (Eds.). *Normal and Deficient Child Language*. Baltimore: University Park Press, 1976.
Collection of reprinted and new papers on phonology, syntax, semantics, cognition, and pragmatics. The editors emphasize current approaches to language deficiency and place the papers in context by means of introductory remarks.

Prûcha, Jan (Ed.). *Soviet Studies in Language and Language Behavior*. Amsterdam: North-Holland, 1976. (Paperback, $30.95.)
Nineteen studies on language function, the psycholinguistics of syntax and semantics, language acquisition, neurolinguistics, and speech pathology. In an introductory chapter, Prûcha surveys contemporary Soviet psycholinguistics.

Lloyd, Lyle L. (Ed.). *Communication Assessment and Intervention Strategies.* Baltimore: University Park Press, 1976.
Collection of articles on interdisciplinary approaches to language disability. Includes seven appendices on information sources, terminology, etc.

Schiefelbusch, Richard L. (Ed.). *The Bases of Language Intervention.* Baltimore: University Park Press, in press. (Publication expected, fall 1977.)

Bloom, Lois (Ed.). *Readings in Language Development.* New York: John Wiley & Sons, forthcoming. (Publication expected, 1977.)

Lahey, Margaret (Ed.). *Readings in Language Disorders.* New York: John Wiley & Sons, forthcoming. (Publication expected, 1977.)

von Raffler-Engel, Walburga (Ed.). *Prospects in Child Language.* The Hague: Mouton, forthcoming.

D Bibliographies and Journals

ABSTRACTS

The following publications reproduce abstracts of articles or dissertations on psychology or language. One journal that specializes in book reviews is also listed.

Child Development Abstracts and Bibliography. Published for the Society for Research in Child Development by The University of Chicago Press, three times yearly.

Contemporary Psychology. Published monthly by the American Psychological Association.
  Reviews of new books; reviews are approximately two pages long.

Dissertation Abstracts International. Monthly compilation of abstracts submitted to the publishers, Xerox University Microfilms.
  Copies of complete texts may be purchased as microfilm or as xerographic prints.

ERIC Clearinghouse on Languages and Linguistics, Center for Applied Linguistics, 1611 North Kent Street, Arlington, Virginia 22209.
  Collects and disseminates information on linguistics and related fields. Abstracts documents and articles for the monthly journals *Resources in Education* and *Current Index to Journals in Education*; acquires and indexes materials; commissions and publishes state-of-the-art papers, selective bibliographies, etc.; provides information services; has microfiche collection and computerized data base.

Language and Language Behavior Abstracts. Published by the University of Michigan Center for Research on Language and Language Behavior, quarterly. (First appeared, 1967.)
  Abstracts of articles in 25 language-related disciplines, from almost 1000 publications in over 30 languages, including technical reports and conference proceedings. There are four indices: author, subject, book review, and source publication. Articles on language acquisition are divided into sections on

child language acquisition, learning disabilities, native language instruction, adult language and speech development, foreign language learning, and translation and interpretation.

Psychological Abstracts. Published by the American Psychological Association, monthly.

Social Sciences Citation Index. Published by the Institute for Scientific Information, Philadelphia, annually.

Useful in literature searches: for a given journal article, lists all articles from over 1000 journals that cite that article.

BIBLIOGRAPHIES

Several bibliographies on child language follow.

Dale, E. & Reichert, D. *Bibliography of Vocabulary Studies* (1st ed.). Columbus: Ohio State University Press, 1949.

Leopold, Werner F. *Bibliography of Child Language.* Evanston, Ill.: Northwestern University Press, 1952.
Annotated.

Dale, E. *Bibliography of Vocabulary Studies* (2nd ed.). Columbus: Ohio State University Press, 1957.

Ervin, Susan. Publications on psycholinguistics. *International Journal of American Linguistics,* 1964a, *30,* 90–93; 184–93.

Sableski, Julia A. A selective annotated bibliography on child language. *The Linguistic Reporter,* 1965, *7,* 4–6.
Twenty-eight items.

DeVito, Joseph A. A bibliography: Speech and language, development and acquisition. Mimeo, Herbert Lehman College, CUNY, New York City, © 1970.

Slobin, Dan I. *Leopold's Bibliography of Child Language* (Revised and augmented ed.). Bloomington: Indiana University Press, 1972.
Based on Leopold (1952), with the annotations and some topics deleted, and references through 1967 added. Attempts to be exhaustive for the topics covered, and includes non-English publications. Alphabetical listing, with indices for language and topic.

The Linguistic Reporter. Published by The Center for Applied Linguistics, 1611 North Kent Street, Arlington, Virginia 22209, nine times yearly.

Information of interest to linguists and related researchers, including bibliographies and reports of new books on various aspects of child language (phonology, syntax, semantics, communicative competence, etc.). See, for example, Vol. 17, Nos. 2 and 5–6; Vol. 18, No. 4. Also, subscribers receive the Child Language Newsletter as a supplement several times a year.

CHILD LANGUAGE PERIODICALS

The following periodicals publish articles on language development exclusively.

Journal of Child Language. Published by Cambridge University Press, twice yearly (first appeared, 1974).
Includes research reports, theoretical articles, notes and discussion, book reviews, and project reports.

Papers and Reports on Child Language Development. Working paper series distributed by the Department of Linguistics, Stanford University, usually twice yearly.
For information write PRCLD, Department of Linguistics, Stanford University, Stanford, California 94305. Some of the papers are available through the ERIC Clearinghouse on Languages and Linguistics (above).

DEVELOPMENTAL PSYCHOLOGY PERIODICALS

The following developmental psychology journals frequently publish articles on child language.

Child Development. Published for the Society for Research on Child Development (SRCD) by The University of Chicago Press, quarterly.

Developmental Psychology. Published by the American Psychological Association, bimonthly.

Human Development. Published by S. Karger, Basel, Switzerland, bimonthly.

Journal of Experimental Child Psychology. Published by Academic Press, bimonthly.

Merrill-Palmer Quarterly of Behavior and Development. Published by The Merrill-Palmer Institute, quarterly.

Monographs of the Society for Research in Child Development. Published for SRCD by the University of Chicago Press, irregularly.

PSYCHOLINGUISTICS PERIODICALS

The following psychology journals publish articles on psycholinguistics, including child language.

Cognition. Published by Elsevier Sequoia, quarterly. (Volumes 1 through 3(2) published by Mouton; the first volume was published in 1972.)

Cognitive Psychology. Published by Academic Press, quarterly.

International Journal of Psycholinguistics. Published by Mouton, twice yearly. (The first volume appeared in 1972.)

Journal of Psycholinguistic Research. Published by Plenum Press, quarterly. (The first volume appeared in 1971.)

Journal of Verbal Learning and Verbal Behavior. Published by Academic Press, bimonthly.

LINGUISTICS PERIODICALS

The following linguistics journals publish articles of interest to psycholinguists. Some occasionally publish an article on child language.

Foundations of Language. Published by D. Reidel Publishing Co., quarterly.

Journal of Linguistics. Published for the Linguistics Association of Great Britain by Cambridge University Press, twice yearly.

Language. Published by the Linguistic Society of America, quarterly.

Lingua. Published by North-Holland, three volumes of three issues each annually.
    Note the "Publications Received" section, ordered by topic.

Linguistic Analysis. Published by American Elsevier, quarterly.
    Articles on formal syntax, semantics, and phonology in a generative linguistics framework.

Linguistic Inquiry. Published by The MIT Press, quarterly. (The first issue appeared in 1970.)

Papers from the Fourth (Fifth, . . .) Regional Meeting of The Chicago Linguistic Society. Published by the Department of Linguistics, The University of Chicago, yearly.

OTHER PERIODICALS

The following are other journals of interest.

Anthropological Linguist. Published by the Archives of Anthropological Linguistics, Indiana University, monthly.

Brain and Language. Published by Academic Press, quarterly.

Journal of Cognitive Science. New interdisciplinary journal (artificial intelligence, psychology, and language). First issue is scheduled for 1977.

Journal of Speech and Hearing Research. Published by the American Speech and Hearing Association, quarterly.

Language and Speech. Published by Kingston Press Services, Ltd., quarterly.

Language in Society. Published by Cambridge University Press, three times yearly.

Psychological Bulletin. Published by The American Psychological Association, monthly.

Psychological Review. Published by The American Psychological Association, bimonthly.

Section 2
GENERAL
BACKGROUND

Language acquisition research has often been influenced by theoretical developments in adjacent fields. In this section, a selection of work in linguistics, psychology, psycholinguistics, artificial intelligence, and philosophy is offered as appropriate background reading. More specific publications relevant primarily to one topic in language acquisition are listed with those topics in Sections 3–12. An attempt has been made to include both introductory and advanced materials in each field and to emphasize approaches that have been most influential in language acquisition research.

A Interdisciplinary Collections of Papers

The following books are collections of articles on language by theorists in fields such as linguistics, psychology, psycholinguistics, and philosophy. Most include a general introduction and short section introductions.

Saporta, Sol (Ed.). *Psycholinguistics: A Book of Readings.* New York: Holt, Rinehart and Winston, 1961.
> Collection of papers by linguists, psychologists, and philosophers on linguistic theory, verbal behavior, speech perception, semantics, language acquisition, pathology, and the Whorfian hypothesis of linguistic relativity.

Fodor, Jerry A. & Katz, Jerrold J. (Eds.). *The Structure of Language.* Englewood Cliffs, N.J.: Prentice-Hall, 1964.
> Collection of papers by philosophers and linguists on general linguistic theory, syntax, semantics, and psychological implications.

Jakobovits, Leon A. & Miron, Murray S. (Eds.). *Readings in the Psychology of Language.* Englewood Cliffs, N.J.: Prentice-Hall, 1967.
> The book has sections on major theories, adult and developmental psycholinguistics, and semantics. Most of the articles represent pretransformational psychological approaches, but others are by transformational linguists and psycholinguists.

Oldfield, R. C. & Marshall, J. C. (Eds.). *Language.* Baltimore: Penguin Books, 1968. (Paperback.)
> Collection of papers on language development, speech perception and production, psycholinguistics, mathematical linguistics, and pathology.

Lyons, John (Ed.). *New Horizons in Linguistics.* Baltimore: Penguin Books, 1970a. (Paperback.)
> Seventeen short introductions written for this volume by experts in various areas of linguistics, psychology, and related areas, including Campbell & Wales on language acquisition. In

addition to an excellent general introduction and a short glossary, each chapter is placed in context by Lyons.

Laird, Charlton & Gorrell, Robert M. (Eds.). *Reading About Language.* New York: Harcourt Brace Jovanovich, 1971. (Paperback.)
Book of readings including dozens of short selections, primarily by traditional and contemporary linguists but also by philosophers, psychologists, lexicographers, and writers.

Dingwall, William O. (Ed.). *A Survey of Linguistic Science* (2nd ed.). College Park, Md.: University of Maryland, 1971. (Paperback, $10.)
Eleven in-depth survey articles written for this volume by experts in linguistic theory, neurolinguistics, psycholinguistics, mathematical and computational linguistics, including Slobin on developmental psycholinguistics.

Carroll, John & Freedle, Roy (Eds.). *Language Comprehension and the Acquisition of Knowledge.* Washington, D.C.: V. H. Winston & Sons, 1972.
Based on a conference; includes articles by psychologists on language processing, discourse memory, and learning from written materials; by linguist Chafe on discourse structure; and by computer scientist Simmons on semantic representation.

Adams, Parveen (Ed.). *Language in Thinking.* Baltimore: Penguin Books, 1972.
Collection of 19 papers by psychologists and linguists on sign language and cognition of the deaf; language acquisition; the Whorfian hypothesis; and the work of Chomsky, Vygotsky, and Piaget.

Miller, George A. (Ed.). *Communication, Language, and Meaning.* New York: Basic Books, 1973.
Includes 25 brief but often effective chapters on a variety of language topics, including Roger Brown on language acquisition. They were written by experts asked by Miller to introduce their fields in a Voice of America lecture series.

Haugen, Einar I. & Bloomfield, Morton W. (Eds.). *Language as a Human Problem.* New York: Norton, 1974.
Set of essays from the summer 1973, issue of *Daedalus.* Includes problems of sociolinguistics, the nature and history of language, language development, applied linguistics, and interdisciplinary topics. Intended for readers with little or no background.

Bever, Thomas G.; Katz, Jerrold J.; & Langendoen, D. Terence
(Eds.). *An Integrated Theory of Linguistic Ability*. New York:
Thomas Y. Crowell, 1976.
   Collection of articles on linguistics and psycholinguistics.

Carterette, Edward C. & Friedman, Morton P. (Eds.). *Handbook of
Perception, Vol. 7. Language and Speech*. New York: Academic
Press, 1976.
   Chapters written by linguists and psychologists for this volume
   on a variety of topics including speech perception and production, psycholinguistics, language development, methodology,
   neurolinguistics, and general linguistic theory.

Cole, Roger W. (Ed.). *Current Issues in Linguistic Theory*. Bloomington: Indiana University Press, in press. (Publication expected,
July 1977.)
   Eight articles on a variety of new directions in linguistic theory
   and related areas.

B Introduction to Language and Linguistic Theory

The following books provide a general introduction to language or linguistic theory, or are useful for reference.

Murray, J. A., et al. (Eds.). *Oxford English Dictionary* (13 Vols.). London: Oxford University Press, 1933. (Originally published, 1888–1933.)

A superb historical dictionary of the English language. A two-volume micrographic reproduction became available in 1971, and can be purchased for $17.50 through a Book-of-the-Month Club offer.

Webster's Third New International Dictionary, Unabridged. Springfield, Mass: G. & C. Merriam, 1961.

The standard reference dictionary in the United States. Some lexicographers prefer the second edition (1934) for its conservatism.

Pei, Mario & Gaynor, Frank. *Dictionary of Linguistics.* New York: Philosophical Library, 1954. (Also in paperback, Totowa, N.J.: Littlefield, Adams & Co., 1969.)

Brief definitions of traditional linguistic terms; also, many languages are identified by region and language family. (See also Pei, 1966.)

Hartmann, R. R. K. & Stork, F. C. *Dictionary of Language and Linguistics.* London: Applied Science Publishers, 1972. (Also in paperback, New York: John Wiley & Sons, 1976.)

Lengthy definitions of linguistic concepts and terms.

Sapir, Edward. *Language.* New York: Harcourt, Brace & World, 1921. (Also in paperback, 1955.)

Sapir offers a vigorous attempt to define the nature of language, made concrete by many examples from a variety of languages. Includes language typology and language change.

Jesperson, Otto. *Language: Its Nature, Development and Origin.* London: Allen and Unwin, 1922; New York: Macmillan, 1949. (Also in paperback, New York: Norton, 1964.)

Jesperson's keen insights and clear exposition transcend linguistic fashions. In addition to this general book, he has writ-

25

ten numerous volumes on the grammar of English and linguistic theory.

Bloomfield, Leonard. *Language*. New York: Holt, Rinehart and Winston, 1933.
Behaviorism applied to linguistic theory; influential at the time but now outdated.

Jakobson, Roman & Halle, Morris. *Fundamentals of Language*. The Hague: Mouton, 1956. (Also in paperback (2nd ed.), New York: Humanities Press, 1971.)

Gleason, Henry A. *An Introduction to Descriptive Linguistics* (rev. ed.). New York: Holt, Rinehart and Winston, 1961.
This traditional textbook is particularly helpful with terminology and concepts that are often taken for granted or ignored in transformational linguistics. Separate workbook.

Sebeok, Thomas A. (Ed.). *Current Trends in Linguistics*. The Hague: Mouton, 1963 to present.
Annual volumes survey work in linguistics and related fields. Volumes 3 (1966) and 12 (1974) are especially relevant.

Lyons, John. *Introduction to Theoretical Linguistics*. London: Cambridge University Press, 1968. (Also in paperback.)
An elegantly written, even-handed treatment of linguistic theory, with deeper coverage than most introductions (519 pages). Emphasizes the relation of traditional linguistics to transformational linguistics.

Palmer, Harold E. & Blanford, F. G. *A Grammar of Spoken English*. London: Cambridge University Press, 1969. (Also in paperback.)

Crystal, David. *Linguistics*. Baltimore: Penguin Books, 1971. (Paperback.)
A 267-page introduction that discusses traditional and generative grammars in the context of pragmatic, historical, and philosophical questions.

Langacker, Ronald W. *Language and Its Structure* (2nd ed.). New York: Harcourt Brace Jovanovich, 1973. (Paperback.)
Exceptionally clear, reliable introduction to linguistic theory, with a transformational linguistics orientation. Exercises; 275 pages.

Syntax and Semantics, Vols. 1–8 (continuing series). New York: Academic Press, 1973–1977.
Editors include Kimball, McCawley, Cole, Morgan, and Sadock. Reports current research in generative grammar; recent

volumes have focused on particular topics (e.g., causatives, Japanese, speech acts).

Parret, Herman. *Discussing Language.* The Hague: Mouton, 1974. (Paperback.)
Dialogues by Parret with Chafe, Chomsky, Greimas, Halliday, Hartmann, G. Lakoff, Lamb, Martinet, McCawley, Saumjan, and Bouveresse.

Fromkin, Victoria & Rodman, Robert. *An Introduction to Language.* New York: Holt, Rinehart and Winston, 1974. (Paperback.)
A highly readable introduction with a transformational linguistics orientation and many "extras" such as animal communication, sociolinguistics, and brain processes. Exercises; 357 pages.

Farb, Peter. *Word Play: What Happens When People Talk.* New York: Alfred E. Knopf, 1974. (Also in paperback, New York: Bantam Books, 1975. Excerpts in *Horizon,* Winter 1974.)
Entertaining, informative, well written, but somewhat shallow and uncritical. A good popularization.

Bolinger, Dwight. *Aspects of Language* (2nd ed.). New York: Harcourt Brace Jovanovich, 1975. (Paperback.)
A popular introductory textbook. Like Lyons, Bolinger puts transformational linguistics in perspective, taking a long-range view in which other approaches are discussed. They differ in that Lyons is deep and Bolinger is broad. 682 pages; separate workbook.

Parisi, Domenico & Antinucci, Francesco. *Essentials of Grammar.* New York: Academic Press, 1976.
An introductory text that differs from the others in that it concentrates on the generative semantics version of generative grammar.

Stewart, Ann Harleman. *Graphic Representation of Models in Linguistic Theory.* Bloomington: Indiana University Press, 1976.
A unique survey and commentary on various graphic models used in linguistics, e.g., tree structures, matrices, and networks.

Stockwell, Robert P. *Foundations of Syntactic Theory.* Englewood Cliffs, N.J.: Prentice-Hall, in press. (Also in paperback. Publication expected, 1977.)
Text with separate workbook.

C Syntax: Chomsky's Transformational Grammar

*The following books present Chomsky's theory of transformational grammar and related studies. His work through the mid-1960's ("Standard Theory") has been most influential in psychology, but some of his later publications ("Extended Standard Theory") are included in the next section (2-D). Some knowledge of transformational grammar is essential for understanding the grammars of child language proposed in the 1960's. The main idea is that **rewrite rules** generate tree-shaped **deep structures** that are modified by **transformations** to produce tree-shaped **surface structures**. **Semantic interpretation rules** apply to deep structure and **phonological rules** apply to surface structure, providing a formal account of the relation between meaning and sound. The major response in adult psycholinguistics has been an attempt to demonstrate the psychological reality of deep structure and transformations (not successful in detail). In developmental psycholinguistics, the formal tools of the grammar were borrowed to describe children's syntactic development, with psychological reality remaining as an issue for discussion (but not resolution).*

Major publications by Chomsky and his interpreters follow. It is best to start with a textbook or summary rather than Chomsky's own publications.

Harris, Zellig S. Co-occurrence and transformation in linguistic structure. *Language,* 1957, *33,* 283–340. (Reprinted in Fodor & Katz, 1964.)

> Harris' original work on transformations, reported in part in this article, influenced his student Chomsky. For later developments, see his 1965 article in *Language* and his 1970 book.

Chomsky, Noam. *Syntactic Structures.* The Hague: Mouton, 1957. (Also in paperback.)

> The little book that sparked a revolution in linguistics. Chomsky rejects finite state grammars and introduces a grammar incorporating phrase structure and transformational rules.

Chomsky, Noam. Formal properties of grammars. In R. D. Luce, R. R. Bush, & E. Galanter (Eds.), *Handbook of Mathematical Psychology,* Vol. 2. New York: John Wiley & Sons, 1963.

> Technical article on properties of automata and grammars.

Miller, George A. & Chomsky, Noam. Finetary models of language users. In R. D. Luce, R. R. Bush, & E. Galanter (Eds.), *Handbook of Mathematical Psychology,* Vol. 2. New York: John Wiley & Sons, 1963.

Chomsky, Noam. *Aspects of the Theory of Syntax.* Cambridge, Mass.: The MIT Press, 1965. (Also in paperback.)

In *Aspects,* Chomsky proposes a substantially revised and elaborated version of transformational grammar (now called "Standard Theory"). Difficult reading, but no other publication by Chomsky has been as influential in psychology.

Chomsky, Noam. *Topics in the Theory of Generative Grammar.* The Hague: Mouton, 1966a. (Paperback.)

Chomsky summarizes the main points of *Aspects* and replies to critics. Originally in Sebeok, 1966.

Chomsky, Noam. *Language and Mind* (enlarged edition). New York: Harcourt Brace Jovanovich, 1972. (Also in paperback. Original edition published, 1968.)

This book is based on a Berkeley lecture series. In addition to providing a simplified account of his transformational grammar, Chomsky discusses issues of interest to psychologists and philosophers.

Jacobs, Roderick A. & Rosenbaum, Peter S. *English Transformational Grammar.* Waltham, Mass.: Blaisdell, 1968.

Introductory textbook.

Reibel, David A. & Schane, Sanford A. (Eds.). *Modern Studies in English.* Englewood Cliffs, N.J.: Prentice-Hall, 1969.

Articles on transformational grammar: general theory, conjunction, pronominalization, relativization, child language, and other topics.

Jacobs, Roderick A. & Rosenbaum, Peter S. (Eds.). *Readings in English Transformational Grammar.* Waltham, Mass.: Ginn and Co., 1970.

Analyses of specific grammatical phenomena which use, extend, or revise the *Aspects* model.

Lyons, John. *Noam Chomsky.* New York: Viking Press, 1970b. (Also in paperback.)

Lyons puts Chomsky in historical context and discusses his major publications and contributions to linguistic theory. An excellent starting point.

McNeill, David. Linguistic appendix to "The development of language." In P. H. Mussen (Ed.), *Carmichael's Manual of Child Psychology* (3rd ed.), Vol. I. New York: John Wiley & Sons, 1970(b).
> Transformational grammar in a nutshell for the novice.

Chomsky, Noam. *Selected Readings* (J. P. Allen & Paul Van Buren, Eds.). London: Oxford University Press, 1971a.
> Extracts arranged and given continuity by the editors.

Greene, Judith. *Psycholinguistics: Chomsky and Psychology*. Baltimore: Penguin Books, 1972. (Paperback.)
> The first half of this book summarizes *Syntactic Structures* and *Aspects*.

Grinder, John T. & Elgin, Suzette H. *Guide to Transformational Grammar*. New York: Holt, Rinehart and Winston, 1973.
> Basic introductory text with many exercises.

Stockwell, Robert P.; Schachter, Paul; & Partee, Barbara Hall. *The Major Syntactic Structures of English*. New York: Holt, Rinehart and Winston, 1973.
> A synthesis of lexicalist and deep case approaches to grammatical theory. This is the most comprehensive attempt to write a transformational grammar of English and is especially useful for reference.

Bach, Emmon. *Syntactic Theory*. New York: Holt, Rinehart and Winston, 1974.
> Intended for graduate courses in syntax; includes exercises.

Wanner, Eric. *On Remembering, Forgetting and Understanding Sentences*. The Hague: Mouton, 1974.
> In the introductory sections, Wanner gives a particularly clear account of the concepts of deep structure, transformational rules, and the issue of their psychological reality.

Akmajian, Adrian & Heny, Frank. *An Introduction to the Principles of Transformational Syntax*. Cambridge, Mass.: The MIT Press, 1975.
> Excellent introduction to Standard Theory.

Chomsky, Noam. *The Logical Structure of Linguistic Theory*. New York: Plenum Press, 1975b.
> Chomsky's original work on generative grammar, published 20 years after it was written.

Emonds, Joseph E. *A Transformational Approach to English Syntax: Root, Structure-Preserving, and Local Transformations.* New York: Academic Press, 1976.

Presents original proposals regarding transformational syntax, including a "structure-preserving constraint" that limits the set of possible derived constituent structures.

Culicover, Peter W. *Syntax.* New York: Academic Press, 1976.

Introductory generative syntax text emphasizing description and theoretical treatment of "core" phenomena of English, with particular emphasis on the relation between constraints on grammars and the learnability of languages.

D Syntax and Semantics: Generative Semantics vs. Interpretive Semantics

Shortly after Aspects *was published, Chomsky's notion of deep structure was challenged by a number of young transformational linguists. In their theory,* **generative semantics**, *rewrite rules generate tree-shaped semantic structures to which transformations apply to produce surface structures. Syntax and semantics are no longer bifurcated by a special level of deep structure; transformational rules performing semantic and syntactic functions are intermixed. There is also no need for the semantic interpretation rules that applied to deep structures, since this work is now performed by transformations. Proposals concerning the form of semantic structures include the incorporation of predicates with variables as arguments, logical quantifiers, and the* **lexical decomposition** *of verbs into constituent predicates. New transformational rules are proposed to transform these abstract semantic structures into surface structures.*

*The idea of lexical decomposition has had some influence in psychology, but the theoretical arguments between generative semanticists and interpretivists have had little impact. (Very recent developments are more promising: major innovations by Chomsky and by Joan Bresnan are starting to draw attention.) The best-known papers from the large generative semantics literature are listed first, followed by counterarguments in defense of Chomsky's interpretive semantics and modifications to that approach (***Extended Standard Theory***). The term* **underlying structure** *is used to refer to the output of rewrite rules— deep structure in the case of Chomsky's theory, and semantic (logical) structure in the case of generative semantics.*

It should be noted that the focus in these papers is primarily syntactic despite the disagreements about semantics. Semantic structures and rules are justified by appeal to syntactic phenomena. In Section 2-F, papers that deal instead with semantics as a separate topic are listed. Also, since about 1972 the generative semanticists have taken on new concerns—e.g. **fuzzy logic** *and* **pragmatics***. This later work is listed with the relevant language acquisition topics in Parts III and IV.*

GENERATIVE SEMANTICS

The papers on generative semantics follow. For a text, see Parisi & Antinucci, 1976.

Lakoff, George. *Irregularity in Syntax.* New York: Holt, Rinehart and Winston, 1970. (Originally a doctoral dissertation, *On the Nature of Syntactic Irregularity,* Indiana University, 1965.)

In an attempt to deal with exceptions to regular rules, Lakoff proposed revisions to Chomsky's (1965) theory that led to the development of generative semantics.

Lakoff, George & Ross, John Robert. Is deep structure necessary? Manuscript, 1968. Available from the Indiana University Linguistics Club, 310 Lindley Hall, Bloomington, Indiana 47401, for $.30 (plus .50 postage for orders under $2.50).

A short paper that presents some of the first arguments for generative semantics.

McCawley, James D. Concerning the base component of a transformational grammar. *Foundations of Language,* 1968, *4,* 243–269.

Another early proposal in generative semantics.

Lakoff, George. Instrumental adverbs and the concept of deep structure. *Foundations of Language,* 1968, *4,* 4–29.

Lakoff argues, on a variety of syntactic grounds, that the following sentences must have the same underlying structure:

1. Seymour sliced the salami with a knife.
2. Seymour used a knife to slice the salami.

Bach, Emmon & Harms, R. (Eds.). *Universals in Linguistic Theory.* New York: Holt, Rinehart and Winston, 1968.

In three long articles, underlying structures more abstract than Chomsky's (1965) deep structure are proposed: C. J. Fillmore, "The case for case"; E. Bach, "Nouns and noun phrases"; J. D. McCawley, "The role of semantics in a grammar." Also, P. Kiparsky ("Linguistic universals and linguistic change") focuses on phonological change and psychological reality of linguistic rules.

Papers from the Fourth (Fifth, . . .) Regional Meeting of the Chicago Linguistic Society. The University of Chicago Linguistics Department, 1968 to present.

Annual volume of short papers; many new developments in generative semantics have been published here first.

Langendoen, D. Terence. *The Study of Syntax.* New York: Holt, Rinehart and Winston, 1969. (Paperback.)

This introductory syntax text emphasizes the generative semantics approach.

Postal, Paul M. The surface verb 'remind'. *Linguistic Inquiry,* 1970, *1,* 37–120.

Postal suggests an underlying structure for one sense of *remind* which involves lexical decomposition and reordering of predicates and arguments: (STRIKE IO (SIMILAR S O)), where IO is surface indirect object, S is surface subject, and O is surface object. The article is not easy to read, but well exemplifies the kinds of arguments generative semanticists have made.

McCawley, James D. English as a VSO language. *Language,* 1970c, *46,* 286–299.

McCawley argues that the order of constituents in the underlying structure of English is VSO (verb-subject-object). For a critical discussion, see A. Berman in *Linguistic Inquiry,* 1974.

McCawley, James D. Semantic representation. In Paul L. Garvin (Ed.), *Cognition: A Multiple View.* New York: Spartan Books, 1970(a).

Underlying structures are suggested that include features of symbolic logic (e.g., predicates with variables as arguments; quantifiers) and involve lexical decomposition of verbs into underlying predicates. Since prelexical transformations are needed, Chomsky's deep structure level does not exist.

McCawley, James D. Where do noun phrases come from? In R. A. Jacobs & P. S. Rosenbaum, 1970(b). (Revised version in D. D. Steinberg & L. A. Jakobovits, 1971.)

Another presentation of McCawley's version of generative semantics. Many of the phenomena discussed in McCawley (1970a) are also discussed here.

Lakoff, George. Global rules. *Language,* 1970, *46,* 627–639.

Lakoff suggests a need for "derivational constraints," a powerful class of rules that includes transformational and phrase structure rules as special cases which are local in application, and also includes global rules that apply over entire derivations.

McCawley, James D. Prelexical syntax. In R. O'Brien (Ed.), *Report of the 22nd Annual Round Table Meeting on Linguistics and Language Studies.* Washington, D.C.: Georgetown University Press, 1972.
In this article McCawley focuses on lexical decomposition (e.g., of the verbs *kill, persuade,* and *hammer*) and the adverb-scope arguments for this type of analysis.

Lakoff, George. On generative semantics. In Steinberg & Jakobovits, 1971(a).
Lakoff summarizes his version of generative semantics and dicusses global derivational constraints involving quantifiers, negatives, adverbs, conjunction reduction, focus, topic, lexical presupposition, and other phenomena. He also discusses proposals made by McCawley, Postal, and R. Lakoff, and criticizes Chomsky.

Lakoff, George. Linguistics and natural logic. *Synthese,* 1971b, *22,* 151–271. (Reprinted in D. Davidson & G. Harman, 1972.)
Lakoff suggests a need to develop a "natural logic" applicable to language; underlying structure should be a form of logical structure rather than Chomsky's (1965) deep structure. Includes discussion of presupposition and lexical decomposition.

Keenan, Edward L. On semantically based grammar. *Linguistic Inquiry,* 1972, *3,* 413–461.
Keenan proposes a fragment of universal grammar in which natural language sentences are syntactically derived from their logical structure.

Shibatani, Masayoshi. Three reasons for not deriving 'kill' from 'cause to die' in Japanese. In J. P. Kimball (Ed.), *Syntax and Semantics,* Vol. 1. New York: Academic Press, 1972.
See also the reply by James D. McCawley and the two contributions on the issue by Michael B. Kac.

Postal, Paul. *On Raising.* Cambridge, Mass.: The MIT Press, 1973.
Postal discusses the "raising" transformation, which combines predicates in preparation for lexical insertion (necessary in derivations involving lexical decomposition).

Green, Georgia. *Semantics and Syntactic Regularity.* Bloomington: Indiana University Press, 1974.

Frantz, Donald G. Generative semantics: An introduction, with bibliography. Manuscript, 1974. Available from the Indiana University

Linguistics Club, 310 Lindley Hall, Bloomington, Indiana 47401, for $1.45 (plus $.50 postage and handling).

A simple presentation of the main points of generative semantics; assumes minimal background knowledge.

McCawley, James D. (Ed.). *Syntax and Semantics, Vol. 7.* New York: Academic Press, 1976.

Collection of classic papers from the "underground literature" of transformational grammar in the 1960's; emphasizes the beginnings of generative semantics.

Li, Charles N. *Computerized Bibliography of Studies in Generative Syntax and Semantics.* Bloomington: Indiana University Research Center, forthcoming.

INTERPRETIVE SEMANTICS

Publications on interpretive semantics follow, including both Standard Theory and Extended Standard Theory approaches.

Fodor, Jerry A. Three reasons for not deriving "kill" from "cause to die." *Linguistic Inquiry,* 1970, *1,* 429–438.

Fodor presents syntactic arguments against the lexical decomposition of *melt* (transitive) and *kill* in underlying structure.

Katz, Jerrold J. Interpretive semantics vs. generative semantics. *Foundations of Language,* 1970, *6,* 220–259.

Katz claims that generative semantics is a notational variant of interpretive semantics.

Chomsky, Noam. Deep structure, surface structure and semantic interpretation. In Steinberg & Jakobovits, 1971(b). (Reprinted in Chomsky, 1972.)

Chomsky responds to the arguments of G. Lakoff, McCawley, and Fillmore, and proposes ways in which surface structure might contribute to semantic interpretation (Extended Standard Theory).

Chomsky, Noam. *Studies on Semantics in Generative Grammar.* The Hague: Mouton, 1972. (Paperback, $10.)

Chomsky discusses topics in his Extended Standard Theory, notably, the introduction of semantic interpretation rules that apply to surface structure.

Jackendoff, Ray S. *Semantic Interpretation in Generative Grammar.* Cambridge, Mass.: The MIT Press, 1972. (Also in paperback.)

Jackendoff adopts a version of interpretive semantics in which semantic interpretation rules apply at various points in the derivation of a sentence, including deep and surface structure. He applies this approach to the analysis of theme, adverbs, pronouns and reflexives, co-reference, focus and presupposition, modal structure, and negation.

Katz, Jerrold J. Interpretive semantics meets the Zombies: A discussion of the controversy about deep structure. *Foundations of Language,* 1973, *9,* 549–596.

The last of three articles in FOL in which Katz and McCawley debate the issue of interpretive vs. generative semantics.

Chomsky, Noam. *Reflections on Language.* New York: Pantheon Books, 1975a. (Also in paperback.)

Directed to a general audience. Chomsky discusses philosophical issues relevant to transformational grammar and introduces his current formulation of transformational grammar, including surface structure semantic interpretation rules and the notion of *traces.*

Chomsky, Noam. Conditions on rules of grammar. In Cole, in press.

Chomsky, Noam. *Essays on Form and Interpretation.* Amsterdam: North-Holland, in preparation.

COMPARISON

Here is a recent comparison in which both theories are rejected.

Brame, Michael K. *Conjectures and Refutations in Syntax and Semantics.* Amsterdam: North-Holland, 1976.

Comparison and criticism of generative semantics, Standard Theory, and Extended Standard Theory.

E Syntax and Semantics: Case Grammar

*About the time that the first papers in generative semantics came out, Fillmore proposed a less radical departure from Chomsky's (1965) theory. In his **deep case** structure, there is no subject noun phrase or predicate; instead, the verb is followed by noun phrases and preposi- tional phrases, each labeled by its semantic role (e.g., agent, instru- ment, dative, locative, object). Transformations introduce certain characteristics of surface structure, such as the distinction between noun phrases and prepositional phrases, and the positioning of one noun phrase as subject. There is still a need for semantic interpreta- tion rules, since the roles noted above are only one aspect of meaning. Deep case grammar has not been widely accepted in linguistics, but it has been adopted and developed by psychologists, developmental psychologists, and computer scientists. In addition to the references that follow, see Brown (1973a, pp. 132–143, 217–226), Bowerman (1973a, 197–228), Schank (1972), Kintsch (1974), and Norman & Rumelhart (1975).*

Fillmore, Charles J. The case for case. In Bach & Harms, 1968(a).
    The classic paper on "deep case" grammar: rather technical.

Fillmore, Charles J. Lexical entries for verbs. *Foundations of Lan- guage,* 1968b, *4,* 373–393. (Reprinted in Steinberg & Jakobovits, 1971 and in F. Kiefer, *Studies in Syntax and Semantics.* Dordrecht, Holland: D. Reidel, 1969.)
    Fillmore discusses the use of predicate-argument descriptions of language and case-grammar assignments for arguments. This may be the best of Fillmore's articles to start with.

Fillmore, Charles J. Toward a modern theory of case. In Reibel & Schane, 1969(a).
    A briefer, more readable presentation of Fillmore's theory than "The case for case."

Fillmore, Charles J. Subjects, speakers and roles. *Synthese,* 1970a, *21,* 251–274.
    Fillmore comments on a wide variety of problems in case grammar and touches on deixis and speech acts.

Fillmore, Charles J. The grammar of *hitting* and *breaking.* In Jacobs & Rosenbaum, 1970(b).
    A case-grammar analysis.

Huddleston, Rodney. Some remarks on case grammar. *Linguistic Inquiry,* 1970, *1,* 501–511.

Huddleston points out similarities between Fillmore's case grammar and Halliday's transitivity component, including their attention to theme, and discusses problems with Fillmore's analysis (especially those due to Fillmore's use of animacy as a criterion for case assignments).

Barron, Nancy M. *Grammatical Case and Sex Role: Language Differences in Interaction.* Unpublished doctoral dissertation, University of Missouri, 1970.

The distributions of case frames differ for men and women teachers, based on videotapes of teacher-student interactions in inner city and suburban classrooms.

Fraser, Bruce. A note on the *spray paint* cases. *Linguistic Inquiry,* 1971, *2,* 604–607.

Fraser discusses the problem of case assignments for sentences like:

1. The man sprayed paint on the wall.
2. The man sprayed the wall with paint.

Anderson, John M. *The Grammar of Case: Towards a Localistic Theory.* London: Cambridge University Press, 1971. (Also in paperback, 1976.)

In a transformational grammar framework, Anderson re-examines the old idea that grammatical cases have locative origins (for example, the dative *to* derives from the goal-of-movement *to*).

Fillmore, Charles J. Some problems for case grammar. *Working Papers in Linguistics* (Department of Linguistics, Ohio State University), 1971a, *10,* 245–265. (Also in O'Brien (Ed.), *Report of the 22nd Annual Round Table Meeting on Linguistics and Language Studies.* Washington, D.C.: Georgetown University Press, 1972.)

Fillmore describes revisions in his deep case grammar, e.g., the introduction of Source (*from*) and Goal (*to*) cases.

Fillmore, Charles J. Verbs of judging: An exercise in semantic description. In Fillmore & Langendoen, 1971(b).

In the description of 12 verbs, Fillmore uses *role structure* (a specific analog to case structure using roles like Judge and Defendant), lexical decomposition, and presupposition.

Suci, George J. & Hamacher, Jane H. Psychological dimensions of case in sentence processing: Action role and animateness. *International Journal of Psycholinguistics,* 1972, *1,* 34–48.

College students and fourth- and sixth-graders performed a task in which they listened to a sentence and then responded "yes" or "no" to a related question. Sentences varied in meaningfulness, case frame, voice, and animacy. Latencies indicated that all subjects differentiated action roles (W. Chafe: agent vs. patient), but only adults reliably differentiated cases (C. Fillmore: agentive, instrumental, dative, and objective).

Stockwell, Robert P.; Schachter, Paul; & Partee, Barbara Hall. *The Major Syntactic Structures of English.* New York: Holt, Rinehart and Winston, 1973.

A synthesis of transformational grammar that incorporates deep case grammar. The consequences for other parts of the grammar of using deep-case base structures can be observed.

Shafto, Michael. The space for case. *Journal of Verbal Learning and Verbal Behavior,* 1973, *12,* 551–562.

In a concept-identification task on case relations, Agent was easiest, followed by Experiencer, Instrument, and Object. Scaling of confusion data revealed a two-feature cognitive structure: living vs. nonliving and active vs. passive. In a recognition task, confusability was a function of similarity of case frames rather than surface or deep structure grammatical functions.

Nilsen, Don L. F. *The Instrumental Case in English.* The Hague: Mouton, 1973.

Nilsen argues that deep cases should be defined by semantic, not syntactic, criteria. The instrumental case is examined in detail, with many summary charts and citations of other literature on cases.

Baron, Dennis E. *Case Grammar and Diachronic English Syntax.* The Hague: Mouton, 1974.

Baron uses case grammar as a framework for studying changes in verb complementation from Old English to Modern English, and discusses general implications.

Bruce, Bertram C. Case systems for natural language. Cambridge, Mass.: Bolt, Beranek, and Newman. BBN Report No. 3010 (A. I. Report No. 23), 1975.

Bruce distinguishes several types of case systems, discusses criteria for evaluation, and surveys systems proposed in linguistics, psychology, and artificial intelligence. A useful source for developments since Fillmore's original proposal.

Gruber, Jeffrey S. *Lexical Structures in Syntax and Semantics.* Amsterdam: North-Holland, 1976. (Paperback, $24.75.)
Innovative proposals on the lexicon, including proposals regarding case relations and theme. Combines a revision of Gruber's 1965 MIT doctoral dissertation, *Studies in Lexical Relations,* and his 1967a work, *Functions of the Lexicon in Formal Descriptive Grammars.*

Fillmore, Charles J. Topics in lexical semantics. In Cole, in press.

F *Linguistic and Philosophical Semantics*

The fields of linguistics and philosophy have very different histories with regard to the study of semantics. The philosophical literature is extensive and technical, due to a long tradition of interest in semantic problems. There has been relative neglect of semantics within linguistics. The recent literature is an extension of work on syntax and therefore is probably more accessible to users of this bibliography. The citations below are divided into linguistic, philosophical, and interdisciplinary references. See Section 2-H for approaches to semantics in psychology and artificial intelligence.

LINGUISTIC SEMANTICS

Most of the contemporary work is associated with Chomsky's Standard Theory (Section 2-C), Chomsky's Extended Standard Theory (Section 2-D), case grammar (Section 2-E), or generative semantics (Section 2-D). The references listed here are those that deal with semantics alone (primarily, those associated with Chomsky's Standard Theory, e.g., Katz & Fodor, 1963). Combined discussions of syntax and semantics are in Sections 2-C, 2-D, and 2-E.

Introductory

The following references provide an introduction to linguistic semantics. See also Fodor, Bever, & Garrett (1974, Chapter 4), Lyons (1968, Chapters 9 and 10), or introductory linguistics texts (Section 2-B).

Greenberg, Joseph H. (Ed.). *Universals of Language* (2nd ed.). Cambridge, Mass.: The MIT Press, 1966b. (Also in paperback.)
> Two different discussions of semantic universals are included, by Weinreich and Ullmann.

Lenneberg, Eric H. *Biological Foundations of Language.* New York: John Wiley & Sons, 1967b.
> Chapter 8 includes a lucid introduction to semantics, as background to a discussion of the Whorfian hypothesis based on color terminology experiments. (Reprinted in Steinberg & Jakobovits, 1971.)

Bierwisch, Manfred. Semantics. In Lyons, 1970a(a).
A general article on semantics; assumes some knowledge of transformational grammar.

Slobin, Dan I. *Psycholinguistics.* Glenview, Ill.: Scott, Foresman, 1971c. (Paperback.)
This introductory textbook includes a readable, interesting chapter on semantics; a good place to start.

Lehrer, Adrienne. Semantics: An overview. *Linguistic Reporter,* 1971, *13,* (Supplement 27), 13–23.
This is another possible starting point; more linguistically oriented than Slobin.

Leech, Geoffrey N. *Semantics.* Baltimore: Penguin Books, 1974. (Paperback.)
Excellent introduction.

Palmer, F. R. *Semantics: A New Outline.* London: Cambridge University Press, 1976. (Also in paperback.)
Based on a 1971 lecture series.

Fodor, Janet Dean. *Semantics: Theories of Meaning in Generative Grammar.* New York: Thomas Y. Crowell, 1977.
The best current text for a more complete treatment than is given by Leech or Palmer.

Fillmore, Charles J. *Introduction to Linguistic Semantics.* New York: Thomas Y. Crowell, in preparation.

Advanced

The following references either provide detailed treatment of specific problems in linguistic semantics or propose semantic theories. See also Sections 2-D and 2-E.

Stern, Gustaf. *Meaning and Change of Meaning.* Bloomington: Indiana University Press, 1964. (Originally published in German, 1931.)
After a general review of work on meaning, Stern discusses seven classes of sense change. The book is old, but it gives a fuller discussion than can be found in contemporary historical linguistics.

Katz, Jerrold J. & Fodor, Jerry A. The structure of a semantic theory. *Language,* 1963, *39,* 170–210. (Reprinted in Fodor & Katz, 1964, and in Jakobovits & Miron, 1967.)

The classic attempt to develop the semantic component of Chomsky's transformational grammar, by means of *projection rules*.

Bolinger, Dwight. The atomization of meaning. *Language,* 1965, *41,* 555–573. (Reprinted in Jakobovits & Miron, 1967.)

Bolinger discusses a number of problems with Katz & Fodor's (1963) theory. He claims that the assumption of a minimal lexical unit (the morpheme) is the weakest point in the theory, since analysis must sometimes be based on larger units (e.g., idioms.)

Weinreich, Uriel. *Explorations in Semantic Theory.* The Hague: Mouton, 1972. (Paperback. Originally published in T. A. Sebeok (Ed.), *Current Trends in Linguistics,* Vol. 3. The Hague: Mouton, 1966.)

A technical book in which Weinreich criticizes Katz & Fodor's theory and suggests an alternative. The critique is reprinted in Steinberg & Jakobovits, 1971.

Bierwisch, Manfred. On certain problems of semantic representations. *Foundations of Language,* 1969, *5,* 153–184.

Bierwisch explores some problems within the framework of Katz & Fodor's (1963) semantic theory. In particular, he suggests that the notion of distinguishers must be abandoned and proposes his own approach to antonymy.

Leech, Geoffrey N. *Towards a Semantic Description of English.* London: Clowes, 1969. (Also published in Bloomington: Indiana University Press, 1970.)

In addition to general material, this book has detailed treatments of time, place, and modality.

Chafe, Wallace L. *Meaning and the Structure of Language.* Chicago: The University of Chicago Press, 1970. (Also in paperback. Reviewed by R. Langacker in *Language,* 1972, *48,* 134–161.)

An ambitious, innovative theory; there is emphasis on the semantic description of change and on case-grammar relations.

Fillmore, Charles J. & Langendoen, D. Terence (Eds.). *Studies in Linguistic Semantics.* New York: Holt, Rinehart and Winston, 1971.

Collection of papers including the topics of presupposition, tense and time, verbs of judging, conjunctions, "even" and "remind."

Waldron, R. A. *Sense and Sense Development.* New York: Academic Press, 1971.

Katz, Jerrold J. *Semantic Theory.* New York: Harper & Row, 1972. (Reviewed by H. Savin in *Cognition,* 1973, *2,* 213–238.)
Technical treatment of selected topics, including semantic markers and distinguishers, linguistic truth, the logic of questions, analyticity and opacity, state and process, and semantics in transformational grammar.

Lehrer, Adrienne. *Semantic Fields and Lexical Structure.* Amsterdam: North-Holland, 1974. (Paperback, $11.50.)
Lehrer reviews research, explores properties of lexical fields, and suggests lexical strategies used by speakers and listeners. Includes chapters on lexical gaps, belief predicates, semantic universals, topics in generative grammar approaches to semantics, and a 16-page bibliography. An analysis of culinary terms is used to illustrate many points.

Jackendoff, R. Toward an explanatory semantic representation. *Linguistic Inquiry,* 1976, *7,* 89–150.

PHILOSOPHICAL SEMANTICS

The following set of references is an entry-level sampling of publications on logic and philosophy of language. The work of major philosophers such as Wittgenstein, Russell, Frege, Quine, Carnap, and Montague can be accessed through them. Most of the theories incorporate syntax as well as semantics.

Reichenbach, Hans. *Elements of Symbolic Logic.* New York: Macmillan, 1947. (Also in paperback, New York: The Free Press, 1966.)
A good introduction to symbolic logic; includes extensive comments on natural language.

Alston, W. P. *Philosophy of Language.* Englewood Cliffs, N.J.: Prentice-Hall, 1964. (Also in paperback, 1967.)
Includes a survey of some important theories of meaning.

Hook, Sidney (Ed.). *Language and Philosophy.* New York: New York University Press, 1969.

Thomason, Richard H. *Symbolic Logic: An Introduction.* Toronto: Macmillan, 1970.

Partee, Barbara; Sabsay, Sharon; & Soper, John. Bibliography: Logic and language. Manuscript, 1971. Available from the Indiana University Linguistics Club, 310 Lindley Hall, Bloomington, Indiana 47401 for $1.80 (plus $.50 postage and handling).

This bibliography is a good guide to the extensive literature in philosophy and linguistics on the philosophy of language, logic, and semantics. Linguists like Partee, McCawley, and G. Lakoff have been influenced by work in philosophy; the bibliography reflects the interdisciplinary trend.

Searle, John R. (Ed.). *Philosophy of Language.* London: Oxford University Press, 1971. (Paperback.)

Harrison, B. *Meaning and Structure: An Essay in the Philosophy of Language.* New York: Harper & Row, 1972. (Reviewed by J. Moravcsik in *Language,* 1975, *51,* 178–185.)

Harrison criticizes an empiricist theory of language and presents his own theory, which is influenced by Wittgenstein and Chomsky. He considers certain issues in linguistics and psychology within this context.

Zierer, Ernesto, *Formal Logic and Linguistics.* The Hague: Mouton, 1972. (Paperback.)

Basic features of modern logic are described for linguists.

Cresswell, M. J. *Logics and Languages.* London: Methuen, 1973.

A text on natural language as viewed by a logician.

Zabeeh, Farhang; Klemke, E. D.: & Jacobson, Arthur (Eds.). *Readings in Semantics.* Urbana: University of Illinois Press, 1974. (Also in paperback.)

Excellent selection of readings in philosophical semantics.

INTERDISCIPLINARY

The following references are interdisciplinary. See also Part 1 of Sebeok, Vol. 12, 1974.

Fodor, Janet Dean. Formal linguistics and formal logic. In J. Lyons, 1970a.

Brief introduction to this topic; a good starting point.

Steinberg, Danny D. & Jakobovits, Leon A. *Semantics: An Interdisciplinary Reader in Philosophy, Linguistics and Psychology.* London: Cambridge University Press, 1971. (Also in paperback.)

A number of relevant papers are included in this book; they vary in difficulty and required background.

Fodor, Jerry A. The ontogenesis of the problem of reference: A review of some theories of linguistic symbols. In Reed, 1971.

Lakoff, George. Linguistics and natural logic. *Synthese,* 1971b, *22,* 151–271. (Reprinted in Davidson & Harman, 1972.)

Lakoff attempts to bring certain notions from logic into generative semantics.

Davidson, D. & Harman G. (Eds.). *Semantics of Natural Language* (2nd ed.). Dordrecht: D. Reidel, 1972. (Paperback, $14.)

Based on a 1969 conference.

Keenan, Edward L. Logic and language. In Haugen & Bloomfield, 1974.

Keenan offers a survey, emphasizing semantic relations between sentences (e.g., entailment) and including a comparison of what can be expressed in Hebrew vs. English relative clauses.

Kempson, Ruth M. *Presupposition and the Delimitation of Semantics.* London: Cambridge University Press, 1975.

Kempson argues that presupposition is a problem in pragmatics and should not be dealt with in the semantic component of a grammar. She comments on linguists Katz, Bierwisch, Karttunen, Fillmore, Keenan, the Lakoffs, and the Kiparskys, and on logicians Strawson, Russell, and Grice.

Rapoport, Anatol. *Semantics.* New York: Thomas Y. Crowell, 1975.

Combines philosophical, linguistic, and psycholinguistic approaches to semantics.

Fodor, Jerry A. *The Language of Thought.* New York: Thomas Y. Crowell, 1975.

Philosophical, linguistic, and psychological arguments are brought to bear on the problem of the internal representation of information.

Keenan, Edward L. (Ed.). *Formal Semantics of Natural Language.* London: Cambridge University Press, 1975.

Papers by philosophers, logicians, and linguists on quantification and reference in natural language, intensional logic and syntactic theory, challenges to model theoretic semantics, pragmatics and context, semantics and surface syntax, tense and aspect. From a 1973 colloquium sponsored by the King's College Research Centre, Cambridge.

Partee, Barbara H. (Ed.). *Montague Grammar.* New York: Academic Press, 1976.

Collection of recent articles on the approach to formal semantics and syntax developed by logician Richard Montague; several articles consider relations to the generative grammars of current linguistic theory. Articles vary in the amount of background assumed.

Miller, George A. & Johnson-Laird, Philip N. *Language and Perception.* Cambridge, Mass.: Harvard University Press, 1976.

See summary in Section 2-H.

Linguistics and Philosophy. Published by D. Reidel Publishing Co., Dordrecht, Holland/Boston, U.S.A., two volumes of three issues yearly. (First appeared, 1976.)

G Cognitive Development

In recent years there has been considerable interest in the relation between cognitive and linguistic development. Much of the work in this area has taken Piaget's theory or experimental tasks as a starting point. Summaries of Piaget's theory, its relation to language development, and other cognitive development theories follow. Publications on specific topics are listed in the appropriate sections of Parts III and IV. See especially Section 10-D.

Piaget, Jean. Language and thought from the genetic point of view. *Acta Psychologia,* 1954, *X,* 51–60. (Reprinted in Adams, 1972, and in J. Piaget, *Six Psychological Studies.* New York: Random House, 1967. Latter is also in paperback, 1968; originally published in French, 1964.)

    A brief summary of Piaget's views, covering the period from infancy to adolescence.

Flavell, John H. *The Developmental Psychology of Jean Piaget.* Princeton, N.J.: Van Nostrand, 1963. (Also in paperback.)

    The standard American summary of Piaget's work; more detailed than most accounts of Piaget's theory.

Piaget, Jean & Inhelder, Bärbel. *The Psychology of the Child.* New York: Basic Books, 1969. (Also in paperback. Originally published in French, 1966.)

    A summary or synthesis of the Genevan work on child development for the general reader. See especially Chapter 3, "The semiotic or symbolic function."

Baldwin, Alfred. *Theories of Child Development.* New York: John Wiley & Sons, 1967.

    The chapter on Piaget is an excellent introduction.

Ginsburg, Herbert & Opper, Sylvia. *Piaget's Theory of Intellectual Development: An Introduction.* Englewood Cliffs, N.J.: Prentice-Hall, 1969. (Also in paperback.)

    An elementary introduction to Piaget's work.

Sinclair-de-Zwart, Hermina. Developmental psycholinguistics. In D. Elkind & J. Flavell (Eds.), *Studies in Cognitive Development.* New York: Oxford University Press, 1969. (Also in paperback. Excerpt in Adams, 1972.)

The role of language in Piaget's theory, from the sensorimotor period to concrete operations. Includes a discussion of Chomsky's generative grammar.

Furth, Hans G. *Piaget and Knowledge.* Englewood Cliffs, N.J.: Prentice-Hall, 1969.

Olson, David R. *Cognitive Development: The Child's Acquisition of Diagonality.* New York: Academic Press, 1970.
Develops an approach to cognitive development by focusing on children's developing ability to deal with diagonals.

Mussen, Paul H. (Ed.). *Carmichael's Manual of Child Psychology* (3rd ed.), Vol. 1. New York: John Wiley & Sons, 1970.
See the articles by Piaget (on Piaget), Langer (on Werner), Flavell (on concept development), and McNeill (on language development).

Reese, Hayne W. (Ed.). *Advances in Child Development and Behavior,* Vols. 6–11 and continuing. New York: Academic Press, 1971–1976.
Series of new reviews and interpretations of active research areas, including cognitive development. See also volumes 1 through 5 (1963–1970), under Reese and other editors.

Riegel, Klaus F. Time and change in the development of the individual and society. In Reese, Vol. 7, 1972.
Reviews the concept of time in the natural sciences and developmental psychology, and argues for the importance of quantitative models of functional changes over time.

Pick, Anne D. (Ed.). *Minnesota Symposia on Child Psychology,* Vols. 6–10 and continuing. Minneapolis: University of Minnesota Press, 1972–1976.
Annual collection of papers presented at the Minnesota Symposia on Child Psychology at University of Michigan's Institute of Child Development. See also volumes 1–5, edited by John P. Hill.

Farnham-Diggory, Sylvia (Ed.). *Information Processing in Children.* New York: Academic Press, 1972.
Papers from the seventh annual symposium in cognition, Carnegie-Mellon University. Includes information processing and artificial intelligence approaches to development of perception, cognition, and memory. The authors include H. A. Simon, R.

H. Pollack, S. Farnham-Diggory, J. W. Hagen, J. J. Goodnow, B. Inhelder, G. Cellérier, A. Newell, D. Klahr, J. G. Wallace, and J. R. Hayes.

Droz, Rémy & Rahmy, Maryanne. *Understanding Piaget*. New York: International Universities Press, 1976. (Originally published in French, 1972.)

Guide to Piaget's publications. Includes an introductory survey, abstracts of his major writings, an annotated bibliography, and suggested reading for people with particular backgrounds and interests.

Battro, Antonio M. *Piaget: Dictionary of Terms*. (S. F. Campbell & E. R. Hermann, Eds.) Oxford: Pergamon Press, 1973. (Also in paperback.)

Bruner, Jerome S. *Beyond the Information Given: Studies in the Psychology of Knowing*. (Jeremy M. Anglin, Ed.). New York: Norton, 1973.

Bruner's body of theoretical and empirical work on the development of perception and thought is probably second only to Piaget's, and there are many similarities between them. In Part 4, Bruner distinguishes three systems of representation, based on action, imagery, and language. He also reports experiments on these systems, in particular, studies of conservation that include linguistic and perceptual variables.

Stone, L. Joseph; Smith, Henrietta T.; & Murphy, Lois B. (Eds.). *The Competent Infant*. New York: Basic Books, 1973.

Collection of 202 previously published papers with organization and commentary supplied by the editors; functions as a handbook on infant development to 15 months.

Wright, John & Kagan, Jerome (Eds.). *Basic Cognitive Processes in Children*. Chicago: The University of Chicago Press, 1973. (Paperback.)

Luria, A. R. *Cognitive Development: Its Cultural and Social Foundations*. Cambridge, Mass.: Harvard University Press, 1976. (Originally published in Russian, 1974.)

In the early 1930's, Luria and his colleagues developed unique methods to show the effect of culture (the introduction of Soviet collectivization) on cognition among remote groups in central Asia. This report includes many excerpts from their interviews.

Case, Robbie. Structures and strictures: Some functional limitations on the course of cognitive growth. *Cognitive Psychology,* 1974, *6,* 544–573.
  Case uses a functional (as opposed to structural) theory of intellectual development as a basis for performance models for certain Piagetian tasks. Data from children, ages 5.6–7.6 and 7.6–8.7, are discussed.

Morehead, Donald M. & Morehead, Ann. From signal to sign: A Piagetian view of thought and language during the first two years. In Schiefelbusch & Lloyd, 1974.
  See summary in Section 10-D.

Moerk, Ernst L. Piaget's research as applied to the explanation of language development. *Merrill-Palmer Quarterly of Behavior and Development,* 1975a, *21,* 151–169.
  See summary in Section 10-D.

Glick, Joseph. Cognitive development in cross-cultural perspective. In F. D. Horowitz (Ed.), *Review of Child Development Research,* Vol. 4. Chicago: The University of Chicago Press, 1975.

Riegel, Klaus F. & Rosenwald, George C. (Eds.). *Structure and Transformation: Developmental and Historical Aspects.* New York: John Wiley & Sons, 1975.
  Papers from a conference at the University of Michigan, August 1972, focusing on the concepts of structure and transformation, particularly in cognitive development and language.

Neimark, Edith D. & Santa, John L. Thinking and concept attainment. *Annual Review of Psychology,* 1975, *26,* 173–205.
  Commentary on selected publications in English, 1970–1973. Topics covered are: problem solving, concept identification, logic and thought, and language and thought; developmental studies are emphasized for the last two topics.

Ginsburg, Herbert & Koslowski, Barbara. Cognitive development. *Annual Review of Psychology,* 1976, *27,* 29–61.
  Commentary on major directions of the field; literature between June 1973 and December 1974 is considered. Topics covered are: language acquisition, Piagetian studies, memory,

humor, social cognition, cross-cultural and social class studies, putative racial differences in intelligence, and applications to education.

Siegler, Robert S. Three aspects of cognitive development. *Cognitive Psychology,* 1976, *8,* 481–520.

The performance of subjects in kindergarten through twelfth grade on balance scale problems was interpreted in terms of their existing knowledge, ability to acquire new information, and process-level differences underlying developmental changes.

Klahr, David & Wallace, J. G. *Cognitive Development: An Information-Processing View.* Hillsdale, N.J.: Lawrence Erlbaum Associates, 1976.

Presents the most recent and complete statement of Klahr & Wallace's information-processing approach, focusing on models of elementary quantification, number concepts, conservation and transitivity. (See also the articles listed in Section 7-A.)

Lawson, Anton E. M-Space: Is it a constraint on conservation reasoning ability? *Journal of Experimental Child Psychology,* 1976, *22,* 40–49.

Performance of children, ages 4.4–6.5 years, on a Backward Digit Span Test (measure of "mental space") compared to four conservation tasks poses difficulties for Pascual-Leone's (in press) theory of cognitive development.

Flavell, John H. *Cognitive Development.* Englewood Cliffs, N.J.: Prentice-Hall, 1977. (Also in paperback.)

Introductory text emphasizing Piagetian tasks and issues. Chapters on infancy, early and middle childhood, adolescence, perception and communication, memory, and diagnosis and issues.

Ault, Ruth L. *Children's Cognitive Development.* New York: Oxford University Press, 1977.

Lower-division undergraduate textbook on Piaget's theory.

Pascual-Leone, J. *Cognitive Development and Cognitive Style.* Lexington, Mass.: Heath Lexington, in press.

Bruner, Jerome S.; Cole, Michael; & Lloyd, Barbara (Eds.). *The Developing Child* (series). Cambridge, Mass.: Harvard University Press, forthcoming. (Published in Great Britain by Open Books.)

The first volumes in this series, aimed toward upper division students and nonpsychologists, should appear in early 1977. Among the volumes are Katherine Nelson, *Learning to Talk*; Peter and Jill de Villiers, *Early Language*; T. G. R. Bower, *Infant Perception*; Ann L. Brown, *Memory*; Jerome S. Bruner, *Attention and Perception*; Catherine Garvey, *Play in Childhood*; and Jacqueline Goodnow, *Children's Symbols*.

H Psycholinguistics, Cognitive Psychology, and Artificial Intelligence

The following is a selected sample of work in psychology and computer science on adult cognition and language. In addition, there are numerous undergraduate-level psycholinguistics texts (e.g., Deese, 1970; Slobin, 1971c; Greene, 1972; Glucksberg & Danks, 1975; Taylor, 1976; Cairns & Cairns, 1976; Kess, 1976).

Ogden, C. K. & Richards, I. A. *The Meaning of Meaning.* New York: Harcourt, Brace & World, 1938.
 A classic treatment.

Morris, Charles. *Signs, Language and Behavior.* New York: Prentice-Hall, 1946.
 This book includes a useful glossary, including the distinction between signs, signals, and symbols.

Miller, George A. *Language and Communication.* New York: McGraw-Hill, 1951. (Also in paperback).
 This and the following two books are classics on pretransformational treatments of language in psychology. (Miller and Brown were among the first psychologists to change their approach after Chomsky's work appeared, however.)

Cherry, Colin. *On Human Communication* (2nd ed.). Cambridge, Mass.: The MIT Press, 1966. (Also in paperback. First edition published, 1957.)
 This book was written when cybernetics information theory (e.g., Shannon & Weaver, 1949) was being applied to human language. The approach has since been discarded, but Cherry's book still makes for interesting reading.

Brown, Roger. *Words and Things.* New York: The Free Press, 1958a. (Also in paperback.)
 Brown is at his captivating best in this volume; see especially Chapters 3, 5, 6, and 7.

Lyons, John & Wales, R. J. (Eds.). *Psycholinguistic Papers: The Proceedings of the 1966 Edinburgh Conference.* Edinburgh: Edinburgh University Press, 1966.
 Five papers on adult and child psycholinguistics.

Rommetveit, Ragnar. *Words, Meanings, and Messages.* New York: Academic Press, 1968.
> Reports psycholinguistic experiments, focusing on word meaning and pragmatics.

Minsky, Marvin (Ed.). *Semantic Information Processing.* Cambridge, Mass.: The MIT Press, 1968.
> Some of the early approaches to semantic representation within artificial intelligence are reported here; Quillian's chapter has been influential in psycholinguistics.

Miller, George A. & McNeill, David. Psycholinguistics. In G. Lindzey & E. Aronson (Eds.), *The Handbook of Social Psychology* (2nd ed.), Vol. 3. Reading, Mass.: Addison-Wesley, 1969.
> Broad, well written survey of transformational linguistics and the following areas of psycholinguistics: mathematical, experimental, developmental, biological and clinical, anthropological (Whorfian hypothesis), and social.

Bower, Gordon H. (Ed.). *The Psychology of Learning and Motivation,* Vols. 4–10 and continuing. New York: Academic Press, 1970–1976.
> Series of integrative papers on their ongoing research by researchers in cognitive psychology, psycholinguistics, and learning. See also volumes 1, 2, and 3, under Bower and other editors, 1967–1969.

Attention and Performance, Vols. I–V and continuing. New York: Academic Press, 1970–1974.
> Under various editors, this series publishes new papers on topics such as attention, reaction time, memory, perception, organization, choice, visual and auditory information processing, and word recognition.

Blumenthal, Arthur L. *Language and Psychology: Historical Aspects of Psycholinguistics.* New York: John Wiley & Sons, 1970. (Also in paperback.)
> Excerpts from the work of Wundt, Stern, Guillaume, Huey, Lashley, and others, including pieces not previously available in English.

Olson, David R. Language and thought: Aspects of a cognitive theory of semantics. *Psychological Review,* 1970, *77,* 257–273.
> Olson argues for a cognitively based approach to semantics; in particular, he notes that word choice depends in part on the set of alternatives from which the referent must be distinguished.

Woods, William. Transition network grammars for natural language analysis. *Communications of the ACM*, 1970, *3*, 591–606.
Woods describes his augmented transition network (ATN) grammar as a competitor to transformational grammar. A version of this type of grammar has been implemented as part of a computer program for natural language understanding (sound to meaning). A final report (five parts, $2.50 each) on the project can be purchased from Ms. Beverly Tobiason, Artificial Intelligence Department, Bolt Beranek and Newman, Inc., 50 Moulton Street, Cambridge, Massachusetts 02138.

Fillenbaum, Samuel. Psycholinguistics. *Annual Review of Psychology*, 1971, *22*, 251–308.
Theory and experiments for the period 1965–1969 on the role of linguistic theory, biological foundations (animal communication, nativism, language universals), language acquisition, and experimental psycholinguistics (about half of the review is on this last topic).

Winograd, Terry. Understanding natural language. *Cognitive Psychology*, 1972, *3*, 1–191. (Also issued as a book by Academic Press, 1972.)
A computer scientist describes his language-understanding program, which gives equal attention to syntax (based on Halliday's theory) and semantics.

Lindsay, Peter H. & Norman, Donald A. *Human Information Processing: An Introduction to Psychology*. New York: Academic Press, 1972.
A second edition of this innovative textbook will appear in 1977. New research trends are explained so well that the book has been consulted by graduate students and researchers in other fields, as well as the intended audience of undergraduates.

Simon, H. & Siklóssy, L. *Representation and Meaning: Experiments with Information Processing Systems*. Englewood Cliffs, N.J.: Prentice-Hall, 1972.

Schank, Roger C. & Colby, Kenneth M. (Eds.). *Computer Models of Thought and Language*. San Francisco: W. H. Freeman & Sons, 1973.
This collection samples recent work in artificial intelligence, with an emphasis on the relevance to human cognition and language.

Dalenoort, G. J. (Ed.). *Process Models for Psychology.* Rotterdam: Rotterdam University Press, 1973.
Lecture notes of the NUFFIC international summer course, 1972. Lecturers included Papert, Reitman, Shaw, Suppes, Tversky, Winograd, and others.

Anderson, John R. & Bower, Gordon H. *Human Associative Memory.* Washington, D.C.: V. H. Winston & Sons, 1973.
Describes a computer-implemented theory of long-term memory and experimental tests, with a review of the historical and current theoretical context.

Hinde, R. A. & Stevenson-Hinde, J. (Eds.). *Constraints on Learning: Limitations and Predispositions.* New York: Academic Press, 1973.
Articles on animal learning and general learning theory, methodology, cognition, and language.

Solso, Robert L. (Ed.). The Loyola Symposium series (various titles; 3 vols.). Hillsdale, N.J.: Lawrence Erlbaum Associates, 1973–1975.
Papers on new developments in cognitive psychology and information processing. The titles are: *Contemporary Issues in Cognitive Psychology* (1973), *Theories in Cognitive Psychology* (1974), and *Information Processing and Cognition* (1975).

Kantowitz, B. H. (Ed.). *Human Information Processing: Tutorials in Performance and Cognition.* Hillsdale, N.J.: Lawrence Erlbaum Associates, 1974.
Each chapter is an overview of method, research, and theory in one research area. Useful primarily for those using an information-processing approach to developmental research. Note especially Pachella's chapter on the analysis of reaction time data, and Smith & Spoehr's paper on letter and word perception.

Winograd, Terry. Five lectures on artificial intelligence. MEMO AIM No. 246, Computer Science Department, Stanford University, Stanford, California, September 1974.

Gregg, Lee W. (Ed.). *Knowledge and Cognition.* Hillsdale, N.J.: Lawrence Erlbaum Associates, 1974.
Papers from the Ninth Annual Symposium on Cognition at Carnegie-Mellon University, May 1973. They reflect an information-processing or artificial intelligence approach. There are other volumes, under other titles, in this series.

Miller, George A. Toward a third metaphor for psycholinguistics. In Weimer & Palermo, 1974.

Miller offers a third metaphor, the notion of procedures, to follow two that have already influenced psycholinguistic research: association and communication.

Johnson-Laird, Philip N. Experimental psycholinguistics. *Annual Review of Psychology,* 1974, *25,* 135–160.

Examines the status of a number of issues and research areas, primarily drawing on literature between 1970 and 1973. Topics covered are the psychological reality of deep structure, organization of semantic memory, representation of word meaning, sentence comprehension, memory for sentences and discourse.

Fodor, Jerry A.; Bever, Thomas G.; & Garrett, Merrill F. *The Psychology of Language.* New York: McGraw-Hill, 1974.

Psycholinguistics textbook oriented toward transformational grammar; for serious beginners. Includes background material on linguistic theory.

Clark, Herbert H. *Semantics and Comprehension.* The Hague: Mouton, 1976. (Originally published in Sebeok, 1974, Part 3; see also other Part 3 papers.)

Good review, with an emphasis on Clark's own work, of the problem of form of representation of linguistic information; processing of negation; semantic representation of locatives; processing of comparatives, especially in three-term series problems; and active and passive sentences.

Weimer, Walter B. & Palermo, David S. (Eds.). *Cognition and the Symbolic Processes.* Hillsdale, N.J.: Lawrence Erlbaum Associates, 1974.

Interesting collection based on a conference, including work in generative semantics, psychology, and psycholinguistics. Chapters 12 and 19 are especially relevant.

Kintsch, Walter. *The Representation of Meaning in Memory.* Hillsdale, N.J.: Lawrence Erlbaum Associates, 1974.

Kintsch proposes that the meaning of text is represented in memory by propositions that include case relations but exclude function words and many other aspects of surface structure. A number of experiments are reported. The most interesting result is evidence that verbatim information from text may co-exist with a more abstract representation for at least several minutes after reading the text.

Norman, Donald A. & Rumelhart, David E. *Explorations in Cognition.* San Francisco: W. H. Freeman & Sons, 1975.

Two cognitive psychologists, their colleagues, and their graduate students describe a computer simulation of cognition and language processing and report associated psychological studies. The syntactic component is based on an augmented transition network (ATN) grammar. The semantic representation includes primitive predicates (the result of a process of lexical decomposition) that are linked to their arguments by case relations. The approach exemplifies recent interdisciplinary influences across cognitive psychology, artificial intelligence, and linguistics.

Kaplan, Ronald. On process models for sentence analysis. In Norman & Rumelhart, 1975.

An excellent introduction to Woods' theory of augmented transition network (ATN) grammar, with comments on psychological reality.

Estes, W. K. (Ed.). *Handbook of Learning and Cognitive Processes.* Hillsdale, N.J.: Lawrence Erlbaum Associates, 1975 and continuing.

A six-volume handbook composed of invited chapters. Most relevant are Volumes 1 (introduction), 4 (memory and attention), 5 (organization in memory, cognitive processes in reading); and 6 (information processing, problem solving, artificial intelligence).

Restle, Frank; Shiffrin, Richard M.; Castellan, N. John; Lindman, Harold R.; & Pisoni, David B. (Eds.). *Cognitive Theory,* Vol. I. Hillsdale, N.J.: Lawrence Erlbaum Associates, 1975.

Collection of papers from the Indiana Conference of 1974, divided into sections on speech perception, judgment, short-term memory, and cognitive structures.

Schank, Roger C. *Conceptual Information Processing.* Amsterdam: North-Holland, 1975.

Reports recent developments in Schank's conceptual dependency theory, including abbreviated versions of the doctoral dissertations of three of his students: C. K. Riesbeck, C. J. Rieger, III, and N. M. Goldman.

Bobrow, Daniel G. & Collins, Allan. *Representation and Understanding: Studies in Cognitive Science.* New York: Academic Press, 1975.

A collection of papers by researchers in artificial intelligence and cognitive psychology on the representation of knowledge, the "frames" approach to memory models, structure of stories and episodes, semantics, and reasoning.

Aaronson, Doris R. & Rieber, Robert W. (Eds.). *Developmental Psycholinguistics and Communication Disorders.* (Annals of the New York Academy of Sciences, Vol. 263.) New York: New York Academy of Sciences, 1975.

Based on a NYAS conference in January 1975. The contributors, primarily psychologists, discuss historical aspects, the role of cognition, mother-infant interaction, the competence-performance issue, and neurolinguistics.

Massaro, Dominic W. (Ed.). *Understanding Language: An Information-Processing Analysis of Speech Perception, Reading, and Psycholinguistics.* New York: Academic Press, 1975.

Massaro proposes an information-processing model of language, followed by more specific articles on speech perception, reading, and psycholinguistics.

Riegel, Klaus F. & Rosenwald, George C. (Eds.). *Structure and Transformation: Developmental and Historical Aspects.* New York: John Wiley & Sons, 1975.

The book is in three parts: historical roots of the concepts of structure and transformation, cognitive development (especially Piaget), and psychological linguistics.

Raphael, Bertram. *The Thinking Computer: Mind Inside Matter.* San Francisco: W. H. Freeman & Sons, 1976. (Also in paperback.)

A textbook on artificial intelligence; provides a good background for reading original reports.

Norman, Donald A. *Memory and Attention,* Second Edition. New York: John Wiley & Sons, 1976. (Also in paperback.)

Provides an excellent overview, including the best of the older work as well as new work on memory for linguistically structured materials.

Neisser, Ulric. *Cognition and Reality.* San Francisco: W. H. Freeman & Sons, 1976.

Theories of information processing are discussed and evaluated, and a new ecologically oriented approach is proposed. See also Neisser's 1967 book, *Cognitive Psychology.*

Crowder, R. G. *Principles of Learning and Memory.* Hillsdale, N.J.: Lawrence Erlbaum Associates, 1976.

Comprehensive survey: theory, methodology, data, historical perspectives.

Bever, T. G.; Katz, J. J.; & Langendoen, D. T. *An Integrated Theory of Linguistic Ability.* New York: Thomas Y. Crowell, 1976.

Wales, R. J. & Walker, Edward (Eds.). *New Approaches to Language Mechanisms.* Amsterdam: North-Holland, 1976. (Paperback, $18.75.)

Collection of articles on psycholinguistic studies, including word meaning acquisition, sentence comprehension and production, lexical access, and neuropsychological aspects of orthographic representation.

Anderson, John. *Language, Memory and Thought.* Hillsdale, N.J.: Lawrence Erlbaum Associates, 1976.

Cofer, Charles N. (Ed.). *The Structure of Human Memory.* San Francisco: W. H. Freeman & Sons, 1976. (Also in paperback.)

Collection of papers on topics such as short-term and long-term memory, prose memory, and artificial intelligence.

Miller, George A. & Johnson-Laird, Philip N. *Language and Perception.* Cambridge, Mass.: Harvard University Press, 1976.

Within an interdisciplinary context, the authors attempt "to lay the foundations for a new field of language study . . . psycholexicology," defining words in a number of semantic fields in terms of mental processes.

Bobrow, Daniel G. & Winograd, Terry. An overview of KRL, a knowledge representation language. *Journal of Cognitive Science,* in press. (Publication expected, early 1977.)

Bobrow, Daniel G.; Kaplan, Ronald M.; Kay, Martin; Norman, Donald A.; Thompson, Henry; & Winograd, Terry. GUS, A frame-driven dialog system. *Artificial Intelligence,* in press. (Publication expected, spring 1977.)

Describes a computer simulation system using knowledge "frames" to aid comprehension in machine-human dialog.

Rosenberg, Sheldon (Ed.). *Sentence Production.* Hillsdale, N.J.: Lawrence Erlbaum Associates, in press.

Clark, Herbert H. & Clark, Eve V. *Psychology and Language: An Introduction to Psycholinguistics.* New York: Harcourt Brace Jovanovich, 1977.
This should be the definitive text on language processing by normal adults and children. Detailed, authoritative consideration of sentence comprehension and usage, memory for prose, speech perception and production, semantic processing, language acquisition, and language and thought.

Chafe, Wallace L. The recall and verbalization of past experience. In Cole, in press.

Rumelhart, David E. *An Introduction to Human Information Processing.* New York: John Wiley & Sons, in press. (Publication expected, 1977.)

I *Mathematical Linguistics*

*Certain types of grammars have been formalized mathematically, yielding advantages such as the means of making explicit comparisons among them. Very little work in child language directly makes use of mathematical formalization, despite its potential value and its applicability to certain basic issues about language learning. Chomsky has been active in the area of **automata theory**, and a full appreciation of modern linguistics requires some knowledge of this aspect. A few references follow, primarily original theoretical papers and textbooks. See also the appropriate publications in Section 2-A (especially Oldfield & Marshall, 1968, Part 4; Dingwall, 1971), Section 2-H, and Section 10-A.*

Chomsky, Noam. Three models for the description of language. *I.R.E. Transactions on Information Theory,* Vol. IT-2, 1956, 113–124.

Chomsky, Noam. Formal properties of grammars. In R. D. Luce, R. R. Bush, & E. Galanter (Eds.), *Handbook of Mathematical Psychology,* Vol. 2. New York: John Wiley & Sons, 1963.

Miller, George A. & Chomsky, Noam. Finetary models of language users. In R. D. Luce, R. R. Bush, & E. Galanter (Eds.), *Handbook of Mathematical Psychology,* Vol. 2. New York: John Wiley & Sons, 1963.

Gross, M. & Lentin, A. *Introduction to Formal Grammars.* New York: Springer-Verlag, 1970. (Originally published in French, 1967.)

Ortiz, Alejandro & Zierer, Ernesto. *Set Theory and Linguistics.* The Hague: Mouton, 1968. (Paperback.)

Suppes, Patrick. The desirability of formalization in science. *Journal of Philosophy,* 1968, *65,* 651–664.

Suppes, Patrick. Stimulus-response theory of finite automata. *Journal of Mathematical Psychology,* 1969, *6,* 327–355.
> Presents a proof and discussion of the theorem that, given any connected finite automaton, there is a stimulus-response model that asymptotically becomes isomorphic to it. Implications for language learning are discussed.

Hopcroft, J. E. & Ullman, J. D. *Formal Languages and Their Relation to Automata.* Reading, Mass.: Addison-Wesley, 1969.

Ginsburg, S. & Partee, B. A mathematical model of transformational grammars. *Information and Control,* 1969, *15,* 297.

Suppes, Patrick. Probabilistic grammars for natural languages. *Synthese,* 1970, *22,* 95–116. (Reprinted in Davidson & Harman, 1972.)

Zierer, Ernesto. *The Theory of Graphs in Linguistics.* The Hague: Mouton, 1970. (Paperback.)
  The tree structures generated by phrase-structure rules are a type of graph. This book introduces basic concepts of graph theory, but for specific material on trees the texts that follow should be consulted.

Brainerd, Barron. *Introduction to the Mathematics of Language Study.* New York: American Elsevier, 1971.
  Formal concepts are introduced, but linguistic examples and applications are emphasized.

Wall, Robert. *Introduction to Mathematical Linguistics.* Englewood Cliffs, N.J.: Prentice-Hall, 1972.
  An excellent text.

Gross, Maurice. *Mathematical Models in Linguistics.* Englewood Cliffs, N.J.: Prentice-Hall, 1972. (Paperback.)

Salomaa, Arto. *Formal Languages.* New York: Academic Press, 1973.
  Emphasizes generative devices (grammars) over recognition devices.

Hintikka, K. J. J.; Moravczik, J. M. E.; & Suppes, P. (Eds.). *Approaches to Natural Language.* Dordrecht, Holland: D. Reidel, 1973.
  Includes articles taking a mathematical approach.

Levelt, W. J. M. *Formal Grammars in Linguistics and Psycholinguistics. Vol. I. An Introduction to the Theory of Formal Languages and Automata.* The Hague: Mouton, 1974.
  Topics include the hierarchy of grammars; probabilistic grammars; finite, push-down, and linear-bounded automata; Turing machines; grammatical inference.

Levelt, W. J. M. *Formal Grammars in Linguistics and Psycholinguistics, Vol. II. Applications in Linguistic Theory.* The Hague: Mouton, 1974.

Topics include phrase-structure grammars, transformational grammars, generative power, probabilistic grammars.

Levelt, W. J. M. *Formal Grammars in Linguistics and Psycholinguistics, Vol. III. Psycholinguistic Applications.* The Hague: Mouton, 1974.

Three problem areas are considered: language use, linguistic intuitions, and language acquisition. Topics include: the language-user as a finite automaton, artificial intelligence, universals of language development, process factors, and conceptual factors in language development.

Part II
SYNTACTIC DEVELOPMENT

Section 3
GRAMMATICAL
DESCRIPTIONS
OF NATURAL SPEECH

In the 1960's, the most important work in child language was done under the influence of Chomsky's syntactic theory. Researchers made audio tape recordings of children's natural speech, usually during interaction with the mother. Working from transcripts of these *corpora*, they wrote grammars. Usually the studies were longitudinal, so that grammars for the same child at different periods could be compared. So that comparisons among children could be made, a measure of linguistic maturity was computed for each speech sample: MLU (mean length of utterance, in morphemes). See Brown (1973a) or Cazden (1972) for rules on computation of MLU. Brown (1973a) has divided early syntactic development into five periods, or stages, on the basis of MLU. He identifies a particular aspect of language learning as characteristic of each stage, though the boundaries are not sharp. The stages are:

Stage	MLU	Focus of language learning
I	1.0–2.0	Major semantic relations, word order
II	2.0–2.5	Modulations of meaning: grammatical morphemes
III	2.5–3.0	Sentence modalities: questions, negation, imperatives
IV	3.0–3.5	Embedding of one sentence within another
V	3.5–4.0	Sentence coordination (e.g., and, but) with appropriate deletions

Stages I and II are covered in Section 3-A, stages III–V are in Section 3-B, and stages I–V for children learning languages other than English are in Sections 3-C and 3-D.

An overview of syntactic development can be obtained from one of the textbooks or review articles in Section 1. Additional information on stages I–V can be found in Sections 4, 6, 10, and 11.

For background reading, see the linguistics publications in Sections 2-A through 2-E and 2-I.

69

A Grammars for Children Learning English at Stages I and II

In the 1960's, syntax was considered in isolation. Word classes and restrictions on their combination were described by phrase-structure grammars or related means, particularly for stage I speech. Less attention was given to the learning of grammatical morphemes (characteristic of stage II), perhaps because English emphasizes word order over morphology as a syntactic device. In the 1970's, some aspects of semantics (e.g., case relations like agent and object) have been incorporated into descriptions of syntax. Furthermore, many researchers use situational and discourse context to help determine the meaning of children's utterances, a procedure made easier by the introduction of videotaping in place of audiotaping. Finally, individual differences are being studied. Some of the more recent publications listed below could equally well be assigned to Part II (Syntax) or Part III (Semantics); due to the historical continuity with syntax studies, they are listed here in Part II.

For background reading, see Section 2-C for an introduction to phrase-structure grammars; Section 2-E for the more recent influence of case grammar; Sections 2-B, 2-C, and the introduction to Section 4-D for morphology.

Leopold, Werner F. Patterning in children's language learning. *Language Learning*, 1953, *5*, 1–14. (Reprinted in Saporta, 1961, and in Bar-Adon & Leopold, 1971.)

> In the second half of this article, Leopold summarizes syntactic and morphological development of his bilingual daughter, Hildegard.

*Braine, Martin D. S. The ontogeny of English phrase structure: The first phase. *Language*, 1963a, *39*, 3–13. (Reprinted in Bar-Adon & Leopold, 1971, and in Ferguson & Slobin, 1973.)

> Braine proposes the notion of pivot construction to account for the early multiword utterances of three children. The idea is that two-word speech has two word classes: pivot words are frequent and appear in a fixed position; open words appear in combination with pivots and with other open words. Each child's corpus is listed.

Brown, Roger & Fraser, Colin. The acquisition of syntax. In C. N. Cofer & B. S. Musgrave (Eds.), *Verbal Behavior and Learning.* New York: McGraw-Hill, 1963, 158–197. (Reprinted in Bellugi & Brown, 1964.)

Like Miller & Ervin, Brown & Fraser identify word classes and their combinations and report some data on morphology. They do not identify a pivot or operator class, but introduce Chomsky's formalism by giving rewrite (phrase structure) rules for one of the two children (Adam and Eve).

*Miller, Wick R. & Ervin, Susan M. The development of grammar in child language. In Bellugi & Brown, 1964. (Reprinted in Bar-Adon & Leopold, 1971, and in Ferguson & Slobin, 1973.)

An independent "pivots" proposal (here, termed *operators*) for two children, plus observations on morphology for a third child. In contrast with Braine's paper, a number of word classes are identified, with tabulation of the ways they can be combined.

Chomsky, Noam. Formal discussion of W. Miller & S. Ervin, "The development of grammar in child language." In Bellugi & Brown, 1964(a).

Dubious of Miller & Ervin's straightforward approach, Chomsky holds that devious methods are required to catch competence in the act of performance.

Brown, Roger; Fraser, Colin; & Bellugi, Ursula. Explorations in grammar evaluation. In Bellugi & Brown, 1964. (Reprinted in Brown, 1970a.)

The authors consider the problem of evaluating grammars based on corpora of children's speech. Grammars for subsets of a 26-hour corpus from a 2-year-old, Abel, are compared.

Gruber, Jeffrey S. Topicalization in child language. *Foundations of Language,* 1967b, *3,* 37–65. (Reprinted in Bar-Adon & Leopold, 1971.)

One child's speech is analyzed as having a topic-comment rather than subject-predicate structure at 26–29 months of age. (See Li, 1976, for background; listed in Section 3-C.)

Cazden, Courtney B. The acquisition of noun and verb inflections. *Child Development,* 1968, *39,* 433–448. (Reprinted in Ferguson & Slobin, 1973.)

Cazden summarizes results from the corpora of Adam, Eve,

and Sarah: acquisition of noun inflections for plurality and possession, and verb inflections for the present progressive (-*ing*), past tense (-*ed*) and present indicative (-*s*). She also presents an error analysis and discusses the role of parental speech.

*Brown, Roger; Cazden, Courtney B.; & Bellugi, Ursula. The child's grammar from I to III. In John P. Hill (Ed.), *Minnesota Symposium on Child Psychology,* Volume 2. Minneapolis: University of Minnesota Press, 1969. (Reprinted in Brown, 1970a; in Bar-Adon & Leopold, 1971; and in Ferguson & Slobin, 1973.)

An overview of the Harvard study of Adam, Eve, and Sarah. Includes a portion of the grammar for Adam at stage III; a less detailed account of development between stages I and III; and sections on segmentation into morphemes, wh-question transformations, and the role of training variables (such as adult expansion of children's "telegraphic" utterances). Fairly technical.

*Bloom, Lois. *Language Development: Form and Function in Emerging Grammars.* Cambridge, Mass.: The MIT Press, 1970.

Bloom argues against pivot grammar, replacing it with a grammar that has different deep structures for different relational meanings of the same words (e.g., "Mommy sock"), determined by situational context. Transformations are used even for stage I speech (e.g., a reduction transformation is responsible for the ambiguity of "Mommy sock"). Very influential.

Slobin, Dan I. (Ed.). *The Ontogenesis of Grammar.* New York: Academic Press, 1971a.

Most of the papers are from a 1965 conference. Data associated with the above articles are discussed by McNeill, Schlesinger, Palermo, and Staats (the last two take a behaviorist approach). Slobin initially describes the data in terms of pivot grammar, but he and Ervin-Tripp comment on recent work (e.g., Bloom, 1970) which challenges that characterization. There are also papers by Braine on language learning and the role of grammars, and by Slobin and by Palermo & Eberhart on experimental studies of morphology.

Bloom, Lois. Why not pivot grammar? *Journal of Speech and Hearing Disorders,* 1971, *36,* 40–50. (Reprinted in Ferguson & Slobin, 1973.)

Summarizes Bloom's arguments against pivot grammar, which
are given at greater length in Bloom (1970).

Schlesinger, I. M. Learning grammar: From pivot to realization rule.
In Huxley & Ingram, 1971(b).
Given an "I-marker" (which specifies concept relations), a
child must *learn* realization rules to express it; they are not
innate. (Note that the same types of relations are represented
in the syntax by Bloom, in the semantics by Bowerman, and at
a separate, nonlinguistic conceptual level by Schlesinger.)

*Schlesinger, I. M. Production of utterances and language acquisi-
tion. In Slobin, 1971a (a).
Schlesinger provides further detail about I-markers and
realization rules.

Bowerman, Melissa. Structural relationships in children's utterances:
syntactic or semantic? In Moore, 1973(b).
Bowerman suggests relationships such as the possible relationships between "Mommy" and "sock" should be regarded
as semantic, not syntactic.

*Brown, Roger. *A First Language: The Early Stages.* Cambridge,
Mass.: Harvard University Press, 1973a.
For stage I speech, Brown adopts the idea of grammars based
on the meaning relations among words, comparing the
approaches of Bloom, Schlesinger, and Fillmore. For stage II
speech he attempts to account for the order of acquisition of
grammatical morphemes. Brown synthesizes a lot of ideas and
data in this re-analysis of the Adam, Eve, and Sarah corpora
and survey of related research. However, the need for additional data is evident, especially for stage II.

*de Villiers, Jill G. & de Villiers, Peter A. A cross-sectional study of
the acquisition of grammatical morphemes. *Journal of Psycholinguistic Research,* 1973a, *2,* 267–278.
Validation of the basic findings of Cazden (1968) on a larger
sample of children (21 children, ages 16–40 months). All 14 of
the morphemes discussed by Brown (1973a) are included.

Morehead, Donald M. & Ingram, David. The development of base
syntax in normal and linguistically deviant children. *Journal of
Speech and Hearing Research,* 1973, *16,* 330–352. (Also in *Papers
and Reports on Child Language Development,* No. 2. Committee
on Linguistics, Stanford University, December 1970.)

Language samples for 15 normal and 15 linguistically deviant children were compared, matching for MLU (2.11–6.5). Few differences between groups were found for general aspects of syntax (e.g., phrase structure rules, frequent transformations, inflections), but differences were found for such criteria as use of infrequent transformations and number of major syntactic categories per construction type. Results are discussed in terms of transformational and cognitive development theory.

*Braine, Martin D. S. Length constraints, reduction rules, and holophrastic processes in children's word combinations. *Journal of Verbal Learning and Verbal Behavior,* 1974a, *13,* 448–456.

Braine accounts for apparent omissions in both single-word and early multiword speech by a word-selection process that becomes more restricted with development (applying first to inappropriately high nodes such as S or VP, eventually to low nodes such as tense). This contrasts with Brown & Fraser's (1963) length constraint and with Bloom's (1970) reduction transformation.

Schlesinger, I. M. Relational concepts underlying language. In Schiefelbusch & Lloyd, 1974.

Schlesinger discusses his theory in relation to recent developments. Recognition of the importance of cognitive structure as a basis for language threatens to become a denial of the distinction between cognitive and linguistic structures.

Schlesinger, I. M. Grammatical development—The first steps. In Lenneberg & Lenneberg, Vol. 1, 1975, 203–222.

Schlesinger briefly surveys the first stages of syntax, describes his realization rules for word order, and discusses learning mechanisms.

Bloom, Lois; Miller, Peggy; & Hood, Lois. Variation and reduction as aspects of competence in language development. In A. D. Pick (Ed.), Vol. 9, 1975.

Children's early sentences involve a variable but systematic "linguistic induction about regularities in the relations between words that are, at once, both semantic and syntactic." Detailed analyses of longitudinal data from four children at MLU of approximately 1.4–3.0 are presented.

Howe, Christine J. The meanings of two-word utterances in the speech of young children. *Journal of Child Language,* 1976, *3,* 29–47.

Howe criticizes Bloom (1970, 1973), Brown (1973a), Schlesinger (1971a), and Slobin (1970) in a theoretical article. She demonstrates that few semantic relations have utterance-internal criteria that are true of all of the utterances cited as examples, and only those utterances. She also argues that the use of adult word-order expansions and situational cues to meaning involve the unjustified imposition of adult syntax and meanings onto children's speech.

Dore, John; Franklin, Margery B.; Miller, Robert T.; & Ramer, Andrya L. H. Transitional phenomena in early language acquisition. *Journal of Child Language,* 1976, *3,* 13–28.

The authors describe transitional phases between babbling, one-word speech, and multiword speech, based on individual videotapes of four children in free play with the mother and teacher for an 8-month period beginning at 0;11–1;4. In the transition to multiword speech, several presyntactic devices were used: phonetically stable or unstable units of one or more phonemes used in combination with a word; rote productions; and reduplication.

Ramer, Andrya L. H. Syntactic styles in emerging language. *Journal of Child Language,* 1976, *3,* 49–62.

Individual audio recordings of seven children in free play situations were made for the period between late single-word speech and an MLU of about 2.0. Age at onset of syntax varied unsystematically, but girls progressed faster than boys. Differences in style were also found: e.g., the four girls quickly learned the basic subject-verb-complement structure, whereas the three boys relied heavily on the presyntactic forms described by Dore et al. (1976).

*Braine, Martin D. S. Children's first word combinations. *Monographs of the Society for Research in Child Development,* 1976, *41* (1, Serial No. 164).

Sixteen corpora of stage I speech (MLU up to 1.7), including English, Samoan, Finnish, Hebrew, and Swedish, show little evidence for broad syntactic rules or word classes. Rather, each child has learned a number of positional formulae that map meaning components into surface structure positions, e.g., *here* + X. They are specific, often quite narrow, in their range. Two sources of free word-order are also noted: "groping" before a formula is learned, and separate learning of two formulae.

Bowerman, Melissa. Semantic factors in the acquisition of rules for word use and sentence construction. In Morehead & Morehead, 1976.

Bowerman reviews theories and data on the meanings of words at the single-word stage and on the relational concepts that underlie early rules for word combination.

Rodgon, Maris Monitz. *Single-Word Usage, Cognitive Development, and the Beginnings of Combinatorial Speech.* London: Cambridge University Press, 1976.

See summary in Section 5-C.

B Acquisition of Syntactic Transformations by Children Learning English at Stages III — V and Beyond

In contrast to research on Stage I speech, there are relatively few naturalistic studies of the acquisition of transformations. Most of these focus on questions and negatives, which develop most rapidly in stage III and are being refined by stage V. The passive transformation is less frequent in preschoolers' speech, but has been studied experimentally (Section 4-B). Transformations involving more than one sentence develop during stages IV, V, and beyond, and have been studied both naturalistically (below) and experimentally (Section 4-C). For background reading, in addition to the sources mentioned above, the following is a classic study of negation.

Klima, Edward S. Negation in English. In Fodor & Katz, 1964.

A number of changes have occurred in transformational grammar since Klima's article was written (e.g., G. Lakoff, 1970; Jackendoff, 1972). Most of the developmental studies are based on the linguistics of the mid-1960's, and their basic conclusions are unaffected by the details of the grammar used to describe developmental changes. However, the conclusions could be challenged on ground external to the grammar. For example, researchers with the view that linguistic learning is not independent of cognitive development (Section 10-C) or that utterances should be viewed as speech acts (Section 11-A) might regard the following studies as too narrowly focused on syntax.

Miller, Wick R. The acquisition of grammatical rules by children. Presented at the annual meeting of the Linguistic Society of America, New York, December 30, 1964. (First published in Ferguson & Slobin, 1973.)

    A study of grammatical transformations in the corpora of five children, approximately 2–3½ years old. Yes/no inversion, negation, and verb ellipsis seemed to develop as a group, though not simultaneously. Questions, relative clauses, passives, and conjunction are also discussed.

Bellugi, Ursula. The development of interrogative structures in children's speech. In K. Riegel (Ed.), *The Development of Language Functions.* University of Michigan Language Development Program, Report No. 8, 1965, 103–138.

*Klima, Edward S. & Bellugi, Ursula. Syntactic regularities in the speech of children. In Lyons & Wales, 1966, 183–208. (Revised version in Reibel & Schane, 1969, and in Bar-Adon & Leopold, 1971.)
  Formal description of the stages of development of questions and of negation, using transformational rules. Examples from the corpora of Adam, Eve, and Sarah are cited.

Bellugi, Ursula. *The Acquisition of Negation.* Unpublished doctoral dissertation, Harvard University, 1967.
  Full report of Bellugi's longitudinal study.

Brown, Roger. The development of Wh questions in child speech. *Journal of Verbal Learning and Verbal Behavior,* 1968, *7,* 279–290.
  Brown describes the development of wh-questions, based on the corpora of Adam, Eve, and Sarah. He emphasizes a stage at which children appear to apply only one of the two required transformations. Less technical than Klima & Bellugi (1966).

Brown, Roger; Cazden, Courtney; & Bellugi, Ursula. The child's grammar from I to III. In J. P. Hill (Ed.), *Minnesota Symposium on Child Psychology,* Vol. 2. Minneapolis: University of Minnesota Press, 1969.
  See summary and list of reprintings in Section 3-A.

*Menyuk, Paula. *Sentences Children Use.* Cambridge, Mass.: The MIT Press, 1969. (Also in paperback.)
  Menyuk obtained speech samples in standard, structured situations from 152 children in the age range 3–7 years. She provides formal linguistic descriptions of the acquisition of base structure rules, phonological rules, morphological rules, and, with special emphasis, transformations. Frequency counts on the population are presented, including data on children's elicited corrections of deviant utterances.

Francis, H. Structure in the speech of a 2½-year-old. *British Journal of Educational Psychology,* 1969, *39,* 291–302.
  Based on notes taken during 10-minute periods on the speech and activity of one child at age 2;7–2;10, speech structure appeared to be more related to the child's activity and to immature processing ability than to hierarchical linguistic

structures. Analysis involved linguistic distinctions among kernels, negatives, interrogatives, imperatives, predicate adjectives, and complements.

*Brown, Roger & Hanlon, Camille. Derivational complexity and order of acquisition in child speech. In Hayes, 1970. (Reprinted in Brown, 1970a.)
   Evidence from the corpora of Adam, Eve, and Sarah supports the view that the linguistic complexity of transformations predicts their order of acquisition.

*Ervin-Tripp, Susan. Discourse agreement: How children answer questions. In Hayes, 1970.
   Based on longitudinal language samples (naturalistic and constrained), Ervin-Tripp presents an order of development for features marking of wh-question words. Data on each word are discussed separately in terms of syntax, semantics, and communicative interaction.

Bellugi, Ursula. Simplification in children's language. In Huxley & Ingram, 1971.
   Children's simplification of the rules of language is considered, focusing on stages of acquisition of auxiliary inversion in questions, negatives, and indefinites, and case marking in personal pronouns. The data are mainly from the longitudinal study of Adam, especially at ages 3–4½ (MLU = 3.5–5.2.)

Limber, John. The genesis of complex sentences. In Moore, 1973.
   Spontaneous speech by 12 children, ages 1;11–3;0, was analyzed to reveal the acquisition by age 3 of complex constructions such as sentence complements, wh-clauses, and conjoined sentences. Several generalizations about the learning sequence could be made.

Lord, Carol. Variations in the acquisition of negation. In *Papers and Reports on Child Language Development,* No. 8. Committee on Linguistics, Stanford University, April 1974, 78–86.
   Lord reports a diary study of the acquisition of negation by her daughter, Jennifer. Contrary to Bellugi (1967) and Bloom (1970), the first marker for negation was intonation. Contrary to Bellugi, the first lexical negative markers were *can't* and *don't* rather than nucleus-external *no* or *not.* Contrary to

Bloom, a sequence of semantic functions (nonexistence, rejection, denial) could not be found.

Wall, Carol. *Predication: A Study of Its Development.* The Hague: Mouton, 1974.

Hypotheses about predication, some based on McNeill's (1970a) distinction between intrinsic and extrinsic predication and his suggested sequence of elaboration of the predicate (predication, modification, direct object, indirect object), were tested on speech samples of 14 children, two each at each 2-month interval from 18 to 30 months. Frequency counts of various predicate structures are given and discussed.

Major, Diana. *The Acquisition of Modal Auxiliaries in the Language of Children.* The Hague: Mouton, 1974.

Children in kindergarten and first, second, and third grades performed several tests designed to elicit responses involving modal verbs (e.g., *could, would, must*), including imitation, conversion, completion, tag-question, and question-asking tasks.

Hurford, James R. A child and the English question formation rule. *Journal of Child Language,* 1975, *2,* 299–301.

Based on Chomsky (1957); Hurford proposes an "Aux Copying Rule" to account for one child's data.

Prideaux, Gary D. A functional analysis of English question acquisition: A response to Hurford. *Journal of Child Language,* 1976, *3,* 417–422.

Certain generalizations based on surface structure can account for the data that Klima & Bellugi (1966) and Hurford (1975) analyzed transformationally.

Kuczaj, Stan A., II. Arguments against Hurford's 'Aux Copying Rule'. *Journal of Child Language,* 1976, *3,* 423–427.

A more parsimonious explanation exists for Hurford's data that accounts for a wider range of data: segmentation problems (in comprehension) and processing limitations (in production).

Limber, John. Unravelling competence, performance and pragmatics in the speech of young children. *Journal of Child Language,* 1976, *3,* 309–318.

Transcripts of children's (ages 2;0–4;0) and adults' speech, and dialogue in literature, show the same asymmetry of noun phrase types for subjects (mostly personal pronouns) vs. objects (mostly inanimate nouns and impersonal pronouns). Only 13% of subject NPs are not pronouns, and therefore potentially modifiable by clauses. Pragmatic factors are responsible for the asymmetry and for the rare occurrence of subject-modifying clauses in children's speech.

C Data for Children Learning Languages Other Than English: The Search for Linguistic Universals

Studies of children learning languages other than English have been important for suggesting universal aspects of language learning. As these are established, the focus should move to the investigation of individual differences and language-related differences in learning. See also Section 10-C.

BACKGROUND PUBLICATIONS: LINGUISTIC UNIVERSALS

The following theoretical publications are useful for background; see also Langacker & Munro (1975).

Greenberg, Joseph H. *Language Universals*. The Hague: Mouton, 1966a. (Paperback. Originally appeared in a briefer version in T. A. Sebeok, Vol. 3, 1966.)

> The search for linguistic universals, extending from phonology to kinship terminology, with special attention to markedness and feature hierarchies. Difficult reading.

Greenberg, Joseph H. (Ed.). *Universals of Language* (2nd ed.). Cambridge, Mass.: The MIT Press, 1966b. (Also in paperback.)

> Papers from a 1961 conference by nontransformational linguists, anthropologists, and psychologists. Topics include phonology, grammar, semantics, language change, general issues, and interdisciplinary considerations.

Greenberg, Joseph H. Some universals of grammar with particular reference to order of meaningful elements. In Greenberg, 1966b(c).

> An anthropological linguist surveys 30 languages to obtain absolute and probabilistic generalizations, particularly with respect to word order and morphology. This is a good source of hypotheses about acquisition of word order and is easier reading than *Language Universals*.

Bach, Emmon. Questions. *Linguistic Inquiry,* 1971, *2,* 153–166.
> Bach discusses substantive linguistic universals regarding word order and the question transformation.

Newnham, Richard. *About Chinese.* Baltimore: Penguin Books, 1971. (Paperback.)
> Though Newnham does not discuss the linguistic theory of universals, comparing his description of Chinese to English is an easy route to some appreciation for the similarities and differences among languages.

Li, Charles N. (Ed.). *Word Order and Word Order Change.* Austin: University of Texas Press, 1975.
> Papers from a conference at the University of California, Santa Barbara, January 1974. Theoretical papers drawing on a variety of languages and focusing on different levels of linguistic analysis.

Li, Charles N. (Ed.). *Subject and Topic.* New York: Academic Press, 1976.
> Note especially Elinor Ochs Keenan & Bambi B. Schieffelin, "Topic as a discourse notion: A study of topic in the conversations of children and adults," and Wallace L. Chafe, "Givenness, contrastiveness, definiteness, subjects, topics, and point of view."

Keenan, Edward L. Towards a universal definition of 'subject'. In Li, 1976.
> Lists about 30 properties that grammatical subjects tend to have, with citations from a number of languages. However, no property is necessary or sufficient, and languages vary in the number of properties their "subjects" exhibit.

Li, Charles N. & Thompson, Sandra A. Subject and topic: A new typology of language. In Li, 1976.
> In addition to the subject-predicate paradigm, there is a topic-comment paradigm. Languages fall into four classes, depending on which paradigm(s) they exhibit. English is primarily subject-predicate; Chinese is primarily topic-comment. Citations from a number of languages are given.

Voegelin, C. F. & Voegelin, F. M. *Classification and Index of the World's Languages.* Amsterdam: North-Holland, 1976.
> A large reference volume.

CHILD LANGUAGE PUBLICATIONS

The naturalistic acquisition studies follow. They emphasize the acquisition of word order and grammatical morphemes in two types of languages: those that rely on word order to determine grammatical relations (e.g., English) and those that are highly inflected (e.g., Russian).

*Leopold, Werner F. *Speech Development of a Bilingual Child: A Linguist's Record. Vol. 1, Vocabulary growth in the first two years. Vol. 2, Sound-learning in the first two years. Vol. 3, Grammar and general problems in the first two years. Vol. 4, Diary from age 2.* Evanston, Ill.: Northwestern University Press, 1939, 1947, 1949a, 1949b.

Leopold's daughter, Hildegard, learned English and German together. His diary study is thorough, trustworthy, and classic.

El'konin, D. B. General course of development in the child of the grammatical structure of the Russian language (according to A. N. Gvozdev). In Ferguson & Slobin, 1973. (Excerpted and translated by D. I. Slobin. Originally published in Russian, 1958.)

Chronological summary of development of sentence structure and parts of speech from 1;0 to 4;4, based on a corpus from one child.

Burling, R. Language development of a Garo and English speaking child. *Word,* 1959, *15,* 45–68.

A linguist's insightful description of the development of phonology, syllabic structure, morphology, syntax, and semantics in his child through age 2;10. Issues of bilingualism are discussed; phonological development is emphasized.

*Slobin, Dan I. The acquisition of Russian as a native language. In Smith & Miller, 1966(a).

Slobin summarizes early syntax and morphology, based on Gvozdev's diary of his son's language development and other Russian studies, and the development of word meaning.

Slobin, Dan I. Grammatical development in Russian-speaking children. In K. Riegel (Ed.), *The Development of Language Functions,* University of Michigan Language Development Program, Report No. 8. Ann Arbor: University of Michigan Press, 1965, 93–101. (Reprinted in Bar-Adon & Leopold, 1971.)

A shorter version of the preceding paper; word meaning is not discussed.

*McNeill, David. The creation of language by children. In Lyons & Wales, 1966(a), 99–115. (Reprinted in Bar-Adon & Leopold, 1971, and in Ferguson & Slobin, 1973).

McNeill relates the innate capacity for language to language universals. He claims that 2-year-olds express abstract grammatical relations such as "subject-of" in their speech, citing naturalistic data from English and Japanese. A reinterpretation of the pivot/open distinction is included. See also McNeill (1970a, 1970b).

McNeill, David. The creation of language. *Discovery*, 1966b, *27*, 34–38. (Reprinted in Oldfield & Marshall, 1968.)

McNeill makes the same argument in this paper as in the preceding paper, but at less length. The pivot/open reinterpretation is not included.

McNeill, D. & McNeill, N. B. What does a child mean when he says 'No?' In E. M. Zale (Ed.), *Proceedings of the Conference on Language and Language Behavior*. New York: Appleton-Century-Crofts, 1968, 51–61. (Reprinted in Adams, 1972, and in Ferguson & Slobin, 1973.)

The development of negation in one Japanese girl from 27 to 34 months of age, analyzed in terms of three semantic dimensions.

Kernan, Keith T. *The Acquisition of Language by Samoan children.* Unpublished doctoral dissertation, University of California, Berkeley, 1969.

Syntactic analysis of the speech of two Samoan children, Sipili (MLU = 1.52) and Tofi (MLU = 1.60).

Blount, Ben G. *Acquisition of Language by Luo Children.* Unpublished doctoral dissertation, University of California, Berkeley, 1969.

Syntactic analysis of the speech of Luo children at several early stages of development.

Kernan, Keith T. Semantic relationships and the child's acquisition of language. *Anthropological Linguist,* 1970, *12*, 171–187.

Analysis of the two-word utterances of a Samoan child based on Fillmore's (1968a) case grammar.

*Slobin, Dan I. Universals of grammatical development in children. In Flores d'Arcais & Levelt, 1970.

Comparative data from several sources suggest a number of universals of language learning.

*Bar-Adon, Aaron & Leopold, Werner F. *Child Language: A Book of Readings.* Englewood Cliffs. N.J.: Prentice-Hall, 1971.

Includes excerpts, translations, or reproductions of 17 articles on children's learning of languages other than English. There are several 19th and 20th century German selections, and also articles on French, Mandarin Chinese, Polish, Hebrew, Russian, and Japanese.

Slobin, Dan I. & Ervin-Tripp, Susan (Directors). *Semantics of Child Speech: Coding Manual.* Berkeley Cross-Linguistic Language Development Project, June 1972.

Describes a semantics-based system for coding utterances in any language, with examples from three of the languages for which the Berkeley project is obtaining child speech corpora.

Dingwall, William O. Government and concord in Russian: A study in developmental psycholinguistics. In B. Kachru, *Papers in Linguistics in Honor of Henry and Renee Kahane.* Urbana: University of Illinois Press, 1972.

*Ferguson, Charles A. & Slobin, Dan I. (Eds.). *Studies of Child Language Development.* New York: Holt, Rinehart and Winston, 1973.

The section on grammar has papers with data from American, Russian, French, German, Latvian, and Japanese children. In addition, Slobin's article contains numerous references and citations of data, international in scope.

*Suppes, P.; Smith, R.; & Leveille, M. The French syntax of a child's noun phrases. *Archives de Psychologie,* 1973, *XLII,* No. 166, 207–269. (Written in English.)

Detailed analysis of 33 one-hour speech samples between 2;2 and 3;4, based on probabilistic grammars and model-theoretic semantics. (See also Suppes, 1974.)

*Brown, Roger. *A First Language: The Early Stages.* Cambridge, Mass.: Harvard University Press, 1973a.

On pages 66 and 70, Brown lists studies (most written in English) based on corpora of utterances from 35 children (American, Finnish, Swedish, French, German, Mexican, Russian, Hebrew, Samoan, Japanese, Korean, and Luo). Brown focuses on the American studies but frequently mentions comparative data, particularly on pp. 156–158 (word order) and pp. 293–298 (morphology).

*Bowerman, Melissa. *Early Syntactic Development: A Cross-linguistic Study with Special Reference to Finnish.* London: Cambridge University Press, 1973a. (Also in paperback. Reviewed by P. Griffiths in *Journal of Child Language,* 1974, *1,* 111–122.)

> Originally a Harvard thesis, this is a detailed study of the development of grammatical relations in a language with free word order and a complex inflectional system; includes a comparison to Kernan's and Blount's (1969) dissertation data.

Lange, S. & Larsson, K. *Syntactical Development of a Swedish Girl, Embla, between 20 and 42 Months of Age. Part I. Age 20–25 Months.* Stockholm: Institutionen för Nordiska Sprak, Stockholm, 1973. (Reviewed by S. Felix in *Journal of Child Language,* 1975, *2,* 329–333.)

> Two grammars, one for utterances between 1;8 and 1;11 (early stage I) and one for 1;11 through 2;1 (early stage I through stage II), are compared, based on the approaches of Brown, Bloom, and Bowerman.

Schaerlaekens, A. M. *The Two-Word Sentence in Child Language Development.* The Hague: Mouton, 1973. (Reviewed by A. Staats in *Journal of Child Language,* 1975, *2,* 322–326.)

> Schaerlaekens analyzes naturalistic speech samples of two sets of Dutch triplets in the period from their first two-word utterances to their first compound sentences. She criticizes pivot grammar and Bloom's use of deep structures more complex than surface structures, and proposes a semantic relations model. She presents grammars and argues that McNeill's idea of a "language acquisition device" is supported.

Roeper, Thomas. Connecting children's language and linguistic theory. In Moore, 1973(a).

> Roeper inquires how children know the positions in deep structure of subject, verb, object, indirect object, negatives, and adverbials, concentrating on German for linguistic reasons. A theoretical linguistic approach is emphasized, though Park's data on stage I German are cited.

*Průcha, Jan. Research on child language in East European countries. *Journal of Child Language,* 1974, *1,* 44–88.

Short review by a Czech psycholinguist of recent studies of language development to age 3. The extensive bibliography refers to papers (some in English) on the acquisition of 11 languages, including Czech, Hungarian, Russian, and Serbo-Croatian.

Bowerman, Melissa F. Cross-linguistic similarities at two stages of syntactic development. In Lenneberg & Lenneberg, Vol. 1, 1975, 267–282.

Comparison of longitudinal data from English, French, Luo, and Samoan at early and late stage I. Certain semantic relations appeared in all of the early samples; others did not appear until late samples for some children. Some constructions tended to be absent through stage I (e.g., adverbs, instrumentals, predicate nominatives). Finnish children lacked yes/no questions; their language does not mark these by a questioning intonation.

Bates, Elizabeth. *Language and Context: The Acquisition of Pragmatics.* New York: Academic Press, 1976a.

Includes discussion of longitudinal speech records for two Italian children, collected by Antinucci, Volterra, and Francesco, for the age periods 1;3–2;9 and 1;4–4;0. In Chapter 12, she argues that a comment-topic pragmatic strategy for word order accounts for the data.

Kanecjan, G. R. An analysis of speech in the six-year-old Armenian child. In Průcha, 1976.

*MacWhinney, Brian. Hungarian research on the acquisition of morphology and syntax. *Journal of Child Language,* 1976, *3,* 397–410.

Reviews findings on morphological analysis, neologisms, order of acquisition of inflections, morpheme order, word order, and agreement, emphasizing data for Hungarian children between $1\frac{1}{2}$ and 3 years of age, but extending to age 6. The word is the first unit; later, semantic analysis precedes morphological analysis of the typically suffixed words. The structural properties of Hungarian make it an excellent choice for testing certain hypotheses about language acquisition.

D Acquisition of Sign Language by Deaf Children

In the search for linguistic universals, it is especially important to consider sign language, e.g., American Sign Language (ASL or Ameslan). Some unique properties derive from the use of the visual and kinesthetic modalities, but this fact strengthens the case for regarding the remaining, shared properties as true universals. Several references on adult Ameslan are listed below, followed by acquisition studies. See also the relevant parts of Lenneberg (1967b) and Kavanagh & Cutting (1975), and the publications of the National Association of the Deaf (814 Thayer Avenue, Silver Spring, Maryland 20910). For attempts to teach Ameslan to chimpanzees and to special human populations, see Section 10-A. For discussion on deaf children's cognition, see Hans Furth, Thinking Without Language. New York: Free Press, 1968.

BACKGROUND PUBLICATIONS: AMERICAN SIGN LANGUAGE

The references on adult ASL follow; note especially the two papers on linguistic universals.

Fant, Louie J., Jr. *Say It with Hands.* Silver Spring, Md.: National Association of the Deaf, 1964. (Paperback.)
Introductory lessons, illustrated.

Stokoe, William C., Jr.; Casterline, D.; & Croneberg, C. G. *A Dictionary of American Sign Language on Linguistic Principles.* Washington, D.C.: Gallaudet College Press, 1965.
A standard reference book. Sign descriptions are based on analysis into *cheremes,* analogous to phonemes in spoken languages.

Schlesinger, I. M. The grammar of sign language and the problem of language universals. Manuscript, Hebrew University of Jerusalem, 1969.

Bellugi, Ursula & Fischer, Susan. A comparison of sign language and spoken language. *Cognition,* 1972, *1,* 173–200.

A sign takes 1½ to 2 times as long to produce as a word, but because fewer signs than words are needed to compose a proposition, little difference occurs in the time required to tell a story in Ameslan vs. English.

Fischer, Susan. Sign language and linguistic universals. In C. Rohrer & N. Ruwet (Eds.), *Actes du Colloque Franco-Allemand de Grammaire Transformationelle.* Tubingen, West Germany: Max Niemeyer, 1974.

Fischer argues that Ameslan does not satisfy a putative linguistic universal suggested by Osgood in Greenberg (1966b). She cites data on word order in support of her position that Osgood's universal is modality specific rather than a true universal. In Ameslan, semantic constraints permit relatively free word order; where there are no such constraints, permissible orders are delimited by certain topicalization transformations.

Stokoe, William C., Jr. Classification and description of sign languages. In T. A. Sebeok, Vol. 12, 1974.

Bellugi, Ursula; Klima, Edward S.; & Siple, Patricia. Remembering in signs. *Cognition,* 1974/75, *3,* 93–125.

Short-term memory errors by deaf college students are associated with formational properties of the signs, paralleling previous findings of phonologically based errors by hearing subjects memorizing words.

Kavanagh, James F. & Cutting, James E. *The Role of Speech in Language.* Cambridge, Mass.: The MIT Press, 1975.

Includes four articles on sign language, by U. Bellugi & E. S. Klima; W. C. Stokoe, Jr.; J. Huttenlocher, and E. S. Klima.

Fischer, Susan. Influences on word order change in American Sign Language. In Li, 1975.

Lane, Harlan; Boyes-Braem, Penny; & Bellugi, Ursula. Preliminaries to a distinctive feature analysis of handshapes in American Sign Language. *Cognitive Psychology,* 1976, *8,* 263–289.

On the basis of clustering and multidimensional scaling analyses of confusion matrices, 11 distinctive features for Ameslan hand configurations are proposed.

Friedman, Lynn A. The manifestation of subject, object, and topic in American Sign Language. In Li, 1976.

Christopher, Dean A. *Manual Communication: A Basic Text and Workbook with Practical Exercises.* Baltimore: University Park Press, 1976. (Paperback, $14.50.)

Basic text, with descriptions and illustrations for fingerspelling and signs; includes exercises. Covers fingerspelling, Ameslan, and English-augmented sign language (Simultaneous Method).

Friedman, Lynn A. *On the Other Hand.* New York: Academic Press, in press. (Publication expected, March 1977.)

Seven papers on the structure of Ameslan by the students and instructor of a 1975 course at University of California, Berkeley.

*Klima, Edward S. & Bellugi, Ursula (Eds.). *The Signs of Language.* Cambridge, Mass.: Harvard University Press, in press.

The chapters of this volume were written by members of the research group on sign language at the Salk Institute in La Jolla, California. Their approach is to apply contemporary linguistic and psycholinguistic research methods to the study of sign language.

Wilbur, Ronnie Bring. *American Sign Language and Sign Systems: Research and Applications.* Baltimore: University Park Press, forthcoming. (Publication expected, November 1977.)

Reviews research on Ameslan and other sign language systems; analyzes relations to educational achievement and use with non-deaf, language-impaired populations; discusses syntactic structures that have not traditionally been attributed to Ameslan (e.g., pronouns and passive voice).

Sign Language Studies. Journal published by the Research Center for the Language Sciences, Indiana University, quarterly. Order from Linstok Press, 9306 Mintwood Street, Silver Spring, Maryland 20901.

CHILD LANGUAGE PUBLICATIONS

Papers on sign language acquisition and related topics follow.

Meadow, Kathryn P. Early manual communication in relation to the deaf child's intellectual, social, and communicative functioning. *American Annals of the Deaf,* 1968, *113,* 29–41.

Evidence is presented that deaf children of deaf (vs. hearing) parents show superior intellectual and social functioning; results on communicative functioning are mixed.

Bellugi, Ursula & Klima, Edward S. The roots of language in the sign talk of the deaf. *Psychology Today*, 1972, *6*, 61–76.
This article on the Salk Institute project includes material on sign language acquisition. See their 1974 NIH grant proposal ("The acquisition of sign language and its structure") for more detail.

Klima, Edward & Bellugi, Ursula. The signs of language in child and chimpanzee. In T. Alloway, L. Krames, & P. Pliner (Eds.), *Communication and Affect*. Academic Press, 1972.
Discussion of Ameslan as a language; the Washoe project; and sign language acquisition by Pola, a deaf child, at 2½ to 4 years.

Sachs, Jacqueline & Johnson, Marie L. Language Development in a Hearing Child of Deaf Parents. Report #2, Language Acquisition Laboratory, University of Connecticut, 1972.
Brief report on the oral speech of a hearing child of deaf, signing parents. The child's MLU at 3;9 was 2.88; his syntax was qualitatively different from that of a control child matched for MLU and was deficient for his chronological age, contrary to Lenneberg (1967b, p. 137).

*Schlesinger, H. S. & Meadow, K. P. *Sound and Sign*. Berkeley: University of California Press, 1972.
Reports a study of the acquisition of sign language in four children, two with deaf parents and two with hearing parents.

Cicourel, Aaron V. & Boese, Robert J. Sign language acquisition and the teaching of deaf children, Parts I and II. *American Annals of the Deaf*, 1972, *117*(1), 27–33; 1972, *117*(3), 403–411.
Deaf children learn sign language by a developmental process similar to that of hearing children learning to speak. It is argued that deaf children should be educated to be bilingual (in sign and speech).

*Bellugi, Ursula. Some aspects of language acquisition. In T. A. Sebeok, Vol. 12, 1974.
This introductory article includes observations about the acquisition of sign language by Pola, a deaf child of deaf parents at ages 2;7–3;0 (MLU = 1.69–2.79).

Goldin-Meadow, S. & Feldman, H. The creation of a communication system: A study of deaf children of hearing parents. Paper presented at the biennial meeting of the Society for Research in Child Development, Denver, April 1975.

The four deaf children studied created their own signs in the absence of language input.

Tervoort, Bernard T. *Developmental Features of Visual Communication: A Psycholinguistic Analysis of Deaf Children's Growth in Communicative Competence*. Amsterdam: North-Holland, 1975.

Based on observations of communication between pairs of children ages 7–17 years. For different children, signs, finger-spelling, and speech improved at different rates.

Meadow, Kathryn P. The development of deaf children. In E. M. Hetherington (Ed.), *Review of Child Development Research,* Vol. 5. Chicago: The University of Chicago Press, in press.

Section 4
EXPERIMENTS ON GRAMMATICAL DEVELOPMENT

In general, naturalistic methods are used to study language development in children younger than 2½–3 years and experimental methods are more common in children older than this. Both approaches have their advantages and disadvantages, even for adult studies, but as a practical matter it is difficult to establish experimental control over syntax in the youngest children, and unwieldy to use naturalistic data from older children.

Many of the following experiments reflect the same concerns as the naturalistic studies: acquisition of correct word order for subject, verb, and object, and acquisition of grammatical morphemes. There are also experiments with older children on more complex constructions, such as embedded clauses, and experiments comparing different types of performance (comprehension, production, elicited imitation, grammaticality judgments).

A Experiments on Competence, Performance, Metalinguistic Awareness, and Grammaticality

The papers in this section report experiments on competence, performance, metalinguistic awareness, and grammaticality, divided into two groups. (A few theoretical papers are included.) In the first group, experiments using comprehension, production, and/or elicited imitation tasks are listed. The major issues are whether comprehension precedes production, and how to interpret elicited imitation data. Many of the papers in Sections 4-B through 4-E also use these tasks, but are more concerned with the results for the grammatical constructions tested than with task differences. The second group of papers in this section focuses on the competence/performance issue and grammaticality. The two groups of papers have in common a concern with linguistic **performance,** *approaching this by comparing different types of performance (first group) or by considering the relation of performance to underlying competence (second group).*

COMPARISON OF DIFFERENT PERFORMANCE TYPES

The first group of papers, comparing comprehension, production, and elicited imitation, follows. For naturalistic studies of presyntactic comprehension and production, see Section 5.

*Fraser, Colin; Bellugi, Ursula; & Brown, Roger. Control of grammar in imitation, comprehension and production. *Journal of Verbal Learning and Verbal Behavior,* 1963, *2,* 121–135. (Reprinted in Brown, 1970a, and in Oldfield & Marshall, 1968.)

    Twelve 3-year-olds were tested on 10 grammatical contrasts, involving plurality, tense, negation, subject vs. object (in reversible active and passive sentences), indirect vs. direct object, and mass vs. count nouns. The order of difficulty of tasks was imitation < comprehension < production.

Maccoby, E. E. & Bee, H. L. Some speculations concerning the lag between perceiving and performing. *Child Development,* 1965, *36,* 367–377.

Children's ability to make perceptual distinctions that they cannot yet match in their copying behavior is discussed primarily with respect to visual forms but also with respect to language comprehension and imitation. Three explanations are considered; the one focusing on number of discriminated attributes is preferred.

Lovell, K. & Dixon, E. M. The growth of the control of grammar in imitation, comprehension, and production. *Journal of Child Psychology and Psychiatry,* 1967, *8,* 31–39.

The results of Fraser, Bellugi, & Brown (1963) were replicated at each age for 100 children, ages 2–6 years, and 80 below-normal "special school" students, ages 6–7 years. Rank difficulty of items tended to be constant across tasks, across age levels within each task, and for items within each task across normal and special school students.

Smith, Carlota S. An experimental approach to children's linguistic competence. In Hayes, 1970. (Reprinted in Ferguson & Slobin, 1973.)

In one of two experiments reported, elicited imitation was used to determine the difficulty of complex sentences in grammatical and ungrammatical versions for 3- to 4-year-old children. Smith argues for the importance of surface structure in processing sentences.

Nurss, Joanne R. & Day, David E. Imitation, comprehension, and production of grammatical structures. *Journal of Verbal Learning and Verbal Behavior,* 1971, *10,* 68–74.

On stimuli used by Fraser, Bellugi, & Brown (1963), high-SES white 4-year-olds performed better than low-SES whites or blacks. Production was harder than comprehension or imitation, which were equal in difficulty.

Rodd, Linda J. & Braine, M. D. S. Children's imitations of syntactic constructions as a measure of linguistic competence. *Journal of Verbal Learning and Verbal Behavior,* 1971, *18,* 430–443.

Four children about 2 years old imitated utterances designed to investigate subject-predicate order, subjectless sentences, and one child's prenominal schwa.

Fernald, Charles D. Control of grammar in imitation, comprehension, and production: Problems of replication. *Journal of Verbal Learning and Verbal Behavior,* 1972, *11,* 606–613.

Although Fraser, Brown, & Bellugi (1963) reported that comprehension of grammatical contrasts was superior to production, removal of a scoring artifact results in no significant difference.

*Slobin, Dan I. & Welsh, Charles A. Elicited imitation as a research tool in developmental psycholinguistics. In Ferguson & Slobin, 1973. (Circulated in 1968 as a working paper.)

Analysis of about 1000 elicited imitations from one precocious child between the ages of 2;3;2 and 2;5;3 suggests that sentence recognition and imitation are filtered through the production system. Many examples are discussed.

Baird, Raymond. On the role of chance in imitation-comprehension-production test results. *Journal of Verbal Learning and Verbal Behavior*, 1972, *11*, 474–477.

A methodological criticism of the approach of Fraser, Bellugi, & Brown (1963).

*Bloom, Lois. Talking, understanding, and thinking. In Schiefelbusch & Lloyd, 1974(a).

Bloom discusses research methods and evidence for an age gap between comprehension and production and provides a theoretical framework for further research.

*Ingram, David. The relationship between comprehension and production. In Schiefelbusch & Lloyd, 1974(a).

Comprehension must precede production, by the nature of these processes. Several alternative hypotheses about the relation between comprehension and production are considered against data and rejected.

Clark, Ruth; Hutcheson, Sandy; & van Buren, Paul. Comprehension and production in language acquisition. *Journal of Linguistics,* 1974, *10*, 39–54.

Critical examination of the assertion that comprehension precedes production, with reference to the speech of one 2-year-old. The role of nonlinguistic cues and a child's difficulty in following another person's line of thought are among the factors discussed.

Kuczaj, Stanley A., II & Maratsos, Michael P. What children *can* say before they *will*. *Merrill-Palmer Quarterly of Behavior and Development,* 1975a, *21*, 89–111. (A related paper is in *Papers and Reports on Child Language Development,* No. 8. Committee on Linguistics, Stanford University, April 1974, 65–77.)

Quantitative data from a longitudinal study of elicited imitation are reported for one child at ages 2;5–2;7 (MLU between 3.01 and 3.25) and at 2;9. The stimuli were various sentence forms incorporating the modal auxiliaries *will* and *can*. The words were imitated correctly in structures more complex than those produced naturally with the words.

Corrigan, Roberta. A scalogram analysis of the development of the use and comprehension of "because" in children. *Child Development,* 1975, *46,* 195–201.

Children ages 3 to 7 years performed production (sentence completion) and comprehension (true/false judgment for correct or reversed sentences) tasks involving three types of context (affective, physical, concrete logical) for *because.* Comprehension of each type of context preceded its production.

Chapman, Robin S. & Miller, Jon F. Word order in early two and three word utterances: Does production precede comprehension? *Journal of Speech and Hearing Research,* 1975, *18,* 355–371.

See summary in Section 4-C.

COMPETENCE, METALINGUISTIC AWARENESS, AND GRAMMATICALITY

The second group of papers is centered on Chomsky's distinction between competence and performance (e.g., Chomsky, 1965, 1968/ 1972) and his use of native speakers' intuitions of grammaticality (metalinguistic awareness) as the primary data source for writing grammars. Competence refers to underlying linguistic knowledge, a "mental grammar" assumed to be accessed whenever language is used. Performance refers to the act of using that knowledge and may vary depending on the type of processing (e.g., free production vs. elicited imitation), memory requirements, etc. Chomsky seems to assume that grammaticality judgments provide good access to linguistic competence, but others have argued that judgment of grammaticality is a type of performance with its own characteristics that must be considered. The usefulness of the competence/performance distinction and the role of grammaticality judgments are issues that have arisen in both adult and developmental psycholinguistics. In addition, grammaticality has been studied as a variable (e.g., in experiments on responses to grammatical vs. nongrammatical sentences).

Background Publications: Linguistics and Adult Psycholinguistics

The following articles provide background from linguistics and adult psycholinguistics for the second group of studies. See also Part IV of Aaronson & Rieber, 1975, which has discussions of the competence/performance issue by D. McNeill, K. Salzinger, D. T. Langendoen, C. A. Miller, and D. Aaronson.

Chomsky, Noam. Formal discussion of W. Miller & S. Ervin, "The development of grammar in child language." In Bellugi & Brown, 1964(a).

> Dubious of the practice of writing grammars of child language on the basis of speech samples, Chomsky holds that devious methods are required to catch competence in the act of performance.

Chomsky, Noam. Current issues in linguistic theory. In Fodor & Katz, 1964(b).

> Discussion of competence and performance, and levels of adequacy of linguistic theories.

Fodor, Jerry A. & Garrett, Merrill. Some reflections on competence and performance. In Lyons & Wales, 1966.

> A review of psycholinguistic data suggests that the relation between competence and performance models is abstract, not direct.

Gleitman, Lila R. & Gleitman, Henry. *Phrase and Paraphrase: Some Innovative Uses of Language.* New York: Norton, 1970.

> After a general overview of linguistics and psycholinguistics, the authors present a grammatical analysis and psycholinguistic investigation of compound nouns. Subjects listened to three-morpheme sequences for which stress patterns determined the segmentation, e.g., "black housebird" vs. "blackhouse bird." Production and recognition of paraphrases varied by subjects' educational level and syntactic and semantic factors. Implications for the competence/performance issue and the status of linguistic intuition are discussed.

Watt, W. C. On two hypotheses concerning psycholinguistics. In Hayes, 1970.

> Watt presents arguments against the Correlation Hypothesis and Strong Inclusion Hypothesis in a discussion of the competence/performance distinction with respect to both children and adults. Some background knowledge is required.

Pylyshyn, Zenon W. Competence and psychological reality. *American Psychologist,* 1972, *27,* 546–552.

Pylyshyn regards a competence theory as an application of the mathematics of symbol manipulation to mental representations. It should be maximally parsimonious for a particular set of observations, whereas a performance theory must be parsimonious for those observations (e.g., grammaticality assignments) plus performance data. Thus, a competence theory cannot be expected to have psychological reality in the usual sense of the term.

Pylyshyn, Zenon W. The role of competence theories in cognitive psychology. *Journal of Psycholinguistic Research,* 1973, *2,* 21–50.

Expanded discussion of the viewpoint presented in Pylyshyn (1972).

Piaget, Jean. *The Grasp of Consciousness.* Cambridge, Mass.: Harvard University Press, 1976. (Originally published in French, 1974.)

Examines how consciousness is acquired in a variety of behavioral situations, based on data from children about 4–12 years old.

Child Language Publications

The developmental studies on grammaticality and on competence vs. performance follow.

*Shipley, Elizabeth F.; Smith, Carlota S.; & Gleitman, Lila R. A study in the acquisition of language: Free responses to commands. *Language,* 1969, *45,* 322–342. (Reprinted in Bloom, forthcoming.)

Eleven children, 18–33 months, were given occasional commands regarding toys in a naturalistic setting. Telegraphic children (median utterance length between 1.4 and 1.85 words) responded (touching, looking, or replying) more often to well-formed commands, whereas holophrastic children (1.06–1.16 words) responded more often to telegraphic commands (e.g., "Throw ball!"). Both groups responded less often, but they repeated the command more often, when a nonsense word was substituted for the verb or indirect object. Implications regarding competence and performance are discussed.

Smith, Carlota S. An experimental approach to children's linguistic competence. In Hayes, 1970. (Reprinted in Ferguson & Slobin, 1973.)

In one of two experiments reported, an attempt was made to determine what kinds of structures stage I children attend to by observing behavioral responses. Though all were producing telegraphic speech, the lower-MLU children responded best to telegraphic commands; the higher-MLU children responded best to well-formed commands. (Same experiment as Shipley, Smith, & Gleitman, 1969.) The other experiment used elicited imitation to determine the difficulty of complex sentences in grammatical and ungrammatical versions for 3- to 4-year-old children.

Love, John M. & Parker-Robinson, Cleo. Children's imitating grammatical and ungrammatical sentences. *Child Development,* 1972, *43,* 309–319.

Children, ages 4 and 6 years, imitated strings of nonsense syllables with noun and verb inflections in grammatical (NVN) and ungrammatical orders. There was an advantage for grammatical orders only when function words were also present.

*Gleitman, Lila; Gleitman, Henry; & Shipley, Elizabeth. The emergence of the child as grammarian. *Cognition,* 1972, *1,* 137–164.

Can young children make grammaticality judgments so that grammars of child speech could be written on the same basis as adult grammars (rather than on the basis of speech samples)? Three children, 2½ years old, showed rudimentary ability. More advanced, adult-like behavior emerges in the period from 5 to 8 years, based on data from a group of seven talented children in that age range.

de Villiers, Peter A. & de Villiers, Jill G. Early judgments of semantic and syntactic acceptability by children. *Journal of Psycholinguistic Research,* 1972, *1,* 299–310.

Children, ages 2–3 years, judged the acceptability of correct ("Throw the stone"), word-order-reversed ("Stone the throw"), and anomalous ("Throw the sky") imperatives. The more advanced children (in MLU) performed above chance on all three types; the less advanced children performed above chance only on the correct and anomalous sentences. The semantic judgment task entails a lag in the evidence for syntactic competence relative to other measures, but it is a promising method for measuring semantic competence.

Schultz, T. P. & Pilon, R. Development of the ability to detect linguistic ambiguity. *Child Development,* 1973, *44,* 728–733.

A study of children, ages 6, 9, 12, and 15, indicates that the age at which children can detect ambiguity depends on the type of ambiguity: first, phonological (6–9 years), then lexical, then surface and deep structure (12 years).

Wetstone, Harriet S. & Friedlander, Bernard Z. The effect of word order on young children's responses to simple questions and commands. *Child Development*, 1973, *44*, 734–740.

Normal, telegraphic, and scrambled sentences were comprehended by the majority of nonfluent 2- and 3-year-olds (due to a preference for highly probable meanings), but fluent children of the same age performed less well on scrambled sentences (due to reliance on word order).

Kramer, Pamela E. Young children's comprehension strategies I–III. Manuscript based on doctoral dissertation, Yeshiva University, 1973.

When children in stages I–III respond to commands, anomalous and ungrammatical commands are harder than well-formed ones. Stage I responses are based on intonation contour and semantic knowledge of the noun.

Clark, Ruth. Performing without competence. *Journal of Child Language*, 1974, *1*, 1–10.

Performance factors are not just restrictions on the expression of linguistic knowledge but affect the manner in which syntactic structures develop. Conversely, linguistic knowledge affects how efficiently psychological processes can be used. Simplification strategies of one boy at 2;9–3;0 are reported.

*de Villiers, Jill G. & de Villiers, Peter A. Competence and performance in child language: Are children really competent to judge? *Journal of Child Language*, 1974, *1*, 11–22.

Four different performance measures (production, comprehension, judgment, and correction) of the same word-order rule (subject-verb-object) give different estimates of the time at which the rule is mastered. Psycholinguists should develop specific models for each performance, not a general competence model.

Blank, Marion. Eliciting verbalization from young children in experimental tasks: A methodological note. *Child Development*, 1975, *46*, 254–257.

When adult experimenters try to elicit children's reasons for responses, children often give irrelevant answers to "why" questions. An alternative method is described that elicits reasons much more successfully.

Eilers, Rebecca E. Suprasegmental and grammatical control over telegraphic speech in young children. *Journal of Psycholinguistic Research,* 1975, *4,* 227–239.

> Contrary to the suggestion of Brown & Fraser (1963), children 18–36 months old imitate more content words than function words even when stress is manipulated to favor function words.

Moore, T. E. Linguistic intuitions of 12 year olds. *Language and Speech,* 1975, *18,* 213–218.

> Like adults, seventh-graders' grammaticality ratings of 162 ungrammatical sentences (on a 20-point scale) provide little support for Chomsky's (1965) theory of degrees of grammaticality based on levels of rules. They differ from adults in their insensitivity to strict-subcategorization violations.

Bohannon, John Neil, III. Normal and scrambled grammar in discrimination, imitation, and comprehension. *Child Development,* 1976, *47,* 669–681.

> Between kindergarten and second grade, the number of children who can discriminate between normal and scrambled sentences increases from 22% to 78%. Discriminators performed better than nondiscriminators on imitation and comprehension of grammatical, but not scrambled, sentences.

Nelson, Nickola W. Comprehension of spoken language by normal children as a function of speaking rate, sentence difficulty, and listener age and sex. *Child Development,* 1976, *47,* 299–303.

Lloyd, Peter & Donaldson, Margaret. On a method of eliciting true/false judgments from young children. *Journal of Child Language,* 1976, *3,* 411–416.

> The authors describe and note the advantages of an experimental procedure in which a child judges and discusses the linguistic errors of a "talking dog," in the context of serving as its tutor. Cooperation is excellent.

B Experiments on the Relations Subject-of and Object-of in Active vs. Passive Sentences

How does a child learn to identify the logical subject and object of transitive sentences? The simplest English sentences are simple, active, affirmative, and declarative (termed SAAD, or **kernel** sentences in the psycholinguistics derived from Chomsky, 1957). The surface structure subject and object correspond to the deep structure (logical) subject and object in the order subject-verb-object (SVO); usually the subject is semantically the agent. With few exceptions, stage I American children use this order in producing their own utterances (Section 3-A). The cross-linguistic evidence is less consistent but indicates at least a strong preference for adult order by children learning a fixed-order language (Section 3-C). The **passive transformation** introduces a mismatch between deep and surface structure order: the logical object is surface subject, and the logical subject is object of the preposition by, or in a **truncated passive,** is deleted by a subsequent transformation. Correctly producing and comprehending both **voices** (active and passive) require a more sophisticated syntactic system than does the stage I regularity.

The following papers experimentally investigate this knowledge. The earlier papers tend to focus on the learning of the passive form as a syntactic transformation. The later papers interpret performance patterns in terms of children's changing strategies, e.g., reliance on semantic factors vs. word order. Most of the studies manipulate reversibility ("The dog bit the cat" is reversible to "The cat bit the dog"; "The dog bit the bone" cannot be reversed to *"The bone bit the dog"). Nonreversible sentences are easier, since semantic constraints alone might underlie correct performance on "The bone was bitten by the dog," but not on "The cat was bitten by the dog." The constraints are often related to the animacy of the noun phrases. (Note: In his 1957 book Chomsky regards these constraints as semantic, but in his 1965 book they are expressed in the syntactic component as **selectional restrictions.**) Another factor (often referred to as the pragmatic factor) is the probability of the event. "The mouse chases the bear" is less probable than the reverse, though either is

105

acceptable. Sentences described as reversible in the studies usually do not change in probability when reversed, but probability is sometimes manipulated as a separate factor.

BACKGROUND PUBLICATIONS: ADULT PSYCHOLINGUISTICS

As background to the developmental studies, some of the many adult studies on active and passive sentences are listed; recent studies are emphasized. One linguistics article is also listed; for additional background see Chomsky (1957, 1965), introductory linguistics books (Section 2-B), and the two books edited by Li (1975, 1976).

Miller, George A. Some psychological studies of grammar. *American Psychologist,* 1962, *17,* 748–762.

    Miller discusses the first psycholinguistic experiments based on Chomsky's (1957) analysis of the passive and other transformations.

Sachs, Jacqueline. Recognition memory for syntactic and semantic aspects of connected discourse. *Perception and Psychophysics,* 1967, *2,* 437–442.

    Eighty syllables (about 27 seconds) after presentation, changes such as sentence voice are not detected significantly more often than chance.

Wearing, A. J. The storage of complex sentences. *Journal of Verbal Learning and Verbal Behavior,* 1970, *9,* 21–29.

    Performance in a recognition memory task was better for unpredictable sentences (e.g., "The ugly boss was grandly entertained by the poor cleaner with Swiss liqueur") than for predictable sentences (e.g., "The weary traveler was soon annoyed by the long delays at the busy airport"). There was no difference for active vs. passive voice.

Clark, Herbert H. Difficulties people have in answering the question "Where is it?" *Journal of Verbal Learning and Verbal Behavior,* 1972, *11,* 265–277.

    Clark presents a theory that predicted parallel response latencies obtained in two experiments: (1) Subjects read instructions like *Blue is lower than pink* and then placed a blue (or pink) object accordingly; (2) Subjects answered questions like *If John is lower than Mary, then where is Mary?* A third experiment provided evidence against Huttenlocher's imagery theory of reasoning. (Background for Huttenlocher et al., below.)

Olson, David R. & Filby, Nikola. On the comprehension of active and passive sentences. *Cognitive Psychology,* 1972, *3,* 361–381.
Prior coding of an event affects ease of processing active vs. passive sentences. Evidence from verification latencies suggests that passives can be comprehended without recovery of the corresponding active or deep structure form.

Anisfeld, Moshe & Klenbort, Irene. On the functions of structural paraphrase: The view from the passive voice. *Psychological Bulletin,* 1973, *79,* 117–126.
Theoretical discussion of semantic and communicative properties of the passive voice.

James, Carlton T.; Thompson, Jack G.; & Baldwin, Jacqueline M. The reconstructive process in sentence memory. *Journal of Verbal Learning and Verbal Behavior,* 1973, *12,* 51–63.
The authors argue that output biases for active over passive voice and for beginning a sentence with the most salient noun (defined by high imagery rating) influenced the results of two sentence recall experiments reported.

Garrod, Simon & Trabasso, Tom. A dual-memory information processing interpretation of sentence comprehension. *Journal of Verbal Learning and Verbal Behavior,* 1973, *12,* 155–167.
Based on response latencies for active or passive questions about active or passive sentences in a preceding paragraph, it is suggested that both surface and deep case structures may be simultaneously represented in long-term memory, while only surface structure is represented in short-term memory.

Anderson, John R. Verbatim and propositional representation of sentences in immediate and long-term memory. *Journal of Verbal Learning and Verbal Behavior,* 1974, *13,* 149–162.
Similar to Garrod & Trabasso (1973), but using a longer memory interval and an additional task in which good recognition memory for sentence voice is found. The two representations are characterized as verbatim and propositional; Anderson argues that the latter cannot be a deep case structure.

Muma, John R.; Perry, Mary Elizabeth; & Gallagher, Joseph W. Some semantic properties in sentence perception. *Psychological Reports,* 1974, *35,* 23–32.

Animateness of noun, but not three other factors, affects comprehension of passive sentences.

Langacker, Ronald W. & Munro, Pamela. Passives and their meaning. *Language,* 1975, *51,* 789–830.

The authors propose an underlying representation for passive sentences in Mojave and Uto-Aztecan and discuss issues in extending their analysis to arrive at a substantive language universal.

CHILD LANGUAGE PUBLICATIONS

The developmental studies of active and passive sentences follow. See also those studies in Section 4-A that include passive sentences (e.g., Fraser, Bellugi, & Brown, 1963, and derivative studies).

Slobin, Dan I. Grammatical transformations and sentence comprehension in childhood and adulthood. *Journal of Verbal Learning and Verbal Behavior,* 1966b, *5,* 219–227.

From Slobin's doctoral thesis. Children, ages 6–12 years, and adults judged the truth of sentences of four types ("kernel," passive, negative, and passive negative) with respect to pictures. Syntactic, semantic, and pragmatic factors interacted to determine response times.

Hayhurst, Hazel. Some errors of young children in producing passive sentences. *Journal of Verbal Learning and Verbal Behavior,* 1967, *6,* 634–639.

Children ages 5–9 years were asked to describe pictures by constructing sentences identical in form with model sentences which were passive or passive negative, full or truncated, and, if full, reversible or nonreversible. Truncated passives were easiest. The most common error was to convert a full passive to its active form. Nonreversibility helped only the older children.

*Turner, Elizabeth A. & Rommetveit, Ragnar. The acquisition of sentence voice and reversibility. *Child Development,* 1967a, *38,* 649–660.

Children ages 4–9 years performed imitation, comprehension, and production tasks. The order of difficulty at all ages was nonreversible active < reversible active < nonreversible passive < reversible passive. Errors frequently involved reversing actor and patient.

Turner, Elizabeth A. & Rommetveit, Ragnar. Experimental manipulation of the production of active and passive voice in children. *Language and Speech*, 1967b, *10*, 169–180.

Children produce more passive sentences when the object, rather than the subject, is scanned first in a picture or is emphasized by the syntactic form of a question about a picture.

Turner, Elizabeth A. & Rommetveit, Ragnar. Focus of attention in recall of active and passive sentences. *Journal of Verbal Learning and Verbal Behavior*, 1968, *7*, 543–548.

Children ages 5–8 years were presented with sentences for recall (reversible and nonreversible actives and passives). The focus of attention, manipulated by pictures presented at storage or recall time, influenced sentence voice in recall.

*Slobin, Dan I. Recall of full and truncated passive sentences in connected discourse. *Journal of Verbal Learning and Verbal Behavior*, 1968, *7*, 876–881.

Children, ages 5–12 years, and adults retold stories presented in full or truncated passive sentences. There was a tendency to use the active voice, though (especially for older subjects) it was weakest for truncated passive originals.

*Huttenlocher, Janellen; Eisenberg, Karen; & Strauss, Susan. Comprehension: Relation between perceived actor and logical subject. *Journal of Verbal Learning and Verbal Behavior*, 1968, *7*, 527–530.

Comprehension of statements about one truck pushing another was tested in 9-year-olds by having them place one truck relative to a fixed truck. It was easier to place the logical subject (the "pusher") for both active and passive sentences. See also Huttenlocher & Weiner (1971).

Herriot, Peter. The comprehension of syntax. *Child Development*, 1968, *39*, 273–282.

Children, ages 5–9, and adults selected pictures (familiar or unfamiliar) to match reversible active and passive affirmative sentences that had nonsense words or English words. Nonsense sentences were more difficult.

Gaer, Eleanor P. Children's understanding and production of sentences. *Journal of Verbal Learning and Verbal Behavior*, 1969, *2*, 289–294.

Children, ages 3–6 years, and adults were tested on sentences varying in type (active, passive, question, negative) and complexity (simple, single-embedded, double-embedded, center-embedded). There was a comprehension task ("yes" or "no" to whether a picture matched the sentence) and a production task (imitation with 5 seconds of counting intervening). Differences for type, complexity, and task were discussed.

Tervoort, Bernard. The understanding of passive sentences by deaf children. In Flores d'Arcais & Levelt, 1970.

Forty-three deaf children viewed pictures and tried to choose the correct one from a set of five sentences (including various types of active, full and truncated passive, and anomalous sentences). They scored 80% correct when the true sentence was active, but only 56% correct when it was passive (27% for children under 13, 74% over 13).

*Bever, Thomas G. The cognitive basis for linguistic structures. In Hayes, 1970. (Also on pp. 1181–1189 of T. G. Bever, The interaction of perception and linguistic structures: A preliminary investigation of neo-functionalism. In Sebeok, Vol. 12, 1974.)

On pages 303–312, Bever reports some results of an experiment in which children, ages 2;0–4;11, used toys to act out reversible, probable, and improbable active and passive sentences. By age 3 children seem to use a processing strategy (strategy C) by which "Constituents are functionally related internally according to semantic constraints," resulting in reversed interpretations of improbable sentences like "The dog pats the mother." At about age 4 children briefly adopt a surface word order strategy for reversible (neutral) sentences, strategy D: "Any NVN sequence within a potential internal unit in the surface structure corresponds to 'actor-action-object.'" Within a few months, performance improves dramatically on reversible sentences but slowly on improbable sentences.

Bever, Thomas G. The nature of cerebral dominance in speech behavior of the child and adult. In Huxley & Ingram, 1971.

Bever presents evidence from adults and children that strategy D (Bever, 1970) is directly available to the dominant, but not the nondominant, ear. Children in the 1970 experiment who had an ear preference in a dichotic-listening test performed worse on reversible passives (i.e., used strategy D) than children with no ear preference.

Jarvella, Robert J. & Sinnott, Joan. Contextual constraints on noun distributions to some English verbs by children and adults. *Journal of Verbal Learning and Verbal Behavior*, 1972, *11*, 47–53.

Third-grade, sixth-grade, and college students supplied subject and object nouns for active and passive sentence frames. Subject nouns were more often animate than objects; children used more animate nouns than adults; and linguistic selectional rules predicted several aspects of the results.

*de Villiers, Jill G. & de Villiers, Peter A. Development of the use of word order in comprehension. *Journal of Psycholinguistic Research*, 1973b, *2*, 331–341.

Children 19–38 months old were asked to act out reversible active and passive sentences with toys. Children with MLU between 1.0 and 1.5 did not use word order; more developed children were correct on active sentences and had an increasing tendency to reverse passives (interpreting the first noun as agent). Below an MLU of 3, children frequently used themselves as agent.

Scholnick, Ellin K. & Adams, Marilyn J. Relationships between language and cognitive skills: Passive-voice comprehension, backward repetition, and matrix permutation. *Child Development*, 1973, *44*, 741–746.

Comprehension of passives by children in kindergarten through second grade did not require reversal to an active form, since children who understood passives did not necessarily pass language and matrix reversal tasks.

Maratsos, Michael P. Children who get worse at understanding the passive: A replication of Bever. *Journal of Psycholinguistic Research*, 1974a, *3*, 65–74.

Children, ages 3–4 years, acted out three passive sentences. The children, at ages 3;8–3;11, performed less well than those younger or older. However, Maratsos criticizes Bever's theoretical interpretation, which identified the dip with the second of three phrases of development, characterized by behavioral strategies.

*Strohner, Hans & Nelson, Keith. The young child's development of sentence comprehension: Influence of event probability, nonverbal context, syntactic form, and strategies. *Child Development*, 1974, *45*, 564–576.

In comprehending active and passive sentences, 3-year-olds

tend to use strategies based on event probabilities and word order (first noun = agent), while 5-year-olds tend to use syntactic information appropriately, performing poorly only on improbable passive sentences.

Ehri, Linnea C. Deep and surface structure in childrens' sentence learning. *Journal of Experimental Child Psychology,* 1974, *17,* 18–36.

Fifth graders studied sentences, half active and half passive, and performed prompted recall with the first or last noun as the prompt. Four types of sentences were used, expressing the cases agent, object, and instrument by different syntactic devices. Children's performance indicated that deep structure information was more easily learned than surface structure.

Whitehurst, G. J.; Ironsmith, M.; & Geldfein, M. Selective imitation of the passive construction through modeling. *Journal of Experimental Child Psychology,* 1974, *17,* 288–302.

Six 4- to 5-year-olds participated in five experimental sessions. Every child who had been exposed to adult models produced some passives on the test trials; children without models never produced passives. Comprehension scores also differed. The procedure involved reinforcement with M&Ms at some points.

Beilin, Harry. *Studies in the Cognitive Basis of Language Development.* New York: Academic Press, 1975.

Includes two chapters on the passive construction (theory and child experiments) with an emphasis on the close relationship between cognition and language.

*Maratsos, Michael P. & Abramovitch, Rona. How children understand full, truncated, and anomalous passives. *Journal of Verbal Learning and Verbal Behavior,* 1975, *14,* 145–157.

In five experiments 3- and 4-year-olds acted out various types of sentences with dolls. Contrary to the suggestion of Watt (1970), truncated passives are not mastered before full passives. Comprehension (and imitation) results for anomalous sentence types (e.g., *The cat is licked of the dog) indicate that children use the preposition as a cue for the passive, contrary to Watt's suggestion that children comprehend passives by processing only the initial segment (*NP be Ved,* which is the same for full and truncated passives).

Powers, James E. & Gowie, Cheryl J. The passive transformation on its own. Presented at the biennial meeting of the SRCD, Denver, April 1975.

Kindergarteners and first graders listened to an active or passive statement, then answered a related active or passive question (repeated for five additional pairs). Active sentences, but not active questions, were easier than passives. Probable sentences were easier than their less probable reversals. Several significant interactions were interpreted as evidence against consistent use of Bever's (1970) strategy D.

Harris, Margaret. The influence of reversibility and truncation on the interpretation of the passive voice by young children. *British Journal of Psychology,* 1976, *67,* 419–427.

Children, at ages 3;1–7;0, performed a two-choice comprehension task with pictures for active and passive sentences. Nonreversible active and passive sentences were easier than reversibles, and truncation also aided comprehension of passives.

Baldie, Brian J. The acquisition of the passive voice. *Journal of Child Language,* 1976, *3,* 331–348.

Children, at ages 3;0–8;0, performed tasks with reversible, nonreversible, and truncated passive sentences, and reversible active sentences. Fraser et al.'s (1963) task order (imitation < comprehension < production) was replicated. Performance was better than that reported by Hayhurst (1967).

Cocking, Rodney R. & Potts, Marion. Social facilitation of language acquisition: The reversible passive construction. *Genetic Psychology Monographs,* 1976, *94,* 249–340.

Eighty children 36–59 months old observed adult or peers modeling tasks involving active and passive reversible sentences. Linguistic comprehension was a prerequisite to imitation; model's status and reinforcement did not affect imitation. Results are discussed in terms of social comparison theory and syntactic rule learning.

Brown, Irvin, Jr. Role of referent concreteness in the acquisition of passive sentence comprehension through abstract modeling. *Journal of Experimental Child Psychology,* 1976, *22,* 185–199. See summary in Section 10-A.

C Experiments on the Relations Subject-of, Object-of, and Indirect-Object-of in Simple Declaratives and Embedded Clauses

The studies in this section are directly concerned with children's early learning of basic grammatical relations and with their later ability to determine the correct subject for embedded clauses that do not specify the subject (due to deletion under a condition of coreference). For early learning, see also McNeill (1966a,b) and Gruber (1967b), which are the naturalistic studies most concerned with the issue of acquisition of the subject-of relation.

*Huttenlocher, Janellen & Strauss, Susan. Comprehension and a statement's relation to the situation it describes. *Journal of Verbal Learning and Verbal Behavior,* 1968, *7,* 300–304.

Children, ages 5, 7, and 9, were asked to place one item relative to a second fixed item (e.g., "Make it so the black block is on top of (under) the orange block."). It was easier to place an item if it was referred to in the subject, not the object, of the statement.

*Chomsky, Carol. *The Acquisition of Syntax in Children from 5 to 10.* Cambridge, Mass.: The MIT Press, 1969. (Also in paperback.)

Interview data from 40 children were used to describe the development of complement structures and pronominalization. The complement structures are of three types: "Ask/tell Sandy what time it is"; "Donald promises Bozo to stand on the book"; "Is the doll easy to see?" (of a blindfolded doll). These structures (except *tell*) are exceptions to the minimal distance principle, by which the implicit subject of the embedded verb is the noun phrase most closely preceding it, and accordingly are difficult.

Cromer, Richard F. 'Children are nice to understand': Surface structure clues for the recovery of a deep structure. *British Journal of Psychology,* 1970, *61,* 397–408.

Children were tested on C. Chomsky's (1969) task, using several types of sentences related to "Is the doll easy to see?"

Young children interpret the surface structure subject as deep structure subject; children above MA of 6;8 could perform correctly and could generalize to nonsense syllable adjectives.

Kessel, F. S. The role of syntax in children's comprehension from ages six to twelve. *Monographs of the Society for Research in Child Development,* 1970, *35* (6).

When asked to indicate which of two pictures matches a sentence, children showed earlier mastery of the *ask/tell* and *easy/eager* contrasts than has been found with other tasks. An experiment on ambiguity is also reported (Section 4-F).

Huttenlocher, Janellen & Weiner, Susan L. Comprehension of instructions in varying contexts. *Cognitive Psychology,* 1971, *2,* 369–385.)

Four experiments are reported extending Huttenlocher's previous work. Fourth graders found it harder to follow instructions of the form "The (color) block is on top of/under the (color) block" when both blocks had to be moved than when one was fixed. A similar result was obtained for "The (color) truck is pushing/pulling the (color) truck" and its passive form with a broader age sample (second, fourth, and sixth graders).

Rodd, Linda J. & Braine, Martin D. S. Children's imitations of syntactic constructions as a measure of linguistic competence. *Journal of Verbal Learning and Verbal Behavior,* 1971, *18,* 430–443.

Four children about 2 years old imitated utterances designed to investigate subject-predicate order, subjectless sentences, and one child's prenominal schwa.

Hornby, Peter A. Surface structure and the topic-comment distinction: A developmental study. *Child Development,* 1971, *42,* 1975–1988.

In picture-choice and picture-description tasks, children at ages 6, 8, and 10 were equally able to mark the topic-comment distinction, but the various surface structure devices were used differentially as a function of age.

Fischer, Susan D. *The Acquisition of Verb-Particle and Dative Constructions.* Doctoral dissertation, MIT, October 1971.

Children, at ages 3;3–4;3, did acceptability judgments, imitation and comprehension tasks. Semantic reversibility had an effect; pronoun objects were easier than full NPs; the dative-movement transformation made sentences more difficult.

McNeill, D.; Yukawa, R.; & McNeill, N. B. The acquisition of direct and indirect objects in Japanese. *Child Development*, 1971, *42*, 237-250.

Errors of 3- to 5-year-old Japanese children in responding to imperatives with direct and indirect objects suggest the operation of certain linguistic universals in the development of linguistic rules.

Brown, H. Douglas. Children's comprehension of relativized English sentences. *Child Development*, 1971, *42*, 1923-1936.

Three syntactic aspects of relative clauses (embeddedness position of the clause; the relative pronoun; and its focus) were incorporated into a picture-cued comprehension task performed by children 3, 4, and 5 years old. Subject focus was easier than object focus; other differences occurred only in interactions.

*Sinclair, Hermina & Bronckart, J. P. S.V.O. a linguistic universal? A study in developmental psycholinguistics. *Journal of Experimental Child Psychology*, 1972, *14*, 329-48.

French children 2-6 years old were presented with uninflected three-word strings of nouns and verbs in the orders NVN (the grammatical order), NNV, and VNN, and acted them out with toys. Strategies, in developmental order, included: (1) interpret the nouns only as objects, with no agent or self as agent, (2) interpret the noun closest to the verb as agent or (other children) as object, and (3) interpret the first noun as agent.

Kramer, Pamela E.; Koff, Elissa; & Luria, Zella. The development of competence in an exceptional language structure in older children and young adults. *Child Development*, 1972, *43*, 121-130.

Subjects 8-20 years of age were tested for competence on *ask* and *tell* sentences similar to those studied by C. Chomsky (1969). About one-third of the older groups performed incorrectly, and stages found by Chomsky for subjects below age 8 were duplicated above age 8. Subjects who were incorrect were retested 2 years later: younger subjects improved no more than the older subjects despite their hypothesized "language plasticity."

Cromer, Richard F. The learning of surface structure cues to deep structure by a puppet show technique. *Quarterly Journal of Experimental Psychology*, 1972a, *24*, 66-76.

Fifty-six children were classified at four levels of comprehension of sentences of the form, "John is easy/eager to please." A few days later they were trained on nonsense words in frames such as "I'm always *ispy* to read to you" and "Reading neckwatches is *riffable*." Different strategies were associated with different levels of comprehension on the pretest. Linguistic markedness is discussed.

Cromer, Richard F. Learning of linguistic surface structure cues to deep structure by educationally subnormal children. *American Journal of Mental Deficiency,* 1972b, *77,* 346–353.

A group of children 7–16 years old, with mean IQ = 62.5, never used a response strategy posited to show a language-specific learning ability, which is found in normal children but not adults (cf. Cromer, 1974a).

Roeper, Thomas. Theoretical implications of word order, topicalization and inflections in German language acquisition. In Ferguson & Slobin, 1973(b).

Imitation and comprehension tasks for 60 sentences were performed by 45 children 4–5 years old. Results on word order, reduced conjoined structures, embedding, and branching are discussed in terms of the child "making decisions" about the language during acquisition. German children have less difficulty with inversions of normal word order than American children, perhaps because it occurs in a wider range of syntactic contexts.

Cromer, Richard F. Child and adult learning of surface structure cues to deep structure using a picture card technique. *Journal of Psycholinguistic Research,* 1974a, *3,* 1–14.

Only adults and higher IQ children performed above chance in learning nonsense words replacing *eager/easy* in the frame "John is —— to please." Children, but not adults, gave evidence of a language-specific learning ability in their strategies.

Cambon, Jacqueline & Sinclair, Hermina. Relations between syntax and semantics: Are they 'easy to see'? *British Journal of Psychology,* 1974, *65,* 133–140.

French children performed one of C. Chomsky's (1969) tasks ("Is the doll easy or difficult to see?"), with a doll-lying-down condition as well as a doll-blindfolded condition. Results are generally consistent with Chomsky's, but certain discrepancies suggested an investigation of a possible parallel development in the semantic interpretation of *see*.

*Maratsos, Michael P. How preschool children understand missing complement subjects. *Child Development,* 1974b, *45,* 700–706.
Four- and 5-year-old children acted out sentences with the verbs *tell, ask,* and *promise.* In the first experiment, they based their responses on a semantic-role principle, not on C. Chomsky's (1969) minimal-distance principle. A second experiment allowed better specification of the use of the semantic-role principle.

Garman, M. On the acquisition of two complex syntactic constructions in Tamil. *Journal of Child Language,* 1974, *1,* 65–76.
Three- to five-year-old Tamil children use strategies sensitive to surface structure order in answering questions requiring correct assignment of subject or object relations in the matrix and embedded clauses of (NV)NV and N(NV)V constructions.

*de Villiers, Jill G. & de Villiers, Peter A. Competence and performance in child language: Are children really competent to judge? *Journal of Child Language,* 1974, *1,* 11–22.
A survey of literature on active (and occasionally passive) sentences reveals that four different performance measures (production, comprehension, judgment, and correction) of the same word-order rule (subject-verb-object) give different estimates of the time at which the rule is mastered. Psycholinguists should develop specific models for each performance, not a general competence model.

Sheldon, Amy. The role of parallel function in the acquisition of relative clauses in English. *Journal of Verbal Learning and Verbal Behavior,* 1974, *13,* 272–281.
Children, at ages 3;8–5;5, performed a comprehension task on four types of sentences with relative clauses. Sentences for which the identical noun phrases had the same function were easier. Position of the embedded clause and word order had no effect, disconfirming a universal proposed by Slobin (1971d). Sheldon proposes a Parallel Function Hypothesis.

Harris, Richard J. Children's comprehension of complex sentences. *Journal of Experimental Child Psychology,* 1975, *19,* 420–433.
Four tasks (imperatives, short-term memory, direct questioning, and anomaly-detection) were performed by children ages 4–12, and the last two tasks by adults, for sentences with verbs

taking sentential complements (e.g., Sally *knew* that she was early). Even the oldest children were not at adult level.

*Cromer, Richard F. An experimental investigation of a putative linguistic universal: Marking and the indirect object. *Journal of Experimental Child Psychology,* 1975, *20,* 73–80.

A putative linguistic universal holds that children should expect a marked linguistic form to be the indirect object. However, in two artificial language experiments, children learning a language in which indirect objects were marked performed no better than children learning a language in which direct objects were marked.

Chapman, Robin S. & Miller, Jon F. Word order in early two and three word utterances: Does production precede comprehension? *Journal of Speech and Hearing Research,* 1975, *18,* 355–371.

Five children each at MLU 1.8, 2.4, and 2.9 were tested on subject-object order for reversible sentences in an object-manipulation paradigm. Performance was better on a production task than on a comprehension task. However, comprehension was near 100% for sentences with animate subject and inanimate object, suggesting the use of semantic strategies.

Goldman, Susan R. Reading skill and the minimum distance principle: A comparison of listening and reading comprehension. *Journal of Experimental Child Psychology,* 1976, *22,* 123–142.

Children in grades three, four, and five performed comprehension tasks for sentences using *tell* and *promise*. C. Chomsky's (1969) stage analysis was supported in a listening, but not in a reading, condition. In a second experiment, half of a group of second and third graders performed differently in a mixed vs. a blocked set of trials.

Morsbach, Gisela & Steel, Pamela M. 'John is easy to see' re-investigated. *Journal of Child Language,* 1976, *3,* 443–447.

Five- and six-year-olds performed well on C. Chomsky's (1969) "easy to see" task when a condition was included in which the doll was placed behind a semitransparent screen.

Cook, V. J. A note on indirect objects. *Journal of Child Language,* 1976, *3,* 435–437.

Children ages 5;0–10;0 acted out sentences with indirect objects. They performed much better with the *to* form than the IO-DO form. The order of difficulty (easiest to hardest) by IO-DO animacy was animate-inanimate, inanimate-animate, inanimate-inanimate.

D Experiments on Inflectional Morphology and Auxiliary Elements

*Most of the papers in this section report on the use of an elicitation procedure to study children's acquisition of grammatical morphemes. A word is composed of one or more **morphemes**, which are the minimal meaning-carrying units of grammatical structure. Nouns, verbs, adjectives, and adverbs are **lexical morphemes**; prepositions, pronouns, conjunctions, articles, and **affixes** (morphemes that cannot occur alone but must be bound to a **root morpheme**) are **grammatical morphemes**. Of the affixes, **inflectional affixes** are those which indicate number (e.g., plurality), tense, aspect, etc. **Derivational affixes** create a word of a different part of speech. For example,* singers *is composed of three morphemes:* sing *is a lexical morpheme (a verb);* -er *is a derivational affix, which when added to the root* sing *creates a noun; and* -s *is an inflectional affix. The developmental studies focus on inflectional affixes (inflections) and on free-standing auxiliary morphemes such as modal verbs (*can, will, *etc.),* not, have, *and* be. *For linguistic treatments see the following books and Section 2.*

BACKGROUND PUBLICATIONS: LINGUISTICS

Matthews, P. H. *Inflectional Morphology*. London: Cambridge University Press, 1972. (Also in paperback.)

Matthews, P. H. *Morphology*. London: Cambridge University Press, 1974. (Also in paperback.)

CHILD LANGUAGE PUBLICATIONS

*Berko, Jean. The child's learning of English morphology. *Word*, 1958, *14*, 150–177. (Reprinted in Bar-Adon & Leopold, 1971, and in Saporta, 1961.)

The classic experimental study of children's acquisition of grammatical morphemes. Children 4–7 years old were led to complete the experimenter's descriptions (requiring inflections) of pictures, using nonsense nouns and verbs as stems. Example: "This is a wug. Now there is another one. There are two of them. There are two ———.''

Ervin, Susan M. Imitation and structural change in children's language. In Lenneberg, 1964b(b).
    Ervin collected longitudinal data from children ages 2–4 years. To test the plural morpheme, she had them describe one or two objects (using a familiar or nonsense root). The past tense morpheme was elicited in interviews. She observed over-regularization when a rule was learned; hence, a child who was using the correct, irregular form *came* would switch to *comed* when the *-ed* inflection was acquired. It was also observed that a nonsense root or phonologically difficult construction delayed performance.

Kernan, Keith T. & Blount, Ben G. The acquisition of Spanish grammar by Mexican children. *Anthropological Linguist,* 1966, *8*(9), 1–14.
    A modification of Berko's procedure for testing morphology was used with Mexican children 4–12 years old.

Anisfeld, M. & Tucker, G. R. English pluralization rules of six-year-old children. *Child Development,* 1967, *38,* 1201–1217. (Reprinted in Ferguson & Slobin, 1973.)
    The results of several production and recognition tasks with kindergarten children are reported.

Anisfeld, Moshe & Gordon, Malcolm. On the psychophonological structure of English inflectional rules. *Journal of Verbal Learning and Verbal Behavior,* 1968, *7,* 973–979.
    Subjects, ages 6, 9, and 19 years, chose from nonsense word pairs the most suitable plural. Preferred words ended in phonemes that shared phonological features with the regular plural suffix. Seven-year-olds judged for past tense.

Palermo, David S. & Eberhart, V. Lynn. On the learning of morphological rules: An experimental analogy. *Journal of Verbal Learning and Verbal Behavior,* 1968, *7,* 337–344.
    College students in a paired-associate learning experiment performed analogously to children learning morphological rules: irregular pairs were learned faster than regular pairs; errors on irregular pairs were overgeneralizations from regular pairs; and pairs presented only on test trials were learned quickly once the regularities of the other pairs had been learned.

Donaldson, M. Developmental aspects of performance with negatives. In Flores d'Arcais and Levelt, 1970.

Five- to seven-year-old children performed sentence-completion and comprehension tasks relating to the description of arrays of colored shapes. Situational variables had an effect on the difficulty of negative descriptions (e.g., "This circle is not red.").

Koziol, S. M. Development of noun plural rules during the primary grades. In *Papers and Reports on Child Language Development,* No. 2. Committee on Linguistics, Stanford University, December 1970.

Slobin, Dan I. On the learning of morphological rules: A reply to Palermo and Eberhart. In Slobin, 1971a(b).

Slobin questions the applicability of Palermo & Eberhart's (1968) experiment to language development and presents previously unpublished data from naturalistic studies in tabular form.

Palermo, David S. & Eberhart, V. Lynn. On the learning of morphological rules: A reply to Slobin. In Slobin, 1971a.

The authors note the results of additional experiments in their reply to Slobin.

Selby, Susan. The development of morphological rules in children. *British Journal of Educational Psychology,* 1972, *42,* 293–299.

Berko's "wug test" was administered to children 4–14 years old. Derivations, the comparative, and the superlative showed the slowest and latest development.

Keeney, Terrence J. & Wolfe, Jean. The acquisition of agreement in English. *Journal of Verbal Learning and Verbal Behavior,* 1972, *11,* 698–705.

Children, ages 3;0–4;11, had correct subject-verb agreement in spontaneous speech and elicited imitation, but nonverbal tests of the verb number inflection indicated they did not understand the singular or plural meaning of the inflections.

Ramer, Andrya L. H. & Rees, Norma S. Selected aspects of the development of English morphology in black American children of low socioeconomic background. *Journal of Speech and Hearing Research,* 1973, *16,* 556–568.

A white examiner gave children, ages 4;10 to 15;7, a modified form of Berko's (1958) test for six morphological rules on which black English and standard American English differ. Black forms decreased and standard forms increased in occurrence with increasing age.

Major, Diana. *The Acquisition of Modal Auxiliaries in the Language of Children.* The Hague: Mouton, 1974. (Reviewed by P. Fletcher in *Journal of Child Language*, 1975, *2*, 318–322).

Children in kindergarten through third grade imitated sentences, converted affirmative sentences to negatives, supplied tag questions, and asked questions of a hand puppet; all sentences included a modal without auxiliary expansion.

Kypriotaki, Lyn. The acquisition of Aux. In *Papers and Reports on Child Language Development*, No. 8. Committee on Linguistics, Stanford University, April 1974, 87–103.

Thirty children, ages 2;1 to 5;1, performed an elicited imitation task for sentences incorporating 16 different combinations of auxiliary elements (perfect, progressive, and passive). The results suggested that children have different strategies rather than the same set of global rules.

Henzl, Věra M. Acquisition of grammatical gender in Czech. In *Papers and Reports on Child Language Development*, No. 10. Department of Linguistics, Stanford University, September 1975, 188–200.

Acquisition of suffixes for gender in Czech was explored by an elicitation procedure with three Czech girls, ages 1;9, 2;10, and 3;8. Adult-like gender morphology is not acquired until age 4 or 5; before then, overgeneralization (especially of non-ambiguous forms) is common. Early gender assignments are based on phonological form of the noun, not sex of referent.

Ivimey, G. P. The development of English morphology: An acquisition model. *Language and Speech*, 1975, *18*, 120–144.

A large sample of English children, ages $3\frac{1}{2}$–$9\frac{1}{2}$ years, performed a task based on Berko (1958). They induced morphological rules only after a lengthy exposure to adult language models and after the learning of specific forms. There are clearly defined stages. Critical factors in adult models are frequency and regularity.

de Villiers, Jill G. & Flusberg, Helen B. Tager. Some facts one simply cannot deny. *Journal of Child Language*, 1975, *2*, 279–286.

Children 2, 3, and 4 years old understand plausible negatives earlier than implausible negatives and have faster reaction times for them.

MacWhinney, Brian. Rules, rote and analogy in morphological

formations by Hungarian children. *Journal of Child Language,* 1975a, *2,* 65–77.

Elicited production of plurals provided evidence for five stages of morphological learning. The major mechanism responsible for performance was the learning and use of rules; analogic formation and rote memorization were of minor importance.

Kuczaj, Stanley A., II & Maratsos, Michael P. What children *can* say before they *will. Merrill-Palmer Quarterly of Behavior and Development,* 1975a, *21,* 89–111.

See summary in Section 4-A.

Marwit, Samuel J. & Marwit, Karen L. Black children's use of non-standard grammar: Two years later. *Developmental Psychology,* 1976, *12,* 33–38.

Between second and fourth grade, both black and white children increased their usage of standard English in a Berko-type test of morphology, but black children still gave more nonstandard responses than white children.

E   Experiments on Other Grammatical Phenomena

The following papers report experiments on grammatical phenomena other than those covered in Sections 4-A through 4-D. Most deal with the changes in syntactic competence during the school years or with acquisition of the pronoun system. On pronouns, see also Huxley (1970) and Tanz (1974).

Menyuk, Paula. Comparison of grammar of children with functionally deviant and normal speech. *Journal of Speech and Hearing Research,* 1964, *7,* 109–121.

> The sentences produced by 10 preschoolers diagnosed as having "infantile speech" were unlike those of normal children at any age. In elicited imitation, the number of omissions was best predicted by sentence length; for 10 normal children of the same IQ and age, the best predictor was sentence complexity.

Ammon, Paul R. The perception of grammatical relations in sentences: A methodological exploration. *Journal of Verbal Learning and Verbal Behavior,* 1968, *7,* 869–875.

> Evidence is reported for phrase structure effects in a reaction time task for both third graders and adults.

Gaer, Eleanor P. Children's understanding and production of sentences. *Journal of Verbal Learning and Verbal Behavior,* 1969, *2,* 289–294.

> Involves actives, passives, questions, negatives, simple, single-embedded, double-embedded, and center-embedded sentences. See Section 4-B for summary.

Riegel, Klaus F. Relational interpretation of the language acquisition process. In Flores d'Arcais & Levelt, 1970.

> Riegel argues for the priority of relations over elements and reports data on children's ability to guess a target word given several relations involving the target. There is improvement from age 7 to 9 to 12, but not to 15.

*Kessel, F. S. The role of syntax in children's comprehension from ages six to twelve. *Monographs of the Society for Research in Child Development,* 1970, *35* (6).

> When asked to indicate which of two pictures matched a sentence, children showed earlier mastery of the *ask/tell* and

125

easy/eager distinctions than has been found in studies using other tasks. Also, when asked to select the two pictures (from a set of four) corresponding to the two readings of ambiguous sentences, lexical ambiguity was detected earlier than surface or underlying structure ambiguity, which were not mastered until age 12.

Hunt, K. W. Syntactic maturity in school children and adults. *Monographs of the Society for Research in Child Development,* 1970, *35* (1). (1, Serial No. 134).

Children in grades 4, 6, 8, 10, and 12 and adults were asked to rewrite "in a better way" a 32-sentence passage, "Aluminum." Changes in length and other structural complexity measures, and changes in frequency of reductions, were examined.

Blasdell, Richard & Jensen, Paul. Stress and word position as determinants of imitation in first-language learners. *Journal of Speech and Hearing Research,* 1970, *13,* 193–202.

Children, ages 28–39 months, imitated four-syllable nonsense strings. Both position and stress affected accuracy: stressed syllables and the last syllable had the fewest errors.

Clay, M. Sentence repetition: Elicited imitation of a controlled set of syntactic structures by four language groups. *Monographs of the Society for Research in Child Development,* 1971, *36* (3, Serial No. 143).

Participants were children of ages 5;0–7;3, from four groups in New Zealand: two Polynesian (Maoris monolingual in English and Samoan bilingual) and two non-Polynesian (Optimum English and Average English). In elicited imitation, memory span for sentences increased with age, and virtually the same orders of difficulty for six sentence types and six variants were found. However, there were group differences in the ratio of grammatical vs. ungrammatical substitutions.

Baird, Raymond. Structural characteristics of clause-containing sentences and imitation by children and adults. *Journal of Psycholinguistic Research,* 1973, *2,* 115–127.

Children, ages 4, 6, and 8 years, and college students attempted to imitate sentences containing combinations of nested and self-embedded clauses. Differences in performance could be attributed to structural characteristics of the sentences.

Roeper, Thomas. Theoretical implications of word order, topicalization and inflections in German language acquisition. In Ferguson & Slobin, 1973(b).

See summary in Section 4-C.

*Maratsos, Michael P. The effects of stress on the understanding of pronominal co-reference in children. *Journal of Psycholinguistic Research*, 1973a, *2*, 1–8.

Children, ages 3, 4, and 5 years, acted out sentences in which presence or absence of stress on a pronoun was critical to its reference (e.g., "Susie bumped into the old woman, and then Harry bumped into *her*."). The children were then divided into three groups based on proficiency in imitating sentences. The least advanced group used a natural cognitive strategy, resulting in high scores on unstressed pronoun sentences and low scores on stressed pronoun sentences. In the other two groups there was improvement on stressed-pronoun sentences because of successful reversal of the role of one actor.

Waryas, Carol L. Psycholinguistic research in language intervention programming: The pronoun system. *Journal of Psycholinguistic Research*, 1973, *2*, 221–237.

Waryas presents a linguistic analysis of the pronoun system in terms of binary syntactic and semantic features. An order of development of the features is proposed (e.g., semantic before syntactic), which is supported by the data of Huxley (1970). Finally, relations to other aspects of language and language training proposals are discussed.

Chipman, Harold H. & de Dardel, Catherine. Developmental study of the comprehension and production of the pronoun "it". *Journal of Psycholinguistic Research*, 1974, *3*, 91–99.

Children ages 3;3–7;0 acted out sentences of the form "There is X on the table, give it to me," where X is a collective noun (clay), count noun (marbles), or a noun that can be either (chocolate). They also performed production and repetition tasks. At ages 3–4, *it* seems to mean *a piece*. The results should be interpreted in the context of cognitive development.

Schwenk, Mary Ann & Danks, Joseph H. A developmental study of the pragmatic communication rule for prenominal adjective ordering. *Memory and Cognition*, 1974, *2*, 149–152.

Preference for the normal (rather than inverted) order of adjectives first appeared in fourth graders in a study of adults and first-, fourth-, and eighth-grade children.

Thieman, Thomas J. Imitation and recall of optionally deletable sentences by young children. *Journal of Child Language,* 1975, *2,* 261–269.

> Children between ages 4 and 5 years, as well as adults, tend to recall sentences in their reduced form, regardless of input form; but the youngest child tested, age 3;8, recalled the sentences in a fully expanded form, supporting Slobin's (1973) linguistic universal E4. Reductions involved the use of a pronoun or proverb (*do*) or the deletion of a relative pronoun (*that*) or indirect object marker (*to*).

Tanz, Christine. Learning how *it* works. In *Papers and Reports on Child Language Development,* No. 10. Department of Linguistics, Stanford University, September 1975, 136–152.

> Children ages 3;1–5;2 had, placed in front of them, items that were labeled by mass nouns (e.g., Playdoh, family) or count nouns (e.g., flowers). They were told, "There is Playdoh (a family, . . .) on the table," followed by "Give it to me," "Give me the Playdoh," or "Give me some." Chipman & de Dardel's (1974) finding that children gave only one piece or item for *it* was not replicated; all of the referent was given equally often for pronoun and noun requests. However, when the pronoun *them* was used in contrast to a plural noun, all of the referent was less often given for pronoun than for noun.

Richardson, K.; Calnan, M.; Essen, J.; & Lambert, L. The linguistic maturity of 11-year-olds: Some analysis of the written compositions of children in the National Child Development Study. *Journal of Child Language,* 1976, *3,* 99–115.

> Compositions of 521 British children were analyzed using Hunt's (1970) mean T-unit length (MTUL) measure (main plus attached subordinate clauses). Composition length was associated with sex, social class, reading comprehension, general ability test scores, and teachers' ratings; however, MTUL was only weakly or not at all associated with these factors or with composition length.

Koenigsknecht, Roy A. & Friedman, Philip. Syntax development in boys and girls. *Child Development,* 1976, *47,* 1109–1115.

> On the Developmental Sentence Scoring procedure for elicited speech samples, administered to children of ages 2–6 years, significant female advantages began showing at age 4.

Part III

SEMANTIC DEVELOPMENT

Section 5
SINGLE-WORD SPEECH

With the renewed interest in semantics characteristic of the 1970's, the period of single-word speech occurring approximately from 9 to 12 months until 18 to 24 months has again become a research focus. In addition to the references given below, many of those in Sections 10-C and 10-D are relevant. For background reading, the following publications on the object concept and the symbolic function cover a broad age range, but they are of special interest with regard to the onset of verbal symbols (early vocabulary).

BACKGROUND READING

*Piaget, Jean. *Play, Dreams, and Imitation in Childhood.* New York: W. W. Norton, 1951. (Also in paperback, New York: Norton, 1962. Originally published in French, 1946.)

Werner, Heinz & Kaplan, Bernard. *Symbol Formation.* New York: John Wiley & Sons, 1963. (Reviewed by J. A. Fodor in *Language,* 1964, *40,* 566–578.)

Cohen, L. B. & Salapatek, P. (Eds.). *Infant Perception: From Sensation to Cognition,* Vol. 2. New York: Academic Press, 1975.
Includes articles on the object concept (thought to be a crucial foundation for early language) by T. G. R. Bower and Gerald Gratch.

Fenson, Larry; Kagan, Jerome; Kearsley, Richard B.; & Zelazo, Philip R. The developmental progression of manipulative play in the first two years. *Child Development,* 1976, *47,* 232–236.
Age differences in play were studied cross-sectionally at 7, 9, 13, and 20 months. The ability to relate two objects, acquired between 9 and 13 months, precedes symbolic play.

Bruner, Jerome S.; Jolly, Alison; & Sylva, Kathy (Eds.). *Play: Its Role in Development and Evolution.* New York: Basic Books, 1976.
Anthology divided into sections on the evolutionary context, the world of objects and tools, the social world, and the world of symbols (including language).

131

A Diary and Case Studies

The first systematic method developed to study early language was the keeping of detailed diaries by parents who were psychologists or linguists. Many such studies in a variety of European languages were done during the first half of this century. In addition, limited observational studies of individual children are still occasionally reported. A few references follow; see Leopold's bibliography (Section 1-D) and E. Clark (1973a), in this section, for further references. A major concern is the phenomenon of overextension in word reference.

Leopold, Werner F. *Speech Development of a Bilingual Child: A Linguist's Record. Volume 1, Vocabulary Growth in the First Two Years.* Evanston, Ill.: Northwestern University Press, 1939.

This is the best and most accessible of the early diary studies. Leopold reports the early speech of his daughter, Hildegard, learning German and English.

Velten, H. V. The growth of phonemic and lexical patterns in infant language. *Language,* 1943, *19,* 281–292. (Reprinted in Bar-Adon & Leopold, 1971.)

Velten describes his daughter Joan's speech up to age 4, giving a number of details and examples. Particularly interesting is his division of her early vocabulary into four stages: (1) words accompanying or calling for action, e.g., "ap" (*up*); (2) a division of hand-eye coordination processes into two classes: "ba" (joining parts of a thing, e.g., buttoning a coat) and "bada´" (successful joining of detached parts, e.g., cups and saucers, shoes and pencils); (3) deictic stage, using "za" to request the naming of every exemplar of a word; (4) classification by size, color, and opposites, using multiword contrasts.

*Leopold, Werner F. Semantic learning in infant language. *Word,* 1948b, *4,* 173–180. (Reprinted in Bar-Adon & Leopold, 1971.)

Leopold summarizes observations on his daughter, Hildegard, emphasizing the idea that semantic overextension is due to small vocabulary, so that the semantic territory embraced by each word shrinks as more words are learned.

Luria, A. R. & Yudovich, F. Ia. *Speech and the Development of Mental Processes in the Child.* Baltimore: Penguin Books, 1959. (Paperback. Originally published in Russian, 1956.)

The influence of training on speech improvement in two language-retarded twins is the focus of the book, but the most interesting part is an analysis of the twins' early vocabulary, including a "private language."

Darley, F. L. & Winitz, Harris. Age of first word: Review of research. *Journal of Speech and Hearing Disorders,* 1961, *26,* 242-90.

Bullowa, Margaret; Jones, Lawrence G.; & Duckert, Audrey R. The acquisition of a word. *Language and Speech,* 1964, *7,* 107-111.
Based on annotated audiovisual records of weekly half-hour observations, six stages (from 9 to 23 months) are identified in one child's acquisition of the word *shoe,* from hearing the word in association with the object to using the word spontaneously with adult pronunciation.

Slobin, Dan I. The acquisition of Russian as a native language. In Smith & Miller, 1966(a).
This summary, based on a Russian diary study by Gvozdev, includes a section on word meaning acquisition.

Bar-Adon, Aaron & Leopold, Werner F. (Eds.). *Child Language: A Book of Readings.* Englewood Cliffs, N.J.: Prentice-Hall, 1971.
Several selections have relevant material; see especially R. Jakobson, "Why 'Mama' and 'Papa'?" (selection 37) and selections 17, 19, 21, 23, and 25.

*Clark, Eve V. What's in a word? On the child's acquisition of semantics in his first language. In Moore, 1973(a).
Clark provides a very useful survey and interpretation of a number of diary studies.

Greenfield, Patricia M. Who is "Dada"? . . . Some aspects of the semantic and phonological development of a child's first words. *Language and Speech,* 1973, *16,* 34-43.
Greenfield used informal training procedures to teach the word's referent after her daughter had begun producing "dada." Changes in an orienting response indicated rapid learning of the referent and also could be used to determine which semantic dimensions (caregiver, sex, parent) were critical at various times for "dada" and "mama." There seemed to be a progression from a phonological representation to development of comprehension (frequent orienting response) to mastery (less frequent orienting response, possibly greater production).

Labov, William & Labov, Teresa. The grammer of "Cat" and

"Mama." Paper presented at the winter meeting of the Linguistic Society of America, December 1974.

Diary study of the first two words of the well known linguist's child.

*Carter, Anne L. The transformation of sensorimotor morphemes into words: A case study of the development of 'more' and 'mine'. *Journal of Child Language,* 1975, *2,* 233–250.

Carter reports an exceptionally detailed, careful longitudinal study of one child. She found that a variety of [m]-initial morphemes, always accompanied by a reaching gesture, were used for general object requests until age 1;5, when two morphemes began to emerge: [mow] meaning "more" (recurrence) and [moy] meaning "mine" (possession). She argues that the phonological differentiation preceded the semantic one.

Thomson, Jean & Chapman, Robin S. Who is 'daddy' (revisited)? The status of two-year-olds' over-extensions in production and comprehension. In *Papers and Reports on Child Language Development,* No. 10. Department of Linguistics, Stanford University, September 1975, 59–68.

Five children at MLU = 1.1–2.5 could correctly choose from pictures corresponding to the referents of some words they overextended in spontaneous speech. A feature analysis of overextended words suggests that the psychological validity of a systematic featural approach is doubtful.

Reich, Peter A. The early acquisition of word meaning. *Journal of Child Language,* 1976, *3,* 117–123.

The development of the concept *shoe* in the author's prelingual child supports the notion that concepts start out very narrow, then generalize until they are overgeneralized. Much of this process may occur before the word is ever produced.

B Recent Theories; Longitudinal and Experimental Studies

In recent years, new theoretical analyses and methods have been introduced. These include analysis of longitudinal speech samples from more than one child, use of diary data supplemented by speech samples, and object naming and sorting under experimenter-arranged conditions. Two papers discuss infants' language comprehension.

Friedlander, Bernard Z. Receptive language development in infancy: Issues and problems. *Merrill-Palmer Quarterly of Behavior and Development,* 1970, *16,* 7–51.

> Theoretical article in four parts: (1) brief review of relevant research, (2) rationale for regarding receptive language development as an important research area, (3) argument for distinguishing this research from general perceptual research, and (4) examination of the psychological and environmental context.

Ingram, David. Transitivity in child language. *Language,* 1971, *47,* 888–910.

> Fillmore's case grammar is applied to the description of one-word utterances (regarded as holophrases) by replacing the VERB category with SEMANTIC TRANSITIVITY. Gestures can be represented as well as words. An analysis of utterances recorded by Leopold shows that early one-word utterances convey states, later ones actions.

*Macnamara, John. Cognitive basis of language learning in infants. *Psychological Review,* 1972, *79,* 1–13.

> Macnamara presents ideas and evidence on how early vocabulary is learned.

*Bloom, Lois. *One Word at a Time.* The Hague: Mouton, 1973. (Reviewed by R. Clark in *Journal of Child Language,* 1975, *2,* 169–183.)

> Bloom's main interest is in the foundation for syntax laid in single-word speech, but material relevant to semantics is also provided. The study is based on speech samples of three children.

*Nelson, Katherine. Structure and strategy in learning to talk. *Monographs of the Society for Research in Child Development*, 1973a, *38* (1–2, Serial No. 149).

Nelson reports a longitudinal study of lexical development extending through the first 50 words of 18 children. Individual differences in the styles of children (referential vs. expressive) and mothers (accepting vs. rejecting) are considered, as are cognitive factors and learning strategies. An appendix shows the developing lexicon for eight children.

Nelson, Katherine. Some evidence for the cognitive primacy of categorization and its functional basis. *Merrill-Palmer Quarterly of Behavior and Development*, 1973b, *19*, 21–39.

Experimental study of object sorting by children 12–24 months old. Nelson argues that children categorize objects before naming them.

Nelson, Keith E. & Bonvillian, John. Concepts and words in the 18-month-old: Acquiring concept names under controlled conditions. *Cognition*, 1973, *2*, 435–450.

Ten children, over a 6-month period, were systematically exposed to referents of 16 nouns; half the referents for each noun were named by the mother. The children's naming behavior was observed and individual differences (e.g., in overgeneralization) noted.

Clark, Eve V. Some aspects of the conceptual basis for first language acquisition. In R. L. Schiefelbusch & L. Lloyd, 1974(a).

Clark reviews the role of cognitive-perceptual factors in the acquisition of word meanings in the presyntactic and syntactic periods, summarizing some of her own studies as well as other work.

Katz, N.; Baker, E.; & Macnamara, J. What's in a name: A study of how children learn common and proper names. *Child Development*, 1974, *45*, 469–473.

Children 17–24 months old learned nonsense names for dolls and blocks. For people, children first discriminate individuals and learn their names; for certain other objects, they do not discriminate individuals and learn only the class name. This is the basis for learning the distinction between common and proper nouns.

*Nelson, Katherine. Concept, word, and sentence: Interrelations in acquisition and development. *Psychological Review,* 1974a, *81,* 267–285.

An important attempt to integrate concept formation theory, semantic feature theory, and Piagetian theory to account for the early translation of meaning into words and the beginnings of syntax.

*Huttenlocher, Janellen. The origins of language comprehension. In R. L. Solso (Ed.), *Theories in Cognitive Psychology.* Hillsdale, N.J.: Lawrence Erlbaum Associates, 1974.

Huttenlocher reports a longitudinal study of receptive language in three children at 10–18 months. The article includes extensive citation of protocols and discussion of theoretical issues such as the gap between language comprehension and production.

*Anglin, Jeremy M. The child's first terms of reference. In S. Ehrlich & E. Tulving (Eds.), *Bulletin de Psychologie,* Special Issue on Semantic Memory, July 1975.

Theoretical paper on the semantic extension of early words. Anglin cites results suggesting that underextension may be as important as overextension.

Clark, Eve V. Knowledge, context, and strategy in the acquisition of meaning. In D. P. Dato (Ed.), *Georgetown University Round Table on Languages and Linguistics 1975.* Washington, D.C.: Georgetown University Press, 1975, 77–98.

Clark discusses new ideas on overextensions and nonlinguistic strategies in children's semantic development, including single-word speech.

*Greenfield, Patricia Marks & Smith, Joshua H. *The Structure of Communication in Early Language Development.* New York: Academic Press, 1976.

The emergence of semantic relations in single-word speech is studied in a group of children in the context of action and the communicative situation. Other literature is reviewed and discussed.

*Dore, John; Franklin, Margery B.; Miller, Robert T.; & Ramer, Andrya L. H. Transitional phenomena in early language acquisition. *Journal of Child Language,* 1976, *3,* 13–28.

The authors describe transitional phases between babbling, one-word and multiword speech for four children, based on videotapes over 8 months starting at 0;11–1;4. In the transition to single words, phonetically consistent forms (not adult words) played four functions (e.g., expressing affect) but did not have objects as referents.

Goldin-Meadow, Susan; Seligman, Martin E. P.; & Gelman, Rochel. Language in the two-year old. *Cognition,* 1976, *4,* 189–202.
On the basis of comprehension and production tasks with 12 children 14–26 months old, three of whom were studied longitudinally, two stages in vocabulary development are identified. In the receptive stage the child produces many fewer nouns than are comprehended; in the productive stage this gap is almost closed, and the first verbs are produced.

Bowerman, Melissa. Semantic factors in the acquisition of rules for word use and sentence construction. In Morehead & Morehead, 1976.
Bowerman reviews theories and data on the meanings of words at the single-word stage and on the relational concepts that underlie early rules for word combination.

Rodgon, Maris Monitz & Rashman, Sue E. Expression of owner-owned relationships among holophrastic 14- to 32-month-old children. *Child Development,* 1976, *47,* 1219–1222.
Children 14–32 months old were shown photographs of familiar and unfamiliar objects and persons. For object photographs, the name of the object was produced much more frequently than the name of the owner.

C Holophrastic Speech

The **holophrastic** controversy—whether or not children's single-word utterances should be regarded as sentences—is scattered through the literature (see, for example, Leopold, Vol. 3, 1949a; de Laguna, 1927; McCarthy, 1954; McNeill, 1970a,b). Dewey (1894) suggests an early form of the holophrase notion. Braine (1974a; see Section 3-A) takes a syntactic approach. Dore (1975) reviews the controversy in the context of speech function and meaning.

Dewey, John. The psychology of infant language. *Psychological Review*, 1894, 2, 63–66.
> Parts of speech in the language of two children (ages 18 and 19 months) are compared to a similar compilation for more than 20 children by Tracy. Dewey argues that many non-verbs function as verbs for the children. He also suggests several complex parts of speech (e.g., nominal-adjectival-verbal).

McNeill, David. Are there specifically linguistic universals? In Steinberg & Jakobovits, 1971(a).
> The concept of a sentence is species-specific and innate. It can be detected during the holophrastic period, since grammatical relations are already apparent. The sentence concept is an example of a strong linguistic universal, since cognition alone is not a sufficient cause. See also McNeill (1970c).

Dore, John. Holophrases, speech acts and language universals. *Journal of Child Language*, 1975, 2, 21–40.
> The holophrastic controversy can be resolved by taking the speech act as the basic unit of linguistic communication.

Rodgon, Maris Monitz. *Single-word Usage, Cognitive Development and the Beginnings of Combinatorial Speech*. London: Cambridge University Press, 1976.
> The holophrase notion is given prominence in this observational study of 10 children beginning at 16–21 months of age.

Section 6
THE SEMANTICS
OF SENTENCES

Most studies of children's sentences have been syntactic rather than semantic, but some recent exceptions are listed here. Some are concerned with arriving at complete semantic descriptions of sentences, others with the difficulties encountered in combining the meanings of words within sentences, and others with the meanings of conjunctions or verbs. See also the semantically oriented grammars listed in Section 3-A; the papers controlling for semantic factors in Section 4-B (active and passive sentences); Kuczaj, 1975; and McNeill's report of his unpublished experiment on semantic anomaly in his 1970b review, pp. 1121–1122. Of the background references in Section 2, Katz & Fodor (1963), Chafe (1970), G. Lakoff (1971a), Katz (1972), Weinreich (1966/1972), Kempson (1975), Kintsch (1974), and the references on logic and artificial intelligence are most relevant.

Suppes, Patrick & Feldman, Shirley. Young children's comprehension of logical connectives. *Journal of Experimental Child Psychology,* 1971, *12,* 304–317.

   Kindergarten and nursery school children were given commands involving conjunctive, disjunctive, and exclusive-or connectives; specific regression models were applied to the data.

Slobin, Dan I. & Ervin-Tripp, Susan (Directors). *Semantics of Child Speech: Coding Manual.* Berkeley Cross-Linguistic Language Development Project, June 1972.

   Describes a semantics-based system for coding utterances in any language, with examples from three of the languages for which the Berkeley project is obtaining child speech corpora.

Nygren, Carolyn. *Children's acquisition of instrumental verbs.* Unpublished doctoral dissertation, Department of Linguistics, The University of Chicago, December 1972.

   Children 3–11 years old answered questions about sentences with instrumental verbs, many of which had a semantically unusual combination of elements; e.g., "Can you chop cheese with an ax?" or "Can you shave wood with an ax?" Theoretical explanations for changes in responses with age are discussed.

Baron, Naomi. Phylogenetic reflections of ontogenetic processes: Contributions to a general theory of linguistic variation and change. Presented at the Summer Linguistics Conference, University of California, Santa Cruz, 1972.

Baron examines development of the periphrastic causative use ("I got the baby to smile") of *have, make* and *get* in historical language change and in children. For children, data from longitudinal corpora (2-year-olds) as well as imitation and comprehension tasks (2- to 5-year-olds) are reported. The theoretical sections, which relate the historical and child data, are carefully reasoned and provocative. Based on a Stanford University doctoral dissertation (1972); the author is now at Brown University.

Jarvella, Robert J. & Sinnott, Joan. Contextual constraints on noun distributions to some English verbs by children and adults. *Journal of Verbal Learning and Verbal Behavior,* 1972, *11,* 47–53.

Third-grade, sixth-grade, and college students supplied subject and object nouns for active and passive sentence frames. Subject nouns were more often animate than objects; children used more animate nouns than adults; and linguistic selectional rules predicted several aspects of the results.

Howe, Herbert E. & Hillman, Donald. The acquisition of semantic restrictions in children. *Journal of Verbal Learning and Verbal Behavior,* 1973, *12,* 132–139.

Children in nursery school through fourth grade judged the nonreversibility of sentences with selectional restrictions. The order of acquisition of restrictions was animate subject, special restrictions, animate object.

James, Sharon L. & Miller, Jon F. Children's awareness of semantic constraints in sentences. *Child Development,* 1973, *44,* 69–76.

Children, ages 4;8–5;3 and 6;8–7;3, judged anomalous and meaningful sentences as "silly" or "okay," and tried to convert the anomalous into meaningful sentences. Both age groups could make the judgments, but 7-year-olds were better at converting sentences and were more aware of selection restriction rules.

*Antinucci, Francesco & Parisi, Domenico. Early language acquisition: A model and some data. In Ferguson & Slobin, 1973.

Using a generative semantics framework, the authors analyze the meanings of single-word and short multiword utterances of an Italian child between ages 1;3 and 1;7.

Bowerman, Melissa. Learning the structure of causative verbs: A study in the relationship of cognitive, semantic and syntactic development. In *Papers and Reports on Child Language Development*, No. 8. Committee on Linguistics, Stanford University, April 1974, 142–178.

Bowerman presents evidence from the natural speech of her daughter, Christy, at ages 2–4, that causative verbs are unanalyzed when they first appear (19 months old) and later gain internal structure (cause a state or change-of-state), as indicated by the appearance of periphrastic causatives and of errors such as "I'm just gonna *fall* this on her" (24 months old). Bowerman also argues for a distinction between the child's cognitive knowledge and linguistic knowledge, in disagreement with Antinucci & Parisi (1973).

*Suppes, Patrick. The semantics of children's language. *American Psychologist*, 1974, *29* (2), 103–114.

Suppes argues that the logical tradition of model-theoretic semantics provides the best framework for analyzing the semantics of children's language; he provides a simple introduction with examples from corpora of children learning English, Mandarin, and French.

Entwisle, Doris R. & Frasure, N. E. A contradiction resolved: Children's processing of syntactic cues. *Developmental Psychology*, 1974, *10*, 852–857.

In an experiment similar to that of McNeill (1970b), children ages 6, 7, 8, and 9 were asked to repeat sentences presented with superimposed noise. The order of difficulty was scrambled (lacking syntax and semantics), anomalous (lacking semantics), and meaningful sentences.

Parisi, Domenico. What is behind child utterances? *Journal of Child Language*, 1974, *1*, 97–105.

Response to Schlesinger's criticisms of Antinucci & Parisi (1973), emphasizing the young child's reliance on the immediate situation and sensorimotor representations.

Farwell, Carol B. Aspects of early verb semantics—Pre-causative development. In *Papers and Reports on Child Language Development*, No. 10. Committee on Linguistics, Stanford University, September 1975, 48–58.

Farwell extends Bowerman's (1974) approach to the analysis of very early verb semantics. Citing naturalistic data from one boy (age $19\frac{1}{2}$–$23\frac{1}{2}$ months), she suggests stages of development culminating in internally structured causatives. In the first stage words like *up* refer to situations that combine action and resultant state; then action and state language develop separately before being recombined in causatives.

*Bloom, Lois; Lightbown, Patsy; & Hood, Lois. Structure and variation in child language. *Monographs of the Society for Research in Child Development,* 1975, *40* (2, Serial No. 160).

The authors describe the natural speech of four children between MLU of 1.0 and 2.5 (ages 19–26 months). Frequency counts and sample utterances for a number of semantic-syntactic categories are presented, with emphasis on verb relations. There is evidence for a constant order of emergence of semantic types but two different syntactic styles (one pronominal, one nominal). There are commentaries by Melissa Bowerman and Michael Maratsos.

Nelson, Katherine. The nominal shift in semantic-syntactic development. *Cognitive Psychology,* 1975, *7,* 461–479.

Nelson argues that there are two contrasting courses of development, one beginning with a lexical emphasis ("referential" children), the other with a syntactic emphasis ("expressive" children), which tend to converge between ages 2 and 3.

Johansson, Bo S. and Sjölin, Barbro. Preschool children's understanding of the coordinators "and" and "or." *Journal of Experimental Child Psychology,* 1975, *19,* 233–240.

Children ages 2;0–7;6 received two tests of their understanding of *and* and *or*; the task for which context helped determine meaning was easier, especially below age 4. In a spontaneous usage test, children used *and* to express enumerations and *or* to express alternatives.

Golinkoff, Roberta M. Semantic development in infants: The concepts of agent and recipient. *Merrill-Palmer Quarterly of Behavior and Development,* 1975, *21,* 181–193.

The author used a habituation procedure to find evidence that infants make case relation distinctions before expressing them in speech.

Antinucci, Francesco & Parisi, Domenico. Early semantic development in child language. In Lenneberg & Lenneberg, Vol. 1, 1975, 189–201.

A view of the relation between cognition and language is

developed, in which performatives, adverbs, and embedded clauses are regarded as specifically linguistic, while the basic predicate-argument structures underlying sentences function nonlinguistically as well.

Nelson, Katherine. Some attributes of adjectives used by young children. *Cognition,* 1976, *4,* 13–30.

In speech samples from 18 children at 24 months, predicate adjectives predominated, referring to transitory states of objects. In samples for 16 of the same children at 30 months, attributive adjectives predominated, used to subdivide classes or specify instances on the basis of physical attributes. Thus, cognitive and communicational usefulness, not syntactic derivation, determines differential use.

Sanches, Mary. Language acquisition and language change: Japanese numeral classifiers. In B. G. Blount & M. Sanches (Eds.), *Sociocultural Dimensions of Language Change.* New York: Academic Press, 1976.

*Osherson, Daniel N. *Logical Abilities in Children, Vol. 4: Reasoning and Concepts.* Hillsdale, N.J.: Lawrence Erlbaum Associates, 1976.

Osherson distinguishes natural concepts from concepts that are merely expressible in language, using the framework of formal logic. Detailed consideration is given to sentential modifiers expressed in English.

Kuhn, Deanna & Phelps, Henry. The development of children's comprehension of causal direction. *Child Development,* 1976, *47,* 248–251.

Children in kindergarten through second grade were shown a picture and asked to choose between two sentences of the form *A because B* and *B because A* (e.g., "The water spills because the chair gets wet.") Kindergarteners performed at a chance level (though an additional group was 84% correct on sentences using *first* in place of *because*), while the older children performed very well. (See also Corrigan, 1975.)

Macnamara, John; Baker, Erica; & Olson, Chester L. Four-year-olds' understanding of *pretend, forget,* and *know:* Evidence for propositional operations. *Child Development,* 1976, *47,* 62–70.

Four-year-olds (mean age, 4;6) showed substantial ability to grasp presuppositions and implications of complex sentences in their answers to questions about stories. It is also argued that they could perform propositional operations at the level of formal logic.

Amidon, Arlene. Children's understanding of sentences with contingent relations: Why are temporal and conditional connectives so difficult? *Journal of Experimental Child Psychology,* 1976, *22,* 423–437.

See summary in Section 9-C.

Section 7
LEXICAL DEVELOPMENT

*The **mental dictionary**, or **lexicon**, specifies (1) the meanings of words, and (2) the relationships between words. Three major approaches to lexical organization and its development have been taken. The first approach emphasizes hierarchical structures. The second emphasizes semantic features or components that are the elements of word meaning. The third and newest approach rejects the first two approaches as too rigid, asserting that category members differ in how well they exemplify the category; hence, categories are "fuzzy." Background reading in other fields is particularly important for this topic and is suggested separately for each of the three approaches.*

A Hierarchical Structure Theories

BACKGROUND PUBLICATIONS:
COGNITIVE DEVELOPMENT AND ADULT PSYCHOLINGUISTICS

The following references provide background on child cognition and   007
adult lexical structure. The emphasis is on hierarchical (paradigmatic)
structures, based on superset-subset or category-member relations.
See also Osherson, 1974.

Vygotsky, L. S. *Thought and Language.* Cambridge, Mass.: The MIT   008
Press, 1962. (Also in paperback. Chapter 5 reprinted in P. Adams,
1972. Originally published in Russian, 1934).
In Chapter 5, Vygotsky discusses his concept-learning experiments using blocks varying on four dimensions. Children use
preconceptual "complexes," which are formed concretely,
rather than the abstract concepts of a mature hierarchical
system.

Inhelder, Bärbel & Piaget, Jean. *The Early Growth of Logic in the*   012
Child. New York: Humanities Press, 1964. (Also in paperback,
New York: Norton, 1969. Originally published in French, 1959.)
The sections on classification describe experiments in which
children are asked to sort items. Sorting into classes appears at
about ages 5–6. A more difficult task involving hierarchies, the
class-inclusion question, is not mastered before age 8.

Miller, George A. Empirical methods in the study of semantics. In   013
Steinberg & Jakobovits, 1971. (Appeared earlier under the title
"Psycholinguistic approaches to the study of communication." In
D. L. Arm (Ed.), *Journey in Science: Small Steps—Great Strides.*
Albuquerque: University of New Mexico Press, 1967).
Introduces the method of cluster analysis for arriving at hierar-
chical semantic structures from similarities data.

Miller, George A. A psycholinguistic method to investigate verbal
concepts. *Journal of Mathematical Psychology,* 1969, *6,* 169–191.
A discussion of cluster analysis and its relation to psycholinguistic theories and data; more technical than the preceding
article.

Collins, Allan M. & Quillian, M. Ross. Retrieval time from semantic memory. *Journal of Verbal Learning and Verbal Behavior*, 1969, *8*, 240–247.
    These researchers found support for a hierarchically structured lexicon with adult reaction-time data, though others have found alternative explanations for their results.

Levelt, Willem J. M. Hierarchical clustering algorithms in the psychology of grammar. In G. B. Flores d'Arcais & W. J. M. Levelt, 1970.
    Brief introduction to the technical aspects of clustering analysis.

Tulving, Endel & Donaldson, Wayne (Eds.). *Organization of Memory*. New York: Academic Press, 1972.
    This volume includes papers by the leading researchers on long-term memory and the organization of the lexicon in adults. It provides much of the necessary background for related research on children.

Klahr, David & Wallace, J. G. Class inclusion processes. In S. Farnham-Diggory, 1972.
    A short review of the literature is followed by an information-processing model.

Klahr, David. An information-processing approach to the study of cognitive development. In A. D. Pick, Vol. 7, 1973.
    Klahr applies production systems from the artificial intelligence research of Newell & Simon to Piagetian tasks such as quantitative comparison, subitizing, class inclusion, and classification.

Carroll, John B. & White, Margaret N. Word frequency and age of acquisition as determiners of picture-naming latency. *Quarterly Journal of Experimental Psychology*, 1973, *25*, 85–95.
    Age of learning, not word frequency, is the best predictor of latency. Word retrieval may be a one-stage process that depends upon the age at which a word was learned.

Garner, Wendell R. *The Processing of Information and Structure*. Hillsdale, N.J.: Lawrence Erlbaum Associates, 1974.
    A theory of pattern perception and classification in which a distinction between integral and separable dimensions is made.

Klahr, David & Wallace, J. G. *Cognitive Development: An Informa-*

tion-Processing View, Hillsdale, N.J.: Lawrence Erlbaum
Associates, 1976.
> The most recent and complete statement of Klahr & Wallace's
> approach.

Kogan, Nathan. *Cognitive Styles in Infancy and Early Childhood.*
Hillsdale, N.J.: Lawrence Erlbaum Associates, 1976.
> Includes chapters on field independence-dependence, reflec-
> tion-impulsivity, breadth of categorization, and styles of con-
> ceptualization, related to Piaget & Inhelder's stages of classifi-
> cation.

Wilkinson, Alexander. Counting strategies and semantic analysis as
applied to class inclusion. *Cognitive Psychology,* 1976, *8,* 64–85.
> A problem processing model that includes a counting strategy
> explains the inclusion errors of preschool children better than
> Piaget's logical model. Also, children understand the semantics
> of inclusion but cannot coordinate this with their counting
> strategy.

CHILD LANGUAGE PUBLICATIONS

Paradigmatic Structure in Word Association Tasks

*The idea that children do not develop hierarchical structures until they
are of school age was originally explored in American psychology by
the coding of word association data for paradigmatic responses
(response word of same part-of-speech as stimulus word).*

*Brown, Roger & Berko, Jean. Word association and the acquisition
of grammar. *Child Development,* 1960b, *31,* 1–14.
> Adults, first-, second-, and third-grade children were given a
> word association test (scored for paradigmatic responses) and a
> usage test (for the ability to use a new word with the appro-
> priate part of speech in a sentence-creation task, given example
> sentences). Scores on the two tests were closely related and
> increased with age, indicating that the child gradually orga-
> nizes vocabulary into parts of speech.

Ervin, Susan M. Changes with age in the verbal determinants of word
association. *American Journal of Psychology,* 1961, *74,* 361–372.
> Children in kindergarten and grades one, three, and six were
> given free and two-choice association tests. There was an

increase with age in the proportion of paradigmatic responses; other findings related to transition probabilities are discussed.

Entwisle, Doris R. *Word Associations of Young Children.* Baltimore: Johns Hopkins Press, 1966.

A standard reference that lists associations for 200 kindergarteners and 280 children each in first, third, and fifth grade to 96 words (mainly nouns, verbs, and adjectives) in three frequency ranges.

Palermo, David S. Characteristics of word association responses obtained from children in grades one through four. *Developmental Psychology,* 1971b, *5,* 118–123.

A 100-item word association test was presented orally to children in grades one through four. Frequency of paradigmatic, contrast, superordinate, and most-popular responses increased with age. Comparisons to a similar written test are made.

Sharp, Donald & Cole, Michael. Patterns of responding in the word associations of West African children. *Child Development,* 1972, *43,* 55–65.

A significant age effect (greater for subjects attending school) and school-attendance effect were found for the proportion of paradigmatic associates produced.

Emerson, Harriet F. & Gekoski, William L. Interactive and categorical grouping strategies and the syntagmatic-paradigmatic shift. *Child Development,* 1976, *47,* 1116–1121.

Children ages 3;0–9;11 performed picture-grouping and word association tasks. Certain cognitive strategies may explain changes in performance with age.

Nelson, Katherine. The syntagmatic-paradigmatic shift revisited: A review of research and theory. *Psychological Bulletin,* 1977, *84,* 93–116.

Nelson compares four classes of theories, points out qualifications on the generality of the phenomenon, and suggests that shifts in both conceptual organization and task interpretation are involved.

Natural Language Categories

The following studies investigate changes with age in the membership of natural language categories. See also Section 5.

Brown, Roger. How shall a thing be called? *Psychological Review,* 1958b, 65, 14–21. (Reprinted in Brown, 1970a, and Oldfield & Marshall, 1968.)

General discussion of how children learn hierarchically related words in the context of their parents' labeling practices.

Saltz, Eli & Medow, Miriam L. Concept conservation in children: The dependence of belief systems on semantic representation. *Child Development,* 1971, *42,* 1533–1542.

Told that a doctor has become a thief (for example), most 8-year-olds deny he is still a doctor. A study with children at ages 5;6–7;8 indicates that the child actually believes that the person is no longer a doctor.

*Saltz, E.; Soller, E.; & Sigel, I. E. The development of natural language concepts. *Child Development,* 1972, *43,* 1191–1202.

Children in kindergarten, third, and sixth grade sorted 72 pictures according to six class labels. Younger children had "fragmented" concepts based on perceptual attributes; concept integration came with age.

Miller, R. The use of concrete and abstract concepts by children and adults. *Cognition,* 1973, *2,* 49–58.

Bruner's theory of cognitive growth, with its hypothesis that younger children tend to define concepts by perceptual or concrete attributes, was not supported in a forced-choice similarities task with first graders and adults.

Neimark, Edith D. Natural language concepts: Additional evidence. *Child Development,* 1974, *45,* 508–511.

Subjects in grades two, six, and college sorted 50 pictures according to the class labels *food, things to eat, clothing,* and *things to wear.* With increasing age, the last two categories diverge, with a decrease in the size of the *clothing* category, in contrast to Saltz, Soller, & Sigel (1972).

Press, Margaret L. Semantic features in lexical acquisition. In *Papers and Reports on Child Language Development,* No. 8. Committee on Linguistics, Stanford University, April 1974, 129–141.

Children, ages 2;8–6;0, chose which of three pictures was most like a standard picture. Each comparison picture shared a different feature with the standard (e.g., shape, color, function, animacy). No feature was consistently high in salience across picture sets. Younger children attended more to perceptual features, older children to function.

*Nelson, Katherine. Variations in children's concepts by age and category. *Child Development,* 1974b, *45,* 577–584.

Nelson analyzed the composition of nine natural language categories in a recall task with subjects of ages 5 and 8 years. There was considerable variation among the categories; there were also age effects.

O'Rourke, Joseph P. *Toward a Science of Vocabulary Development.* The Hague: Mouton, 1974.

In this study, focusing on school-age vocabulary development, hierarchical structure is only one of many organizing principles discussed.

Riegel, Klaus F. Semantic basis of language: Language as labor. In Riegel & Rosenwald, 1975.

Markman, Ellen M. Children's difficulty with word-referent differentiation. *Child Development,* 1976, *47,* 742–749.

Kindergarteners and first graders perform better on certain questions about word meaning when the symbol is as tangible as its referent. Other hypotheses regarding the cognitive demands of the questions are also evaluated, but this is complicated by second-grade results. "Nominal realism" (the belief that the word is an attribute of its referent) is an unnecessary explanation.

Winters, John J., Jr. & Brzoska, Mary Anne. Development of the formation of categories by normal and retarded persons. *Developmental Psychology,* 1976, *12,* 125–131.

Children in kindergarten, fourth, and ninth grades and retarded children (mean CA, 11.89 years; MA, 8.46 years) labeled and categorized 480 slides of objects. With increased age, the number of superordinates, congruency with adult criteria, superordinate category size, and category fragmentation increased. The retarded children were less efficient in forming reliable categories.

Kail, Robert V., Jr. Children's encoding of taxonomic classes and subclasses. *Developmental Psychology,* 1976, *12,* 487–488.

Children in grades two, three, and six seemed to use both specific and general taxonomic classes in performing a memory task.

*Markman, Ellen M. & Seibert, Jeffrey. Classes and collections: Internal organization and resulting holistic properties. *Cognitive Psychology,* 1976, *8,* 561–577.

Children, ages 4–7, performed better on tasks involving concepts characterized as collections than on classes in tasks on part-whole relationships and internal concept structure.

*Rosch, Eleanor; Mervis, Carolyn B.; Gray, Wayne D.; Johnson, David M.; & Boyes-Braem, Penny. Basic objects in natural categories. *Cognitive Psychology,* 1976, *8,* 382–439.

A number of experiments were performed showing that basic objects are the most inclusive categories whose members (1) possess many attributes in common, (2) have similar motor programs, and (3) have similar shapes. They (4) can be identified from averaged shapes, (5) can be represented by a concrete image, (6) are perceived first, and (7) are most codable and necessary in language. Based on a triads task with children of ages 3–10, they are the earliest categories named and sorted by children.

Anglin, Jeremy M. *Word, Object, and Conceptual Development.* New York: Norton, 1977.

Experiments on Hierarchical Lexical Structure

In the following studies, experimental tasks are used to explore the development of hierarchical lexical structures in children. See also the theoretical discussions in McNeill (1970a) and E. Clark (1973a) in Section 7-B.

*Anglin, Jeremy M. *The Growth of Word Meaning.* Cambridge, Mass.: The MIT Press, 1970.

Anglin reports the results of sorting, free recall, and free association experiments with subjects at ages 9, 13, 17, and adult, using materials hierarchically structured by semantic features of increasing abstractness (e.g., human, animal, living, entity). He argues for the generalization hypothesis, that as children get older they acquire broader classes based on more abstract features, as opposed to McNeill's view that as children get older they form finer discriminations.

Schaeffer, Benson; Lewis, Joan A.; & Van Decar, Annette. The growth of children's semantic memory: Semantic elements. *Journal of Experimental Child Psychology,* 1971, *11,* 296–309.

First and fifth graders' performance on semantic oddity problems supports the position that children learn superordinate elements later than subordinate ones.

Loftus, Elizabeth F. & Grober, Ellen H. Retrieval from semantic memory by young children. *Developmental Psychology,* 1973, *8,* 310.

Like adults, children 72–93 months take longer to produce a category instance to a stimulus like "an animal that's enormous" than to "an enormous animal," suggesting that their semantic memory is organized and accessed primarily by noun categories.

Nelson, Keith E. & Kosslyn, Stephen M. Semantic retrieval in children and adults. *Developmental Psychology,* 1975, *11,* 807–813.

Sentences of the form "A lion has a mane" are verified more quickly for high-salient properties and for low-specificity properties, for subjects at ages 8, 11, 13, and adult, contrary to Collins & Quillian (1969). Noun-property association strength was controlled.

Steinberg, Esther R. & Anderson, Richard C. Hierarchical semantic organization in 6-year-olds. *Journal of Experimental Child Psychology,* 1975, *19,* 544–553.

A picture recall task using hierarchically related verbal cues was performed by 58 six-year-olds. The results are interpreted as evidence for class-inclusion hierarchies in the lexical structure at this age, contrary to previous studies.

Harris, Paul. Inferences and semantic development. *Journal of Child Language,* 1975, *2,* 143–152.

Children ages 5–7 years were given information of the form "A mib is a bird" and were able to make appropriate inferences regarding attributes of the "mib" and distinguish it from other members of the class in an interview situation.

B Semantic Component Theories

There are various formulations of the idea that word meanings can be broken down into **components** *(features, semantic primitives). For linguistic approaches, a good introduction is given in Chapter 6 of Leech (1974). See also the papers on generative semantics (Section 2-D), Katz & Fodor (1963), Lyons (1968, pp. 470–481), Bierwisch in Lyons (1970a), and the following.*

BACKGROUND PUBLICATIONS

Linguistics

Postal, Paul M. Review of André Martinet, *Elements of General Linguistics. Foundations of Language,* 1966, *2,* 151–186.

> Postal hypothesizes that a set of universal semantic primitives underlie all languages.

Bendix, Edward H. *Componential Analysis of General Vocabulary: The Semantic Structure of a Set of Verbs in English, Hindi, and Japanese.* Bloomington, Ind.: Research Center for the Language Sciences, 1966. (Reviewed by C. J. Fillmore in *General Linguistics,* 1969b, *9,* 41–65.)

> Bendix uses several kinds of semantic tests to obtain data for an analysis of possession verbs using relational semantic components.

Bierwisch, Manfred. On classifying semantic features. In M. Bierwisch & K. E. Heidolph (Eds.), *Progress in Linguistics.* The Hague: Mouton, 1970(b). (Reprinted in Steinberg & Jakobovits, 1971.)

> This article is more technical than Bierwisch's article in Lyons (1970a).

Talmy, Leonard. *Semantic structures in English and Atsugewi.* Unpublished doctoral dissertation, University of California, Berkeley, 1972.

> Talmy suggests semantic tree structures for several types of situations which, by appropriate transformations, can be related to the surface structures of two dissimilar languages.

Lehrer, Adrienne. Componential analysis. Chapter III, Lehrer, 1974. Review of componential semantic analysis in linguistics, emphasizing Katz & Postal (1964) and derivatives. Culinary terms are analyzed as an example.

Talmy, Leonard. Semantics and syntax of motion. In J. P. Kimball (Ed.), *Syntax and Semantics,* Vol. 4. New York: Academic Press, 1975.

Nida, Eugene A. *Componential Analysis of Meaning: An Introduction to Semantic Structures.* The Hague: Mouton, 1975. (Reviewed by A. Lehrer in *Language,* 1976, *52,* 972–976, with two other books on semantics by Nida.)
Introductory textbook on lexicography, including problems and a glossary.

Parisi, Domenico & Antinucci, Francesco. Componential analysis. Chapter 4 in Parisi & Antinucci, 1976.

Nida, Eugene A.; Louw, Johannes, P.; & Smith, Rondal B. Semantic domains and componential analysis of meaning. In Cole, in press.

Cognitive Psychology and Artificial Intelligence

Other approaches have been taken in cognitive psychology and artificial intelligence. In addition to the following references, see Kintsch (1974, Chapter 11) and Norman & Rumelhart (1975).

Anisfeld, M. & Knapp, M. Association, synonymity, and directionality in false recognition. *Journal of Experimental Psychology,* 1968, *77,* 171–179.
This memory experiment is one of the first pieces of evidence for decomposition of words into semantic components.

Perfetti, Charles A. Psychosemantics: Some cognitive aspects of structural meaning. *Psychological Bulletin,* 1972, *78,* 241–259.
Developments in transformational grammar are contrasted to the idea of semantic features as components of lexical meaning. Evidence for such components and limitations on the idea (e.g., due to semantic deep structure; reference) are discussed.

Miller, George. English verbs of motion: A case study in semantics and lexical memory. In A. W. Melton & E. Martin (Eds.), *Coding Processes in Human Memory.* Washington, D.C.: V. H. Winston & Sons, 1972.
Miller introduces a method of semantic analysis (incomplete

definition by paraphrase) that can be viewed as a componential analysis.

Schank, Roger. Conceptual dependency: A theory of natural language understanding. *Cognitive Psychology,* 1972, *3,* 552–631.
Outlines a computer-implemented theory of language processing in which verbs are broken down into primitive components, and inferences are stored indistinguishably from the original assertions.

Thorndyke, Perry W. Conceptual complexity and imagery in comprehension and memory. *Journal of Verbal Learning and Verbal Behavior,* 1975, *14,* 359–369.
Comprehension latencies in two experiments indicate that number of conceptual components predicts processing difficulty only when there is not a control for imagery value of the word.

Fodor, Janet Dean; Fodor, Jerry A.; & Garrett, Merrill F. The psychological unreality of semantic representations. *Linguistic Inquiry,* 1975, *6,* 515–531.
Presents data and argues against a semantic component theory of semantic processing.

Abrahamson, Adele A. Experimental analysis of the semantics of movement. In Norman & Rumelhart, 1975.
Proposes that analysis of memory errors can be used to uncover semantic components, exemplified by an analysis of errors in memory for sentences about movement from a text. Some suggestions about the memory processes are also made.

Multidimensional Scaling

Multidimensional scaling is a technique that has often been used to arrive at componential representations of adult word meaning. In the future it will probably be applied to children's lexicons. A few references follow.

Henley, Nancy M. A psychological study of the semantics of animal terms. *Journal of Verbal Learning and Verbal Behavior,* 1969, *8,* 176–184.
A good example of the semantic application of multidimensional scaling.

Green, Paul E. & Carmone, Frank J. *Multidimensional Scaling and Related Techniques in Marketing Analysis.* Boston: Allyn & Bacon, 1970.

Despite the title, this is the only good textbook for beginners currently available. Includes some material on cluster analysis also.

Fillenbaum, Samuel & Rapaport, Amnon. *Structures in the Subjective Lexicon.* New York: Academic Press, 1971.
Introductory chapters on multidimensional scaling and cluster analysis are followed by results on color names, kinship terms, emotion names, and various parts of speech or verb classes.

Shepard, Roger N.; Romney, A. Kimball; & Nerlove, Sara Beth (Eds.). *Multidimensional Scaling: Theory and Applications in the Behavioral Sciences,* Vols. 1 & 2. New York: Seminar Press, 1972.
These volumes are not for beginners, but they usefully bring together a good deal of information on multidimensional scaling.

Burton, Michael L. & Romney, A. Kimball. A multidimensional representation of role terms. *American Ethnologist,* 1975, *2,* 397–407.
Burton & Romney illustrate multidimensional scaling with a study of English role terms.

Arabie, Phipps; Kosslyn, Stephen M.; & Nelson, Keith E. A multidimensional scaling study of visual memory of 5-year-olds and adults. *Journal of Experimental Child Psychology,* 1975, *19,* 327–345.
Includes critical discussion of the scaling techniques.

CHILD LANGUAGE PUBLICATIONS

A few of the relevant papers on child language follow. Many others are listed among the references on polar, relational, and spatio-temporal terms (Sections 8 and 9).

General

*McNeill, David. *The Acquisition of Language.* New York: Harper & Row, 1970a.
McNeill gives an elementary survey in his chapter on semantic development, including a proposal that children begin with a sentence-meaning dictionary and later switch to a word-meaning dictionary. Two hypotheses about the addition of semantic features (horizontal vs. vertical development) are suggested.

Stross, Brian. Tzeltal: Acquisition and componentiality. In *Papers from the Sixth Regional Meeting of the Chicago Linguistic Society,* The University of Chicago Linguistics Department, 1970.

Stross examines 2000 utterances of a Tzeltal child at age 2;6, finding no evidence that semantic components have been abstracted by the child.

*Clark, Eve V. What's in a word? On the child's acquisition of semantics in his first language. In Moore, 1973(a).

Clark proposes a Semantic Feature Hypothesis (briefly, that children initially attribute only one or two semantic features to a word, adding additional features until the adult meaning is attained), compares it to other theories, and reviews supporting data from single-word through school-age speech.

Baron, Jonathan. Semantic components and conceptual development. *Cognition,* 1973, *2,* 299–317.

Baron argues for component-by-component acquisition of word meaning and extends his theory to general concept learning by defining a concept as a habitual plan and a component as a subplan. Applications to logical concepts and physical and moral reasoning are discussed. The theory contrasts with stage theories.

*Baron, Jonathan & Kaiser, Anne. Semantic components in children's errors with pronouns. *Journal of Psycholinguistic Research,* 1975, *4,* 303–317.

In the presence of the experimenter and two dolls, children ages 3–5 years responded to instructions such as "point to my (your, his, her, our, their) feet" and to corresponding instructions for subject and indirect object pronouns. Errors more frequently involved shared semantic components than would be predicted by a response-bias model.

Gentner, Dedre. Evidence for the psychological reality of semantic components: The verbs of possession. In D. A. Norman & D. E. Rumelhart, 1975.

Gentner asked children ages $3\frac{1}{2}$–$8\frac{1}{2}$ to act out with toys sentences using the verbs *give, take, pay, trade, spend, buy,* and *sell.* Performance was worse for verbs with more semantic components, and semantic components were often missing for the more complex words (e.g., *sell* interpreted as *give*; components concerning transfer of money not yet part of the lexical entry).

Kuczaj, Stan A., II. On the acquisition of a semantic system. *Journal of Verbal Learning and Verbal Behavior*, 1975, *14*, 340–358.

Levels of acquisition for the words *always, never, usually, seldom,* and *sometimes* were determined by a comprehension task and a judgment and imitation task with children 40–61 months; incorrect polarity often was observed.

Applications of the Semantic Differential

The semantic differential is a componential theory for connotative (rather than denotative) meaning. It was the major pretransformational approach to meaning in psychology and has occasionally been applied to language development.

Osgood, C. E.; Suci, G. J.; & Tannenbaum, P. H. *The Measurement of Meaning.* Urbana: University of Illinois Press, 1957.

A survey of the semantic differential technique by those who developed it. See also Snider & Osgood (1969) and Osgood, May, & Miron (1975).

Ervin, Susan M. & Foster, G. The development of meaning in children's descriptive terms. *Journal of Abnormal and Social Psychology*, 1960, *61*, 271–275.

Children confuse the meanings of terms that are similar on the semantic differential, first graders more than sixth graders.

Di Vesta, Francis J. A developmental study of the semantic structure of children. *Journal of Verbal Learning and Verbal Behavior*, 1966, *5*, 249–259.

Reports an investigation of connotative meaning using the semantic differential scales. The three most salient semantic factors found in adult studies (evaluation, potency, activity) were found even for second graders (through sixth graders), but children had some nonadult factors among their less salient factors (e.g., warmth).

Gordon, Lucy H. & Williams, John E. Secondary factors in the affective meaning system of the preschool child. *Developmental Psychology*, 1973, *8*, 25–34.

Evidence for an evaluation factor, but not the other two factors usually found with the semantic differential, was found in preschoolers.

C Fuzzy
Concept Theories

*According to this last approach, category members differ in how well they exemplify the category. Some members are **focal** (typical, central); others are **boundary** (atypical, peripheral) members. The following references give theoretical background and some adult studies.*

BACKGROUND PUBLICATIONS:
LINGUISTICS AND PSYCHOLINGUISTICS

Berlin, Brent & Kay, Paul. *Basic Color Terms: Their Universality and Evolution.* Berkeley: University of California Press, 1969. (Reviewed by G. A. Collier in *Language,* 1973, *49,* 245–248.)
   Detailed statement of the method and results for finding focal and boundary colors that was the basis for Rosch's work.

Lakoff, George. Hedges and meaning criteria. In R. McDavid & A. R. Duckert (Eds.), *Lexicography in English.* New York: New York Academy of Sciences, 1973. (Or see—Hedges: A study in meaning criteria and the logic of fuzzy concepts. *Papers from the Eighth Regional Meeting of the Chicago Linguistic Society,* The University of Chicago Linguistics Department, 1972.)
   There are various criteria for category membership, exemplified by hedges such as *"Technically,* a whale is a mammal" and *"Loosely speaking,* a whale is a fish." These can be related to Zadah's fuzzy set theory, which assigns degrees of membership to various items rather than a binary member/ nonmember relation.

Rips, Lance J.; Shoben, Edward J.; & Smith, Edward E. Semantic distance and the verification of semantic relations. *Journal of Verbal Learning and Verbal Behavior,* 1973, *12,* 1–20.
   Ratings of semantic relatedness among subordinate and super-ordinate categories predicted reaction time for verifying statements of the form "An X is a Y." A multidimensional scaling of the terms, based on the ratings, predicted reaction time for a same/different category judgment task and predicted analogy solutions. The dimensions, e.g., size and ferocity for animals, are *characteristic* rather than *defining* features. A two-stage

model is proposed in which (1) all and (2) defining features only are accessed. This is the simplest presentation of the authors' theory; more technical treatments with broader discussion of the semantic memory literature appear in *Psychological Review*, 1974, *81*, 214–241 and in G. Bower (Ed.), *The Psychology of Learning and Motivation*, Vol. 8, 1974.

Labov, W. The boundaries of words and their meanings. In C.-J. N. Bailey & R. W. Shuy (Eds.), *New Ways of Analyzing Variation in English*. Washington, D.C.: Georgetown University Press, 1973(b).

Rosch, Eleanor H. On the internal structure of perceptual and semantic categories. In Moore, 1973(a).

Rosch explains the ideas that categories do not have well defined boundaries and that some members are better exemplars of their category than others. She summarizes a good deal of her recent research, including (1) studies on color and shape categories with the Dani, who have only two color terms ("dark" and "light"); and (2) American studies relating "exemplariness" ratings and reaction times for statements like "A pear is a fruit."

Rosch, Eleanor H. Natural categories. *Cognitive Psychology*, 1973b, *4*, 328–350.

Shorter presentation of the ideas and data in the Moore chapter.

Schmidt, C. The relevance to semantic theory of a study of vagueness. In *Papers from the Tenth Regional Meeting of the Chicago Linguistic Society*. The University of Chicago Linguistics Department 1974.

Glass, Arnold L. & Holyoak, Keith J. Alternative conceptions of semantic theory. *Cognition*, 1974/75, *3*, 313–339.

The feature-comparison model of Smith, Shoben, & Rips (1974) and a marker-search model based on Katz (1972) are evaluated. A major prediction of the feature-comparison model is not confirmed in verification reaction time experiments.

Collins, Allan M. & Loftus, Elizabeth F. A spreading-activation theory of semantic processing. *Psychological Review*, 1975, *82*, 407–428.

An extended version of Quillian's (1968) semantic theory can account for recent experimental results. Alternative theories are criticized, including the model of Rips, Shoben, & Smith.

Rosch, Eleanor H. & Mervis, Carolyn B. Family resemblances: Studies in the internal structure of categories. *Cognitive Psychology*, 1975, *7*, 573–605.
> Further development of Rosch's theory; several experiments are reported. See also Rosch's other paper in the same volume.

Rosch, Eleanor H. Universals and cultural specifics in human categorization. In R. Brislin, S. Bochner, & W. Lonner (Eds.), *Cross-cultural Perspectives on Learning*. New York: Sage/Halsted, 1975.

Kaufmann, Arnold. *Introduction to the Theory of Fuzzy Subsets. Vol. 1: Fundamental Theoretical Elements*. New York: Academic Press, 1975.
> A mathematical treatment.

Zadeh, Lofti A.; Fu, King-Sun; Tanaka, Kokichi; & Shimura, Masamichi (Eds.). *Fuzzy Sets and Their Applications to Cognitive and Decision Processes*. New York: Academic Press, 1975.
> Papers from a conference.

Hersh, Harry M. & Caramazza, Alfonso. A fuzzy set approach to modifiers and vagueness in natural language. *Journal of Experimental Psychology: General*, 1976, *105*, 254–276.
> Applications of fuzzy set theory to natural language are discussed, and in particular, experiments are reported on natural language operators on fuzzy sets (e.g., *not very large*), providing a series of membership functions.

Brown, Roger. Reference: In memorial tribute to Eric Lenneberg. *Cognition*, 1976, *4*, 125–153.
> Brown discusses work on reference between the 1950's and the present, focusing on color terms. Rosch's work provides a new interpretation of this literature. The article is Section I of a book in preparation, *The New Paradigm of Reference*.

CHILD LANGUAGE PUBLICATIONS

Only a few developmental studies taking this approach exist at present.

Heider, Eleanor R. "Focal" color areas and the development of color names. *Developmental Psychology*, 1971, *4*, 447–455.
> American children prefer to show an adult focal rather than nonfocal colors and perform better on a color-matching task with focal colors than with nonfocal colors. (Heider is Rosch's previous name.)

Mervis, Carolyn B.; Catlin, Jack; & Rosch, Eleanor H. Development of the structure of color categories. *Developmental Psychology,* 1975, *11,* 54–60.

Subjects in kindergarten, third grade, and college were asked to select the referents of various color terms from a color array. The foci (centers) of the color categories become established earlier than the boundaries.

*Andersen, Elaine S. Cups and glasses: Learning that boundaries are vague. *Journal of Child Language,* 1975a, *2,* 79–103.

Children ages 3, 6, 9, and 12 years named and sorted 25 drinking vessels; then for the words *cup* and *glass* they gave definitions and chose the best exemplars. These were three stages: (1) overextension of *cup,* (2) discrete boundaries based on certain perceptual attributes, and (3) vague boundaries based on awareness of functional properties also.

Carson, Margaret T. & Abrahamson, Adele A. Some members are more equal than others: The effect of semantic typicality on class-inclusion performance. *Child Development,* 1976, *47,* 1186–1190.

Children ages 7–10 have more difficulty with Piaget's class-inclusion task when the problem includes atypical exemplars of categories. However, correct sorting performance suggests that the difficulty is semantic, not conceptual.

WORD MEANING DEVELOPMENT
OVERVIEW OF SECTIONS 8 AND 9

The references in Section 7 (lexical development) included some studies of the development of meaning for specific words. These studies were used to argue for one or another view of lexical structure. In the following two sections many additional studies of word meaning development are cited. Some of them are associated with particular views of lexical organization; others are more concerned with the relationship of word meaning development to cognitive development. Almost all of the words are relational; they relate two objects (e.g., A bigger *than B), two people (A* daughter *of B), or two events (*E_1 *before* E_2). *Many also occur in polar pairs, with an* **unmarked** *(positive) and* **marked** *(negative) term (*big/small, before/after). *Because so many different words have been studied, they are divided here into two sections. Section 8 covers comparative adjectives (especially dimensional adjectives) and kinship terms. Section 9 has studies on spatial, temporal, and deictic terms. Dimensional adjectives refer to dimensions of objects (e.g., height, width), whereas the spatial terms in Section 9 refer to location or orientation in space.*

Section 8
WORD MEANING DEVELOPMENT OF ADJECTIVES AND KINSHIP TERMS

In recent years, a great deal of experimental effort has been devoted to children's acquisition of dimensional adjectives in their basic form (e.g., tall) as well as their relational forms (comparative, e.g., taller, and superlative, e.g., tallest). Related work has been done on the general comparative adjectives, more/less and same/different. There are also a few studies on kinship terms, which are relational nouns. Piaget used relational terms in many of his studies of concrete operations, a cognitive stage beginning at about age 7. Recent studies have been more concerned with the successive acquisition of meaning components, especially positive versus negative polarity (e.g., tall vs. short) and dimensional differences (e.g., tall vs. long). The background readings for Section 7, especially 7-B (semantic component theories), are relevant to these recent studies. Additional background reading is suggested separately for some of the topics in this section and in Section 9.

A Comparative Adjectives in Cognitive Development Research

Several tasks used by Piaget and others typically include comparative (or superlative) adjectives in the instructions or questions posed to the child. In a typical seriation task, a child is given a series of sticks and must arrange them from shortest to longest. A second task is transitive inference: If stick A is longer than stick B, and B longer than C, can the child conclude that stick A is longer than stick C? Finally, in conservation studies children must understand that a relationship of identity or equality is invariant (is conserved) under certain transformations. For example, if a quantity of water is poured from a shallow dish into a narrow tube, is the amount of water "the same"? Or is it "more"? Correctly responding to these terms requires fairly complicated cognitive operations.

Piaget, Jean & Szeminska, Alina. *The Child's Conception of Number.* New York: Humanities Press, 1952. (Also in paperback, New York: Norton, 1965. Originally published in French, 1941.)

Some of Piaget's work on seriation and conservation is reported here.

Piaget, Jean; Inhelder, Bärbel; & Szeminska, Alina. *The Child's Conception of Geometry.* New York: Basic Books, 1960. (Originally published in French, 1948.)

Includes an investigation of transitivity of length.

Inhelder, Bärbel & Piaget, Jean. *The Early Growth of Logic in the Child.* New York: Humanities Press, 1964. (Also in paperback, New York: Norton, 1969. Originally published in French, 1959.)

The sections on seriation are relevant.

Elkind, David. Children's discovery of the conservation of mass, weight and volume: Piaget Replication Study II. *Journal of Genetic Psychology,* 1961a, *98,* 219–227.

Piaget's findings of regular, age-related differences in performance were replicated for children in grades kindergarten through sixth, his three-stage theory summarized, and one of his methodological assumptions verified.

Elkind, David. Discrimination, seriation, and numeration of size and dimensional differences in young children: Piaget Replication Study VI. *Journal of Genetic Psychology*, 1964, *104*, 275–296.

Piaget's findings of regular, age-related differences in performance were replicated for children ages 4;0–6;7, and his theory summarized. Dimensionality (one-, two- or three-dimensional) of materials affected ease of success, but not sequence of success, on the three tasks.

Bruner, Jerome S.; Olver, Rose R.; & Greenfield, Patricia M. *Studies in Cognitive Growth*. New York: John Wiley & Sons, 1966.

This book is a collection of research reports based on collaborative research by 12 individuals at Harvard's Center for Cognitive Studies. The studies reported include experiments on seriation, conservation, and the use of the terms *fuller than* and *emptier than*.

*Mehler, Jacques & Bever, Thomas G. Cognitive capacity of very young children. *Science*, 1967, *158*, 141–142.

This is the first in a series of articles on conservation. A U-shaped age function is reported, with good performance at about age 3;0 followed by a decline. The next two articles in the series are in *Science*, 1968, *162*, 920–924.

*Piaget, Jean. Quantification, conservation and nativism. *Science*, 1968, *162*, 976–981. (With a reply by J. Mehler and T. G. Bever.)

This reply by Piaget closes the series. Piaget objects that Mehler & Bever's task was testing something other than conservation, and he reports new experiments of his own.

Farnham-Diggory, Sylvia & Bermon, Maurice. Verbal compensation, cognitive synthesis, and conservation. *Merrill-Palmer Quarterly of Behavior and Development*, 1968, *14*, 215–227.

Kindergarteners and first graders were asked to describe the difference between two objects differing in two dimensions; the taller one was always the narrower one. Almost every child who previously passed a conservation-of-liquids task mentioned both dimensions; many of those who failed the conservation task mentioned only one dimension. Conservers were also better at synthesizing logograph sequences into sentences.

Gelman, Rochelle. Conservation acquisition: A problem of learning to attend to relevant attributes. *Journal of Experimental Child Psychology*, 1969, *7*, 167–187.

Conservation failure may often be due to the child's attention to attributes (e.g., length) irrelevant to the task. Training with 32 six-trial oddity problems with feedback, alternating number and length as the relevant attributes, resulted in considerable improvement in kindergarteners' performance and explanations.

Gelman, Rochelle. The nature and development of early number concepts. In H. W. Reese (Ed.), *Advances in Child Development and Behavior,* Vol. 7. New York: Academic Press, 1972.

Gelman summarizes previous theories (e.g., Piaget's), introduces a distinction between operators and estimators, and reports new experiments in which young children show rudimentary skill at operations on arrays that are small in number.

Klahr, David & Wallace, J. G. The role of quantification operators in the development of conservation of quantity. *Cognitive Psychology,* 1973, *4,* 301–327.

Formal theoretical analysis of quantitative processes involved in conservation of quantity. Not linguistically oriented. (See also their publications listed in Section 7-A.)

Bryant, P. E. What the young child has to learn about logic. In R. A. Hinde & J. Stevenson-Hinde (Eds.), *Constraints on Learning: Limitations and Predispositions.* New York: Academic Press, 1973.

Bryant reports several experiments on transitive inference performed with children ages 4–6.

Inhelder, Bärbel; Sinclair, Hermina; & Bovet, Magali. *Learning and the Development of Cognition.* Cambridge, Mass.: Harvard University Press, 1974.

A number of forms of conservation are discussed, as well as the influence of training on class inclusion.

Steiner, Gerhard. On the psychological reality of cognitive structures: A tentative synthesis of Piaget's and Bruner's theories. *Child Development,* 1974, *45,* 891–899.

Piaget's and Bruner's explanations of classification, conservation, and logical multiplication are compared and synthesized.

Osherson, Daniel. *Logical Abilities in Children, Volume 1. The Organization of Length and Class Concepts in Children: Empirical Consequences of a Piagetian Formalism.* Hillsdale, N.J.: Lawrence Erlbaum Associates, 1974.

Osherson uses Grice's axiomatization of the grouping as the

basis of a theory to predict development of class-inclusion and length relations. In addition to a transitivity of length task, several new tasks for class concepts are introduced. Osherson eventually rejects the logical model as adequate for prediction, and in Volume 2 switches to a process model for reasoning in older children.

Baron, Jonathan; Lawson, Glen; & Siegel, Linda S. Effects of training and set size on children's judgments of number and length. *Developmental Psychology,* 1975, *11,* 583–588.

When children are asked to compare two rows of dots in length or number, some respond consistently as if they were asked about number and some as if about length. The number strategy is more probable with small than large dot arrays. Apparently children have both strategies available, and factors such as array size, bias, and situation-induced set influence which is used.

*Trabasso, T. & Riley, C. A. On the construction and use of representations involving linear order. In R. L. Solso (Ed.), *Information Processing and Cognition: The Loyola Symposium.* Hillsdale, N.J.: Lawrence Erlbaum Associates, 1975.

A number of experiments on transitive inference are summarized, including Bryant & Trabasso (*Nature,* 1971), Riley & Trabasso (*Journal of Experimental Child Psychology,* 1974), and Trabasso, Riley, & Wilson (in Falmagne, 1975). New experiments using six sticks varying in length are analyzed with respect to processing models which predict both adult and child data and conflict with Piaget. Also see Riley in *Journal of Experimental Child Psychology,* 1976, *22,* 1–22.

Harris, Paul L. & Bassett, Elizabeth. Transitive inferences by 4-year-old children? *Developmental Psychology,* 1975, *11,* 875–876.

Two experiments rule out an alternative explanation of Bryant and Trabasso's results.

Miller, Scott A. Nonverbal assessment of Piagetian concepts. *Psychological Bulletin,* 1976, *83,* 405–430.

Miller reviews studies that reduced linguistic or other performance demands in Piagetian tasks. Some (not all) of the studies are suggestive that concepts such as conservation and transitivity might emerge earlier than Piaget indicated.

Beilin, Harry. Constructing cognitive operations linguistically. In H. W. Reese (Ed.), *Advances in Child Development and Behavior,* Vol. 11. New York: Academic Press, 1976.

Presents data in support of the hypothesis that conservation can be trained by linguistic means, and reviews some of the more general research on conservation and training.

B Two- and Three-Term Series Problems

Two- and three-term series problems are a verbal means of determining children's ability to make **transitive inferences.** For example, a three-term problem used by Piaget is: "Edith is fairer than Suzanne; Edith is darker than Lili. Which of the three has the darkest hair?" An easier form of the problem would have as its first premise: "Suzanne is darker than Edith." A few references follow, with Piaget primarily interested in the general problem form and later writers primarily trying to account for differences among problem forms for adults. See also Kavanaugh, 1976a.

*Piaget, Jean. *Judgment and Reasoning in the Child*. London: Routledge & Kegan Paul, 1928. (Also in paperback, Totowa, N.J.: Littlefield, Adams & Co., 1959. Originally published in French, 1924.)
Piaget briefly discusses children's performance on three-term series problems (pp. 87–90).

Huttenlocher, Janellen. Constructing spatial images: A strategy in reasoning. *Psychological Review*, 1968, *75*, 550–560.
Huttenlocher gives a theoretical account of processing of three-term series problems, based on the construction of spatial images. The theory predicts differences in reaction times and errors for alternative forms of the problem.

Clark, Herbert H. Linguistic processes in deductive reasoning. *Psychological Review*, 1969, *76*, 387–404.
Clark gives a theoretical account of processing of two- and three-term series problems, based on the extraction and comparison of propositional representations. The theory predicts differences in reaction times and errors for alternative forms of the problem. The disagreement between Clark and Huttenlocher extends through the 1972 volume of *Psychological Review*.

Johnson-Laird, Philip N. The three-term series problem. *Cognition*, 1972, *1*, 57–82.
Johnson-Laird reviews three theories of adult processing and suggests that subjects change their strategy during the experimental session.

Potts, George R. & Scholz, Karl W. The internal representation of a three-term series problem. *Journal of Verbal Learning and Verbal Behavior*, 1975, *14*, 439–452.

When three-term series problems are presented so that premise study time can be measured independent of question reaction time, marked and unmarked adjectives are stored in the same form and the two premises are integrated into a unified representation. Huttenlocher's and H. Clark's theories are compared; neither can account for the results.

Ehri, L. C. & Ammon, P. R. Children's comprehension of comparative sentence transformations. *Child Development*, 1974, *45*, 512–516.

Children ages 4–8 years performed surprisingly well on two-term relational problems (e.g., "John is bigger than Bill. Who is smaller?"). Marked adjectives and negation made problems harder, but lack of congruence between assertion and question adjective did not.

C Children's Acquisition of Dimensional Adjectives

The following studies of dimensional adjectives emphasize semantic factors influencing age of acquisition of various terms. This is in contrast to Section 8-A, which emphasizes the relational thinking reflected in certain tasks regardless of which term is used. The major issue here, as in Sections 8-D and 8-F, is whether semantically marked words are learned later than the corresponding unmarked words. Other papers focus on the assignment of words to particular dimensions of objects. For some overviews, see Section 8-F; for background, see the first papers in Section 7-B and the following.

BACKGROUND PUBLICATIONS: LINGUISTICS

Bierwisch, Manfred. Some semantic universals of German adjectivals. *Foundations of Language,* 1967, *3,* 1–36.
> Bierwisch presents an elegant semantic analysis of a number of German polar adjective pairs. The pairs differ in the location of the implicit norm. He gives examples of semantic representations for dimensional and spatial adjectives, in which semantic features such as (+vertical) are arranged in dependency trees.

Teller, P. Some discussion and extension of Manfred Bierwisch's work on German adjectivals. *Foundations of Language,* 1969, *5,* 185–217.
> Teller explores problems with Bierwisch's analysis, using the corresponding English adjectives, e.g., *long, high, tall, wide, big, top, front, side,* and *end.*

CHILD LANGUAGE PUBLICATIONS

The developmental studies follow.

Lumsden, Ernest A., Jr., & Poteat, Barbara W. S. The salience of the vertical dimension in the concept of "bigger" in five- and six-year-olds. *Journal of Verbal Learning and Verbal Behavior,* 1968, *7,* 404–408.
> Children ages 5 and 6 years and high school seniors performed a forced-choice comprehension task for the word *bigger.* The

children tended to choose the figure with greatest vertical extent, not greatest area. This may be a confounding factor in size conservation tasks.

*Wales, Roger & Campbell, Robin. On the development of comparison and the comparison of development. In Flores d'Arcais & Levelt, 1970.

Children in a longitudinal study performed comprehension and production tasks on dimensional adjectives at mean ages 3;5 and 4;8. A fairly detailed analysis and theoretical discussion are offered, focusing on longitudinal aspects. (See also the articles in the same volume about adult processing of comparatives by H. Clark and Flores d'Arcais.)

*Clark, Eve V. On the child's acquisition of antonyms in two semantic fields. *Journal of Verbal Learning and Verbal Behavior,* 1972, *11,* 750–758.

Children at ages 4;0–5;5 were given words (dimensional adjectives and spatiotemporal terms) and were asked to respond with their opposites (antonyms). Difficulty was related to relative complexity of meaning, and simpler words (e.g., *big*) were often used where a more complex word (e.g., *tall*) was required.

Klatzky, Roberta L.; Clark, Eve V.; & Macken, Marlys. Asymmetries in the acquisition of polar adjectives: linguistic or conceptual? *Journal of Experimental Child Psychology,* 1973, *16,* 32–46.

Children ages 3;7–4;11 took longer to learn nonsense syllable labels for the negative poles of four dimensions than for the positive poles. Thus, an underlying conceptual asymmetry is responsible for findings that negative words are learned later than their positive counterparts.

*Clark, Herbert H. Space, time, semantics and the child. In Moore, 1973.

Clark discusses dimensional adjectives in the context of a theoretical discussion of space and time terms. Previous experimental results are used to evaluate the theory.

*Maratsos, Michael P. Decrease in the understanding of the word "Big" in preschool children. *Child Development,* 1973b, *44,* 747–752.

Children were shown pairs of rectangles in which the larger rectangle was either shorter than or of equal height to the smaller rectangle. Three-year-olds performed above chance in choosing the "big one," but 4- and 5-year-olds seemed to define "big" in terms of tallness.

Peisach, Estelle. Relationship between knowledge and use of dimensional language and achievement of conservation. *Developmental Psychology,* 1973, *9,* 189–197.

Children in kindergarten, first, and second grades were tested for conservation of quantity and for comprehension and production of dimensional adjectives. There was a significant correlation, but an expected difference between conservers and nonconservers in degree of degeneration of dimensional language during a conservation task was not found. Dimensional language is a necessary but not sufficient condition for conservation.

Maratsos, Michael P. When is a high thing the big one? *Developmental Psychology,* 1974c, *10,* 367–375.

Seven experiments with children ages 3;0–5;11 established that the height of the top point of an object (rather than distance between bottom point and top point) affects use of *big, tall,* and *high* increasingly with age.

Eilers, Rebecca E.; Oller, D. Kimbrough; & Ellington, Judy. The acquisition of word-meaning for dimensional adjectives: The long and short of it. *Journal of Child Language,* 1974, *1,* 195–204.

Children at ages 2;3–3;7 performed in a comprehension task on the pairs *big/little, long/short, wide/narrow.* Order of acquisition corresponded with semantic generality. More errors were made on unmarked than marked adjectives, contrary to other studies.

Nelson, Katherine & Benedict, Helen. The comprehension of relative, absolute, and contrastive adjectives by young children. *Journal of Psycholinguistic Research,* 1974, *3,* 333–342.

Children ages 3;10–6;7 performed a two-choice comprehension task with pictures for relative (e.g., *tall, short, light, dark*), contrastive (e.g., *happy, sad*), and absolute (e.g., *cloudy, round*) adjectives. Comparative forms (e.g., *taller*) were harder than standard forms (e.g., *tall*), by error frequency and latency, except relative-term latency. The three classes of adjectives are processed differently.

Bausano, Mary K. & Jeffrey, Wendell E. Dimensional salience and judgments of bigness by three-year-old children. *Child Development,* 1975, *46,* 988–991.

The results of Maratsos (1973b) can be explained on the grounds that 3-year-olds choose on the basis of the most salient dimension (the one with the greatest difference among stimuli, using ratios). Such an effect was demonstrated in a three-alternative choice task with 30 children ages 2;11–3;11. Salience determined whether the tallest or widest rectangle was chosen; the biggest was never the tallest or widest and was less frequently chosen.

Coots, James H. Polarity and complexity in spatial adjective acquisition. Paper presented at the biennial meeting of the Society for Research in Child Development, Denver, April 10–13, 1975.

Preschoolers and kindergarteners performed two-alternative production and comprehension tasks for the terms *bigger/smaller, higher/lower, longer/shorter, taller/shorter, wider/narrower,* and *thicker/thinner.* Overall, the hypotheses were not supported that negative polar terms are learned later than positive ones and that they take the meaning of the corresponding positive term at some stage. (For similar conclusions on other terms, see Kuczaj & Maratsos, 1975b, in Section 9-C; and Carey, 1976, and Glucksberg et al., 1976, in Section 8-D.)

Brewer, William F. & Stone, J. Brandon. Acquisition of spatial antonym pairs. *Journal of Experimental Child Psychology,* 1975, *19,* 299–307.

In a comprehension task, children ages 3;6–5;3 seemed to acquire the polarity of a term before its dimension, based on six dimensional pairs. Unmarked terms were learned earlier than marked terms.

Townsend, David J. & Erb, Melinda. Children's strategies for interpreting complex comparative questions. *Journal of Child Language,* 1975, *2,* 271–277.

Children ages 3–6 answered questions of the form "Which box is Xer than it is Y?" where Xer was *taller, shorter, fatter,* or *thinner* and Y was *tall* or *fat,* with respect to five rectangles. The largest rectangle was most often chosen. Older children often chose the Xest rectangle, indicating that they attended to the first, but not the second, clause.

Tinder, Paula A.; Arnold, Marjorie R.; & Abrahamson, Adele A. Development of spatial adjectives in nursery-school children. Paper presented at the annual meeting of the Eastern Psychological Association, New York City, April 1976.

Children ages 3;5–4;11 were tested for comprehension of six dimensional and spatial adjective pairs. As an alternative to a stage of reliance on the vertical dimension reported by Maratsos (1973b), some children used dimension-of-greatest-extent as the criterion for some words. Also, results on *high* v. *tall* differed in part from those of Maratsos (1974c).

Ehri, Linnea C. Comprehension and production of adjectives and seriation. *Journal of Child Language,* 1976, *3,* 369–384.

Data on adjectives from children of ages 4–8 years indicated that vocabulary and comprehension tasks were better than production tasks in distinguishing seriators from nonseriators. Adjective forms included uninflected (e.g., *tall*), comparative (e.g., *taller than, as tall as,* and their negations), and coordinated (*tall and skinny*). These and other results are related to Sinclair-de-Zwart (1969) and H. Clark (1970a).

Kavanaugh, Robert D. Developmental changes in preschool children's comprehension of comparative sentences. *Merrill-Palmer Quarterly of Behavior and Development,* 1976a, *22,* 309–318.

Children ages 3–5½ years performed a task testing comprehension of *taller/shorter* and *happier/sadder* using a simpler procedure than the three-term series problem. They pointed out the referents of the subject and object of simple sentences from a five-picture array. The results indicate that they can process the relational information, though it is more difficult for arrays in which the two referents are near the opposite poles rather than the same pole of the scale.

D Children's Acquisition of General Comparative Adjectives

The following studies are on children's use of same/different and more/less. The earlier studies emphasize the cognitive concept of conservation (see the references on conservation in Section 8-A), while the later ones emphasize the acquisition of word meaning. See also Sections 7-B, 8-C, and 8-F.

Griffiths, J. A.; Shantz, C. A.; & Sigel, I. E. A methodological problem in conservation studies: The use of relational terms. *Child Development,* 1967, *38,* 841–848.

> Preschool children were tested on *same, more,* and *less.* For comparison of number and weight, correct use of the terms was most often an elicited response; for length, children tended to use the words correctly spontaneously. *Same* was the most difficult term, and length the easiest dimension of comparison. Implications for Piaget's verbal methods of testing conservation are discussed.

*Donaldson, Margaret & Balfour, George. Less is more: A study of language comprehension in children. *British Journal of Psychology,* 1968, *59,* 461–471.

> This is the original study suggesting that preschoolers interpret *less* as meaning *more.* A variety of questions were asked regarding two trees with the same or a different number of apples.

Harasym, Carolyn R., Boersma, Frederick J. & Maguire, Thomas O. Semantic differential analysis of relational terms used in conservation. *Child Development,* 1971, *42,* 767–779.

> Children in grades one, two, and three were compared on semantic differential judgments of *more/less* and *same/different.* Ability to judge the terms appears to be related to conservation level.

Palermo, David S. More about less: A study of language comprehension. *Journal of Verbal Learning and Verbal Behavior,* 1973, *12,* 211–221.

> The findings of Donaldson & Balfour (1968) were replicated

for both discrete and continuous substances for children ages 3–7; semantic differential ratings were also obtained.

Palermo, David S. Still more about the comprehension of "less." *Developmental Psychology,* 1974, *10,* 827–829.
On four different tasks (apples on trees; linear array of poker chips; water; weight), most 3- and 4-year-olds who did not know the meaning of *less* consistently acted as though it meant *more.*

Weiner, Susan. On the development of 'more' or 'less.' *Journal of Experimental Child Psychology,* 1974, *17,* 271–287.
Children were asked which of two rows of toys had more/less toys, after viewing an addition or subtraction which made the changed row have more or less toys than the static row. The manipulation had little effect. Other results and theoretical issues are also discussed.

Donaldson, M. & McGarrigle, J. Some clues to the nature of semantic development. *Journal of Child Language,* 1974, *1,* 185–195.
Comprehension of *all* and *more* was tested for children ages 3–5 years. The results suggest a new interpretation of performance on conservation tasks, emphasizing the operation of "local rules" (e.g., length is more important than density).

Webb, Roger A.; Oliveri, Mary Ellen; & O'Keeffe, Lynda. Investigations of the meaning of "different" in the language of young children. *Child Development,* 1974, *45,* 984–991.
Two cross-sectional and one longitudinal study covering the approximate period 3–5.5 years supported a four-stage model, in which *different* (1) means *same,* (2) means *another,* (3) requires a dimension of similarity, and (4) has adult meaning.

Roeper, T. On the acquisition of *all* and *some.* In *Papers and Reports on Child Language Development,* No. 9. Committee on Linguistics, Stanford University, April 1975.

*Holland, V. Melissa & Palermo, David S. On learning "less": Language and cognitive development. *Child Development,* 1975, *46,* 437–443.
Children at ages 4 and 5 rapidly learn the *more/less* distinction when given training. The training does not, however, lead to improved performance on a conservation task.

Clark, Eve V. Knowledge, context, and strategy in the acquisition of meaning. In D. P. Dato (Ed.), *Georgetown University Round Table on Languages and Linguistics 1975.* Washington, D.C.: Georgetown University Press, 1975, 77–98.

Clark discusses the role of nonlinguistic strategies affecting comprehension tests for words such as *more, less, in, on,* and *under.*

*Glucksberg, Sam; Hay, Anne; & Danks, Joseph H. Words in utterance contexts: Young children do not confuse the meanings of *same* and *different. Child Development,* 1976, *47,* 737–741.

With children ages 2;8–3;3, the authors replicated the findings of Donaldson & Wales (1970) that preschoolers comprehend *same* but are systematically wrong on *different.* However, it was also shown that many adults in one experimental context respond to *different* by choosing another object of the same kind, and that in other experimental contexts preschoolers perform equally well on *same* and *different.* Thus, when situational contexts and utterances are sampled, no overall evidence exists that *same* is acquired earlier than *different.*

Carey, Susan. Less may never mean more. In Campbell & Smith, Proceedings of the Stirling Conference on Language, Stirling, Scotland, 1976.

In a tea party situation, children responded to instructions like "Make it so there's——tea in here." Whether the blank was filled with *more, less,* or a nonsense word, children responded appropriately for *more.* Using the words in a different sentence frame, *more* and *less* were responded to appropriately.

Kavanaugh, Robert D. On the synonymity of *more* and *less*: Comments on a methodology. *Child Development,* 1976b, *47,* 885–887.

The idea that children interpret *less* as a synonym of *more* is not supported by a procedure in which 3- and 4-year-olds placed objects (e.g., apples on trees) in response to instructions like "Make this tree have more (less) apples than this tree." The error of placing equal numbers of objects was about as frequent as the reversal error.

Wales, R. J.; Garman, M. A. G.; & Griffiths, P. D. More or less the same: A markedly different view of children's comparative judgments in three cultures. In Wales & Walker, 1976.

Discusses the performance of 3- and 4-year-olds speaking English, Tamil (Dravidian), and Lun Bawang (Malayo-Polynesian) on comprehension tasks using the words *more, less, same,* and *different* (or their equivalents in each language).

E Kinship Terms

A good deal of theoretical effort, and some experimental effort, has been placed in the study of kinship terms. Chapter 11 of Leech, 1974 (Section 2-F) summarizes much of the theoretical work, and some primary sources can be found in Tyler (1969). The child development studies have used kinship terms as a convenient set of relational terms, supplementing studies of comparative adjectives. A few theoretical background references are followed by the developmental studies.

BACKGROUND PUBLICATIONS: ANTHROPOLOGY

Tyler, Steven A. (Ed.). *Cognitive Anthropology.* New York: Holt, Rinehart and Winston, 1969.

> Analysis of terms in a semantic field (e.g., kinship terms) according to semantic components (e.g., of sex and generation) was aggressively pursued in anthropology in the 1960's. This volume includes the most important papers. Most relevant to psychologists are the papers on psychological reality by A. F. C. Wallace & J. Atkins ("The meaning of kinship terms," *American Anthropologist,* 1960, *62,* 58–80) and A. K. Romney & R. G. D'Andrade ("Cognitive aspects of English kin terms," *American Anthropologist,* 1964, *66,* No. 3, Part 2 (Special Publication), 146–170).

Burling, Robbins. American kinship terms once more. *Southwestern Journal of Anthropology,* 1970, *26,* 15–24.

> Formal analyses of kinship terms have had several deficiencies. Burling suggests capitalizing on people's verbal definitions in analyzing the terms, incorporating a sequence of principles that seems to correspond to the way children learn the terms.

Brown, Cecil H. Psychological, semantic and structural aspects of American English kinship terms. *American Ethnologist,* 1974, *1,* 415–436.

> Reviews componential analysis, offering a new analysis incorporating aspects of Romney & D'Andrade (1964) and Goodenough (1965). Recent literature is also remarked on, in particular those articles suggesting relational analyses or dealing with the problem of psychological reality. A distinction between necessary and contingent facts is made, roughly cor-

responding to the formal relational logic of a kinship system and to its use in practice, respectively.

Winkelman, John H. Semantic representation of kinship systems. *Journal of Psycholinguistic Research,* 1975, *4,* 133–140.

An algebraic system is argued to be preferable to associative, semantic feature and logical predicate representations. For example, P · P^{-1} (Tom) means parent (P) of (·) child (P^{-1}) of Tom.

CHILD LANGUAGE PUBLICATIONS

*Piaget, Jean. *Judgment and Reasoning in the Child.* London: Routledge & Kegan Paul, 1928. (Also in paperback, Totowa, N.J.: Littlefield Adams & Co., 1959. Originally published in French, 1924.)

Piaget analyzes children's understanding of the terms *brother* and *sister* in the context of a general discussion of reversibility and egocentrism. He identifies three stages: categorical (a sister is a little girl), relational (a sister has the same parents), and reciprocal (to be a sister, you must have a sister or brother).

Danziger, K. The child's understanding of kinship terms: A study in the development of relational concepts. *Journal of Genetic Psychology,* 1957, *91,* 213–232.

An interview task was conducted with 41 Australian children ages 5–8, testing five kinship terms. In addition to three stages similar to those of Piaget (1924/28), Danziger observed an earlier stage (precategorical).

Elkind, David. Children's conceptions of brother and sister: Piaget replication study V. *Journal of Genetic Psychology,* 1962, *100,* 129–136.

Elkind tested 210 children ages 5–11 in an interview task on the terms *brother* and *sister.* Results generally agreed with those of Piaget, but Elkind makes a distinction between the class concept and the relational concept, each of which has three developmental stages.

*Haviland, Susan E. & Clark, Eve V. 'This man's father is my father's son': A study of the acquisition of English kin terms. *Journal of Child Language,* 1974, *1,* 23–47.

An analysis of 15 kinship terms based on Bierwisch's relational components (PARENT-OF and CHILD-OF) generally predicts order of acquisition of the terms by children ages 3;0–8;10, as measured by verbal definitions.

Chambers, James C., Jr., & Tavuchis, Nicholas. Kids and kin: Children's understanding of American kin terms. *Journal of Child Language,* 1976, *3,* 63–80.

Children of mean ages 7;0 and 9;1 answered several questions in an interview format about each of 17 terms. Several types of difficulties or misconceptions were observed, especially in younger boys. Performance was best on nuclear family terms.

Landau, Barbara S. *The Acquisition of Kinship Terms.* Unpublished Ed.M. thesis, Rutgers University, 1976.

See also Landau's paper to be presented at the annual meeting of the Eastern Psychological Association, spring 1977.

F *Studies Combining Terms from Sections C, D, and E*

Donaldson, M. and Wales, R. J. On the acquisition of some relational terms. In Hayes, 1970. (Reprinted in Adams, 1972.)

Theoretical discussion and partial summary of experiments on *same/different, more/less,* and dimensional adjectives. Positive terms (e.g., *more, long*) are learned earlier than their negative counterparts (e.g., *less, short*). The individual papers on these topics cited above are more complete.

*Clark, Herbert H. The primitive nature of children's relational concepts. In Hayes, 1970(a).

Commentary on Donaldson & Wales (same volume), interpreting the advantage for positive terms in terms of semantic markedness (positive terms being unmarked) and suggesting three stages of meaning for the terms studied.

Swartz, Karyl & Hall, Alfred. Development of relational concepts and word definition in children five through eleven. *Child Development,* 1972, *43,* 239–244.

Children at ages 5, 7, 9, and 11 answered questions about *left/ right,* the kinship term *brother,* and the judgment of comparison (*taller/shorter*). Stages of development were compared to those found by Piaget and Elkind.

Townsend, David J. Children's comprehension of comparative forms. *Journal of Experimental Child Psychology,* 1974, *18,* 293–303.

Children between ages 3½ and 5½ performed a comprehension task for the words *taller, shorter, more,* and *less* in five different types of sentences. Syntactic complexity affected performance.

Townsend, David J. Do children interpret 'marked' comparative adjectives as their opposites? *Journal of Child Language,* 1976, *3,* 385–396.

Children ages 2;6–4;0 answered questions about arrays of five objects using comparative or superlative forms of marked/ unmarked adjective pairs (e.g., *shorter/taller, less/more*) or negative/positive pairs (*lighter/darker, skinnier/fatter*). It is argued that linguistic marking is not the correct explanation for the performance on marked/unmarked pairs. The object of greater extent was not frequently chosen in error for marked adjective questions, contrary to the Clarks' theory (cf. Kavanaugh, 1976a).

Section 9
WORD MEANING DEVELOPMENT OF SPATIAL, TEMPORAL, AND DEICTIC TERMS

Deixis refers to certain language uses in which the interpretation depends on knowing the speaker's or addressee's position in space or time, social standing, etc. The meaning is anchored in a particular situation to which the sentence is applied. For example, the location of the speaker determines the referent of here, there, this *or* that. *Adverbs like* soon *and the choice of verb tense require consideration of one or more points in time including the moment of speech. Professors address students differently than students address professors, and the referents of* I *and* you *depend on who is speaking. These are examples of place deixis, time deixis, and social deixis, respectively. Not all spatial and temporal terms involve deixis (and some terms have both deictic and nondeictic uses, e.g.,* front *and* back). In *is a nondeictic spatial term; it has the same meaning regardless of the speaker's location.* On July 4, 1776 *is a nondeictic temporal phrase; it has the same meaning regardless of the time of speech. Likewise, the progressive tense form and aspectual terms such as the habitual* always *need no situational anchoring. However, deictic phenomena are pervasive enough that they will figure prominently in any comprehensive description of temporal and spatial language.*

For background reading, see Section 7-B on semantic component theories, and from Section 2 see the relevant parts of Leech (1969, Chapters 7 and 8 on temporal and spatial language), Fillmore (1970a), Katz (1972), McCawley in Fillmore & Langendoen (1971), Lyons (1968, Chapter 7), and Reichenbach (1947). Other background reading is listed separately for each topic below.

First, general overviews of deixis and studies of social deixis are cited. These are followed by papers on verb tense and general temporal language. Finally, papers on the temporal terms before *and* after *and on spatial terms are listed. Moerk (1977) has sections relevant to each of these topics.*

A Overview of Deixis; Studies of Social Deixis

BACKGROUND PUBLICATIONS: LINGUISTICS

The following papers provide general linguistic analyses of deixis. Several concentrate on come *and* go, *which involve time, place, and social deixis.*

Fillmore, Charles J. Deictic categories in the semantics of 'come.' *Foundations of Language,* 1966, *2,* 219–227.
    Introduction to deixis ("those aspects of language whose interpretation is relative to the occasion of utterance"), and a preliminary analysis of *come* (later expanded).

Weinreich, Uriel. On the semantic structure of language. In J. H. Greenberg, *Universals of Language* (2nd ed.). Cambridge, Mass.: The MIT Press, 1966b. (Also in paperback.)
    Introduces several types of deixis in addition to other topics related to semantic universals.

Rommetveit, Ragnar. *Words, Meanings and Messages.* New York: Academic Press, 1968.
    As part of a broader treatment of "the embeddedness of the utterance in a communication setting," the Norwegian psycholinguist discusses deixis of person, place, and time. See especially pp. 46–54, 86–88, and 185–197.

Fillmore, Charles J. Santa Cruz lectures on deixis. Presented at University of California, Santa Cruz, 1971c. Available from Indiana University Linguistics Club, 310 Lindley Hall, Bloomington, Indiana 47401, for $3.00 plus $.65 postage and handling. (For an additional $.55 another paper on deixis, "The grammar of facing" by John Kimball, can be obtained.)
    There are six separate lectures, entitled "May we come in?", "Space," "Time," "Deixis I," "Deixis II," and "Coming and Going." ("Space" and "Time" cover nondeictic forms.) A theoretical position is outlined, but there are also numerous specific observations about the use of many different language forms, including some from non-Indo-European languages.

Lakoff, Robin. Language in context. *Language,* 1972, *48,* 907–927.
    To predict correctly the applicability of many linguistic rules, one must be able to refer to assumptions about the social

context of an utterance as well as to other implicit assumptions made by the discourse participants.

Fillmore, Charles J. How to know whether you're coming or going. In *Studies in Descriptive and Applied Linguistics.* Tokyo: International Christian University, 1972, *5,* 3–17.

Sinha, Anjani K. On the deictic use of *coming* and *going* in Hindi. In *Papers from the Eighth Regional Meeting of the Chicago Linguistic Society,* The University of Chicago Linguistics Department, 1972, 351–358.

Kurylowicz, Jerzy. The role of deictic elements in linguistic evolution. *Semiotica,* 1972, *22,* 151–271.

> Discusses pronouns, noun cases (particularly the localist theory of case), and verb tense using examples from several languages. Some knowledge of grammatical terminology for these topics is presupposed.

Givón, Talmy. The time-axis phenomenon. *Language,* 1973, *49,* 890–925.

> Givón introduces a theoretical framework that encompasses a variety of linguistic phenomena not previously viewed as related. He associates the presupposition/implication distinction with the before/after time-of-verb distinction; this allows him to make several generalizations about tense, negation, and modality as well as deictic verbs such as *come* and *go.*

Clark, Eve V. Normal states and evaluative viewpoints: More on *come* and *go. Language,* 1974b, *50,* 316–332.

> In idiomatic uses, the deictic center (corresponding to the goal of *come*) is provided by some normal state of being, whereas *go* marks departure from a normal state. *Come* and *go* may also be used in an evaluative deixis (good and bad, respectively). Both uses derive from the basic deictic contrast between *ego* and *non-ego.*

Lyons, John. Deixis as the source of reference. In E. L. Keenan, 1975.

Chafe, Wallace L. Givenness, contrastiveness, definiteness, subjects, topics, and point of view. In Li, 1976.

CHILD LANGUAGE PUBLICATIONS

The following papers report psycholinguistic studies involving social deixis with children or adults. Some also deal with other kinds of deixis.

Kernan, Keith T. The acquisition of formal and colloquial styles of speech by Samoan children. *Anthropological Linguist,* 1966, *16* (3), 107–119.

There are three stages in acquisition of the two phonologically contrasting styles. Initially one of the styles is used in all situations; by the third stage the styles are used in appropriate situations but the formal style is over-regularized.

Shipley, E. F. & Shipley, T. E., Jr. Quaker children's use of thee: A relational analysis. *Journal of Verbal Learning and Verbal Behavior,* 1969, *8,* 112–117.

In nine of 16 Quaker families, the children used standard English pronouns rather than *thee, thy,* or *thine.* Even when used, the terms often seemed to be identified with the parental role (e.g., the child used them only to address younger siblings).

Huxley, Renira. The development of the correct use of subject personal pronouns in two children. In Flores d'Arcais & Levelt, 1970.

Longitudinal, naturalistic data between ages 2;3 and about 4 are analyzed with special concern for problems of deixis and egocentrism. Example utterances are listed in an appendix.

Bates, Elizabeth. Acquisition of pragmatic competence. *Journal of Child Language,* 1974, *1,* 277–281.

Longitudinal and cross-sectional data for Italian children ages 2;0–6;0 are briefly examined with respect to emphasis and word order, deixis, conditional and subjunctive verbs, polite forms, and attitudinal inflections.

Brewer, William F. & Harris, Richard J. Memory for deictic elements in sentences. *Journal of Verbal Learning and Verbal Behavior,* 1974, *13,* 321–327.

Adult subjects memorized sentences containing words from one of five deictic categories (e.g., certain determiners, adverbs, verbs). These deictic words were harder to remember than nondeictic words only when the sentences were presented isolated from deictic context.

Clark, Eve V. & Garnica, Olga K. Is he coming or going? On the acquisition of deictic verbs. *Journal of Verbal Learning and Verbal Behavior,* 1974, *13,* 559–572.

Children ages 5;6–9;5 were asked to identify the speaker or the addressee of utterances containing one of four deictic verbs. Even the youngest children were correct on *come* and *bring,* but not on *go* and *take.* Error patterns suggested four stages in their strategies.

*Clark, Eve V. From gesture to word: On the natural history of deixis in language acquisition. In J. S. Bruner & A. Garton (Eds.), *Human Growth and Development: Wolfson College Lectures 1976.* London: Oxford University Press, in press.

Clark traces the development of deixis, presenting data suggesting that the order of mastery (between about 1 and 9 years of age) is: gesture, pronouns (*I/you*), locatives (*here/there*), demonstratives (*this/that*), intransitive verbs (*come/go*), and causative verbs (*bring/take*).

B Verb Tense and General Time Language

BACKGROUND PUBLICATIONS: LINGUISTICS, LOGIC, COGNITIVE DEVELOPMENT, ADULT PSYCHOLINGUISTICS

Several background references follow, from the fields of linguistics, logic, cognitive development, and adult psycholinguistics.

Jesperson, Otto. *The Philosophy of Grammar.* New York: Henry Holt, 1924.

Chapters 19 and 20 have an excellent linguistic treatment of time and tense.

Piaget, Jean. *The Child's Conception of Time.* London: Routledge & Kegan Paul, 1969. (Also in paperback, New York: Ballantine Books, 1971. Originally published in French, 1927.)

Piaget's research on children's understanding of time, and his general cognitive theory, have been the basis for predictions in some studies of children's acquisition of language about time.

Fraisse, P. *The Psychology of Time.* New York: Harper & Row, 1963.

See especially Part II ("The Perception of Time") and Chapter 8 ("The Notion of Time"; reviews Piaget's findings).

Prior, Arthur N. *Time and Tense.* Oxford: The Clarendon Press, 1968a.

An important treatment of time and verb tense within the framework of modern logic. Technical. (See also Prior's other books on time logic, by Clarendon Press, in 1957, 1967, and 1968b.)

Huddleston, Rodney. Some observations on tense and deixis in English. *Language,* 1969, *45,* 777–806.

The distinction between "full verbs" and "auxiliaries" (e.g., Palmer, 1965) is rejected. Deep tense, a ternary system, is contrasted with the binary surface tense system.

Clark, Herbert H. & Stafford, Richard A. Memory for semantic features in the verb. *Journal of Experimental Psychology,* 1969, *80,* 326–334.

Adult errors in memory for verb tense are analyzed in terms of loss of marked semantic (rather than syntactic) features.

Lakoff, Robin. Tense and its relation to participants. *Language,* 1970, *46,* 838–849.

An adequate theory of tense must be able to incorporate concepts such as the interrelationship of the actual time of occurrence of events with the involvement of the speaker, hearer, or other participant in these events.

McCawley, James D. Tense and time reference in English. In Fillmore & Langendoen, 1971.

McCawley suggests a refinement of Ross' analysis of English auxiliaries. On the basis of semantic phenomena of presupposition and quantification, he proposes that tenses are verbs in underlying structure.

Rescher, N. & Urquhart, A. *Temporal Logic.* New York: Springer-Verlag, 1971. (Summarized in Miller & Johnson-Laird, 1976.)

Harris, Richard J. & Brewer, William F. Deixis in memory for verb tense. *Journal of Verbal Learning and Verbal Behavior,* 1973, *12,* 590–597.

Sentences in six tenses were studied for a cued recall test; tense was changed in 45% of the responses. In a second experiment, temporal adverbs were added to provide some deictic context, and tense errors decreased substantially, suggesting that Clark and Stafford's explanation in terms of semantic features is wrong.

Hurtig, Richard. Abstract ideas: The relation of linguistic time and psychological time. *ETS Research Bulletin,* RB-74-54, December 1974.

A tense logic is incorporated into the grammatical description of time language. This model predicts memory errors better than the derivational theory of complexity, due to tense shift laws.

Palmer, F. R. *The English Verb.* London: Longman, 1974. (Also in paperback. First edition was published as *A Linguistic Study of the English Verb.* Austin: University of Texas Press, 1965.)

Palmer analyzes the English verb system, emphasizing the traditional grammatical categories: auxiliaries, tense, phase, aspect, voice, and modals. He also discusses catenative verbs, e.g., *kept* (talking), *saw* (John leaving); compound verbs, e.g., *give in*; and deictic tenses in reportative speech (pp. 44–47).

Åqvist, L. Formal semantics for verb tenses as analysed by Reichenbach. In van Dijk, 1975.

Comrie, Bernard. *Aspect.* London: Cambridge University Press, 1976. (Also in paperback.)
Introductory overview with examples from various languages; traditional rather than generative grammar approach. Very helpful.

Clifford, John E. *Tense and Tense Logic.* The Hague: Mouton, 1976. (Paperback, $15.25.)

CHILD LANGUAGE PUBLICATIONS

Lewis, M. M. The beginnings of reference to past and future in a child's speech. *British Journal of Educational Psychology,* 1937, *7,* 39–56. (Reprinted in Bar-Adon & Leopold, 1971.)
Lewis discusses the way in which reference to past and future becomes differentiated in children approximately between ages 1 and 2½.

Ames, L. B. The development of the sense of time in the young child. *Journal of Genetic Psychology,* 1946, *68,* 97–125.
Children's verbal expressions of time were compiled for ages 18 months to 8 years.

Bradley, N. C. The growth of the knowledge of time in children of school age. *British Journal of Psychology,* 1947, *38,* 67–78.
Stages of development between ages 5 and 7 are suggested, based on several tasks and a range of temporal concepts including intervals and end points of intervals.

Schecter, D. E.; Symonds, M.; & Bernstein, I. Development of the concept of time in children. *The Journal of Nervous and Mental Disease,* 1955, *121,* 301–311.
Spontaneous speech and speech elicited in story-telling and picture-describing situations, as well as responses to direct questioning about time, were analyzed for children ages 3–6. Younger children were more egocentric, emphasized immediate personal experience, and were more concrete, e.g., in referring to time units such as seasons, days of week, hours. A hypothesis concerning the origin of the concepts of past, present, and future was suggested.

Lovell, K. & Slater, A. The growth of the concept of time: A comparative study. *Child Psychology and Psychiatry*, 1960, *1*, 179–190.
Seven Piagetian experiments were replicated. Children of below average intelligence (ages 8–11 and 15) showed the same sequence of development as children of at least average intelligence (ages 5–9 years), but delayed by several years.

Cromer, Richard F. *The Development of Temporal Reference during the Acquisition of Language.* Unpublished doctoral dissertation, Department of Social Relations, Harvard University, 1968.
Cromer reports data on the emergence of temporal features from the longitudinal studies of Adam and Sarah at Harvard University. Many temporal forms appear at age 4–4½. Also, the study summarized in the following article is described in detail.

Herriot, Peter. The comprehension of tense by young children. *Child Development*, 1969, *40*, 103–110.
Children ages 36–48 months can comprehend the difference between past and future tense when contrasted to one another but not to the present progressive. A second experiment showed that comprehension of future tense in contrast to the present progressive is not attained until age 6. An attention factor is suggested.

*Cromer, Richard F. The development of the ability to decenter in time. *British Journal of Psychology*, 1971, *62*, 353–365.
Children performed a task intended as a temporal-ordering analog to Piaget's three-mountain task. Preschoolers failed to decenter. Based on part of Cromer's 1968 Harvard dissertation.

*Bronckart, J. P. & Sinclair, Hermina. Time, sense and aspect. *Cognition*, 1973, *2*, 107–130.
Seventy-four French children at ages 2;11–8;7 described 11 actions performed by the experimenter with toys. Choice of verb tense was affected by aspectual factors (type of result, repeated vs. continuous, duration) as well as simultaneity or sequence, though aspectual effects decreased with age.

Beilin, Harry. *Studies in the Cognitive Basis of Language Development.* New York: Academic Press, 1975.
Includes one chapter on temporal concepts and language, considering Piaget's view and empirical studies.

Nussbaum, N. J. & Naremore, Rita C. On the acquisition of present perfect "have" in normal children. *Language and Speech*, 1975, *18*, 219–226.

Children ages 4–6 years have not stabilized the use of *have*, though the form is used frequently by age 4;6, in five different tasks eliciting production or imitation (imitation is easiest). Use varied with task and syntactic form (e.g., question vs. declarative). A variety of substitutions for the present perfect were observed.

Harner, Lorraine. Yesterday and tomorrow: Development of early understanding of the terms. *Developmental Psychology*, 1975, *11*, 864–865.

Children were asked to "show me a toy from yesterday/for tomorrow," where toys used on the previous, same, or succeeding day were the choices. The 2-year-olds did poorly; the 3-year-olds understood *yesterday* better than *tomorrow* and made fewer choices of the same-day toys; the 4-year-olds performed equally well on both terms. E. Clark's (1973a) semantic feature hypothesis was partly supported.

Harner, Lorraine. Children's understanding of linguistic reference to past and future. *Journal of Psycholinguistic Research*, 1976, *5*, 65–84.

Children ages 2, 3, and 4 years performed in two comprehension experiments. Linguistic forms studied were verb tense and *before* and *after*. Situations involved immediate or remote (1 day) past and future events. For future tense, performance was best for events in the immediate future. *Before* and *after* were best understood when referring to the next event from the present. For past tense there were no differences. Based on a Columbia University doctoral dissertation.

Ginsberg, Erika Hoff & Abrahamson, Adele A. Children's comprehension of sentences expressing simultaneity and sequentiality. Paper presented at the annual meeting of the American Psychological Association, September 1976.

See summary in Section 9-C.

Geodakjan, I. M. Expression of the category of time in the speech of a young child. In Průcha, 1976.

C Spatial and Temporal Terms

BACKGROUND PUBLICATIONS: LINGUISTICS

Several linguistic treatments of spatial and temporal terms (particularly prepositions) are given first as background.

Teller, P. Some discussion and extension of Manfred Bierwisch's work on German adjectivals. *Foundations of Language,* 1969, *5,* 185–217.
Teller argues that certain words have two different uses, deictic and nondeictic (e.g., *front* and *side*).

Parisi, Domenico & Antinucci, Francesco. Lexical competence. In Flores d'Arcais & Levelt, 1970.
Includes a suggested componential analysis of Italian spatial prepositions and related adult data.

Geis, Jonnie E. Lexical insertion of locative and time prepositions. In *Papers from the Sixth Regional Meeting of the Chicago Linguistic Society,* The University of Chicago Linguistics Department, 1970.
Problems in the linguistic description of locative and time prepositions are discussed.

Geis, Michael L. Time prepositions as underlying verbs. In *Papers from the Sixth Regional Meeting of the Chicago Linguistic Society,* The University of Chicago Linguistics Department, 1970.
Geis argues that *before, after, until,* and *since* are derived from the underlying verbs *earlier than, later than, end,* and *begin,* respectively.

Chapin, Paul G. What's in a word? Some considerations in lexicological theory. *Papers in Linguistics,* 1971, *4,* 259–277.
Chapin suggests comparing the sets of contexts in which words are used across languages as a basis for proposing semantic primitives, using locative prepositions as examples.

Bennett, David. *Spatial and Temporal Uses of English Prepositions: An Essay in Stratificational Semantics.* New York: Longman, 1975.
Linguistic analysis performed within the framework of stratificational grammar, including consideration of deictic and nondeictic uses of the same preposition.

CHILD LANGUAGE PUBLICATIONS: TEMPORAL CONNECTIVES

Developmental studies of temporal prepositions and conjunctions have focused recently on before *and* after, *with some studies including additional terms. Two reports of adult memory for these terms are also listed below. Some of the linguistic papers listed as background reading in Section 9-A are also relevant here.*

Clark, Herbert H. & Clark, Eve V. Semantic distinctions and memory for complex sentences. *The Quarterly Journal of Psychology,* 1968, *20,* 129–138.

> Adult recall errors for two-clause sentences conjoined by *before, after, and then,* and *but first* indicated that subjects remember three semantic distinctions (temporal order, order of mention, and main-subordinate clause relation) and forget semantic markedness, preferring the unmarked form in recall.

Clark, Eve V. How young children describe events in time. In Flores d'Arcais & Levelt, 1970.

> This article is similar to Clark (1973b), but it is shorter and less complete in reporting the data. The idea that simultaneity is recognized before sequence is discussed. (Two articles on adult processing of temporal order in sentences also appear in the volume.)

Hatch, Evelyn. The young child's comprehension of time connectives. *Child Development,* 1971, *42,* 2111–2113.

> Kindergarten and second-grade children comprehended *and then/but first* commands better than *before/after* commands.

Ferreiro, Emilia & Sinclair, Hermina. Temporal relationships in language. *International Journal of Psychology,* 1971, *6,* 39–47.

> Four-year-olds acted out, produced, and imitated French sentences expressing temporal order, and answered *when-*questions. Three hierarchically-ordered response patterns were found and discussed in the context of Piaget's theory.

*Clark, Eve V. On the acquisition of the meaning of *before* and *after. Journal of Verbal Learning and Verbal Behavior,* 1971, *10,* 266–275.

> Forty children ages 3;0–5;0 acted out two-clause sentences conjoined by *before* or *after,* and answered when-questions. There were three comprehension stages: noncomprehension, comprehension of *before* (using order-of-mention for *after,* or interpreting it as synonymous with *before*), and comprehension

of both words. The stages were interpreted in terms of the separate acquisition of three hierarchically related semantic features.

*Amidon, Arlene & Carey, Peter. Why five-year-olds cannot understand before and after. *Journal of Verbal Learning and Verbal Behavior,* 1972, *11,* 417–423.

Fifty kindergarteners ages 5;4–6;3 acted out two-clause sentences expressing the temporal order of two events. Performance was much better for "S_1 first; S_2 last" than for the four types of sentences using *before* or *after* (both clause orders were used). Subordinate clauses were acted out less often than main clauses, and *before* and *after* did not differ. Feedback improved performance, but intonational stress of the conjunction did not. An explanation in terms of main-clause salience rather than semantic features was suggested.

Clark, Eve V. How children describe time and order. In Ferguson & Slobin, 1973(b).

In the naturalistic speech of 15 children observed longitudinally between ages 3½ and 4, temporal order descriptions appeared first as coordinate-clause constructions, then as subordinate-clause-second constructions, finally as subordinate-clause-first constructions. This was interpreted in terms of principles of order of mention, derivational simplicity and choice of theme. Based on a doctoral dissertation, University of Edinburgh, 1969.

Barrie-Blackley, Sandie. Six-year-old children's understanding of sentences adjoined with time adverbs. *Journal of Psycholinguistic Research,* 1973, *2,* 153–165.

Twenty-four sentences with the conjunctions *after, before,* and *until* were presented to 6-year-olds. They performed best on *after; until* was easier with a negative marker than without one; *before* was nonsignificantly easier than *until.*

Keller-Cohen, Deborah. *The Acquisition of Temporal Reference in Pre-school Children.* Unpublished doctoral dissertation, State University of New York at Buffalo, 1974. Available from Indiana University Linguistics Club, 310 Lindley Hall, Bloomington, Indiana 47401, for $4.15 plus $.60 postage and handling.

Preschoolers acted out and imitated sentences expressing temporal order, and answered when-questions. Sequentiality (*before, after, and then, first . . . last*) was easier than simultaneity (*while, at the same time*), a result interpreted in connection with Piaget's work on time. Portions of the study were reported at the 1974 winter meeting of LSA and the 1975 biennial meeting of SRCD.

Hurtig, Richard. Abstract ideas: The relation of linguistic time and psychological time. *ETS Research Bulletin,* RB-74-54, December 1974.

> Hurtig's tense logic model correctly predicts that there are more errors in adults' memory for tense in sentences with an ordering conjunction (e.g., *before*) than in sentences with other conjunctions (e.g., *while, but*).

Coker, Pamela L. On the acquisition of temporal terms: *Before* and *After.* In *Papers and Reports on Child Language Development,* No. 10. Department of Linguistics, Stanford University, September 1975, 166–177.

> Coker presents evidence from comprehension tasks with kindergarteners and first graders that children learn *before* and *after* first as prepositions, than as conjunctions, and that 5-year-olds use a main clause strategy (Amidon & Carey, 1972) or (both ages) an order-of-mention strategy. She found no support for Clark's hypothesis of a semantic advantage for *before.*

Johnson, Helen L. The meaning of *before* and *after* for preschool children. *Journal of Experimental Child Psychology,* 1975, *19,* 88–99.

> Three different tasks in which children acted out sentences varied in difficulty and predominant types of errors. Also, order of mention was more important than coordinate-subordinate relations or semantic markedness in determining errors.

Harner, Lorraine. Children's understanding of linguistic reference to past and future. *Journal of Psycholinguistic Research,* 1976, *5,* 65–84.

> See summary in Section 9-B.

Amidon, Arlene. Children's understanding of sentences with contingent relations: Why are temporal and conditional connectives so difficult? *Journal of Experimental Child Psychology,* 1976, *22,* 423–437.

> Children ages 5, 7, and 9 years performed two comprehension tasks with two-clause sentences using *when, as soon as, before,*

after, if, if . . . not, unless, and *unless . . . not.* Improvement with age was attributed to an increased ability to retain information in the subordinate clauses. At all ages, *unless* was treated like *if,* and *unless . . . not* like *if . . . not.*

Ginsberg, Erika Hoff & Abrahamson, Adele A. Children's comprehension of sentences expressing simultaneity and sequentiality. Paper presented at the annual meeting of the American Psychological Association, September 1976.

Kindergarteners, second, and fourth graders listened to sentences with the terms *at the same time, last . . . first, while,* and *before,* and judged whether they correctly described videotaped situations with two simultaneous or sequential events. Sentences expressing simultaneity were easier, contrary to Keller-Cohen (1974). In a forthcoming article, performance on sentences with past progressive or past perfect verb forms is predicted by these data, plus data on linguistic descriptions of unequal duration and cessation.

BACKGROUND PUBLICATIONS: SPATIAL DEVELOPMENT

The following analyses of children's spatial development provide cognitive background for the linguistic development studies.

Piaget, Jean & Inhelder, Bärbel. *The Child's Conception of Space.* London: Routledge & Kegan Paul, 1956. (Also in paperback, New York: Norton, 1967. Originally published in French, 1948.)

The discussion of spatial egocentrism is a good background for work on the acquisition of spatial terminology.

Laurendeau, Monique & Pinard, Adrien. *The Development of the Concept of Space in the Child.* New York: International Universities Press, 1970.

Laurendeau & Pinard replicated several of Piaget and Inhelder's tasks (all nonverbal) and Piaget's *left/right* task (verbal), using the same sample of children ages 2 to 12 years.

Pufall, Peter B. & Shaw, Robert E. Analysis of the development of children's spatial reference systems. *Cognitive Psychology,* 1973, *5,* 151–175.

Four-, six-, and ten-year-old children were asked to copy an object's location and orientation on their own layout when the experimenter's layout was in the same orientation or rotated

180°. Results generally support Piaget and Inhelder; additional findings are noted.

Masangkay, Zenaida S.; McCluskey, Kathleen A.; McIntyre, Curtis W.; Sims-Knight, Judith; Vaughn, Brian E.; & Flavell, John H. The early development of inferences about the visual percepts of others. *Child Development,* 1974, *45,* 357–366.

There are two levels of inference about others' visual percepts. At level 1, present as young as 2–3 years, children can infer that another person sees an object that is not visible to themselves. At level 2, which appears later, children can infer how an object appears to a person with a different spatial perspective.

Eliot, John & Salkind, Neil J. (Eds.). *Children's Spatial Development.* Springfield, Ill.: Charles C Thomas, 1975.

The book includes four papers on neurophysiological and linguistic factors; 40 journal abstracts; and a 98-page bibliography. David Olson's article, "On the relations between spatial and linguistic processes," is of special interest.

Eliot, John & Dayton, C. Mitchell. Egocentric error and the construct of egocentrism. *Journal of Genetic Psychology,* 1976, *128,* 275–289.

Based on the performance of hundreds of first and fifth graders and undergraduates on board/block adaptations of Piaget's three-mountain task, it is argued that egocentric errors result from response bias.

Salatas, Harriet & Flavell, John H. Perspective taking: The development of two components of knowledge. *Child Development,* 1976, *47,* 103–109.

Kindergarteners understood that one observer has one unique view, while second graders also understood that one view cannot be seen from more than one position, in a task using an array of three dolls. This understanding of views is a separate achievement from coordination of spatial dimensions.

Acredolo, Linda P. Developmental changes in the ability to coordinate perspectives of a large-scale space. *Developmental Psychology,* 1977, *13,* 1–8.

Children ages 3, 4, and 5 years participated in three experiments using a large-scale space or a model to test *left* and *right.* Differences based on age and type of space were found.

CHILD LANGUAGE PUBLICATIONS: SPATIAL TERMS

Piaget, Jean. *Judgment and Reasoning in the Child.* London: Routledge & Kegan Paul, 1928. (Also in paperback, Totowa, N.J.: Littlefield, Adams & Co., 1959. Originally published in French, 1924.)

Children's understanding of *left* and *right* is discussed on pp. 107-113, with special attention to the listener's need to use the speaker's spatial perspective for correct use of the terms, and the greater difficulty of dealing with a middle object (which is left of one object but right of the other).

Ames, Louise Bates & Learned, Janet. The development of verbalized space in the young child. *Journal of Genetic Psychology,* 1948, *72,* 63-84.

Children ages 1½-4 years were observed during play in a nursery school over a 9-month period, with all language about space recorded stenographically. These and other children also answered 36 questions about space (e.g., "Where do you live?"; "What is under the floor?"). A general developmental sequence is suggested, and individual differences discussed.

Elkind, David. Children's conception of right and left: Piaget replication study IV. *Journal of Genetic Psychology,* 1961b, *99,* 269-276.

Children ages 5-11 years were tested on six types of *left/right* problems, four of which had been used by Piaget (1924/28). Elkind's results were similar to those of Piaget.

Huttenlocher, Janellen & Strauss, Susan. Comprehension and a statement's relation to the situation it describes. *Journal of Verbal Learning and Verbal Behavior,* 1968, *7,* 300-304.

Children ages 5, 7, and 9 years were asked to place one block relative to a second fixed block by stating the outcome in sentences of the form X *is on top of/is under Y.* It was easiest to comply when X (the grammatical subject) was the block to be moved.

*Laurendeau, Monique & Pinard, Adrien. *The Development of the Concept of Space in the Child.* New York: International Universities Press, 1970.

Includes a detailed report of acquisition of *left* and *right.*

Harris, Lauren Jay & Strommen, Ellen A. The role of front-back features in children's "front," "back," and "beside" placements of objects. *Merrill-Palmer Quarterly of Behavior and Development,* 1972, *18,* 259-271.

Children as young as 4;9 are similar to adults in their use of *front* and *back* for both fronted and nonfronted objects.

Clark, Eve V. Non-linguistic strategies and the acquisition of word meanings. *Cognition*, 1973c, *2*, 161–182.

Comprehension of some words is at first dependent on a combination of linguistic hypotheses about a word's meaning and certain nonlinguistic strategies. This is illustrated in an experiment on the words *in, on,* and *under* performed by children ages 1;6–5;0.

Reich, Peter A.; Rice, Karen; & Pressner, Ute Schneider. Acquisition of ambiguous prepositions. Manuscript, University of Toronto Centre for Linguistic Studies, March 1974.

According to Bennett (1975), a number of spatial prepositions have two related meanings, one direct ("There are some helicopters over the hill") and one deictic ("There are some helicopters over the hill [from you])." In a comprehension task, 6-year-olds performed better on the direct meaning of *along* and *across*; there was no difference for *over*. This supports Bennett's linguistic analysis better than it supports an egocentrism analysis.

de Villiers, Peter A. & de Villiers, Jill G. On this, that, and the other: Nonegocentrism in very young children. *Journal of Experimental Child Psychology*, 1974, *18*, 438–447.

In comprehension and production tasks for *this/that, here/there, my/your,* and *in front of/behind* with children ages 2½–4½ years, it was found that by age 3 children could perform correctly when they and the experimenter had opposite perspectives.

*Wilcox, Stephen & Palermo, David S. "In," "On," and "Under" Revisited. *Cognition*, 1974/75, *3*, 245–254.

Children ages 1;6–1;11 make the simplest motor response to requests of the form "Can you put the X (in/on/under) the Y?" By age 2;6–2;11 they tend rather to respond according to the most usual relation of two objects, e.g., boat under bridge. With neutral objects, percent correct is 64% for *on*, 61% for *in*, and 27% for *under*. Only *under* improves with age (8–42%).

*Kuczaj, Stan A., II & Maratsos, Michael P. On the acquisition of *Front, Back* and *Side*. *Child Development*, 1975b, *46*, 202–210.

Children ages 2½–4 years performed several comprehension tasks. Contrary to expectation, they learn the meanings of *front* and *back* at the same time (earlier than they learn *side*). Age of correct use varies with the situation (e.g., fronted vs. nonfronted objects).

Grimm, Hannelore. On the child's acquisition of semantic structure underlying the wordfield of prepositions. *Language and Speech,* 1975, *18,* 97–119.

The spontaneously produced prepositional phrases of German preschoolers (2;7–5;11) and first graders are analyzed, with special attention to anomalous combinations. The developmental sequence concurs with Piaget's findings on spatiogeometric properties. Temporal prepositions are rarer than spatial ones, and only those that are also used locatively occur.

*Webb, Pamela A. & Abrahamson, Adele A. Stages of egocentrism in children's use of *this* and *that*: A different point of view. *Journal of Child Language,* 1976, *3,* 349–367.

Four- and seven-year-olds performed a comprehension task for *this* and *that.* Error patterns were similar to those found by Laurendeau & Pinard (1970) for *left* and *right,* at similar ages, contrary to de Villiers & de Villiers (1974). More than half the 7-year-olds had difficulty when facing the speaker with objects between them, despite the theoretical possibility of performing correctly on the basis of topological representations controlled by preschoolers.

Windmiller, Myra. A child's conception of space as a prerequisite to his understanding of spatial locatives. *Genetic Psychology Monographs,* 1976, *94,* 227–248.

Twenty-four children ages $2\frac{1}{2}$–$7\frac{1}{2}$ performed a Piagetian spatial task (stereognostic recognition of shapes) and comprehension and production tasks for three groups of words, designed to correspond to topological, projective, or Euclidean spatial representations. In a final task, the child moved his or her own body rather than an object in response to the verbal instructions. The results support the idea that "cognition precedes and is a prerequisite to certain language forms."

Clark, Eve V. From gesture to word: On the natural history of deixis in language acquisition. In J. S. Bruner & A. Garton (Eds.), *Human Growth and Development: Wolfson College Lectures 1976.* London: Oxford University Press, in press.

See summary in Section 9-A.

CHILD LANGUAGE PUBLICATIONS:
SPATIAL AND TEMPORAL TERMS COMBINED

Clark, Eve V. On the child's acquisition of antonyms in two semantic fields. *Journal of Verbal Learning and Verbal Behavior,* 1972, *11,* 750–758.

Reports results of an antonym-eliciting task; see summary in Section 8-C.

*Clark, Herbert H. Space, time, semantics and the child. In Moore, 1973.

Clark presents a theoretical description of the properties of perceived space and time and of language describing space and time, arguing that the child learning the linguistic terms benefits from *a priori* perceptual knowledge. A number of predictions about acquisition are made and evaluated against results in the literature.

Feagans, D. L. The comprehension by young children of some temporal and spatial linguistic structures. In *Papers from the Tenth Regional Meeting of the Chicago Linguistic Society.* The University of Chicago Linguistics Department, 1974.

Friedman, William J. & Seely, Pamela B. The child's acquisition of spatial and temporal word meanings. *Child Development,* 1976, *47,* 1103–1108.

In comprehension tasks for spatial and temporal uses of *before/after, first/last, ahead of/behind,* and *together,* difficulty of positive vs. negative words and spatial vs. temporal use varied with the word pair.

Part IV

BEYOND GRAMMAR

Section 10
EXPLANATIONS OF
LANGUAGE LEARNING

*The papers in this section are primarily theoretical. Their authors are seeking to determine the general principles that account for the way in which language emerges and matures. Currently, most attention is being given to biological and cognitive approaches. Before the late 1960's, discussion centered instead on the differences between approaches characterized as **empiricist** vs. **rationalist**. The empiricist (or behaviorist) approach favored nurture over nature, a passive role for the learner, and the application of learning theory. The rationalist approach favored **nativism** (nature over nurture), an active role for the learner (e.g., in inducing linguistic rules), and the application of transformational grammar. The labels can be misleading, however; they roughly distinguish two views of learning mechanisms but not research strategy. The current biological and cognitive approaches take an intermediate position on learning mechanisms, but are based on empirical data of higher quality and greater quantity than were the older theories (e.g., videotaping is now commonplace). The empiricist/ rationalist controversy is no longer a central issue in language research. The narrowly empiricist learning theory approach was most attractive when the least was known about language learning, and it now has little influence. The biological approach has always shared with learning theory an emphasis on observable events but has differed in having a tendency to nativism. Finally, most of those who took a linguistic approach are now trying to integrate the linguistic and cognitive perspectives. Empiricist vs. rationalist aspects can still be identified in current work, but the controversy has lost its force.*

A   *Theories and Issues*

This section is divided into three parts: (1) papers on the rationalist/ empiricist controversy, (2) other theoretical and experimental publications, and (3) research on aspects of the parent/child interaction which may be important for language learning.

THE RATIONALIST/EMPIRICIST CONTROVERSY

The rationalist/empiricist controversy has largely been defined by Chomsky, who views his transformational grammar as a return to the rationalist position in 17th-century philosophy. Publications on both sides of the general issue are listed below, followed by papers that focus on children learning language.

Background Publications: Linguistics and Psychology

Skinner, B. F. *Verbal Behavior.* New York: Appleton-Century-Crofts, 1957.

> Skinner takes on the challenge of accounting for language learning and behavior within the framework of his operant conditioning theory.

Chomsky, Noam. Review of *Verbal Behavior* by B. F. Skinner. *Language,* 1959, *35,* 26–58. (Reprinted in Fodor & Katz, 1964, and in Jakobovits & Miron, 1967.)

> A point-by-point criticism of Skinner's analysis.

Miller, G. A.; Galanter, E.; & Pribram, K. H. *Plans and the Structure of Behavior.* New York: Holt, Rinehart and Winston, 1960.

> This book signaled the "cognitive revolution" in experimental psychology, replacing the behaviorist view of intelligent behavior with the beginnings of a system based on active, internal processes.

Miller, George A. Some preliminaries to psycholinguistics. *American Psychologist,* 1965, *20,* 15–20. (Reprinted in Oldfield & Marshall, 1968.)

> Miller summarizes seven aspects of human language that lead to the conclusion that "language is exceedingly complicated" and has not been adequately characterized in behaviorist theories.

Fodor, Jerry A. Could meaning be an r_m? *Journal of Verbal Learning and Verbal Behavior,* 1965, *4,* 73–81. (Reprinted in Oldfield & Marshall, 1968, and in Steinberg & Jakobovits, 1971.)
 Criticism of mediation learning theories of referential meaning.

Chomsky, Noam. *Cartesian Linguistics: A Chapter in the History of Rationalist Thought.* New York: Harper & Row, 1966b.
 Chomsky presents in detail his view of the relation of transformational grammar to the theories of Descartes and other rationalist philosophers.

Chomsky, Noam. *Language and Mind* (enlarged edition). New York: Harcourt Brace Javanovich, 1972. (Also in paperback. Original edition published, 1968.)
 In Part 1, Chomsky gives a clear account of his views on rationalism vs. empiricism. (These views are summarized in Chapter 9 of Lyons, 1970b.)

Dixon, Theodore R. & Horton, David L. (Eds.). *Verbal Behavior and General Behavior Theory.* Englewood Cliffs, N.J.: Prentice-Hall, 1968.
 Collection of papers from a 1966 conference; includes theoretical papers on the behavior theory approach to language as well as criticisms of that approach.

Staats, Arthur W. *Learning, Language, and Cognition.* New York: Holt, Rinehart and Winston, 1968.
 Staats marshals empirical evidence for the view that language and cognition follow the laws of learning and conditioning. See also his 1971 book, *Child Learning, Intelligence and Personality.*

MacCorquodale, Kenneth. On Chomsky's review of Skinner's *Verbal Behavior. Journal of the Experimental Analysis of Behavior,* 1970, *13,* 83–99.
 Skinner has not directly responded to Chomsky's review, but MacCorquodale has.

Child Language Publications

The papers on rationalist vs. empiricist theories of children's language learning follow. Many other publications discuss the issue in the context of particular studies, but are not listed here. See also McNeill (1970a,b) for a nativist position, as well as other general texts (Section 1-A) for summaries of the issue.

*Braine, Martin D. S. On learning the grammatical order of words. *Psychological Review,* 1963b, *70,* 323–348. (Reprinted in Bar-Adon & Leopold, 1971, and in Jakobovits & Miron, 1967.)
Braine reports experiments on the learning of word order and parts of speech, arguing for "context generalization" as a mechanism (similar to stimulus generalization in learning theory).

Jenkins, James J. & Palermo, David S. Mediation processes and the acquisition of linguistic structure. In Bellugi & Brown, 1964.
Application of mediation learning theory to structural aspects of language, including a discussion of experiments on adults learning artificial languages, and of the grammars of child language becoming available at that time.

Bever, Thomas G.; Fodor, Jerry A.; & Weksel, William. On the acquisition of syntax: A critique of "contextual generalization." *Psychological Review,* 1965a, *72,* 467–482. (Reprinted in Bar-Adon & Leopold, 1971, and in Jakobovits & Miron, 1967.)
The processes suggested by Braine cannot account for what children learn about the structure of sentences.

Braine, Martin D. S. On the basis of phrase structure: A reply to Bever, Fodor, and Weksel. *Psychological Review,* 1965, *72,* 483–492.
Bever et al. did not present sufficient evidence that the order of elements in simple declarative sentences is a deformation of order in the underlying string. Learning of word class is also discussed.

*Bever, Thomas G.; Fodor, Jerry A.; & Weksel, William. Is linguistics empirical? *Psychological Review* 1965b, *72,* 493–500.
The last of the *Psychological Review* series of four articles, which began with Braine (1963b). The authors respond to Braine, presenting arguments for analyzing the English declarative as transformationally generated and discussing the grounds on which claims made by grammars can be confirmed.

Schlesinger, I. M. A note on the relationship between psychological and linguistic theories. *Foundations of Language,* 1967, *3,* 397–402.
Schlesinger comments on the *Psychological Review* controversy, suggesting that Braine's model might be correct for the first stages of language learning though perhaps not for later development. He also discusses the competence/performance issue.

Slobin, Dan I. *The Ontogenesis of Grammar.* New York: Academic Press, 1971a.

A behaviorist approach is taken by Palermo and Staats and criticized by Ervin-Tripp; a nativist approach is taken by McNeill; and approaches more difficult to classify are discussed by Schlesinger and Braine.

*Ervin-Tripp, Susan. An overview of theories of grammatical development. In D. I. Slobin, *The Ontogenesis of Grammar.* New York: Academic Press, 1971a.

Ervin-Tripp marshals arguments against a stimulus-response theory of language learning, citing data on characteristics of parental speech, early syntax, morphology, and semantics, and ending with an emphasis on processing models.

Furth, Hans G. Two aspects of experience in ontogeny: Development and learning. In H. W. Reese, Vol. 9, 1974.

Considers the nature-nurture issue from a Piagetian perspective.

Segal, Evalyn F. Psycholinguistics discovers the operant: A review of Roger Brown's *A First Language: The Early Stages. Journal of the Experimental Analysis of Behavior,* 1975, *23,* 149–158.

Brown's analyses of stage I and stage II speech are restated or interpreted in terms of Skinner's *tacts* and covert autoclitic verbal behavior.

Munsinger, Harry & Douglass, Arthur, II. The syntactic abilities of identical twins, fraternal twins, and their siblings. *Child Development,* 1976, *47,* 40–50.

Monozygotic and dizygotic twins and their siblings were administered two standard tests of syntactic ability and the WISC (Wechsler Intelligence Scale for Children). Results suggest that heritability, rather than environmental effects, accounts for much more of the variation in syntactic performance.

Schlesinger, I. M. Grammatical development—The first steps. In Lenneberg & Lenneberg, Vol. 1, 1975, 203–222.

Includes a short discussion of learning mechanisms: reinforcement, hypothesis testing, passive learning, and imitation.

THEORIES AND EXPERIMENTS ON LANGUAGE LEARNING

In the next group of publications, explanations for language learning are offered on the basis of theories such as transformational grammar;

others papers criticize these approaches. Some of the explanations are formalized mathematically or are computer implemented; others are based on psychological data from adults or children.

Guillaume, Paul. *Imitation in Children.* Chicago: The University of Chicago Press, 1968. (Originally published in French, 1926.)

*Fodor, Jerry A. How to learn to talk: Some simple ways. In Smith & Miller, 1966.

The child induces rules of language by applying an intrinsic structure to the sample of sentences he or she hears.

Brown, Roger & Hanlon, Camille. Derivational complexity and order of acquisition in child speech. In Hayes, 1970. (Reprinted in Brown, 1970a.)

On the basis of a transformational grammar, sentence types involving negation, questioning, deletion, and tags (e.g., "We had a ball, didn't we?" where "didn't we" is a tag) were ordered by complexity. Order of acquisition, determined from speech samples of Adam, Eve, and Sarah, was generally predicted by order of linguistic complexity.

Hebb, D. O.; Lambert, W. E.; & Tucker, G. R. Language, thought and experience. *Modern Language Journal,* 1971, *15,* 212–222.

Learning and heredity collaborate in language development; the role of learning is emphasized in this article. Hebb's cell-assembly theory is applied, particularly the use of second- and third-order assemblies as a mechanism for abstraction, and for S-S (latent) learning of word-referent pairs. The approach also clarifies problems such as the role of imitation, use of new plural forms, the basis of the passive transformation, and the child's understanding of "nounness."

Ingram, Elisabeth. The requirements of model users. In Huxley & Ingram, 1971.

Desirable characteristics of a theoretical model for application to child language are outlined, and transformational grammar is unfavorably evaluated as such a model.

*Moeser, Shannon D. & Bregman, Albert S. Imagery and language acquisition. *Journal of Verbal Learning and Verbal Behavior,* 1973, *12,* 91–98.

Two subjects each at ages 12, 15, and 18 were presented with sentences in a miniature artificial language. One subject at each age had pictures presented with the sentences; they learned the syntax rapidly and thereafter could learn class membership of new words in a purely verbal context (no pictures). The other subjects saw no pictures and failed to learn the syntax. Thus, early syntax learning seems to be mediated through an understanding of the reference field.

*Wexler, K. & Hamburger, H. On the insufficiency of surface data for the learning of transformational grammar. In Hintikka, Moravcsik, & Suppes, 1973.

Stemmer, Nathan. *An Empiricist Theory of Language Acquisition.* The Hague: Mouton, 1973.

Stemmer's methodology is based on the logician Carnap, not on psychology. He distinguishes three kinds of learning processes (isolated ostensive, contextual ostensive, and contextual verbal) and applies his ideas to a range of topics, from animal language to lexical ambiguity to innate ideas.

Derwing, B. L. *Transformational Grammar as a Theory of Language Acquisition.* London: Cambridge University Press, 1973. (Reviewed by J. McCawley in *Canadian Journal of Linguistics,* 1974, *19,* 177–187, and by N. Smith in *Journal of Linguistics,* 1975, *11,* 261–269. Also in paperback.)

Critical theoretical examination by a nontransformational linguist.

van der Geest, Ton. *Evaluation of Theories on Child Grammars.* The Hague: Mouton, 1974. (Paperback.)

Huttenlocher, Janellen. The origins of language comprehension. In R. L. Solso (Ed.), *Theories in Cognitive Psychology.* Hillsdale, N.J.: Lawrence Erlbaum Associates, 1974.

Huttenlocher raises the question of how language comprehension develops in infants and how this comprehension relates to their speech production. She reports results of a longitudinal study with three infants, beginning about 10 months, mainly by reproducing portions of her session notes. She also discusses methodological problems.

Clark, Eve V. What should *LAD* look like? Some comments on Levelt. In *Papers and Reports on Child Language Development,* No. 7. Committee on Linguistics, Stanford University, April 1974c, 53–66.

Clark suggests incorporating semantic mechanisms into LAD (language acquisition device), discusses the nature of linguistic input to the child (i.e., parental speech), and notes some non-linguistic strategies and knowledge used in language learning.

Hamburger, Henry & Wexler, Kenneth. A mathematical theory of learning transformational grammar. *Journal of Mathematical Psychology,* 1975, *12,* 137–177.

The authors present a formal characterization of the language learning process and the language environment in which it operates, and a formal proof that the process, acting on the input it receives, learns the language. The reader's knowledge of elementary set theory is presupposed.

*Anderson, John R. Computer simulation of a language acquisition system: A first report. In R. L. Solso (Ed.), *Information Processing and Cognition: The Loyola Symposium.* Hillsdale, N.J.: Lawrence Erlbaum Associates, 1975.

Anderson reports on LAS.1, a preliminary computer program for inducing an augmented transition network grammar from matched sentence/situation input, relying on existing correspondences between syntax and semantics. He claims that a child learning language benefits from many of the same constraints that an ultimately successful version of his program would embody.

Fabens, William & Smith, Donald. A model of language acquisition using a conceptual base. Technical Report CBM-TR-55, Department of Computer Science, Rutgers University, New Brunswick, N.J., September 29, 1975.

The first report on a computer simulation of early syntactic learning. Rules for expression and parsing are associated with conceptual graphs based on case relations such as agent and object.

Leonard, L. B. The role of nonlinguistic stimuli and semantic relations in children's acquisition of grammatical utterances. *Journal of Experimental Child Psychology,* 1975, *19,* 346–357.

Children ages 28–40 months were trained to produce two-word subject-verb utterances. The task was easier if the utterances were related to ongoing events, and in that case, having a variety of case relations across utterances was no harder than agent-only utterances. If they were not so related, the varied condition was harder.

MacWhinney, Brian. Rules, rote and analogy in morphological

formations by Hungarian children. *Journal of Child Language,* 1975a, *2,* 65–77.

Elicited production of plurals provided evidence for five stages of morphological learning. The major mechanism responsible for performance was the learning and use of rules; analogic formation and rote memorization were of minor importance.

Brown, Irvin, Jr. Role of referent concreteness in the acquisition of passive sentence comprehension through abstract modeling. *Journal of Experimental Child Psychology,* 1976, *22,* 185–199.

Children ages 3;6–5 years heard a model narrate a series of events in passive sentences (verbal modeling) and performed two comprehension tasks. When the model simultaneously enacted the events, children performed best; with no referent the scores were less consistent across comprehension measures than with pictorial referents. Other results suggest that verbal modeling alone or with pictorial referents facilitates comprehension; verbal modeling with enactment promotes learning.

Fromberg, Doris. Syntax model games and language in early education. *Journal of Psycholinguistic Research,* 1976, *5,* 245–260.

Fromberg describes "syntax model games" for developing the language skills of children ages 5–9 years. They are based on the method of induction and reflect concern with developmental style and transformational grammar.

Wexler, K.; Culicover, P.; & Hamburger, H. Learning-theoretic foundations of linguistic universals. *Theoretical Linguistics,* in press.

Derwing, B. L. What kind of rules can children learn? In W. von Raffler-Engel (Ed.), *Prospects in Child Language.* The Hague: Mouton, in press.

ROLE OF PARENT-CHILD INTERACTION AND IMITATION

The last group of papers report research on aspects of the parent/child interaction that may be important for language learning. Some of the papers in Section 11-C are relevant here also. One important issue is the role of the child's imitations of parental utterances (usually reductions rather than complete). Over the last 20 years of American theory, imitation has been regarded successively as passive, irrelevant, and active. The active view is often presented in the context of Piaget's theory. Some papers also consider whether there is anything the parent can do to improve language learning, e.g., expand immature utterances into grammatical ones, model new utterances on a topic related to the child's last utterances, be accepting (or rejecting) of ungrammatical utterances, use short utterances. The final evidence is not in for these and other possibilities. In addition to the items listed below, see Brown, Cazden, & Bellugi (1969); Nelson (1973a); Moerk (1977); and Newport, Gleitman, & Gleitman (in press). For background, see Guillaume (1926/1968), Piaget (1946/1951), and Werner & Kaplan (1963).

*Brown, Roger & Bellugi, Ursula. Three processes in the child's acquisition of syntax. *Language and Learning* (special issue of *Harvard Educational Review*), 1964, *34*, 133–151. (Reprinted in Lenneberg, 1964b; Brown, 1970a; and Bar-Adon & Leopold, 1971.)
   Discusses the role in language learning of adult expansions of child utterances, child reductions of adult utterances, and the child's induction of the latent structure of language.

*Ervin, Susan M. Imitation and structural change in children's language. In Lenneberg, 1964b(b).
   In the natural speech of five children younger than age 3, there is no evidence that imitations are grammatically progressive, since they could be described by the same grammar as free utterances in the same corpus.

Cazden, Courtney. *Environmental Assistance to the Child's Acquisition of Grammar.* Unpublished doctoral dissertation, Harvard University, 1965.
   Three matched groups of four preschoolers each received 40 minutes daily of adult expansion of child utterances, of adult modeling of new but related utterances, or no training. After 12 weeks, the modeling group showed the most improvement on language tests.

*Slobin, Dan I. Imitation and grammatical development in children. In N. S. Endler, L. R. Boulter, & H. Osser (Eds.), *Contemporary Issues in Developmental Psychology.* New York: Holt, Rinehart and Winston, 1967, 437–443.
   Argues for a functional analysis of the role of imitation, attempting to reconcile rule-learning theory and an active-imitation theory. Cites data from Adam and Eve.

Aronfreed, Justin. The problem of imitation. In L. P. Lipsitt & H. W. Reese (Eds.), *Advances in Child Development and Behavior*, Vol. 4. New York: Academic Press, 1969.

Reviews research and theory on the role and mechanism of imitation in animal and children's learning.

Sherman, J. A. Imitation and language development. In Hayes W. Reese (Ed.), *Advances in Child Development and Behavior*, Vol. 6. New York: Academic Press, 1971, 239–272.

Reviews evidence that imitation can be a helpful device in language learning, particularly in the context of highly structured reinforcement procedures with language-deficient children.

*Nelson, Keith E.; Carskaddon, Gaye; & Bonvillian, John D. Syntax acquisition: Impact of experimental variation in adult verbal interaction with the child. *Child Development*, 1973, *44*, 497–504.

Syntax acquisition of 32- to 40-month-olds was facilitated by 22 sessions of verbal interaction. The experimenter recast the subject's sentences, retaining basic meaning but providing new syntactic information.

Ryan, J. Interpretation and imitation in early language development. In R. A. Hinde and J. Stevenson-Hinde (Eds.), *Constraints on Learning: Limitations and Predispositions*. New York: Academic Press, 1973.

Ryan briefly reviews and criticizes various views on language learning and discusses aspects of adult-child interaction in language learning. In particular, evidence is cited that imitation may play a role in the acquisition of new words and grammatical constructions. Piaget's view of the function of imitation is summarized.

*Bloom, Lois; Hood, Lois; & Lightbown, Penny. Imitation in language development: If, when, and why? *Cognitive Psychology*, 1974, *6*, 380–420.

Analysis of the natural speech of six children (primarily at MLU between 1 and 2) reveals consistent intersubject differences in extent of imitation. Imitators selected for imitation those words or structures that they were in the process of learning. Imitation might support learning by enabling further mapping between the utterance and aspects of the referent situation.

Seitz, Sue & Stewart, Catherine. Imitations and expansions: Some developmental aspects of mother-child communications. *Developmental Psychology,* 1975, *11,* 763–768.
See summary in Section 11-C.

Whitehurst, Grover J. & Vasta, Ross. Is language acquired through imitation? *Journal of Psycholinguistic Research,* 1975, *4,* 37–59.
Evidence previously cited against the importance of imitation is countered by proposing a process of selective imitation that follows comprehension and precedes production of a grammatical form, and by citing operant conditioning data.

Nicholich, Lorraine. *Development of Mental Representation and Language Production in Early Childhood.* Unpublished doctoral dissertation, Rutgers University, 1975.
See summary in Section 10-D.

*Rees, Norma S. Imitation and language development: Issues and clinical implications. *Journal of Speech and Hearing Disorders,* 1975, *40,* 339–350.
Clinicians have tended to emphasize the role of imitation, e.g., in modeling procedures, while psycholinguists have de-emphasized it. A review of the literature reveals great variation in terminology, definitions, and explanations. It is suggested that clinical imitation procedures have greater significance for the acquisition of communication skills than for development of linguistic structure.

Abravanel, Eugene; Levan-Goldschmidt, Eileen; & Stevenson, Marguerite B. Action imitation: The early phase of infancy. *Child Development,* 1976, *47,* 1032–1044.
A study of action imitation in children ages 6–18 months. Actions with objects were more frequently imitated than actions without objects. Imitation and object concept performance were unrelated when age was controlled. The effects of other variables are reported.

Scollon, Ronald. *Conversations with a One-year-old: A Case Study of the Developmental Foundation of Syntax.* Honolulu: University of Hawaii Press, 1976.
Includes consideration of the role of repetition and imitation.

Leonard, Lawrence B. & Kaplan, Linda. A note on imitation and lexical acquisition. *Journal of Child Language,* 1976, *3,* 449–455.
Eight children were exposed to four new words (names of toys)

under controlled conditions during each of four videotaping sessions about six weeks apart. (MLU was 1.00–1.26 morphemes at the start, 2.38–2.56 at the end.) Well over half of the children's first productions of the words were spontaneous rather than imitative, and no other evidence was found for a crucial role of imitation.

Newport, Elissa L. & Gleitman, Henry. Maternal self-repetition and the child's acquisition of language. Paper presented at the First Annual Boston University Conference on Language Development, Boston, October 1976.

In a naturalistic and an experimental situation, mothers generated sequences of related utterances (e.g., "Bring me the dog. The dog. Bring it here.") and unrelated utterances. The probability that 2-year-olds responded to a given utterance was independent of the number of preceding utterances. Thus, repetition is helpful only in increasing the number of opportunities for a response; there are no additional cumulative effects.

Ruder, Kenneth F.; Hermann, Patricia; & Schiefelbusch, Richard L. Effects of verbal imitation and comprehension training on verbal production. *Journal of Psycholinguistic Research,* 1977, *6,* 59–72.

American first and second graders performed best on a Spanish-noun production task (picture labeling) when it was preceded by a comprehension task (forced-choice among pictures) followed by an imitation task (no referents), as opposed to the order imitation-comprehension-production.

B Biological Views of Language Learning

Various biological approaches to language are referenced below, with an emphasis on developmental topics. Case studies and reports of sign language learning by chimpanzees and language-deficient humans follow. Many of the articles are based on studies of **aphasia,** *the loss or disturbance of language due to brain damage (lesions), usually caused by stroke or a severe blow to the head. Others focus on the concept of a* **critical period** *(ending around puberty) during which the brain is especially suited to learn language; it has been hypothesized that language input during the critical period is essential to language learning. In addition to the publications listed, see Part V of Aaronson & Rieber (1975).*

GENERAL

Luria, A. R. & Vinogradova, O. An objective investigation of the dynamics of semantic systems. *British Journal of Psychology,* 1959, *50,* 89–105.

A habituation measure (change in size of blood vessels) was used in several experiments, including studies of semantic generalization. See also the two reviews of Soviet research listed in Section 1-B.

Lenneberg, Eric H. On explaining language. *Science,* May 9, 1964a, *164,* 635–643.

A summary of Lenneberg's view of language as a biological process: milestones of development, environment vs. innate capacity in determining vocalization of deaf infants, determinants of language development, maturation, critical age, species specificity.

Lenneberg, Eric H. A biological perspective of language. In Lenneberg, 1964b(c).

Summarizes the views and data that Lenneberg discusses in more detail in his 1967b book, and in less detail in the preceding article.

Lenneberg, Eric H. The biological foundations of language. *Hospital Practice,* 1967a, *2,* 59–67. (Reprinted in T. D. Spencer & N. Kass

(Eds.), *Perspectives in Child Psychology*. New York: McGraw-Hill, 1970.)
> Short, simple presentation of Lenneberg's main ideas and summary of development.

*Lenneberg, Eric H. *Biological Foundations of Language*. New York: Wiley, 1967b.
> Lenneberg views language as a species-specific biological process. Many specific language functions are discussed, with an emphasis on biological constraints, language pathology, and clinical cases, and with considerable attention to developmental topics.

Salzinger, K. & Salzinger, S. (Eds.). *Research in Verbal Behavior and Some Neurophysiological Implications*. New York: Academic Press, 1967.
> Includes articles on aphasia.

Gazzaniga, M. S. *The Bisected Brain*. New York: Appleton-Century-Crofts, 1970.
> Gazzaniga reports the effects on humans of having a severed *corpus collosum*. The two brain hemispheres cannot communicate so that, for example, an object can be named if held in the right hand but not the left hand. See also his 1967 *Scientific American* article.

Geschwind, N. The organization of language and the brain. *Science,* 1970, *170*, 940–944.
> Geschwind introduces the localist theory of brain organization, associating particular kinds of language disturbances in aphasia with particular cortical areas. For example, speech production tends to be disturbed when there are lesions in Broca's area.

McAdam, Dale W. & Whitaker, Harry A. Language production: Electroencephalographic localization in the normal human brain. *Science,* 1971, *172,* 499–502.
> Slow negative potentials were recorded over Broca's area when eight normal subjects spontaneously produced polysyllabic words, beginning up to 1 second before articulation.

Hutt, S. J. Constraints upon learning: Some developmental considerations. In R. A Hinde & J. Stevenson-Hinde (Eds.), *Constraints on Learning: Limitations and Predispositions*. New York: Academic Press, 1973.

Discusses development stage as a constraint on language learning.

Marshall, John C. Language, learning and laterality. In R. A. Hinde & J. Stevenson-Hinde (Eds.), *Constraints on Learning: Limitations and Predispositions.* New York: Academic Press, 1973.
Discusses language performance level as a function of hemispheric lateralization and localization of processes within a hemisphere.

Goodglass, Harold & Blumstein, Sheila. *Psycholinguistics and Aphasia.* Baltimore: The Johns Hopkins University Press, 1973.
Collection of articles on classification of aphasias, phonology, syntax, semantics, etc.

Razran, Gregory. Symboling and semantic conditioning: Anthropogeny. In P. Pliner, L. Krames, & T. Alloway. *Communication and Affect.* New York: Academic Press, 1973.
Razran presents a view of language learning and cognition influenced by the Russian view (e.g., Luria, 1969, listed in Section 1-B), and summarizes experiments using conditioning and physiological measures.

Lenneberg, Eric H. The neurology of language. In Haugan & Bloomfield, 1974.

*Lenneberg, Eric H. & Lenneberg, Elizabeth (Eds.). *Foundations of Language Development* (2 vols.). New York: Academic Press, 1975.
In volume 1, see the papers by E. H. Lenneberg, F. Nottebohm, M. Jacobson, A. R. Lecours, and O. L. Zangwill. Volume 2 focuses on language disorders.

Whitaker, Harry. Neurobiology of language. In E. C. Carterette & M. P. Friedman, Vol. 7, 1976(b).
See also Whitaker's other chapter in this volume ("Disorders of speech production mechanisms") and his survey article in Dingwall, 1971.

Harnad, Steven R.; Doty, Robert W.; Goldstein, Leonide; Jaynes, Julian; & Krauthamer, George (Eds.). *Lateralization in the Nervous System.* New York: Academic Press, 1976.
Collection of papers surveying what is known about differences in the functions of the two brain hemispheres, including the left-hemisphere control of language. Note especially the papers on infant development by Gerald Turkewitz and by Martin F. Gardiner & Donald O. Walter.

Whitaker, Haiganoosh & Whitaker, Harry A. *Studies in Neuro-linguistics.* New York: Academic Press, Vols. 1 & 2, 1976; Vol. 3, in press. (Publication expected, May 1977.)

Articles on aphasia and the neural basis of language, with occasional articles on topics like deafness and reading problems.

CASE STUDIES

Case studies of unusual "experiments in nature" provide otherwise unavailable evidence on theoretical questions.

Lenneberg, Eric H. Understanding language without ability to speak: A case report. *Journal of Abnormal and Social Psychology,* 1962, *65,* 419–425. (Reprinted in Bar-Adon & Leopold, 1971.)

Babbling and imitation may be important for development of speech motor skills, but are neither sufficient nor necessary for acquisition of grammar. Understanding and production of language both reflect a single set of organizing principles (grammatical rules); either performance is evidence of language acquisition.

Fromkin, Victoria; Krashen, Stephen; Curtiss, Susan; Rigler, D.; & Rigler, M. The development of language in Genie: A case of language acquisition beyond the "critical period." *Brain and Language,* 1974, *1,* 81–107.

Genie was isolated in a small room from about 20 months to almost 14 years of age. This report on her progress from silence to simple utterances considers the implications for the biological notion of a critical period for language learning. Results of dichotic listening tests suggest that Genie is right-lateralized, i.e., uses her right rather than left hemisphere for language.

*Curtiss, Susan; Fromkin, Victoria; Krashen, Stephen; Rigler, D.; & Rigler, M. The linguistic development of Genie. *Language,* 1974, *50,* 528–554.

This article has more descriptive detail on Genie's language than the preceding article, including an appendix presenting the results of comprehension tests.

Curtiss, Susan; Fromkin, Victoria; Harshman, Richard; & Krashen, Stephen. Language development in the mature (minor) right hemisphere. Paper presented at the winter meeting of the Linguistic Society of America, San Francisco, December 1975.

> The authors report further evidence for right-lateralization in Genie.

Lane, Harlan. *The Wild Boy of Aveyron.* Cambridge, Mass.: Harvard University Press, 1976.

> Lane brings together and evaluates information on the case of Victor, a mute and wild boy discovered in the woods of 17th-century France at about age 12. A young doctor, Itard, had partial success in training Victor to more human behavior. Lane discusses implications for special education, including the controversy over teaching sign language to deaf children.

Curtiss, Susan, et al. *Genie: A Linguistic Study of a Modern Day "Wild Child."* New York: Academic Press, in press. (Publication expected, spring 1977.)

TEACHING LANGUAGE TO CHIMPANZEES

The following publications discuss recent attempts to teach human-defined languages to chimpanzees. Major publications from three different projects are included, plus debate on whether it has been demonstrated that the chimpanzees have actually learned language. The Gardners are in the best position to explicitly compare chimpanzee and child performance, since they are using an existing language (American Sign Language, or Ameslan). However, the Premacks and Rumbaugh also are interested in interspecies implications. Note that all the successful projects use the visual or gestural modalities; previous attempts to teach vocal language failed.

*Gardner, R. Allen & Gardner, Beatrice T. Teaching sign language to a chimpanzee. *Science,* 1969, *165,* 664–672. (Reprinted in Adams, 1972.)

> An early report of the first attempt to teach a sign language (Ameslan) to a great ape. Training procedures and results are described. The Gardners' approach is to make the learning situation as comparable as possible to that of a child learning language; later reports explicitly compare Washoe's performance to that of human children.

Bronowski, Jacob & Bellugi, Ursula. Language, name and concept. *Science,* 1970, *168,* 669–673.

The authors argue that Washoe's use of Ameslan falls short of the accomplishments of human children, who have the advantage of the particular evolution of the human mind.

Brown, Roger. The first sentences of child and chimpanzee. In Brown, 1970a(b). (Reprinted in Ferguson & Slobin, 1973.)

Brown compares Washoe's sign utterances to those of human children at stage I. He notes semantic similarities and some evidence that Washoe's utterances are syntactically structured, but he is concerned over the variable word order and undemonstrated ability to use syntax appropriately in utterances displaced from immediate context. For Brown's more recent views, see the introduction to his 1973a book or the language chapter of his introductory psychology book (Brown & Herrnstein, 1975).

Neurosciences Research Program Bulletin, 1971, *9*(5).

Special issue on the learning of language by chimpanzees.

Lenneberg, Eric H. Of language, knowledge, apes, and brains. *Journal of Psycholinguistic Research,* 1971, *1*, 1–29.

Mathematical thought is similar to language; both are species-specific to human beings. The studies of Washoe and Sarah are critically evaluated.

Gardner, Beatrice T. & Gardner, R. Allen. Two-way communication with an infant chimpanzee. In A. Schrier & F. Stollnitz (Eds.), *Behavior of Nonhuman Primates.* New York: Academic Press, 1971.

Provides a more complete description of Washoe's training than does the *Science* article.

Premack, David. On the assessment of language competence in the chimpanzee. In A. M. Schrier & F. Stollnitz (Eds.), *Behavior of Nonhuman Primates,* Vol. 4. New York: Academic Press, 1971.

Provides a more complete description of Sarah's training than does the *Scientific American* article.

*Premack, Ann James & Premack, David. Teaching language to an ape. *Scientific American,* 1972, *227,* 92–99.

Summarizes the methods and results used to train a chimpanzee, Sarah, to communicate by means of plastic "words" placed in order on a magnetic board.

Klima, Edward & Bellugi, Ursula. The signs of language in child and

chimpanzee. In T. Alloway, L. Krames, & P. Pliner (Eds.), *Communication and Affect,* Academic Press, 1972.
> Discussion of Ameslan as a language; the Washoe project; and sign language acquisition by Pola, a deaf child, at 2½–4 years.

Fouts, Roger S. Acquisition and testing of gestural signs in four young chimpanzees. *Science,* 1973, *180,* 978–980.
> Four chimpanzees at the Institute for Primate Studies, University of Oklahoma, each learned 10 Ameslan signs, passing a double-blind test.

*Rumbaugh, D. M.; Gill, E. V.; & von Glasersfeld, E. C. Reading and sentence completion by a chimpanzee (Pan). *Science,* 1973, *182,* 731–733.
> Summarizes four experiments demonstrating that a chimpanzee, Lana, can read the beginnings of "Yerkish" sentences, as indicated by her ability to complete them. She is being trained in a controlled, interactive-computer environment; words in Yerkish correspond to computer console keys. See also the criticism by Mistler-Lachman & Lachman and reply by the authors in *Science,* 1974, *185,* 871–873.

Gardner, R. Allen & Gardner, Beatrice T. Early signs of language in child and chimpanzee. *Science,* 1974a, *187,* 752–753.
> Summarizes features of a new sign project with newborn chimpanzees. Signs are produced as early as 13 weeks, in comparison with 5–6 months for human infants exposed to sign language.

Gardner, Beatrice T. & Gardner, R. Allen. Comparing the early utterances of child and chimpanzee. In A. Pick (Ed.), *Minnesota Symposium on Child Psychology,* Vol. 8. Minneapolis: University of Minnesota Press, 1974.
> The Gardners summarize Washoe's performance on vocabulary (double-blind tests), wh-questions, sign combinations (semantic relations expressed; order), negation, and other aspects of Ameslan. Some of the similarities with the development of human children are pointed out.

Gardner, Beatrice T. & Gardner, R. Allen. Evidence for sentence constituents in the early utterances of child and chimpanzee. *Journal of Experimental Psychology: General,* 1975, *104,* 244–267.
> At age 5, 84% of Washoe's answers to wh-questions (*who, what, where, whose*) contained appropriate sentence

constituents, which compares favorably with the behavior of human children at stage III.

Premack, Ann James. *Why Chimps Can Read.* New York: Harper & Row, 1976.
Premack describes Sarah's training program and discusses its possible usefulness for language-deficient children.

Premack, David. *Intelligence in Ape and Man.* Hillsdale, N.J.: Lawrence Erlbaum Associates, 1976.

Osherson, Daniel N. & Wasow, Thomas. Task-specificity and species-specificity in the study of language: A methodological note. *Cognition,* 1976, *4,* 203–214.
Are there certain processes specific to language processing and acquisition? Theoretical and methodological issues are discussed with reference to the chimpanzee language and other studies.

Rumbaugh, Duane M. *Language Learning by a Chimpanzee: The LANA Project.* New York: Academic Press, 1977.
In chapters by 13 researchers, the findings of the Lana project and its theoretical context are described. Lana was taught Yerkish, a specially constructed language of visual pattern sequences, in a computer-controlled environment.

THERAPEUTIC APPLICATIONS OF THE CHIMPANZEE STUDIES

In addition to theoretical implications, the chimpanzee language studies are beginning to have a practical payoff. New methods of language training are being developed for nonverbal humans (certain retarded persons, aphasics, and autistic children). These methods, using sign language or plastic symbols, are often successful where purely oral methods have failed. If the visual/kinesthetic symbols are paired with words during training, improvement in oral speech often occurs as well.

Larson, Thalia. Communication for the nonverbal child. *Academic Therapy,* 1971, *6,* 305–312.
The author discusses selection of candidates to learn sign language and outlines her program, developed for special education schools.

*Bricker, Diane D. Imitative sign training as a facilitator of word-object association with low-functioning children. *American Journal of Mental Deficiency,* 1972, *76,* 509–516.

> Imitative-sign movements were taught, then paired with appropriate words followed by pairing with appropriate objects. Improvement on a 90-item two-choice task for word-object association was greater than for an untrained control group.

*Gazzaniga, Michael S.; Glass, Andrea Velletri; & Premack, David. Artificial language training in global aphasics. *Neuropsychologia,* 1973, *11,* 95–103.

> The language training procedure developed for Sarah had some success with global aphasics.

Wilson, Paula Starks. Sign language as a means of communication for the mentally retarded. Paper presented at the annual convention of the Eastern Psychological Association, Philadelphia, 1974.

> Sign training was given to 26 nonverbal residents of an institution for the mentally retarded (CA = 12–26 years). Over a 7-month period both receptive and productive language were demonstrated.

Fouts, Roger S. & Fulwiler, Robert L. Acquisition of American Sign Language by a non-communicating autistic child. Paper presented at the Southwestern Psychological Association Meeting, El Paso, May 1974.

> After 20 hours of training, an autistic child used several signs and sign combinations appropriately, even outside the training situation; vocal speech also increased.

Moores, Donald F. Nonvocal systems of verbal behavior. In Schiefelbusch & Lloyd, 1974.

> Moores describes Ameslan, reviews studies of sign language acquisition and training, and notes its potential for use by other populations.

Premack, David & Premack, Ann James. Teaching visual language to apes and language-deficient persons. In Schiefelbusch & Lloyd, 1974.

> The Premacks review aspects of Sarah's training program with a plastic-token language and summarize the training program of two other chimpanzees and an 8-year-old autistic child diagnosed as "retarded nonremedial." For example, the child learned to use the plural token and could transfer this to comprehension of spoken English if the word "plural" were used rather than the plural affix.

Kopchick, George A.; Romback, D. W.; & Smilovitz, R. A total communication environment in an institution. *Mental Retardation,* 1975, *13*(3), 122-123.

> After only 6 months, three of 11 nonverbal retarded residents began communicating in sign phrases; all learned single signs (45-134 signs).

Richardson, Toni. Sign language for the SMR and PMR. *Mental Retardation,* 1975, *13*(3), 17.

> Severely or profoundly retarded residents of an institution achieved receptive or productive use of signs in a classroom program.

Bonvillian, John D. & Nelson, Keith E. Sign language acquisition in a mute autistic boy. *Journal of Speech and Hearing Disorders,* 1976, *41,* 339-347.

Knast, Jerome F. Manual communication with severely mentally retarded. Paper presented at the International Convention of the Council for Exceptional Children, Chicago, April 6, 1976.

> Four nonverbal, severely retarded young adults learned more than 30 Ameslan signs and made some progress towards productive use of two- and three-sign utterances, in a program incorporating a total communication approach and re-inforcement training. (Written report in preparation with A. Abrahamsen.)

C Cognitive Basis of Linguistic Universals

A number of researchers have recently adopted the view that language is not independent of the general cognitive system; it develops according to constraints and strategies that also govern nonverbal behavior. Many universals of language and its development (Section 3-C) might be the result of universal concepts and cognitive processes. Some papers exploring this idea are listed below; see also Greene (1975), Schlesinger (1974), and E. Clark (1973a). A different approach is taken by Blank (1974), who argues that language may influence thinking in the preschool years.

Vygotsky, L. S. *Thought and Language.* (E. Hanfmann & G. Vakar, Eds. and trans.). Cambridge, Mass.: The MIT Press, 1962. (Also in paperback. Parts reprinted in Adams, 1972. Originally published in Russian, 1934.)

Since Americans neglected the relation between thought and language in children for so many years, Vygotsky's book is still worth reading; interesting and not difficult. See especially Chapters 3, 4, and 7.

*Bever, Thomas G. The cognitive basis for linguistic structures. In Hayes, 1970. (Revised version: The interaction of perception and linguistic structures: A preliminary investigation of neo-functionalism. In Sebeok, Vol. 12, 1974.)

Bever distinguishes three aspects of cognition and how they affect language development. In developmental order, they are: basic capacities, behavioral strategies, and epistemological structures. He suggests particular behavioral strategies in discussing how clauses are isolated and assigned internal structure in speech perception. Developmental implications are discussed, particularly in Bever's summary of his experiment on children's comprehension of passive sentences.

*Sinclair, Hermina. The transition from sensory-motor behaviour to symbolic activity. *Interchange,* 1970, *1,* 119–126.

Sinclair contrasts Piaget's theory to other views of single-word speech and reports a study in which children at ages 12–26 months progress from learning objects' uses to pretending with them in sequenced play.

McNeill, David. Language before symbols: Very early children's grammar. *Interchange,* 1970c, *1,* 127–133.

Responding to Sinclair (1970), McNeill distinguishes between strong linguistic universals (a linguistic ability is a necessary cause) and weak linguistic universals (a cognitive or other non-linguistic ability is a necessary and sufficient cause). He argues that the syntactic categories of noun and verb are strong and weak linguistic universals, respectively. Holophrastic speech relies on the noun category and therefore can antedate the emergence of the symbolic function, which is an aspect of cognitive development. See also McNeill (1971a).

Nelson, Katherine. The cognitive basis of early speech: A reply to McNeill. *Interchange,* 1971a, *2,* 91–94.

Nelson points out objections to McNeill's (1970c) arguments, concluding that there is just as much evidence for early emergence of verbs as for nouns and that the linguistic and cognitive systems develop interdependently. A final exchange of views follows (McNeill, pp. 94–98; Nelson, pp. 98–99).

Church, Joseph. Methods for the study of early cognitive functioning. In Huxley & Ingram, 1971.

Church reviews a number of measures of cognitive development and discusses their relation to linguistic development with reference to cross-cultural studies. He eschews the approaches of both Piaget and Chomskian psycholinguists as too fragmented, arguing for his version of a Whorfian approach.

Fodor, Jerry A. Some reflections on L. S. Vygotsky's *Thought and Language. Cognition,* 1972, *1,* 83–95.

A contemporary psycholinguist's criticisms of Vygotsky, with responses by Leontiev & Luria and by Sinclair.

*Macnamara, John. Cognitive basis of language learning in infants. *Pychological Review,* 1972, *79,* 1–13.

Young children learn language by first determining the speaker's intended meaning, then working out its relationship to the speaker's utterance. Macnamara presents evidence from both vocabulary and syntactic development.

Olson, Gary M. Developmental changes in memory and the acquisition of language. In Moore, 1973.

Olson reviews characteristics of short-term memory and considers their application to language acquisition. Increase in immediate memory span and increase in MLU reflect the same underlying change; Olson offers some speculations on its nature.

*Ervin-Tripp, Susan. Some strategies for the first two years. In Moore, 1973(b).

Suggests several prerequisites to language learning, related to environmental factors, knowledge of concepts such as recurrence and possession (similar to Bloom's 1970 analysis), and information storage factors. These ideas are applied to data on acquisition of grammatical morphemes and word order.

*Slobin, Dan I. Cognitive prerequisites for the development of grammar. In Ferguson & Slobin, 1973.

Slobin suggests seven "operating principles" by which very young children act on the language they hear, resulting in a number of putative universals of language acquisition. Citations from a variety of languages support the universals.

Tanz, Christine. Cognitive principles underlying children's errors in pronominal case-marking. *Journal of Child Language,* 1974, *1,* 271–276.

Tanz uses two of Slobin's operating principles to account for an asymmetry in case-marking errors in English.

Clark, Ruth. Performing without competence. *Journal of Child Language,* 1974, *1,* 1–10.

One boy in the age period 2;9–3;0 used strategies for simplifying his speech production (e.g., incorporating a prior utterance, concatenating two related utterances).

*Blank, Marion. Cognitive functions of language in the pre-school years. *Developmental Psychology,* 1974, *10,* 229–245.

Language plays a functional role even in the preschool years, especially by helping the child to perform in situations in which other skills are useless. Blank considers three areas as examples: concept formation, communication, and problem solving.

*Cromer, Richard F. The development of language and cognition: The cognition hypothesis. In B. Foss (Ed.), *New Perspectives in Child Development.* London: Penguin Education Series, 1974(b).

Cromer's hypothesis is that a given linguistic structure can be comprehended and produced only when cognitive abilities are sufficiently developed; even then, a simpler linguistic form might be grasped before a more complex form.

*Slobin, Dan I. The more it changes . . . On understanding language by watching it move through time. In *Papers and Reports on Child Language Development,* No. 10. Department of Linguistics, Stanford University, September 1975a.

See summary in Section 11-B.

Aaronson, Doris & Rieber, Robert W. (Eds.). *Developmental Psycholinguistics and Communication Disorders.* (Annals of the New York Academy of Sciences, Vol. 263.) New York: New York Academy of Sciences, 1975.

Part II ("The Role of Cognition in the Acquisition and Development of Language") has articles by Marion Blank, Paula Menyuk, and H. G. Furth, and discussions by Thomas G. Bever and Lawrence Raphael.

Rieber, Robert W. The role of language and thought in developmental psycholinguistics—An historical review. In Aaronson & Rieber, 1975.

Riegel, Klaus F. Semantic basis of language: Language as labor. In Riegel & Rosenwald, 1975.

Huttenlocher, Janellen & Burke, Deborah. Why does memory span increase with age? *Cognitive Psychology,* 1976, *8,* 1–31.

Performance of children ages 4, 7, 9, and 11 years on ordered recall of auditory digits differing in sound pattern and temporal grouping indicates that increased span with age is attributable to improvement in identification of items and encoding of their order, not to the emergence of active strategies. There were large temporal grouping and primacy effects at all ages.

Kaper, Willem. Pronominal case-errors. *Journal of Child Language,* 1976, *3,* 439–441.

Presents counterevidence to Tanz (1974) from Dutch and German.

Cromer, Richard F. The cognitive hypothesis of language acquisition and its implications for child language deficiency. In Morehead & Morehead, 1976.

Once children acquire certain meanings, they use existing linguistic forms and learn new ones to express the meanings. A variety of studies suggesting cases of cognitive influence and cases of lack of influence on language are cited.

Greenfield, Patricia Marks & Smith, Joshua H. *The Structure of*

Communication in Early Language Development. New York: Academic Press, 1976.

See summary in Section 5-B.

McNeill, David. Forthcoming book. This new synthesis of ideas on language and thought extends McNeill (1975a). McNeill analyzes the action of speech formation as a network of signs, building on the ideas of the philosopher Peirce. Piagetian notions are also incorporated, particularly in the proposal that speech is organized at a sensorimotor level: concepts such as entity, state, action, and location are used to organize even highly abstract utterances. A model for representing conceptual structures is proposed, and various types of evidence (including gesture) are examined.

D Relationship of Piaget's Cognitive Theory to Language Development

*Like the preceding group of papers (Section 10-C), the papers in this section explore the relation between language development and cognition. However, they take Piaget's theory of cognitive development as a starting point (not always uncritically). In Piaget's theory, development is divided into four major periods: **sensorimotor** (ends at 1½–2 years), **preoperational** (ends at 7 years; the emergence of the symbolic function is one of the earliest attainments), **concrete operational** (ends at 11 years), and **formal operational** (11 years and older). Most of the discussions focus on foundations for language laid in the sensorimotor period and on very early language. The three most relevant books by Piaget are listed; for language in older children, see Piaget's publications in Section 11-D. Several papers by Hermina Sinclair (simplified from Sinclair-de-Zwart) are listed. A colleague of Piaget's, she has played an important role in developing a Piagetian approach to psycholinguistics. Other relevant publications are in Section 2-G (background reading on cognitive development) and in Part III (semantics). Many recent publications listed in other sections show a Piagetian influence.*

Piaget, Jean. *The Origins of Intelligence in Children.* New York: International Universities Press, 1952. (Also in paperback, New York: Norton, 1963. Originally published in French, 1936.)

Describes major accomplishments of the sensorimotor period.

Piaget, Jean. *The Construction of Reality in the Child.* New York: Basic Books, 1954. (Also in paperback, New York: Norton, 1962. Originally published in French, 1936.)

Companion to the preceding volume; also on the sensorimotor period.

*Piaget, Jean. *Play, Dreams and Imitation in Childhood.* New York: Norton, 1951. (Also in paperback. Originally published in French, 1946.)

Development of the symbolic and representational functions following the sensorimotor period.

*Sinclair-de-Zwart, Hermina. Developmental psycholinguistics. In D.

Elkind & J. Flavell (Eds.), *Studies in Cognitive Development.* New York: Oxford University Press, 1969. (Also in paperback. Excerpt in Adams, 1972.)

> The role of language in Piaget's theory, from the sensorimotor period to concrete operations. Includes a discussion of Chomsky's generative grammar.

Sinclair, Hermina. The transition from sensory-motor behavior to symbolic activity. *Interchange,* 1970, *1,* 119–126.

> See summary in Section 10-C.

Sinclair, Hermina. Sensorimotor action patterns as a condition for the acquisition of syntax. In Huxley & Ingram, 1971.

> Sinclair argues that linguistic universals are due to prior thought structures, which are universal. Piaget's observations of several children are cited.

Mehler, J. Studies in language and thought development. In Huxley & Ingram, 1971.

> Mehler discusses competence and performance, arguing that linguistic processing is not completely separate from cognitive processing. Experiments are cited on memory for series of lines of different heights, conservation, comprehension of active and passive sentences, and recall of affirmative and negative sentences, using subjects 2–6 years old.

Sinclair, Hermina. Some remarks on the Genevan point of view on learning with special reference to language learning. In R. A. Hinde & J. Stevenson-Hinde (Eds.), *Constraints on Learning: Limitations and Predispositions.* New York: Academic Press, 1973(a).

> Sinclair reviews constraints on language learning suggested by Piaget's theory and discusses several ways language can be regarded within the framework of that theory.

Sinclair, Hermina. Language acquisition and cognitive development. In Moore, 1973(b).

> Children's expression of basic grammatical relations depends on the prior establishment of action patterns in sensorimotor development. Includes a summary of Sinclair & Bronckart's (1972) experiment.

Bloom, Lois. *One Word at a Time.* The Hague: Mouton, 1973. (Also in paperback.)

> Single-word speech is not a unitary stage; cognitive development in this period lays a foundation for the beginning of

syntax. Bloom is influenced by Piaget's analysis of the development of mental representation. Data from three children are presented.

Edwards, Derek. Sensory-motor intelligence and semantic relations in early child grammar. *Cognition*, 1973, *2*, 395–434.

A system of semantic clause-types based on case grammar shows correspondence to concepts in Piaget's theory. The nature of sensorimotor intelligence constrains the range of relational meanings expressed in two-word speech.

*Nelson, Katherine. Concept, word and sentence: Interrelations in acquisition and development. *Psychological Review*, 1974a, *81*, 267–285.

An important attempt to integrate concept formation theory, semantic feature theory, and Piagetian theory to account for the early translation of meaning into words.

Morehead, Donald M. & Morehead, Ann. From signal to sign: A Piagetian view of thought and language during the first two years. In Schiefelbusch & Lloyd, 1974.

The authors summarize the six substages of the sensorimotor stage of development, place some recent studies of early language development in that context, and discuss training for language-deficient children.

Moerk, Ernst L. Piaget's research as applied to the explanation of language development. *Merrill-Palmer Quarterly of Behavior and Development*, 1975a, *21*, 151–169.

Moerk outlines how a number of Piaget's basic principles apply to language development, including the epigenetic principle, horizontal and vertical décalage, assimilation and accommodation, equilibration, transformation, abstraction and classification, representation, coordination of schemes, the object and action concepts, and relations. The article focuses on topics different than those in Sinclair's articles and therefore supplements them well for the reader with some knowledge of Piaget's theory.

*McNeill, David. Semiotic extension. In Solso, 1975(a).

The organization of language is based on Piaget's sensorimotor level of development. (See also McNeill, forthcoming, Section 10-C.)

Nicolich, Lorraine McCune. *Development of Mental Representation and Language Production in Early Childhood.* Unpublished doctoral dissertation, Rutgers University, 1975.

Five females, ages 14–19 months at the study's beginning, were videotaped monthly until about age 24 months (MLU = 1.0 to less than 2.0). Symbolic play level (based on Piaget, 1946/51) was associated with certain linguistic milestones. Imitation increased with time and was selective.

Edmonds, Marilyn H. New directions in theories of language acquisition. *Harvard Educational Review,* 1976, *46,* 175–198.

Edmonds reviews and criticizes nativistic theories of language acquisition (e.g., McNeill 1970a,b). An approach incorporating semantics and cognition as well as syntax avoids the problems of nativism. A sequence of early cognitive and linguistic development is suggested in the context of Piaget's theory. (See a related book in preparation, *Language Acquisition and Sensori-motor Development* or the author's doctoral dissertation of the same title, University of Nebraska, 1975.)

Inhelder, Bärbel. Observations on the operational and figurative aspects of thought in dysphasic children. In Morehead & Morehead, 1976.

Bates, Elizabeth. *Language and Context: The Acquisition of Pragmatics.* New York: Academic Press, 1976a.

See summary in Section 11-B.

Rodgon, Maris Monitz. *Single-word Usage, Cognitive Development, and the Beginnings of Combinatorial Speech.* London: Cambridge University Press, 1976.

See summary in Section 5-C.

Furth, Hans G. & Youniss, James. Formal operations and language: A comparison of deaf and hearing adolescents. In Morehead & Morehead, 1976.

Moerk, Ernst L. *Pragmatic and Semantic Aspects of Early Language Development.* Baltimore: University Park Press, 1977.

See summary in Section 11-B.

Section 11
PRAGMATICS AND THE ATTAINMENT OF COMMUNICATIVE COMPETENCE

*Communicative competence refers to language **in use** as an effective communication system in a social context. In the preceding sections (Parts II and III), acquisition of language **structure** is the object of study, and theoretical grounding is found primarily in linguistic descriptions of language as an abstract system of syntactic and semantic rules. Even the attempts to relate language development to cognitive development do not consider the social context of speech. In contrast, the studies in this section focus on language **function**. Language is viewed as one form of interpersonal interaction, in which particular utterances can perform various functions, e.g., soliciting information, directly or indirectly requesting an action. Furthermore, a particular utterance may be appropriate or inappropriate in its social context. These considerations traditionally have been in the province of sociolinguistics, but the linguist Halliday also emphasizes language function in his work. Going a step further, philosophers Austin and Searle have regarded utterances as acts (**speech acts**). For example, "You better watch out" may involve an **illocutionary** act of warning (speaker's intent) and a **perlocutionary** act of creating fear (utterance's effect). Another philosopher, Grice, has worked out various shared assumptions that govern conversation (**conversational principles** or postulates), e.g., an assumption that requests are sincere. Finally, there has traditionally been a wastebasket category of linguistic theory called **pragmatics,** to which aspects of language too untidy for semantic theories have been relegated. Pragmatics includes nonsocial factors, such as the use of knowledge of the world when producing and interpreting utterances, and also encompasses the social aspects of language mentioned above.*

The 1970's have been marked by a revival of interest in language in use, not only in linguistics and philosophy but also in child lan-

guage. Some background references on theoretical approaches are given below. These are followed by child studies, divided into those emphasizing theory or preverbal communication, and those emphasiz-   009 ing empirical investigations of parent-child speech. A last group of studies are based on a different but related theory from the 1920's, Piaget's concept of communicative egocentrism.

A Theory of Pragmatics and Speech Acts

Most of the following publications are by philosophers or socio-linguists and are useful for background reading.

Austin, John L. *How to Do Things with Words.* London: Oxford University Press, 1962. (Also in paperback, J. O. Urmson & G. J. Warnock (Eds.), 1965.)
> Austin did much of the original work on speech acts in philosophy.

Hymes, Dell (Ed.). *Language in Culture and Society.* New York: Harper & Row, 1964.
> Selection of previously published papers, with extensive editorial commentary and bibliography.

Grice, H. P. *Logic and Conversation.* Mimeographed, 1968a.
> Grice discusses his conversational principles in detail. Some linguistics and philosophy departments have a copy of the manuscript.

Grice, H. P. Utterer's meaning, sentence-meaning and word-meaning. *Foundations of Language,* 1968b, *4,* 225–242.
> Focuses on "timeless meaning"; technical.

Grice, H. P. Utterer's meaning and intentions. *The Philosophical Review,* 1969, *78,* 147–177.

Searle, John R. *Speech Acts: An Essay in The Philosophy of Language.* London: Cambridge University Press, 1969. (Also in paperback, 1970.)
> Searle has further developed the theory of speech acts, and his work has had interdisciplinary influence.

Bernstein, Basil. A sociolinguistic approach to socialization: with some reference to educability. In F. Williams (Ed.), *Language and Poverty.* Chicago: Markham, 1970. (Similar paper in J. J. Gumperz & D. Hymes (Eds.), *Directions in Sociolinguistics.* New York: Holt, Rinehart and Winston, 1972.)
> Bernstein discusses his distinction between restricted and elaborated codes and its relation to family type and social class.

Halliday, M. A. K. Language structure and language function. In Lyons, 1970a.
Brief summary of Halliday's approach. He distinguishes three grammatically relevant functions: ideational (propositional content), interpersonal (e.g., mood and modality), and textual (discourse structure and relations to situations).

Bar-Hillel, Yehoshua (Ed.). *Pragmatics of Natural Language.* Dordrecht, Holland: D. Reidel, 1971. (Also in paperback, $13.)

Ferguson, Charles A. *Language Structure and Language Use.* (Essays selected and introduced by Anwar S. Dil.) Stanford: Stanford University Press, 1971.

Huxley, Renira & Ingram, Elisabeth (Eds.). *Language Acquisition: Models & Methods.* New York: Academic Press, 1971.
The section on sociolinguistics has papers by Hymes, Ervin-Tripp, Cazden, Robinson, and Bernstein.

Carswell, E. A. & Rommetveit, Ragnar (Eds.). *Social Contexts of Messages.* New York: Academic Press, 1971.
Collection of research reports by European psychologists.

Gordon, David & Lakoff, George. Conversational postulates. In *Papers from the Seventh Regional Meeting of the Chicago Linguistic Society.* The University of Chicago Linguistics Department, 1971.
Two linguists formalize some of Grice's conversational principles as part of a theory of grammar. An article of the same title is in Cole & Morgan, 1975.

Langendoen, D. Terence & Savin, Harris B. The projection problem for presuppositions. In Fillmore & Langendoen, 1971, 54–60.

Hymes, D. On communicative competence. In J. B. Pride & J. Holmes (Eds.), *Sociolinguistics.* Baltimore: Penguin Books, 1972. (Paperback.)

Labov, William. Some principles of linguistic methodology. *Language and Society,* 1972, *1,* 97–120.

Lakoff, Robin. Language in context. *Language,* 1972, *48,* 907–927.
Discussion of contextually linked linguistic phenomena including honorifics, polite forms, and modal verbs.

Labov, William. *Sociolinguistic Patterns.* Philadelphia: University of Pennsylvania Press, 1973a. (Also in paperback.)
Collection of papers by Labov, suggesting alternatives to an

intuition-based method and developing techniques for the study of linguistic variation.

Halliday, M. A. K. *Explorations in the Functions of Language.* London: Arnold, 1973. (Paperback.)

Ervin-Tripp, Susan M. Sociolinguistics. Reprinted in B. G. Blount (Ed.), *Language, Culture and Society.* Cambridge, Mass.: Winthrop Publishers, 1974(a).
Introduction to the field. Includes a brief but useful appendix on tape-recording techniques.

Langendoen, D. Terence. The problem of linguistic theory in relation to language behavior: A tribute and reply to Paul Goodman. In Haugen & Bloomfield, 1974.
A linguist discusses pragmatics, competence vs. performance, and the contrast between Chomsky's emphasis on conventional meaning and Grice's emphasis on conversational meaning.

Hymes, Dell. *Foundations in Sociolinguistics: An Ethnographic Approach.* Philadelphia: University of Pennsylvania Press, 1974.
Collection of articles in which Hymes defines and explores sociolinguistics.

Cherry, Colin (Ed.). *Pragmatic Aspects of Human Communication.* Dordrecht, Holland: D. Reidel, 1974. (Also in paperback, $13.50.)

Rommetveit, Ragnar. *On Message Structure: A Framework for the Study of Language and Communication.* New York: John Wiley & Sons, 1974.
Rommetveit argues for an approach to the psychology of meaning that takes into account the social and psychological contexts of utterances, in contrast to the approach taken by linguists at Harvard and MIT (e.g., Chomsky).

Cicourel, Aaron V. *Cognitive Sociology: Language and Meaning in Social Interaction.* New York: Free Press, 1974.
Reprints five of Cicourel's essays on the ethnomethodological analysis of social interaction and language; may serve as an introduction to this challenging approach in sociology.

Bauman, Richard & Sherzer, Joel (Eds.). *Explorations in the Ethnography of Speaking.* London: Cambridge University Press, 1974. (Also in paperback.)
Papers from a Conference on the Ethnography of Speaking held in Austin in April 1972. Theoretical and empirical papers on the patterns and functions of speech in communities.

Cohen, L. Jonathan. Speech acts. In Sebeok, Vol. 12, 1974.

Sadock, Jerrold M. *Toward a Linguistic Theory of Speech Acts.* New York: Academic Press, 1974. (Reviewed by John R. Searle in *Language*, 1976a, *52*, 966–971; he disagrees.)

> Sadock discusses speech acts in the framework of a modified version of generative semantics. He includes discussion of the range of illocutionary forces encoded by questions and imperatives, performatives, indirect speech acts, adverbs, transderivational constraints, and idioms vs. metaphors.

Halliday, M. A. K. Learning how to mean. In Lenneberg & Lenneberg, Vol. 1, 1975.

Cole, P. & Morgan, J. (Eds.). *Syntax and Semantics, Vol. 3. Speech Acts.* New York: Academic Press, 1975.

> Articles contributing to the theory of speech acts, by linguists such as Georgia Green, Susan Schmerling, David Gordon, George Lakoff, and John Ross; philosophers H. P. Grice and John Searle; the editors; and other contributors.

Searle, John R. Speech acts and recent linguistics. In Aaronson & Rieber, 1975.

Lakoff, George. Pragmatics in natural logic. In Keenan, 1975.

van Dijk, Teun A. (Ed.). *Pragmatics of Language and Literature.* Amsterdam: North-Holland, 1975. (Paperback, $18.)

> An interdisciplinary collection, including such papers as S.-Y. Kuroda, "Reflections on the foundations of narrative theory from a linguistic point of view"; I. Kummer & W. Kummer, "Logic of action and the structure of practical discourse"; and N. Kasher & A. Kasher, "Speech acts, contexts and valuable ambiguities."

Bernstein, Basil. *Class, Codes, and Control: Theoretical Studies Towards a Sociology of Language* (3 vols.). London: Routledge & Kegan Paul, 1975. (Vol. 1 revised edition; also in paperback, New York: Schocken, 1975.)

> Collection of Bernstein's papers over a 12-year period.

Collins, Allan; Warnock, Eleanor H.; & Passafiume, Joseph J. Analysis and synthesis of tutorial dialogues. In G. H. Bower, Vol. 9, 1975.

> Analysis of strategies used in tutorial dialogues by the method of dialogue analysis, which can be applied to other conversational situations as well.

Sanches, Mary & Blount, Ben G. (Eds.). *Sociocultural Dimensions of Language Use.* New York: Academic Press, 1975.
Collection of papers on anthropological linguistics, offering analyses of verbal behavior in a variety of contexts (jokes, magic, courtship, the Japanese Theater, etc.). Includes a paper by Claudia Mitchell-Kernan and Keith T. Kernan, "Children's insults: America and Samoa."

Hass, Wilbur A. Pragmatic structures of language: Historical, formal and developmental issues. In Riegel & Rosenwald, 1975.

Kempson, Ruth M. *Presupposition and the Delimitation of Semantics.* London: Cambridge University Press, 1975. (Also in paperback.)
Kempson argues that pragmatics (including presupposition) should not be incorporated into a theory of grammar; she discusses Grice's theory in Chapters 7 and 8.

Wilson, Deirdre. *Presuppositions and Non-truth-conditional Semantics.* New York: Academic Press, 1975.
Critical analysis of the logical and the psychological/pragmatic approaches to presuppositional semantics.

Katz, Jerrold J. & Langendoen, D. Terence. Pragmatics and presupposition. *Language,* 1976, *52,* 1–17.
Argues that presupposition can be accounted for semantically, so that contextual accounts are unnecessary, contrary to Karttunen and others.

Schweller, Kenneth G.; Brewer, William F.; & Dahl, Deborah A. Memory for illocutionary forces and perlocutionary effects of utterances. *Journal of Verbal Learning and Verbal Behavior,* 1976, *15,* 325–337.
College students hearing sentences containing reported utterances confused these with new sentences consistent in their illocutionary force (recall) or perlocutionary effect (recognition) in memory tests.

Verschueren, Jef. Speech act theory: A provisional bibliography with a terminological guide. Manuscript, 1976. Available from the Indiana University Linguistics Club, 310 Lindley Hall, Bloomington, Indiana 47401, for $2.25 plus $.50 postage.

Halliday, M. A. K. *System and Function in Language: Selected Papers.* London: Oxford University Press, 1976. (Paperback, $16.)

Bever, T. G.; Katz, J. J.; & Langendoen, D. T. (Eds.). *An Integrated Theory of Linguistic Ability.* New York: Thomas Y. Crowell, 1976.
Includes articles on presupposition and semantics.

Freedle, R. (Ed.). *Discourse Relations: Comprehension and Production.* Hillsdale, N.J.: Lawrence Erlbaum Associates, 1976.
Includes an article by John Dore, "Children's illocutionary acts."

Searle, J. A classification of illocutionary acts. *Language in Society,* 1976b, *5,* 1–23.

Goffman, E. Replies and responses. *Language in Society,* 1976, *5,* 257–313.

Ervin-Tripp, Susan. Is Sybil there? The structure of some American English directives. *Language in Society,* 1976, *5,* 25–66. (Originally titled "Wait for Me, Roller-Skate!")

Labov, William & Fanshel, David. *Therapeutic Discourse.* New York: Academic Press, in press. (Publication expected, April 1977.)

Journal of Pragmatics. Published by North-Holland Publishing Co., quarterly. (First issue, spring 1977.)
Articles on the theory of pragmatics and its applications, including language acquisition; book reviews. Examples to appear in volume 1: D. Wunderlich, "Assertions, conditional speech acts, and practical inferences"; A. Kasher, "What is a theory of use?"; F. Pasierbsky, "The concept of function in recent Soviet linguistics"; K. Sornig, "On the concept of communicative competence: Some consequences for the teaching of language"; Th. Kotschi, "On the distinction between presuppositions and conversational implications."

Fishman, Joshua A. The sociology of language: Yesterday, today, and tomorrow. In Cole, in press.

Williams, Edwin. On discourse grammar. *Linguistic Inquiry,* 1977, *8,* in press.

Bach, Kent & Harnish, Robert M. *A Theory of Speech Acts.* New York: Thomas Y. Crowell, forthcoming.

Katz, Jerrold J. *Propositional Structure: A Study of the Contribution of Sentence Meaning to Speech Acts.* New York: Thomas Y. Crowell, forthcoming.

B Toward a Theory of Adult-Child Communication

The view that language is communicative is taken as a starting point by these investigators. They offer the beginnings of a theoretical framework and examine data suggestive of its usefulness.

*Gruber, Jeffrey S. Correlations between the syntactic constructions of the child and of the adult. In Ferguson & Slobin, 1973(a). (Presented as a conference paper, 1967. A similar article is: J. S. Gruber, Performative-constative transition in child language development. *Foundations of Language,* 1975, *12,* 513–527.)

> For a corpus beginning at age 1.24 years, all utterances in the first 9 weeks were performatives (related to ongoing acts, e.g., "see kitty"), composed of theme (*kitty*) and complement (*see*). In the 10th week, reportative utterances appear also (e.g., "shoe all gone").

Williams, Frederick (Ed.). *Language and Poverty.* Chicago: Markham, 1970.

> Selection of previously published and new articles by linguists, psycholinguists, and sociolinguists in which an attempt is made to bridge the gap between theory and practice. Some of the papers focus on family-child speech interactions.

Eveloff, Herbert H. Some cognitive and affective aspects of early language development. *Child Development,* 1971, *42,* 1895–1907.

> Normal and abnormal language development depends largely on the infant-mother relationship. Eveloff discusses his own and other ideas on important affective and cognitive parameters, e.g., mother-child symbiosis, transitional phenomena, and novelty.

Cazden, Courtney B.; John, Vera; & Hymes, Dell (Eds.). *Functions of Language in the Classroom.* New York: Teachers College Press, 1972. (Also in paperback.)

> Papers written for this volume were meant to "illuminate the communicative demands of the school and the sociolinguistic discontinuities between a child's home community and school culture." Topics include nonverbal communication (including sign language acquisition), varieties of language (including

Black English and bilingualism), varieties of communicative strategies (including studies of American Indian children, and the meaning of questions and narratives for Hawaiian children).

Lewis, Michael & Freedle, Roy. Mother-infant dyad: The cradle of meaning. In P. Pliner, L. Krames, & T. Alloway, *Communication and Affect*. New York: Academic Press, 1973.

The authors analyzed the interaction between mothers and their 3-month-old infants, using a checklist observation procedure over 2–4 hours. They argue that the communication system observed is the precursor of the later linguistic system.

Ferguson, Charles A. *Studies in Child Language and Development*. New York: Holt, Rinehart and Winston, 1973.

Collection of papers by Ferguson.

Blank, Marion. *Teaching Learning in the Preschool: A Dialogue Approach*. Columbus, Ohio: Charles E. Merrill, 1973. (Paperback.)

In approaching the problem of preschoolers with poor cognitive functioning, Blank analyzes in detail tutorial dialogues between teachers and children.

Ryan, J. Early language development: Towards a communicational analysis. In. M. P. M. Richards (Ed.), *The Integration of a Child into a Social World*. London: Cambridge University Press, 1974.

Cicourel, Aaron V.; Jennings, Kenneth H.; Jennings, Sybillyn, H. M.; Leiter, Kenneth C. W.; MacKay, Robert; Mehan, Hugh; & Roth, David R. *Language Use and School Performance*. New York: Academic Press, 1974.

Based on doctoral theses using an ethnomethodological approach; analyzes actual communicative interactions among children and teachers. Seemingly objective phenomena, e.g., test scores, are shown to be variable and subjective products of the interaction.

Dore, John. A pragmatic description of early language development. *Journal of Psycholinguistic Research,* 1974, *4,* 423–430.

Connolly, Kevin & Bruner, Jerome (Eds.). *The Growth of Competence*. New York: Academic Press, 1974.

See especially the articles by Ainsworth & Bell and Richards on mother-infant interaction and by Cazden, McNeill, and Tizard on language acquisition.

Lewis, Michael & Rosenblum, Leonard A. (Eds.). *The Effect of the Infant on its Caregiver.* New York: John Wiley & Sons, 1974.
Eleven original papers involving mother-infant communication and adaptation; useful as background for the topic of linguistic communication.

Menyuk, Paula. Early development of receptive language: From babbling to words. In Schiefelbusch & Lloyd, 1974.
The second half of this article reviews research on comprehension of language function and parent-infant communication.

Davison, Anni. Linguistics play and language acquisition. In *Papers and Reports on Child Language Development,* No. 8. Committee on Linguistics, Stanford University, April 1974, 179–187.
Some understanding and use of Grice's sincerity principle are reflected in the playful speech of two French-speaking girls at ages 24–26 months (MLU = 1.78–2.16) and 38–40 months (MLU = 3.37–4.15), but not in the single-word speech of a 22- to 25-month-old boy.

*Bruner, Jerome S. From communication to language—A psychological perspective. *Cognition,* 1974/75, *3,* 255–287.
Four examples of nonspeech precursers of language characteristics are discussed: the mother's interpretation of the infant's intent, joint referential devices en route to deixis, the infant's enlistment of aid, and topic-comment organization.

*Slobin, Dan I. The more it changes . . . On understanding language by watching it move through time. In *Papers and Reports on Child Language Development,* No. 10. Department of Linguistics, Stanford University, September 1975a.
Slobin discusses four ground rules for a language, two of which favor precision (be clear, be humanly processible in ongoing time) and two of which favor complexity (be quick and easy, be expressive). Creoles and child language emphasize the first two ground rules; surface structure is regular and explicit. The second two ground rules compete with the first two and provide the expressive power of a mature language. Examples of language change and child language processes are cited from a variety of languages.

Bruner, Jerome S. The ontogenesis of speech acts. *Journal of Child Language,* 1975, *2,* 1–19.

Bruner suggests it is time to turn from the emphasis on language structure (e.g., syntax) to the study of language function. Linguistic concepts are originally realized in action, for example, the rituals of mutual play between mother and child.

*Dore, John. Holophrases, speech acts and language universals. *Journal of Child Language,* 1975, *2,* 21–40.

The holophrastic controversy (should children's one-word utterances be regarded as sentences?) can be avoided by taking the speech act, rather then the sentence, as the basic linguistic unit. Three language universals are proposed: communicative functions, referring expressions, and predicating expressions.

Bates, Elizabeth; Camaioni, L.; & Volterra, V. The acquisition of performatives prior to speech. *Merrill-Palmer Quarterly of Behavior and Development,* 1975, *21,* 205–226.

Videotaped samples of behavior of three Italian infants younger than 1½ years were analyzed for cognitive, social, and communicative development using a speech act framework. Three phases are described: perlocutionary (nonintentional communication), illocutionary (intentional communication, performatives), and locutionary (illocutionary structures carry propositions with a referential value).

Slobin, Dan I. On the nature of talk to children. In Lenneberg & Lenneberg, Vol. 1, 1975(b).

A review of preliminary findings on differences between adult-directed and child-directed speech in syntax, semantics, style, and manner, with examples from several languages.

*Shatz, Marilyn. The comprehension of indirect directives: Can two-year-olds shut the door? In *Pragmatics Microfiche,* 1975a, 1.5.

Five mother-child dyads (18–34 months) were each videotaped in a 15-minute interaction. Even the youngest children responded appropriately to directives given syntactically in question form (indirect speech acts) as often as they responded appropriately to directives given in imperative form. They used a simple action-response strategy in which they produced a plausible action involving a referent of the sentence.

Halliday, M. A. K. Learning how to mean. In Lenneberg & Lenneberg, Vol. 1, 1975, 239–265.

Discusses three stages in a sociosemantic view of language development, with data from the longitudinal record of one child from 9 to 24 months of age: (1) functional origins, (2) vocabulary and syntax, and (3) dialogue.

Lewis, M. & Lee-Painter, Susan. The origin of interactions: Methodological issues. In Riegel & Rosenwald, 1975.

Gewirtz, Jacob L. & Boyd, Elizabeth F. Mother-infant interaction and its study. In H. W. Reese (Ed.), *Advances in Child Development and Behavior,* Vol. 11. New York: Academic Press, 1976.
Discusses theoretical models and methodology.

Mahoney, Gerald J. & Seely, Pamela B. The role of the social agent in language acquisition: Implications for language intervention. In N. R. Ellis (Ed.), *International Review of Research in Mental Retardation,* Vol. 8. New York: Academic Press, 1976.

Keenan, Elinor Ochs & Schieffelin, Bambi B. Topic as a discourse notion: A study of topic in the conversations of children and adults. In Li, 1976.
See also the other articles in Li for background on the topic-comment distinction.

*Bates, Elizabeth. *Language and Context: The Acquisition of Pragmatics.* New York: Academic Press, 1976a.
A speech act approach to the relation of nonlinguistic to linguistic factors, organized by Piaget's stages of cognitive development. Includes chapters on the development of presupposition, performatives, word order, counterfactual conditions, and polite forms. Some chapters are based on longitudinal records for two Italian children, collected by Antinucci, Volterra, and Francesco, for the periods 1;3–2;9 and 1;4–4;0.

Bates, Elizabeth. Pragmatics and sociolinguistics in child language. In Morehead & Morehead, 1976(b).

*Greenfield, Patricia Marks & Smith, Joshua H. *The Structure of Communication in Early Language Development.* New York: Academic Press, 1976.
This longitudinal study of the emergence of semantic relations in the single-word speech of two children emphasizes the communicative and action context.

Moerk, Ernst L. *Semantic and Pragmatic Aspects of Early Language Development.* Baltimore: University Park Press, 1977.
A process-oriented analysis of early language development, with emphasis on biological and conceptual antecedents of lan-

guage, Piagetian theory, pragmatics, and parent-child interaction. Moerk reviews relevant research, including the
European literature.

Ramge, H. Language acquisition as the acquisition of speech act
competence. *Journal of Pragmatics,* in press. (Publication expected,
1977, *1*(2).)

Halliday, M. A. K. *Explorations in the Development of Language.*
Amsterdam: North-Holland, in press. (Publication expected, February 1977.)

*Mitchell-Kernan, Claudia & Ervin-Tripp, Susan (Eds.). *Child Dis-
course.* New York: Academic press, in press. (Publication expected,
March 1977.)

    Collection of papers on speech events, function and act, and
social meaning in children's discourse.

Gelman, Rochelle & Shatz, Marilyn. Appropriate speech adjustments:
The operation of conversational constraints on talk to two-year-
olds. In M. Lewis & L. Rosenblum, in press.

    Similar to the findings of Shatz & Gelman, in press, for 4-year-
olds (Section 11-D), mothers' speech to 2-year-olds is simplified functionally (which is responsible for the apparent finding of syntactic simplification). The meanings they express
include those expressed by 4-year-olds. The concept of functional appropriateness is discussed.

Lewis, Michael & Rosenblum, Leonard. *Interaction, Conversation,
and the Development of Language.* New York: John Wiley & Sons,
in press. (Publication expected, early 1977.)

Shatz, Marilyn. On the development of communicative understand-
ing: An early strategy for interpreting and responding to messages.
In J. Glick & K. A. Clarke-Stewart (Eds.), *Studies in Social and
Cognitive Development.* New York: Gardner Press, forthcoming.

    In conversation with children 19–34 months old, the experi-
menter systematically produced declaratives, questions, and
imperatives. As in Shatz (1975a), children gave action responses
much more often than informing responses to questions,
though the questions could be interpreted as either directives or
requests for information. Preceding a question by non-
ambiguous requests for information increased the number of
informing responses, especially for the older children, but
action responses still predominated.

C Empirical Studies of Adult-Child Speech

The following articles report empirical studies of parental speech, child speech, or parent-child speech interaction. (See also Part III of Aaronson & Rieber, 1975.) Most involve coding speech samples for quantitative variables like MLU or qualitative variables like number of utterances of various functional types (e.g., question, report, request). An attempt is made in many of the studies to establish correlations between parental and child speech characteristics or between some of the speech characteristics and nonspeech variables such as child's age and parents' social class. Many of the investigators discuss theoretical implications of their findings. For attempts to determine what types of interaction facilitate language development, see also Section 10-B.

GENERAL

McCarthy, Dorothea. Some possible explanations of sex differences in language development and disorders. *Journal of Psychology,* 1953, *35,* 155–160.

McCarthy claims small but important differences favoring girls over boys in language development and suggests explanations, particularly based on sex differences in parent-child interaction.

*Ferguson, Charles A. Baby talk in six languages. *American Anthropologist,* 1964, *66,* 103–114. (Reprinted in Ferguson, 1971.)

Cross-cultural comparison of adult speech to infants ("baby talk"), based on already existing and new source material.

*Brown, Roger & Bellugi, Ursula. Three processes in the child's acquisition of syntax. *Harvard Educational Review* (Special issue on Language and Learning), 1964, *34,* 133–150. (Reprinted in Lenneberg, 1964b; in Brown, 1970a; and in Bar-Adon & Leopold, 1971.)

Discusses adult expansions of children's utterances, and children's reductions of adult utterances.

Language, Society and The Child. Working Paper No. 13, Language-Behavior Research Laboratory, University of California, Berkeley, 1968.

See the papers by Drach, Kobashigawa, and Pfuderer on parental speech.

Bynon, J. Berber nursery language. *Transactions of the Philological Society,* 1968, 107–161.

Detailed description and discussion of the language used by Berber adults and siblings to address infants up to the age of about 3 years, including phonological, syntactic, semantic, and communicative adjustments.

Rebelsky, Freda & Hanks, Cheryl. Fathers' verbal interaction with infants in the first three months of life. *Child Development,* 1971, *42,* 62–68.

Microphone recordings over a 24-hour period biweekly from 10 infants between 2 weeks and 3 months of age indicate that fathers spend little time vocalizing to their infants; several factors were associated with amount of interaction.

*Snow, Catherine E. Mothers' speech to children learning language. *Child Development,* 1972, *43,* 549–565.

College-graduate mothers of children ages 2;0–3;4 and 9;5–12;4 were paired and then were audiorecorded while speaking (1) to their own child, (2) to the other mother's child, and (3) with no child present but as though they were talking to children of these ages. Speech to 2-year-olds was simpler and more redundant than speech to 10-year-olds, but speech was modified less when the child was absent than when present. A nonmother control group for the 2-year-old absent condition modified speech almost as much as mothers.

*Friedlander, Bernard Z.; Jacobs, A. C.; Davis, B. B.; & Wetstone, H. S. Time sampling analysis of infants' natural language environments in the home. *Child Development,* 1972, *43,* 730–740.

The home language environment of two 12-month-old infants was recorded by means of a time-sampling tape recorder for 1 week. Analysis of all language input to the infants and of categories of parent-infant language interactions showed notable similarities and differences between the families. The link between infants' receptive and productive language is discussed.

Blount, Ben G. Parental speech and language acquisition: Some Luo and Samoan examples. *Anthropological Linguist,* 1972, *14*(4), 119–130.

Parental speech to three children ages 2½ years (two Luo, one Samoan) has a high proportion of interrogatives, a lower proportion of imperatives, and a very low proportion of declarative sentences, in contrast to adult-adult speech (70% declaratives in Luo). This may be because adult-to-child speech primarily controls behavior. Analysis of children's responses and comparisons to American studies are made.

Moerk, Ernst L. Principles of dyadic interaction in language learning. *Merrill-Palmer Quarterly of Behavior and Development*, 1972, *18*, 229-257.

Broen, Patricia A. The verbal environment of the language-learning child. *Monographs of the American Speech and Hearing Association*, 1972, *17*.

Phillips, J. R. Syntax and vocabulary of mothers' speech to young children: Age and sex comparisons. *Child Development*, 1973, *44*, 182-185.

Nelson, Katherine. Structure and strategy in learning to talk. *Monographs of the Society for Research in Child Development*, 1973a, *38* (1-2, Serial No. 149).

Individual differences in the styles of children beginning speech (referential vs. expressive) and mothers (accepting vs. rejecting) are described.

Clarke-Stewart, K. Alison. Interactions between mothers and their young children: Characteristics and consequences. *Monographs of the Society for Research in Child Development*, 1973 (6-7, Serial No. 153).

Over a 9-month period, 36 mothers and their first-born children (9 months old at the start) were observed interacting. Measures of infants' cognitive, linguistic, and social behavior were related to maternal care.

Farwell, Carol B. The language spoken to children. In *Papers and Reports on Child Language Development*, No. 5. Committee on Linguistics, Stanford University, April 1973, 31-62.

Farwell summarizes what is known about parental and older-child speech to young children, discusses issues (e.g., whether comprehension precedes production; whether aspects of parental speech influence child language development), and suggests directions for research. (See also the note by Weeks in the same volume.)

van der Geest, T.; Gerstel, R.; Appel, R.; & Tervoort, B. Th. *The Child's Communicative Competence.* The Hague: Mouton, 1973. (Also in paperback, New York: Humanities Press, 1973. Reviewed by J. Průcha in *Journal of Child Language,* 1976, *3,* 135–137.)

The speech of lower-class and middle-class boys was recorded in nursery playrooms. In addition to the usual quantitative measures (e.g., mean sentence length), a Syntactic Complexity Score was devised. The groups did not differ in their language structure, but middle-class boys were better at using the structures in various situations (i.e., they had superior communicative competence).

Ling, D. & Ling, A. H. Communication development in the first three years of life. *Journal of Speech and Hearing Research,* 1974, *17,* 146–159.

Time-sampled behavior of 48 children aged 1 month to 3 years was analyzed for eight modes of mother-child and child-mother communication in relation to child's age, sex, and position in the family.

Bates, Elizabeth. Acquisition of pragmatic competence. *Journal of Child Language,* 1974, *1,* 277–281.

See summary in Section 9-A.

Moerk, Ernst L. Changes in verbal child-mother interactions with increasing language skills of the child. *Journal of Psycholinguistic Research,* 1974, *3,* 101–116.

A one-hour recording of natural speech interaction was studied in detail for each of five children, ages 2;2–5;0. Both syntax and content of mothers' speech were more complex with increasing MLU. The use of situational constraints and the presence of individual differences were observed.

Holzman, M. The verbal environment provided by mothers for their very young children. *Merrill-Palmer Quarterly of Behavior and Development,* 1974, *20,* 31–42.

Giattino, Jill & Hogan, Jeanne G. Analysis of a father's speech to his language-learning child. *Journal of Speech and Hearing Disorders,* 1975, *40,* 524–537. (Comments, pp. 545–546.)

Daily speech samples of father-daughter interaction totaling 18 hours during the 2 weeks after the child's third birthday (MLU = 4.5 words) were analyzed with respect to the father's sentence types and imitation and expansion, which were rare.

Declaratives (35%) and interrogatives (34%) were the most frequent types.

Ferguson, Charles A. Baby talk as a simplified register. In *Papers and Reports on Child Language Development*, No. 9. Committee on Linguistics, Stanford University, April 1975.

Andersen, E. S. A selected bibliography on language input to young children. In *Papers and Reports on Child Language Development*, No. 9. Committee on Linguistics, Stanford University, April 1975b. (Expanded version published by Center for Applied Linguistics: ERIC/CLL Series on Languages & Linguistics, No. 22, 1975.)

Papers and Reports on Child Language Development, No. 10. Department of Linguistics, Stanford University, September 1975.
There are several papers on mother-child speech interaction and pragmatics in this volume, by E. O. Keenan; J. Gleason & S. Weintraub; M. Shatz; E. Newport, L. Gleitman, & H. Gleitman; T. Cross; and B. MacWhinney.

Cherry, Louise. The preschool teacher-child dyad: Sex differences in verbal interaction. *Child Development*, 1975a, *46*, 532–535.
The speech of four female preschool teachers in interactions with 16 female and 22 male preschoolers was recorded. Teachers verbally interacted more, verbally initiated more, and used more attention-marked utterances with boys; they used more verbal acknowledgments with girls.

Thorne, Barrie & Henley, Nancy. *Language and Sex: Difference and Dominance*. Rowley, Mass.: Newbury House Publishers, 1975.
Collection that includes two papers by Jacqueline Sachs and Louise Cherry, on sex differences in adult-child interaction. Also includes an annotated bibliography with a section on language acquisition (available separately as *She said, He said* by Henley & Thorne, published by KNOW, Inc., Box 86031, Pittsburgh, Pennsylvania 15221).

Cherry, Louise J. Sex differences in child speech: McCarthy revisited. Research Bulletin, ETS, Princeton, New Jersey, February 1975b.
Cherry criticizes several decades of studies claiming sex differences in language use or acquisition, suggesting that the dyad should be used as the unit of analysis.

Moerk, Ernst L. Verbal interactions between children and their mothers during the preschool years. *Developmental Psychology*, 1975b, *11*, 788–794.

Tape recordings with written contextual commentary were made for a 1-hour interaction between 20 child-mother pairs at ages 2–5 years. Analyses of utterance length and frequency counts of speech function (e.g., mother answers question, child imitates mother) suggest close mutual adaptation between mother and child.

Fraser, Colin & Roberts, Naomi. Mothers' speech to children of four different ages. *Journal of Psycholinguistic Research,* 1975, *4,* 9–16.

Speech of 32 middle-class mothers to their children aged 1½, 2½, 4, and 6 years was analyzed on five different measures (total words, MLU in words, number of words in disfluencies, grammatical complexity, and number of different words) in two different arranged tasks. For every measure but disfluency, task and age had significant effects; child's sex and birth order did not.

*Seitz, Sue & Stewart, Catherine. Imitations and expansions: Some developmental aspects of mother-child communications. *Developmental Psychology,* 1975, *11,* 763–768.

Eighteen child-mother pairs were videotaped in a 15-minute free-play interaction; the children were 18–26 months and 48–61 months old. Utterance length and frequency counts of types of children's and mothers' utterances were analyzed. Mothers' expansions and sentence length were positively correlated with children's imitations and children's frequency of responding to questions, respectively, for the younger age range only.

Wulbert, Margaret; Inglis, Susan; Kriegsmann, Elinor; & Mills, Barbara. Language delay and associated mother-child interaction. *Developmental Psychology,* 1975, *11,* 61–70.

There is less mother-child interaction for language-delayed children than for normal or Down's syndrome children.

Snow, Catherine E.; Arlman-Rupp, A.; Hassing, Y.; Jobse, J.; Joosten, J.; & Vorster, J. Mother's speech in three social classes. *Journal of Psycholinguistic Research,* 1976, *5,* 1–20.

Speech of Dutch mothers to their 2-year-olds showed the same characteristics of simplicity and redundancy found in other languages. In a free-play situation (but not in a book-reading situation), academic and white-collar mothers produced more expansions and substantive deixis, and fewer imperatives and modal verbs, than working-class mothers.

Cherry, Louise & Lewis, Michael. Mothers and two-year-olds: A study of sex-differentiated aspects of verbal interaction. *Developmental Psychology,* 1976, *12,* 278–282.

Speech between 12 mothers and their 2-year-olds was taped in free-play interactions. Mothers of females talked more, asked more questions, repeated child utterances more often, and used longer utterances than mothers of males, who ($p < .07$) used more directives. Differences between male and female children were marginal or nonsignificant.

Moerk, Ernst L. Processes of language teaching and training in the interactions of mother-child dyads. *Child Development,* 1976, *47,* 1064–1078.

Recordings of a 1-hour verbal interaction between each of 20 mothers and her child, ages 1.9–5.0 years, indicate that mothers actively teach syntax, morphology, and other aspects of language. The dyad is described as a self-regulating, relatively closed system with feedback cycles and calibration processes. It is suggested that aspects of the interaction affect the learning process.

Scollon, Ronald. *Conversations with a One-year-old: A Case Study of the Developmental Foundation of Syntax.* Honolulu: University of Hawaii Press, 1976.

Study of one child's English between ages 1 and 2 years. Includes consideration of phonology, speech acts, conversation, and the role of repetition and imitation.

*Bloom, Lois; Rocissano, Lorraine; & Hood, Lois. Adult-child discourse: Developmental interaction between information processing and linguistic knowledge. *Cognitive Psychology,* 1976, *8,* 521–552.

Longitudinal data from four children approximately 21–36 months of age were used to analyze discourse interaction with adults. The analysis is in terms of utterance content and linguistic and contextual relations. Distinctions include child utterances adjacent vs. nonadjacent to an adult utterance and, if adjacent, contingent vs. noncontingent. Contingent speech increased over time. The effects of differential information processing requirements are discussed.

Reichle, Joe Ernest; Longhurst, Thomas M.; & Stepanich, Lyanne. Verbal interaction in mother-child dyads. *Developmental Psychology,* 1976, *12,* 273–277.

Analysis of tape recordings of play interactions of mothers with their children indicates that mothers of 2-year-olds (23–35 months) used fewer complex expatiations and modeled questions than mothers of children 35–37 months old. Mothers' expansions and direct imitation did not differ by age, but 2-year-olds produced more imitations with reductions.

Cohen, Sarale E. & Beckwith, Leila. Maternal language in infancy. *Developmental Psychology,* 1976, *12,* 371–372.

Naturalistic time-sampled observations of mothers' speech to preterm infants at 1, 3, and 8 months past the expected delivery date indicate that maternal language varies with the infant's age and ordinal position and the mother's education. Relations between maternal speech at 1 month and later were also analyzed.

Buium, Nissan. Interrogative types in parental speech to language-learning children: A linguistic universal? *Journal of Psycholinguistic Research,* 1976, *5,* 135–142.

Four American and four Israeli mothers produced different wh-question types in similar relative frequency to their 24-month-old children; this may be related to the children's concept development. Israeli mothers produced more wh-questions than yes/no questions.

Weist, Richard M. & Kruppe, Betty. Parent and sibling comprehension of children's speech. *Journal of Psycholinguistic Research,* 1977, *6,* 49–58.

Ten utterances (mean length = 2.2–7.0) were edited from videotapes of each of 12 children ages 25–42 months. Parents and siblings comprehended the utterances better than did control subjects.

Garnica, Olga K. Nonverbal concomitants of language input to children: Clues to meaning. In *Working Papers in Linguistics,* No. 22, Ohio State University, 1977.

The volume contains Garnica's Stanford University doctoral dissertation, *Some Prosodic Characteristics of Speech to Young Children.* For more information see Section 12-A.

*Ferguson, Charles A. & Snow, Catherine E. (Eds.). *Talking to Children.* London: Cambridge University Press, in press.

Collection of articles.

Newport, Elissa; Gleitman, Henry; & Gleitman, Lila. Mother, I'd rather do it myself: Some effects and non-effects of motherese. In Ferguson & Snow, in press.

Reports evidence that indices of universal aspects of language (e.g., number of noun phrases per utterance) are not affected by parental speech characteristics, but that language-specific structures (e.g., auxiliary elements) are affected.

QUESTIONS AS A COMMUNICATIVE DEVICE

The remaining articles focus on the development of questions as a communicative device. For studies of the acquisition of the syntax of questions, see Section 3-B. Some linguistic treatments are listed first as background.

Background Publications: Linguistics

Hudson, Richard A. The meaning of questions. *Language,* 1975, *51,* 1–31.

Yes/no and tag questions have a very small number of syntactic and semantic categories but a virtually unlimited number of illocutionary forces.

Kearsley, Greg P. Questions and question asking in verbal discourse: A cross-disciplinary review. *Journal of Psycholinguistic Research,* 1976, *5,* 355–375.

The review covers linguistic, psychological, and social aspects of questions; classification systems; empirical research; and discourse contexts.

Belnap, Nuel D., Jr. & Steel, Thomas B., Jr. *The Logic of Questions and Answers.* New Haven, Conn.: Yale University Press, 1976.

Baumert, M. The classification of question-answer structures in English. *Journal of Pragmatics,* in press. (Publication expected, 1977, 1 (1).)

Child Development Studies

The developmental studies follow. See also Shatz (1975a; forthcoming) in Section 11-B.

*Ervin-Tripp, Susan. Discourse agreement: How children answer questions. In Hayes, 1970.

Based on longitudinal language samples (naturalistic and constrained), Ervin-Tripp presents an order of development for features marking of wh-question words. Data on each word are discussed separately in terms of syntax, semantics, and communicative interaction.

Holzman, M. The use of interrogative forms in the verbal interaction of three mothers and their children. *Journal of Psycholinguistic Research,* 1972, *1,* 311–336.

Twelve samples of 100 utterances were obtained for the mothers of Adam, Eve, and Sarah—two samples for each mother for child at MLU = 2 and at MLU = 4. Interrogatives comprised 15–33% of the samples. All mothers (and the children at MLU = 3) sometimes used the interrogative to make suggestions and reports (indirect speech acts).

Ervin-Tripp, Susan. The comprehension and production of requests by children. In *Papers and Reports on Child Language Development,* No. 8. Committee on Linguistics, Stanford University, 1974b, 188–196.

Ervin-Tripp discusses children's increasingly sophisticated linguistic forms for the directive speech function, particularly focusing on question forms. She cites examples from English and Turkish.

Savić, Svenka. Aspects of adult-child communication: The problem of question acquisition. *Journal of Child Language,* 1975, *2,* 251–260.

Question acquisition was observed in a pair of twins between the ages of 1;1 and 3;0. Until the twins were about 27 months, questions were the most frequent type of adult utterance to the twins. Examination of adult and child frequencies for specific question forms suggests that child-adult communication is an interaction, with mutual influence occurring.

Endsley, Richard C. & Clarey, Susan A. Answering young children's questions as a determinant of their subsequent question-answering behavior. *Developmental Psychology,* 1975, *11,* 863.

Kindergartners in 6-minute sessions designed to elicit information-seeking behavior asked 20.2 questions per session when reinforced by informative replies, but only 12.6 questions when the adult consistently responded, "I don't know."

Mischler, Elliot G. Studies in dialogue and discourse: II. Types of discourse initiated by and sustained through questioning. *Journal of Psycholinguistic Research,* 1975, *4,* 99–121.

Three discourse types are defined and applied to conversations in first-grade classrooms. When adults initiate a conversation with a question, they retain control by further questioning (chaining); when children do so, the adult regains control by responding with a question (arching). Child-to-child speech is more balanced.

Crosby, Faye. Early discourse agreement. *Journal of Child Language,* 1976, *3,* 125–126.

A 17½-month-old boy at the single-word speech stage, was recorded during a 10-day period. His responses were different for yes/no and wh-questions, and "no" seemed primarily to indicate rejection.

D Communicative Competence and the Function of Language for Children

The references in this section approach three related issues:
1. *What function does speech serve for the developing child?*
2. *Do children speak* **egocentrically***?*
3. *How do children learn to give adequate descriptions of objects and events?*

The first question emphasizes **private speech** *(external speech for oneself); the second question emphasizes* **interpersonal** *or* **social speech** *(speech for communication to others); and the third question emphasizes* **referential speech** *(speech that describes an object or event; when this is done for the benefit of another person, it is also a specific type of interpersonal speech called* **referential communication***).*

FUNCTION OF SPEECH FOR CHILDREN

The first question, that of speech function, has been important in Russian psychology, but there have also been some non-Russian reports. Only a few of the many publications on this topic are listed.

Luria, Alexander R. The role of language in the formation of temporary connections. In B. Simon (Ed.), *Psychology in the Soviet Union*. London: Routledge & Kegan Paul, 1957. (Originally published in Russian, 1955.)

> Luria discusses the progression from external to internal regulative speech in children and experiments on the role of speech in establishing connections such as "Press for a short signal, do not press for a long one."

Luria, Alexander R. *The Role of Speech in the Regulation of Normal and Abnormal Behavior.* (J. Tizard, Ed.) New York: Pergamon Press, 1961. (Excerpts reprinted in Bar-Adon & Leopold, 1971. Originally published in Russian, 1956.)

> Luria discusses experiments on the regulative function of speech and his theoretical interpretations.

Luria, Alexander R. The directive function of speech in development and dissolution. *Word,* 1959, *15,* 341–352; 453–464; (Reprinted in Oldfield & Marshall, 1968.)

Jarvis, P. E. Verbal control of sensory-motor performance: A test of Luria's hypothesis. *Human Development*, 1968, *11*, 172–183.

Children in nursery school through first grade were asked to push a button for a blue light and refrain from pushing for a yellow light. Three different instructions were used for each child at different times: say "push" and push for blue light; say "don't push" and don't push for yellow light; no verbalization requested. The instructions had no significant effect.

Wozniak, R. H. Verbal regulation of motor behavior—Soviet research and non-Soviet replications. *Human Development*, 1972, *15*, 13–57.

Wozniak sympathetically discusses Luria's theory of verbal regulation of action, especially his notion of verbal inhibition of perseveration. Non-Soviet failures to replicate the associated Soviet experimental work are attributed to inappropriate methodology and to misunderstanding of assumptions. There is sufficient evidence for the general outlines of the Soviet approach, but more research on Luria's inhibition notion is needed.

Bronckart, J.-P. The regulating role of speech: A cognitivist approach. *Human Development*, 1973, *16*, 417–439.

Bronckart criticizes Luria (and Wozniak's commentary on Luria), preferring the perspectives of Piagetian cognitive theory (in which cognition and speech are separate) and modern psycholinguistics (in which syntactic complexity is considered). Experiments with silent control conditions do not support Luria's theory. Results supporting his hypothesis of verbal inhibition can be explained in terms of competition between vocal and manual motor systems.

van Duyne, H. John & Scanlan, David. Gender differences in the development of the regulatory function of language. *The Journal of Genetic Psychology*, 1976, *128*, 17–26.

Boys vs. girls in the age range 3–5 years showed differences in the integration of functional systems when performing a task requiring verbal regulatory control of nonverbal behavior.

Rondal, Jean A. Investigation of the regulatory power of the impulsive and meaningful aspects of speech. *Genetic Psychology Monographs*, 1976, *94*, 3–33.

Experiments with children 3–8 years old, 10–13 years old, and adults replicated the basic findings reported in Luria (1956/61), but did not confirm predictions derived from Luria's hypothesis about the regulatory function of speech in its meaningful (rather than impulsive or rhythmic) aspect.

Bain, Bruce. Verbal regulation of cognitive processes: A replication of Luria's procedures with bilingual and unilingual infants. *Child Development*, 1976, *47*, 543–546.

COMMUNICATIVE EGOCENTRISM

The following references explore the second question, that of com-municative egocentrism. They fall into two groups: older publications in which Piaget's and Vygotsky's contrasting notions of egocentric speech are debated, and newer publications (beginning with Flavell, et al.) in which Piaget's notion is supported or challenged in experi-mental studies. The debate can be partly resolved by noting that Vygotsky's egocentric speech is private speech used to regulate behavior, whereas Piaget's egocentric speech is speech in the presence of others that is not adequately social (e.g., the child does not take into account the listener's perspective and limitations). Some of the references (Vygotsky; Kohlberg through Beaudichon) would therefore have been listed with the above papers on the regulative function of speech were it not for the debate.

Note that communicative egocentrism is only one manifestation of a more general childhood egocentrism in Piaget's theory; preopera-tional children are also limited by their own perspective in their systems of time and space, and in their use of words for relations (e.g., left/right, brother/sister), causation (e.g., because), and deixis (a recent suggestion, e.g., come/go). See Sections 8 and 9 for experi-ments on these other manifestations of egocentrism.

The Piaget/Vygotsky Debate

*Piaget, Jean. The Language and Thought of the Child. London: Routledge & Kegan Paul, 1926. (Also in paperback, New York: World Publishing, 1955. Originally published in French, 1923.)

   In one of his earliest books, Piaget introduces the notion of communicative egocentrism. He classifies types of egocentric speech observed in child-to-child speech at ages 4–7; analyzes egocentrism in the speech of children at ages 6–8 retelling stories or explaining how a device works; discusses verbal syn-cretism in children at ages 9–11; and analyzes the questions asked by a 6-year-old.

*Vygotsky, L. S. *Thought and Language.* Cambridge, Mass.: The MIT Press, 1962. (Also in paperback. Originally published in Russian, 1934.)

The late Russian psychologist criticizes Piaget's view that children progress from presocial to egocentric to socialized speech. Rather, speech is social from the beginning, but children go through a stage of externalized thinking-out-loud prior to internalizing speech as "inner speech." In the last two stages speech has a directive function.

Piaget, Jean. Comments on Vygotsky's critical remarks concerning "The Language and Thought of the Child" and "Judgment and Reasoning in the Child." Cambridge, Mass.: The MIT Press, 1962.

This is one of the best sources on Piaget's later views on egocentrism. It was distributed as an insert in the cloth edition of Vygotsky (1962).

*Kohlberg, Lawrence; Yaeger, Judy; & Hjertholm, Else. Private speech: Four studies and a review of theories. *Child Development,* 1968, *39,* 691–736.

The views of Piaget, Vygotsky, G. H. Mead, and Flavell are examined and related to experimental data. Mental age and task difficulty are primary determinants of amount of private speech (not sex, chronological age, etc.). Vygotsky's hypothesis of a curvilinear course of development (due to the role of private speech in the transition between outer speech and thought) is supported over Piaget's view of monotonic decline. Finally, seven types of private speech are defined; consistent with Mead's theory, they form a developmental hierarchy.

Conrad, R. The chronology of the development of covert speech in children. *Developmental Psychology,* 1971, *5,* 398–405.

Conrad argues that private speech and inner speech develop independently during the preschool years; when private speech disappears at school age, inner speech is already well established.

Deutsch, Francine & Stein, Aletha H. The effects of personal responsibility and task interruption on the private speech of preschoolers. *Human Development,* 1972, *15,* 310–324.

Children at ages 4;0–5;2 were asked to perform a cognitive task under one of three conditions. Quantity and quality of private speech were higher in the personal-failure condition than the task interruption or success conditions, and for children with high mental age.

Beaudichon, Janine. Nature and instrumental function of private speech in problem solving situations. *Merrill-Palmer Quarterly of Behavior and Development,* 1973, *19,* 117–135.

Children at ages 5;6–6;8 showed a positive correlation between amount of "immediate regulatory" self-guiding speech and task performance for complex problems, but not for simple ones. Total number of utterances produced was not related to performance level and decreased with age for complex problems.

Greene, Judith. *Thinking and Language.* London: Methuen, 1975. (Also in paperback.)

Chapter 5 includes a discussion of Piaget's and Vygotsky's views.

General

The articles not involved in the Piaget-Vygotsky debate follow.

*Flavell, J. H.; Botkin, P. T.; Fry, C. L.; Wright, J. W.; & Jarvis, P. E. *The Development of Role-taking and Communication Skills in Children.* New York: John Wiley & Sons, 1968.

A large number of experiments on egocentrism, including communicative egocentrism, are reported.

Huxley, Renira. The development of the correct use of subject personal pronouns in two children. In G. B. Flores d'Arcais & W. J. M. Levelt, 1970.

Weekly speech samples for two children from 2;3 to about 4 years provide data on the appearance of personal pronouns. Sometimes "me" was used where "I" was correct, but the reverse error did not occur, nor did a confusion of "I" and "you." A quantitative summary and an appendix of sample utterances are supplied. (For a different explanation, see Tanz, 1974.)

Mueller, E. The maintenance of verbal exchanges between young children. *Child Development,* 1972, *43,* 930–938.

Contrary to the claim that preschoolers' speech is egocentric, in videotapes of 24 pairs of children ages 3½–5½ covering 20–60 minutes of free play, the children almost always displayed social interest and gave replies, especially when more than one of several causal indicators was present (e.g., technical quality of message, visual attention of listener at beginning).

Garvey, Catherine & Hogan, Robert. Social speech and social interaction: Egocentrism revisited. *Child Development,* 1973, *44,* 562–568.

Eighteen dyads of children, ages 3½–5, were videotaped in 15-minute play sessions. There was a high level of mutual responsiveness in speech and behavior.

*Gleason, Jean Berko. Code switching in children's language. In Moore, 1973.

Analysis of conversations in five families indicates that children talk differently to different people (switch codes), as do their parents.

*Shatz, Marilyn & Gelman, Rochelle. The development of communication skills: Modifications in the speech of young children as a function of listener. *Monographs of the Society for Research in Child Development,* 1973, *38,* (5, Serial No. 152).

Four-year-olds performed poorly on standard tests of communicative egocentrism (Glucksberg et al., 1966) and spatial perspective, but adjusted their speech so that it was simpler when talking to 2-year-olds than to other 4-year-olds or adults.

Rubin, Kenneth H. Egocentrism in childhood: A unitary construct? *Child Development,* 1973, *44,* 102–110.

Children in grades kindergarten, two, four, and six were given tests of communicative, cognitive (private speech), role-taking and spatial egocentrism, and of conservation. Factor analysis revealed a "decentration" factor for all of the tasks except cognitive egocentrism.

*Maratsos, Michael P. Preschool children's use of definite and indefinite articles. *Child Development,* 1974d, *45,* 446–455.

Children 3–4 years old were tested for their understanding of definite and indefinite articles in two kinds of story-telling tasks. The children could distinguish between specific and non-specific reference, but only a subgroup of 4-year-olds could take into account the referential knowledge of the listener.

Deutsch, F. Observational and sociometric measures of peer popularity and their relationship to egocentric communication in female preschoolers. *Developmental Psychology,* 1974, *10,* 745–747.

*Schachter, Frances F.; Kirshner, Kathryn; Klips, Bonnie; Friedricks,

Martha; & Sanders, Karin. Everyday preschool interpersonal speech usage: Methodological, developmental, and sociolinguistic studies. With commentary by Courtney B. Cazden and Lois Bloom. *Monographs of the Society for Research in Child Development,* 1974, *39* (3, Serial No. 156).

Spontaneous speech at preschool centers was recorded for a longitudinal sample of four and a cross-sectional sample of 170 children ages 2–5. Before age 3, most speech is egocentric, focusing on desires, reporting, and naming. After age 3 sociable speech functions increase, and by ages $4\frac{1}{2}$–$5\frac{1}{2}$ speech adapted to the listener's needs emerges. Advantaged white and black children of above-average IQ score higher in the last category than do lower-IQ disadvantaged black children.

Keenan, Elinor O. Conversational competence in children. *Journal of Child Language,* 1974, *1,* 163–183.

Recordings of early morning conversations between twin boys at about 3 years indicate that they can sustain a coherent conversation over a number of turns. Contrary to Piaget (1923/26), they generally attend to one another's utterances. A partial formalization of young children's discourse procedure is presented.

Keenan, Elinor & Klein, Ewan. Coherency in children's discourse. *Journal of Psycholinguistic Research,* 1975, *4,* 365–380.

Recordings of the same boys as in the preceding reference, at ages 2;9–3;9, are analyzed with respect to a number of discourse categories involving attention to context. Conversational coherence is maintained, often by focusing on the phonological shape of the other's last utterance and modifying it (mutual sound play). Again, Piaget (1923/26) is not supported.

Garvey, Catherine. Requests and responses in children's speech. *Journal of Child Language,* 1975, *2,* 41–63.

An aspect of communicative competence was studied in the spontaneous speech of 36 children ages 3;6–5;7, observed in pairs. Evidence from the contexts of direct requests (e.g., "Give me the hammer") indicated that speaker and addressee shared an understanding of the interpersonal meaning factors in the communication. These factors were also the basis for indirect requests.

Sachs, Jacqueline & Devin, Judith. Young children's use of age-appropriate speech styles in social interaction and role-playing. *Journal of Child Language,* 1976, *3,* 81–98.

Individual audio recordings were made for four children ages 3;9–5;5 talking to different listeners and role-playing a baby. Quantitative (e.g., MLU) and functional (e.g., proportion of imperatives) measures varied for speech to mother, peer, baby, and baby doll, usually in predicted directions. The children had some success at role playing, but were inconsistent.

Maratsos, Michael P. *The Use of Definite and Indefinite Reference in Young Children.* London: Cambridge University Press, 1976a.

Maratsos reports the results of a variety of tasks performed by 40 three- and four-year-old children, showing that they used an abstract semantic distinction (specific vs. nonspecific reference) in their use of *a* and *the.* He also discusses egocentricity in the use of this distinction and methodological problems related to task differences.

Mossler, Daniel G.; Marvin, Robert S.; & Greenberg, Mark T. Conceptual perspective taking in 2- to 6-year-old children. *Developmental Psychology,* 1976, *12,* 85–86.

By age 4, more than 50% of children can make simple judgments of what another person knows or does not know about an ongoing event.

Rubin, Kenneth H. Social interaction and communicative egocentrism in preschoolers. *The Journal of Genetic Psychology,* 1976, *129,* 121–124.

Preschoolers (mean age, 56 months) showed a negative correlation between egocentric speech and frequency of peer interaction in a naturalistic setting.

Warden, David A. The influence of context on children's use of identifying expressions and references. *British Journal of Psychology,* 1976, *67,* 101–112.

Three experiments on children's ability to use indefinite (*a*) and definite (*the*) articles indicate that even 3-year-olds correctly use *the* for the second mention of a referent, but correct use of *a* (in a situation where the listener would not have knowledge of a referent) is still developing at age 9 (82% correct).

Welkowitz, Joan; Cariffe, Gerald; & Feldstein, Stanley. Conversational congruence as a criterion of socialization in children. *Child Development,* 1976, *47,* 269–272.

Congruence in the duration of speech pauses in children's con-

versations was investigated as an alternative measure of socio-
centric (vs. egocentric) speech for children ages 5.4–6.1 and
6.4–7.2 years.

Brown, Ann L. The construction of temporal succession by preopera-
tional children. In A. D. Pick, Vol. 10, 1976.
   Analysis of children's recall of stories and series of items, and
   other tasks involving temporal succession, in a Piagetian
   framework.

Shatz, Marilyn & Gelman, Rochelle. Beyond syntax: The influence of
conversational constraints on speech modifications. In Ferguson &
Snow, in press.
   A reanalysis of the data reported in Shatz & Gelman (1973)
   indicates that the few syntactically complex constructions used
   by 4-year-olds talking to 2-year-olds were simple semantically
   or functionally. Simplification is functional, with the result that
   most but not all utterances are syntactically simple as well. See
   Gelman & Shatz (in press), Section 11-B, for a similar finding
   with adult speakers.

Journal of Communication. Special issue on children's communication skills, in press. (Publication expected, April 1977.)

REFERENTIAL SPEECH

*The following references explore the third question, that of referential
speech. All of the tasks are communicative: the child must describe an
object or form to another person. Some of the researchers relate their
results to Piaget's notion of egocentric speech (see above). There are
few recent experimental studies of adult referential speech; see Osgood
(1971), below, and Olson (1970). There are also some adult studies primarily conceived as tests of the **Whorfian hypothesis** of linguistic
relativity; see Lenneberg (1967b, Chapter 8) and Greene (1972, selections 4 and 13).*

*Glucksberg, Sam; Krauss, Robert M.; & Weisberg, Robert.
Referential communication in nursery school children: Method and
some preliminary findings. *Journal of Experimental Child
Psychology,* 1966, *3,* 333–342.
   This paper reports a method for studying referential communication which has been influential. A speaker must communicate to a listener behind a screen a stacking order for blocks

marked with forms. Children at 33–49 months could not perform the task; children at 46–63 months could perform with familiar forms but not with novel forms. The idiosyncratic descriptions given can be viewed as instances of egocentrism.

Kaplan, Eleanor & Yonas, Patricia. Communication requirements and children's production of relational words. *Journal of Experimental Child Psychology,* 1967, *5,* 142–151.

An attempt was made to elicit spatial prepositions in preschoolers' descriptions of line drawings, using four different questions. A three-alternative forced-choice task and variations on the production task were also used. Two factors affected performance: (1) verbal information about the situational demands and the communicative adequacy of responses, and (2) nonverbal information specified by the stimulus situation.

Krauss, Robert M. & Glucksberg, Sam. The development of communication: Competence as a function of age. *Child Development,* 1969, *40,* 255–266.

Pairs of children in kindergarten, first, third, and fifth grades performed the task described in the preceding reference, with novel forms. Children began at about the same level of communication accuracy, but kindergarteners did not improve, while older children did. Accuracy of adults in matching the children's labels to the forms was a positive function of the child's age.

Pascual-Leone, Juan & Smith, June. The encoding and decoding of symbols by children: A new experimental paradigm and a Neo-Piagetian model. *Journal of Experimental Child Psychology,* 1969, *8,* 328–355.

Predictions based on Piaget's theory (but not those based on Bruner's theory) predict children's performance in two referential communication tasks using words or gestures. The paper has a theoretical and integrative focus.

Osgood, Charles E. Where do sentences come from? In Steinberg & Jakobovits, 1971.

Osgood discusses results of his "simply describing" task. For example, characteristics of preceding events affect choice of determiners, pronouns, and adjectives in descriptions of a just-completed event.

Peterson, Carole L.; Danner, Fred W.; & Flavell, John H. Developmental changes in children's response to three indications of communicative failure. *Child Development,* 1972, *43,* 1463–1468.

When explicitly requested to rephrase their message, both 4- and 7-year-olds did so; when implicitly requested, only 7-year-olds did so; when facial gesture of noncomprehension was used as a request, neither age responded.

Martin, J. E. & Molfese, Dennis L. Preferred adjective ordering in very young children. *Journal of Verbal Learning and Verbal Behavior,* 1972, *11,* 287–292.

Nursery school children imitated sentences with normal and inverted adjective orders; younger children (mean age, 3;5) made fewer errors than older children (mean age, 4;6), but there was no significant difference between orders. In a production task, the children exhibited order preferences that did not exactly correspond to those of older children and adults.

Maratsos, Michael P. Nonegocentric communication abilities in preschool children. *Child Development,* 1973c, *44,* 697–700.

Children ages 3–5 years performed a simple referential communication task. Those communicating to an apparently blind experimenter were more explicit verbally than those communicating to an experimenter who could see.

Houston, Susan H. Syntactic complexity and information transmission in first-graders: A cross-cultural study. *Journal of Psycholinguistic Research,* 1973, *2,* 99–114.

First-graders performed a task based on Piaget (1923/26). The experimenter told a story to one child, who told it to a second child, who told it to the experimenter. Results were analyzed in terms of childhood syncretism and faulty mastery of difficult syntactic constructions. Differences in performance relating to race and social class are discussed.

Schwenk, Mary Ann & Danks, Joseph H. A developmental study of the pragmatic communication rule for prenominal adjective ordering. *Memory and Cognition,* 1974, *2,* 149–152.

Subjects in first, fourth, and eighth grades, and college indicated preference for normal or inverted adjective orders in picture descriptions. Preference for normal order first appeared with the fourth graders. When a color adjective was required for discriminating the referent from a nonreferent, college students increased their preference for the inverted order, indicating a separation of the linguistic rule from its utilization in communication.

Bearison, David J. & Cassel, Thomas Z. Cognitive decentration and social codes: Communicative effectiveness in young children from differing family contexts. *Developmental Psychology,* 1975, *11,* 29–36.

On five measures of form and content of messages to sighted and blindfolded listeners, children from families with a person-oriented social code accommodated to the listener's perspective better than those from position-oriented families.

*Glucksberg, Sam; Krauss, Robert M.; & Higgins, E. Tory. The development of referential communication skills. In F. D. Horowitz (Ed.), *Review of Child Development Research,* Vol. 4. Chicago: The University of Chicago Press, 1975.

The authors provide a theoretical framework and literature review on communicative speech, including a number of their own studies.

Ford, William & Olson, David. The elaboration of the noun phrase in children's description of objects. *Journal of Experimental Child Psychology,* 1975, *19,* 371–382.

Children ages 4–7 years were required to describe an object relative to alternatives differing on one to five dimensions. They did not give invariant labels, but their descriptions tended to encode the attributes varied in the experiment as a whole rather than those critical on a particular trial. Older children gave longer, more informative descriptions than younger children when more than three adjectives were required.

Asher, Steven R. Children's ability to appraise their own and another person's communication performance. *Developmental Psychology,* 1976, *12,* 24–32.

In a communication task with second, fourth, and sixth graders, younger children were less accurate appraisers of their own and others' effectiveness as well as being less effective. They appeared to base their appraisal on the degree of association between message and referent rather than the relative association of message to referent and nonreferent.

Asher, Steven R. & Oden, Sherri L. Children's failure to communicate: An assessment of comparison and egocentrism explanations. *Developmental Psychology,* 1976, *12,* 132–139.

Poor communicators in third and fifth grades were not as able to identify referents from their own messages as were good communicators.

Robinson, E. J. & Robinson, W. P. The young child's understanding of communication. *Developmental Psychology,* 1976, *12,* 328–333.
Children ages 5½–8 years were asked to judge fault for communication failure. Developmental trends were to blame the listener (youngest subjects), the experimenter, and finally the speaker (some of the oldest children).

Meissner, Judith A. & Apthorp, Helen. Nonegocentrism and communication mode switching in black preschool children. *Developmental Psychology,* 1976, *12,* 245–249.
In a task requiring communication of an object choice, the majority of 4- and 5-year-old black children responded appropriately on blindfolded and nonblindfolded experimenter trials.

Garmiza, Carol & Anisfeld, Moshe. Factors reducing the efficiency of referent-communication in children. *Merrill-Palmer Quarterly of Behavior and Development,* 1976, *22,* 125–136.
First and second graders participated in a procedure similar to that of Krauss & Glucksberg (1969) using pairs of pictures differing on one dimension. Results suggest that children often fail to adjust to a listener's perspective because it requires shifting away from an existing perspective, not because it is a new perspective or a different person's perspective. The lack of concrete contextual support for a listener's perspective also is a source of difficulty.

Whitehurst, Grover J. The development of communication: Changes with age and modeling. *Child Development,* 1976, *47,* 473–482.
Children in kindergarten, first, second, and fourth grades described objects varying in number of contrasting vs. same attributes. Descriptions increased in redundancy and in focus on contrasting attributes with age. In a second experiment, first-graders imitated aspects of a modeled style, but used a principle of least effort in their analysis of stimulus arrays.

Krauss, Robert M. & Glucksberg, Sam. Social and nonsocial speech. *Scientific American,* 1977, *236*(2), 100–105.

SOCIOLINGUISTIC STUDIES

Higgins, E. Tory. Social class differences in verbal communicative accuracy: A question of "which question?" *Psychological Bulletin,* 1976, *83,* 695–714.

> Previous studies of children and adults were examined "to determine which communication task and social class sample variables increase the likelihood of finding social class differences in communicative accuracy." A number of conclusions were drawn on the issues in this literature.

Edelsky, Carole. The acquisition of communicative competence: Recognition of linguistic correlates of sex roles. *Merrill-Palmer Quarterly of Behavior and Development,* 1976, *22,* 47–59.

> Children in first, third, and sixth grades, and adults, were asked to judge the likely sex of the speaker of statements containing sex-typed phrases such as "oh dear" (female) and "damn it" (male). Some subjects were also interviewed. There was gradual development of this aspect of sociolinguistic competence.

Gay, Judy & Tweney, Ryan D. Comprehension and production of standard and black English by lower-class black children. *Developmental Psychology,* 1976, *12,* 262–268.

> Results of black kindergarteners, third and sixth graders on a modification of the Fraser, Bellugi, & Brown (1963) tasks and a picture-description task suggest that they "code switch." Also, semantic constraints seemed to affect the results of the younger children.

James, Linda B. Black children's perceptions of Black English. *Journal of Psycholinguistic Research,* 1976, *5,* 377–387.

> Urban black first graders performed a discrimination task on pairs of 20-second speech excerpts. Accuracy on both style (suprasegmental characteristics) and content (syntax and lexicon) contrasts was related to their language variety preference and register maintenance.

Part V
PHONOLOGY
AND
ORTHOGRAPHY

Section 12
PHONOLOGICAL DEVELOPMENT AND SPEECH PERCEPTION

There is currently no widely accepted, integrated theory of speech perception or production, but some interesting theoretical principles and research paradigms have assured lively discussion in this area. It is difficult to understand most of this literature without some basic background in phonetics and phonology. A simplified overview is given here.

*At the most detailed level, speech sounds can be described acoustically. A sound spectrogram shows the amount of energy at each sound frequency over time. In speech sounds, the energy tends to be concentrated in certain frequency regions called **formants**. Rapid frequency changes at the beginning or end of syllables (**formant transitions**) are often important for the identification of consonants. At the next level, different acoustic patterns can be grouped according to shared characteristics. For example, voiced initial consonants tend to have strong formant transitions for both the first and second formant; the first formant loses its transition for unvoiced initial consonants (plus some additional differences). Acoustically this dimension is called **voice onset time (VOT)**.*

*These acoustic characteristics reflect the articulatory differences in the production of these sounds (for voicing, whether there is a delay in vocal cord vibration relative to opening the vocal tract). Another distinction is **place of articulation**, based on where the vocal tract constricts, and reflected in the direction of the first and second formant transitions. In a linguistic analysis, characteristics such as voicing and place of articulation are the basis for **features**. At the phonetic level, a segment called a **phone** is specified by a particular combination of these features. The p in pin is represented [p^h] and includes the features unvoiced, bilabial (place of articulation: the two lips), and aspirated. The "h" superscript represents the aspiration feature (corresponding to a puff of air), which is absent from the phone [p], as in spin.*

285

Finally, there is a phonological level of analysis in which the corresponding segments are **phonemes,** *which we may think of loosely as corresponding to the vowels and consonants of the written language. They are defined by the* **distinctive features,** *which are features that, if changed, result in a different word (e.g., a voicing change distinguishes* pin *from* bin*). One phoneme may be exemplified by different phones (its* **allophones***). For example, [pʰ] and [p] are allophones of the phoneme /p/, since aspiration is not a distinctive feature of English. Two speech signals contrasting only in aspiration would always exemplify the same word in English; a pair contrasting only on one distinctive feature would exemplify two different words with different meanings (a* **minimal pair***).*

Chomsky & Halle's (1968) **generative phonology** *is concerned with abstract phonemic (phonological) representations of morphemes and words, including the distinctive features. It also specifies* **phonological rules** *that operate on the abstract representations to generate phonetic representations. These rules account for various influences that adjacent phonemes have on one another (e.g., whether /p/ is aspirated depends on its context). Some phonological theories distinguish between morphophonemic and phonemic rules, with the morphophonemic rules doing some of the work that Chomsky & Halle accomplish by having very abstract phonemic representations. Hence, their phonemes are less abstract than those of Chomsky & Halle, but more abstract than phones. Finally,* **suprasegmental phonology** *deals with prosodic characteristics of speech, e.g., stress, intonation, and rhythm.*

This leads us to a distinction between prelinguistic and linguistic periods of infant development. The prelinguistic period, earlier than about 1 year, is marked by various kinds of vocalization. The most advanced form is babbling, which can be described phonetically. The linguistic period is marked by the onset of words and is often analyzed phonologically. However, there is a great deal of variation among researchers. Some insist on an absolute discontinuity between prelinguistic and linguistic development (e.g., Jakobson); others do phonetic analyses and are uninterested in whether the sounds are used in words (e.g., Irwin). The distinction between phone and phoneme is often not honored and varies with the phonological theory. I have retained the authors' own terminology in my annotations.

Phonological theory is also important in the area of speech perception, since the major interest is in development of the ability to discriminate among phonemes in a particular language. In addition, a good deal of the developmental work is based on the theoretical and experimental work on adult speech perception, which is itself based on psycholinguistics and acoustic phonetics. The first three subsections below list background reading in these fields. (Section 12-A also has some developmental references.) The remaining sections present research on the prelinguistic period (emphasizing speech perception studies) and on the linguistic period (emphasizing speech production studies).

A   Collections and Bibliographies

Smith, Frank & Miller, George A. (Eds.). *The Genesis of Language.* Cambridge, Mass.: The MIT Press, 1966. (Also in paperback.)
See the articles by Weir, Templin, Fry, Hirsh, Lenneberg, and Chase.

Lyons, John (Ed.). *New Horizons in Linguistics.* Baltimore: Penguin Books, 1970a.
Includes brief introductions to speech perception (D. B. Fry), speech production (John Laver), and phonology (E. C. Fudge).

Papers and Reports on Child Language Development. Department of Linguistics, Stanford University, 1970 to present.
Numerous papers on speech perception and production have appeared in this series. Numbers 1, 3, and 6 are devoted entirely to these topics; see also numbers 7, 8, 9, and 10.

Bar-Adon, Aaron & Leopold, Werner F. (Eds.). *Child Language: A Book of Readings.* Englewood Cliffs, N.J.: Prentice-Hall, 1971.
In addition to the articles given separate listings here, there are short selections based on German (Wilhelm Wundt, Fritz Schultze), English (Frederick Tracy), and French (Antoine Grégoire, Marcel Cohen).

Macken, Marlys A. Readers, books and articles on child phonology: A selected bibliography. In *Papers and Reports on Child Language Development,* No. 7. Committee on Linguistics, Stanford University, April 1974a, 101–112.
Annotated. See also Macken, M. A., Child phonology. *Linguistic Reporter,* 1974b, *16*(10), 9–12.

*Kavanagh, James F. & Cutting, James E. (Eds.). *The Role of Speech in Language.* Cambridge, Mass.: The MIT Press, 1975.
Collection of papers, primarily on the evolution of speech, speech perception, phonology, and American Sign Language.

Working Papers in Linguistics, No. 22. Ohio State University, 1977. (Department of Linguistics, 1841 Millikin Road, Columbus, Ohio 43210, $3.50 to "OSU College of Humanities.")
Includes "Phonological variation in children's speech: The trade-off phenomena" by Olga K. Garnica & Mary Louise Edwards; *Some Prosodic Characteristics of Speech to Young Children,* Stanford University doctoral dissertation by Olga K. Garnica; and *Phonological Differentiation in a Bilingual Child,* Ohio State University masters thesis by Roy Major.

B Phonological Theory in Linguistics

The following publications provide introductory and advanced treatments of phonology and phonetics. For a brief overview, see the introductory books on linguistics in Section 2-B (Fromkin & Rodman's chapter is especially readable and reliable). For suggested phonological universals, see Greenberg (1966a,b). For phonological analyses of sign language, see Section 3-D, including Klima (1975).

Journal of Phonetics. Published by Academic Press, quarterly.

Jakobson, Roman; Fant, C. Gunnar M.; & Halle, Morris. *Preliminaries to Speech Analysis* (2nd ed.). Cambridge, Mass.: The MIT Press, 1963. (Paperback. Originally published as Technical Report No. 13, MIT Acoustics Laboratory, May 1952.)
Offers a distinctive feature analysis based on both articulatory and acoustic distinctions.

Pike, K. L. *Phonetics* (2nd ed.). Ann Arbor: University of Michigan Press, 1962.

Chomsky, Noam & Halle, Morris. *The Sound Pattern of English.* New York: Harper & Row, 1968.
Proposes a phonological theory including a binary feature system (based on articulatory distinctions) and phonological rules, applied to an account of the phonology of English. Difficult reading, but of great importance; see textbooks such as Schane (1973) for a simpler presentation.

Schane, Sanford A. *Generative Phonology.* Englewood Cliffs, N.J.: Prentice-Hall, 1973. (Also in paperback.)
An excellent, 127-page introduction, based on Chomsky & Halle (1968).

Fant, Gunnar. *Speech Sounds and Features.* Cambridge, Mass.: The MIT Press, 1973.
Collection of articles by Fant on acoustics, phonetics, and phonology. Half of the book is on feature systems.

Fromkin, Victoria A. (Ed.). *Speech Errors as Linguistic Evidence.* The Hague: Mouton, 1973.
Includes papers arguing that speech errors are evidence for certain phonological analyses.

Anderson, Steven R. *The Organization of Phonology.* New York: Academic Press, 1974.
A comprehensive overview of generative phonology incorporating advances made since Chomsky & Halle (1968).

O'Connor, J. D. *Phonetics*. Baltimore: Penguin Books, 1974. (Paperback.)

Ladefoged, Peter. *A Course in Phonetics*. New York: Harcourt Brace Jovanovich, 1975. (Paperback.)
    Excellent introduction including segmental and suprasegmental phonetics, articulation, acoustic phonetics, and feature systems.

Kiparsky, Paul. Comments on the role of phonology in language. In Kavanagh & Cutting, 1975.

Schnitzer, Marc L. The role of phonology in linguistic communication: Some neurolinguistic considerations. In H. Whitaker & H. A. Whitaker, Vol. 1, 1976.

Lass, Roger. *English Phonology and Phonological Theory*. London: Cambridge University Press, 1976b.

Singh, Sadanand & Singh, Kala S. *Phonetics: Principles and Practices*. Baltimore: University Park Press, 1976.
    Innovative graphic aids are used to teach acoustic and articulatory phonetics, including high-speed motion picture frames with matching line drawings and sound spectrograms.

Wang, William S.-Y. *Phonetics*. Englewood Cliffs, N.J.: Prentice-Hall, in press.

Catford, J. C. *Fundamental Problems in Phonetics*. Bloomington, Ind.: Indiana University Press, in press. (Publication expected, May 1977.)
    A textbook.

C Speech Processing Theories and Research

The following publications, primarily on speech perception, were written by researchers in acoustic phonetics, psycholinguistics, and related fields.

Miller, G. A. & Nicely, P. E. An analysis of perceptual confusions among some English consonants. *Journal of the Acoustical Society of America,* 1955, *27,* 338–352. (Reprinted in Saporta, 1961.)

Fant, Gunnar. *Acoustic Theory of Speech Production.* The Hague: Mouton, 1960.
   A classic reference on the theory of sound production by the human vocal tract.

Stevens, K. N. Toward a model for speech recognition. *Journal of the Acoustical Society of America,* 1960, *32*(1), 47–55.
   Proposes the analysis-by-synthesis model of speech perception. See also Stevens & Halle in Wathen-Dunn, 1967.

Ladefoged, Peter. *Elements of Acoustic Phonetics.* Chicago: The University of Chicago Press, 1962. (Also in paperback.)
   A well written introduction to speech spectography, perception, and production, with glossary.

Denes, Peter B. & Pinson, Elliot N. *The Speech Chain: The Physics and Biology of Spoken Language.* Murray Hill, N.J.: Bell Telephone Laboratories, 1963. (Also published in a commercial paperback edition. New York: Anchor/Doubleday, 1973.)
   An exceptionally clear introduction, which covers topics similar to the preceding book. Both are becoming dated, however.

Liberman, A. M.; Cooper, F. S.; Shankweiler, D. P.; & Studdert-Kennedy, Michael. Perception of the speech code. *Psychological Review,* 1967, *74,* 431–461.
   Presents a review and synthesis of nearly 20 years of research on speech at Haskins Laboratory.

Wathen-Dunn, W. (Ed.). *Models for the Perception of Speech and Visual Form.* Cambridge, Mass.: The MIT Press, 1967.

Lenneberg, Eric H. *Biological Foundations of Language.* New York: John Wiley & Sons, 1967b.

Lenneberg gives detailed consideration to aspects of human biology relevant to phonological development, e.g., physiological structures and functions, maturation, and temporal patterning.

Gibson, Eleanor J. *Principles of Perceptual Learning and Development.* New York: Appleton-Century-Crofts, 1969.
Presents a general psychological theory that has been influential in studies of perceptual development. Examples are drawn primarily from visual perception.

Liberman, Alvin M. The grammars of speech and language. *Cognitive Psychology,* 1970, *1,* 301–323.
Introduces issues and research on speech perception and its relation to the acoustic signal to a psychological audience. Good entry point to the literature, though it should be supplemented by a more recent review.

Stevens, Kenneth N. The quantal nature of speech: Evidence from articulatory-acoustic data. In E. E. David, Jr. & P. B. Denes (Eds.), *Human Communication: A Unified View.* New York: McGraw-Hill, 1972.
Proposal that phonetic features have their basis in acoustic attributes with quantal properties that are well matched to the auditory system.

Flanagan, J. L. *Speech Analysis, Synthesis and Perception* (2nd ed.). New York: Academic Press, 1972.

Liberman, Alvin M.; Mattingly, Ignatius G.; & Turvey, Michael T. Language codes and memory codes. In Melton & Martin, 1972.
Good overview of the relationship between the acoustic signal and the phonemic structure of language, with an emphasis on issues of speech perception.

Studdert-Kennedy, Michael; Shankweiler, D.; & Pisoni, D. B. Auditory and phonetic processes in speech perception: Evidence from a dichotic study. *Cognitive Psychology,* 1972, *3,* 455–466.
Presents evidence that the facilitation in dichotic presentation of shared features (place of articulation and voicing) is due to a phonetic, not auditory, level of speech processing. Laterality effects are also discussed.

Minifie, Fred D.; Hixon, Thomas J.; & Williams, Frederick. *Normal Aspects of Speech, Hearing, and Language.* Englewood Cliffs, N.J.: Prentice-Hall, 1973.

Edited undergraduate textbook on speech and hearing. Basic and applied information on acoustics, articulation, physiology, and phonetics.

Studdert-Kennedy, Michael. The perception of speech. In Thomas A. Sebeok (Ed.), *Current Trends in Linguistics,* Vol. 12. The Hague: Mouton, 1974.
Useful review concentrating on studies of adult speech perception. See also the other phonetics papers in the volume.

Studdert-Kennedy, Michael. From continuous signal to discrete message: Syllable to phoneme. In Kavanagh & Cutting, 1975.

Lieberman, Philip. *On the Origins of Language.* New York: Macmillan, 1975. (Paperback.)
Though this book primarily considers how vocal speech evolved in humans (and did not evolve in apes), useful chapters on acoustics, physiology of speech, phonetic features, and cognitive factors are included.

Lenneberg, Eric H. & Lenneberg, Elizabeth (Eds.). *Foundations of Language Development,* Vol. 1. New York: Academic Press, 1975.
See especially the biologically oriented articles, such as those by A. A. Leontiev and F. Nottebohm.

Cohen, A. & Nooteboom, S. (Eds.). *Structure and Process in Speech Perception.* Heidelberg: Springer-Verlag, 1975.
Proceedings of a recent conference on developments in speech perception research.

Reddy, D. R. *Speech Recognition.* New York: Academic Press, 1975.
Artificial intelligence offers an alternative strategy for learning how humans process speech signals: attempting to build automatic speech recognition systems on computers. These papers from the 1974 IEEE symposium include general overviews as well as reports on specific systems.

Restle, Frank; Shiffrin, Richard M.; Castellan, N. John; Lindman, Harold R.; & Pisoni, David B. (Eds.). *Cognitive Theory: Volume I.* Hillsdale, N.J.: Lawrence Erlbaum Associates, 1975.
Part 1, on contemporary issues in speech perception, has articles by Michael Studdert-Kennedy ("The nature and function of phonetic categories"), William E. Cooper ("Selective adaptation to speech"), Charles C. Wood ("A normative model for redundancy gains in speech"), and David B. Pisoni ("Dichotic listening and processing phonetic features").

Carterette, Edward C. & Friedman, Morton P. (Eds.). *Handbook of Perception, Vol. VII. Language and Speech.* New York: Academic Press, 1976.
> Includes articles by P. MacNeilage & P. Ladefoged ("The production of speech and language"), C. J. Darwin ("The perception of speech"), W. A. Wickelgren ("Phonetic coding and serial order"), and H. A. Whitaker ("Disorders of speech production").

Lass, Norman J. (Ed.). *Contemporary Issues in Experimental Phonetics.* New York: Academic Press, 1976a.
> Chapters provide information on research methods, peripheral mechanisms, theory and research on speech production and perception, acoustic phonetics, and other topics. Assumes a basic background.

Studdert-Kennedy, Michael. Speech perception. In Lass, 1976a.
> A review of the literature.

Fant, Gunnar & Tatham, M. A. A. (Eds.). *Auditory Analysis and Perception of Speech.* New York: Academic Press, 1976.
> Selected papers from an international symposium of the same title in Leningrad in August 1973, grouped into sections on vowel perception, consonant perception and temporal organization of connected speech. The papers focus on the perceptual relevance of aspects of the speech wave.

Massaro, Dominic W. Auditory information processing. In Estes, Vol. 4, 1976.
> Review of the literature, including speech perception, in the framework of an information-processing theory emphasizing a sequence of memory stores and recording processes.

Fry, D. B. *Acoustic Phonetics.* London: Cambridge University Press, 1976.

Singh, Sadanand (Ed.). *Measurement Procedures in Speech, Hearing, and Language.* Baltimore: University Park Press, 1976a.

Green, David M. *An Introduction to Hearing.* Hillsdale, N.J.: Lawrence Erlbaum Associates, 1976.
> Covers sound, physiology of hearing, psychoacoustics, and speech perception for beginning students in upper division or graduate courses.

Bullock, Theodore H. (Ed.). *Recognition of Complex Acoustic Signals.* Berlin: Dahlem Konferenzen, 1977.

An interesting collection of papers on developmental and comparative research dealing with biologically significant acoustic signals, including speech.

Hardcastle, W. J. *Physiology of Speech Production.* New York: Academic Press, 1977.

Textbook with extensive bibliography.

Pisoni, David B. Speech perception. In Estes, Vol. 6, in press. (Publication expected, 1977.)

Excellent introduction.

D *Prelinguistic Period: Infant Vocalization*

Only a few of the many articles on early infant vocalization and adult responses are listed here, including some linguistically oriented studies of babbling. Issues include the relative importance of segmental vs. suprasegmental aspects of speech, the sequence of changes in vocalizations, and the relevance of phonological analysis. For further comments on this period, see review articles such as those of Nakazima, 1975 (Section 12-F) and Menyuk, 1974 (Section 12-G); research reports that span both periods, e.g., Irwin & Chen, 1946 and Leopold, 1947 (Section 12-F); some of the articles on suprasegmental development in Section 12-H; and the overviews of language development in Sections 1-A and 1-B (e.g., Lewis, 1951).

Irwin, Orvis C. & Chen, Han Piao. Speech sound elements during the first year of life: A review of the literature. *Journal of Speech Disorders,* 1943; *8,* 109–121.

Mowrer, H. O. Speech development in the young child: The autism theory of speech development and some clinical applications. *Journal of Speech and Hearing Disorders,* 1952, *17,* 263–268.
    Learning theory approach emphasizing the child's self-reinforcement process.

*Lenneberg, Eric H.; Rebelsky, Freda G.; & Nichols, Irene A. The vocalizations of infants born to deaf and hearing parents. *Human Development,* 1965, *8,* 23–37.
    Based on 24-hour tape recordings made every other week for the first 3 months of life; no differences were found in the vocalizations of six infants of deaf parents (all but one hearing) vs. 10 hearing infants of hearing parents.

Wasz-Hoeckert, O., et al. *The Infant Cry: A Spectrographic and Auditory Analysis.* Philadelphia: J. B. Lippincott, 1968.

Siegel, Gerald M. Vocal conditioning in infants. *Journal of Speech and Hearing Disorders,* 1969, *34,* 3–19.
    Discussion of learning theoretic approaches to the transition from "reflexive vocalization" to babbling.

Blount, Ben G. The pre-linguistic system of Luo children. *Anthropological Linguistics,* 1970, *12,* 326–342.

The speech of three Luo children was recorded over a period of several months: 0;7–1;0, 0;8–1;2, and 1;3–1;8, plus one sample from a fourth child at 0;10. Phonetic development and intonation are discussed. Contrary to Jakobson, the children converged toward a similar, reduced inventory of sounds late in the babbling phase.

*Kaplan, Eleanor & Kaplan, George. The prelinguistic child. In J. Eliot (Ed.), *Human Development and Cognitive Processes.* New York: Holt, Rinehart and Winston, 1971, 359–381.
Critical overview of theory and research on production and perception of speech in the first year of life, including summaries of chronological stages.

Lieberman, P.; Crelin, E. S.; & Klatt, D. H. Phonetic ability and related anatomy of the newborn and adult human, Neanderthal man, and the chimpanzee. *American Anthropologist,* 1972, *74*(4), 287–307.

Gruber, Jeffrey S. Playing with distinctive features in the babbling of infants. In Ferguson & Slobin, 1973(b).
In the babbling of one child at age 1;1 on one day, initial segments of syllables generally increase in markedness from beginning to end of each syllable sequence.

Stone, L. Joseph; Smith, Henrietta T.; & Murphy, Lois B. (Eds.). *The Competent Infant: Research and Commentary.* New York: Basic Books, 1973.
Reprinted papers on infant vocalization by P. H. Wolff; A. J. Brodbeck & O. C. Irwin; E. H. Lenneberg; H. L. Rheingold, J. L. Gewirtz & H. W. Ross; and L. Beckwith.

Kewley-Port, Diane & Preston, Malcolm S. Early apical stop production: A voice onset time analysis. *Journal of Phonetics,* 1974, *2,* 195–210.

Müller, Eric; Hollien, Harry; & Murry, Thomas. Perceptual responses to infant crying: Identification of cry types. *Journal of Child Language,* 1974, *1,* 89–95.

Murry, Thomas; Hollien, Harry; & Müller, Eric. Perceptual responses to infant crying: Maternal recognition and sex judgments. *Journal of Child Language,* 1975, *2,* 199–204.

Stark, Rachel E.; Rose, Susan N.; & McLagen, Margaret. Features of infant sounds: The first eight weeks of life. *Journal of Child Language,* 1975, *2,* 205–221.

Segmental features in the recorded vocalizations of two female infants were different for "vegetative" sounds vs. cry and discomfort sounds, but did not vary with increasing age for the 8 weeks studied.

Olney, Rachel L. & Scholnick, Ellin K. Adult judgments of age and linguistic differences in infant vocalization. *Journal of Child Language,* 1976, *3,* 145–155.

College students were 88% accurate at judging the relative ages of pairs of vocalizations (from Chinese or American infants 0;6, 1;0, and 1;6), but could not distinguish Chinese from American infants at each age (or adults instructed to babble).

Oller, D. Kimbrough; Wieman, Leslie A.; Doyle, William J.; & Ross, Carol. Infant babbling and speech. *Journal of Child Language,* 1976, *3,* 1–11.

Contrary to Jakobson (1941/68), the phonetic content of babbling in five infants at ages 0;6–0;8 and 1;0–1;1 exhibits many of the same preferences found in early speech.

E Prelinguistic Period: Infant Speech Perception

This subsection focuses on the developmental course of the receptive mastery of phonemes. The performances involved are **phoneme discrimination** *(in which two different phonemes are perceived as different) and* **phoneme identification** *(in which a phoneme is correctly labeled). Adults in speech perception studies are generally asked to give active responses: a verbal same/different judgment ("those sound the same") or identification ("that's an* m*"), or a button-push. Procedures involving passive responses have been recently developed, making it possible to study discrimination between phonemes (or between pairs of nonlinguistic sounds) by infants as young as 1 month. The procedures are generally modifications of the conjugate reinforcement methodology developed by Siqueland & DeLucia (1969) and are often referred to as a* **habituation-dishabituation** *paradigm (Eimas, 1974a, prefers the description "satiation and release-from-satiation"). In Eimas' version, an infant is reinforced for high amplitude sucking by presentation of a speech sound. (In studies of consonant discrimination, the stimuli are actually syllables because shorter acoustic segments do not sound like speech.) Eventually the speech sound becomes familiar and presumably less reinforcing; sucking rate decreases. A new speech sound is introduced, and it is assumed that sucking rate will increase if the sound is perceived as different. In a similar procedure, cardiac deceleration (part of the orienting response) is used as the dependent variable. These methods have revolutionized the study of infant speech perception, but the first has been criticized by Trehub (1973) on the grounds that reinforcement as well as discrimination are necessary conditions. This problem is avoided by a modified procedure in which the speech sound signals a reinforcing visual event, and the infant's anticipatory head-turn toward the location of the visual event is the dependent variable (e.g., Fodor, Garrett, & Brill, 1975; Aslin & Pisoni, 1976).*

One class of questions that could be addressed with these procedures involves the order of phoneme discriminations (e.g., are the distinctive features of phonological theory relevant, or is the order based on some other factor?). However, most attention has focused on the issue of how early phonemic (or phonetic) discriminations are made, in general. A number of recent experiments report that lin-

guistic discriminations between various pairs of phonemes are made very early (as early as 1 month). This would be uninteresting, however, if such discriminations were due to a general ability to discriminate sounds (including acoustically different examples of the same phoneme). Thus, much excitement has been caused by the finding of **categorical perception** *of speech sounds at this age. The phenomenon was originally reported for adults. As an example, if voice onset time is systematically varied in synthesized syllables, adults show a sharp boundary in their identification of the syllables at a VOT of 25–30 milliseconds. Furthermore, if they are asked to discriminate pairs of syllables differing by a constant VOT value, they perform well for pairs that straddle the identification boundary but poorly for pairs within the same identification category. Since VOT is a continuous dimension, but perception is discontinuous in a way related to the phonemic categories of the language, it was originally concluded that the categorical perception phenomenon resulted from specifically linguistic perceptual processes. Infants also showed the effect with respect to the adult identification boundary, and so a linguistic interpretation of early phonemic discrimination was suggested. However, similar results have recently been reported in animal studies, and with certain nonlinguistic stimuli, so that many researchers now prefer a psychophysical explanation. Such an explanation has implications for understanding the role of experience in infant speech perception and the way in which the sound systems of language have evolved.*

BACKGROUND PUBLICATIONS:
THE CATEGORICAL PERCEPTION PHENOMENON IN ADULTS

For background, many of the papers on categorical perception in adults and animals are listed first. The publications in Section 12-C are relevant at a more general level.

Liberman, A. M.; Harris, K. S.; Hoffman, H. S.; & Griffith, B. C. The discrimination of speech sounds within and across phoneme boundaries. *Journal of Experimental Psychology,* 1957, *54,* 358–368.
  An early report of the categorical perception phenomenon for place of articulation using synthesized stimuli.

Mattingly, Ignatius G.; Liberman, Alvin M.; Syrdal, Ann K.; & Halwes, Terry. Discrimination in speech and nonspeech modes. *Cognitive Psychology,* 1971, *2,* 131–157.

The categorical speech phenomenon was obtained for syllables varying (in their second-formant transitions) between [bæ], [dæ], and [gæ], but not for the chirp-like transitions alone. Results on three related types of nonspeech stimuli are also reported.

Eimas, Peter D.; Cooper, William E.; & Corbit, John D. Some properties of linguistic feature detectors. *Perception and Psychophysics,* 1973, *13,* 247-252.
Interprets results from selective adaptation experiments.

Pisoni, David B. Auditory and phonetic memory codes in the discrimination of consonants and vowels. *Perception and Psychophysics,* 1973, *13,* 253-260.
In a delayed comparison discrimination task, amount of delay affected accuracy on synthetic vowels but not consonants, both within and between phonetic categories, providing evidence for phonetic as well as auditory memory codes.

Cutting, James E. & Rosner, Burton S. Categories and boundaries in speech and music. *Perception and Psychophysics,* 1974, *16,* 564-570.
Reports categorical perception for nonspeech stimuli (sawtooth stimuli differing in rise time), using an ABX discrimination paradigm.

Pisoni, David B. & Tash, Jeffrey. Reaction times to comparisons within and across phonetic categories. *Perception and Psychophysics,* 1974, *15,* 285-290.
Given pairs of synthetic speech sounds ranging between /ba/ and /pa/, subjects' "same" responses were fastest for acoustically identical stimuli; "different" responses across a phonetic boundary were fastest for large differences. Thus, an acoustic encoding level is available as well as the phonetic code accessed in other tasks.

Kuhl, P. K. & Miller, J. D. Speech perception by the chinchilla: Voiced-voiceless distinction in alveolar plosive consonants. *Science,* 1975, *190,* 69-72.
Chincillas learned to respond differentially to the consonants /d/ and /t/ in three different vowel contexts and could generalize to synthesized speech stimuli. Their identification functions were similar to those of English speakers. (However, no discrimination data were collected.)

Lisker, Leigh. Is it VOT or a first-formant transition detector? *Journal of the Acoustical Society of America*, 1975, *57*(6), 1547–1551.

A first-formant frequency shift has been suggested to be responsible for perceptual results with stimuli designed to vary on another parameter, voice onset time (VOT) (Stevens & Klatt, 1974), but new experiments show that the shift is neither a necessary nor sufficient condition for a change in phoneme identification.

Morse, Philip A. & Snowdon, Charles T. An investigation of categorical speech discrimination by rhesus monkeys. *Perception and Psychophysics*, 1975, *17*, 9–16.

Eight rhesus macaques discriminated place of articulation differences within categories, and to a greater extent between categories, based on changes in heart rate in a habituation-dishabituation paradigm. A feature-detector model of auditory perception provides the most likely explanation.

Miyawaki, Kuniko; Strange, Winifred; Verbrugge, Robert; Liberman, Alvin M.; Jenkins, James J.; & Fujimura, Osamu. An effect of linguistic experience: The discrimination of [r] and [l] by native speakers of Japanese and English. *Perception and Psychophysics*, 1975, *18*, 331–340.

Sinnot, J. M.; Beecher, M. D.; Moody, D. B.; & Stebbins, W. C. Speech sound discrimination by monkeys and humans. *Journal of the Acoustical Society of America*, 1976, *60*, 687–695.

Based on response accuracy and latency in a discrimination task, it is concluded that monkeys and humans share similar sensory capacities but that humans also have unique speech-processing capacities.

Waters, R. S. & Wilson, W. A., Jr. Speech perception by rhesus monkeys: The voicing distinction in synthesized labial and velar stop consonants. *Perception and Psychophysics*, 1976, *19*, 285–289.

Monkeys showed evidence of identifying synthesized speech sounds in a shock avoidance procedure. The results resembled speech-boundary phenomena found in humans, except that boundaries shifted when the stimulus range was varied.

Cutting, James E.; Rosner, Burton S.; & Foard, Christopher F. Perceptual categories for musiclike sounds: Implications for theories of speech perception. *Quarterly Journal of Experimental Psychology*, 1976, *28*, 361–378.

Reports further investigation of music-like nonspeech sawtooth stimuli, in experiments using a new criterion for categorical perception (interstimulus interval effects) or a selective adaptation task.

DEVELOPMENTAL STUDIES

The following publications on speech perception in infancy include experimental reports, particularly on the categorical perception phenomenon; reviews; and theoretical discussions.

Siqueland, E. R. & DeLucia, C. A. Visual reinforcement of non-nutritive sucking in human infants. *Science,* 1969, *165,* 1144–1146.
Describes the conjugate reinforcement methodology that was modified for categorical perception studies.

Friedlander, Bernard Z. Receptive language development in infancy: Issues and problems. *Merrill-Palmer Quarterly of Behavior and Development,* 1970, *16,* 7–51. (Reprinted in Stone, Smith, & Murphy, 1973.)
Reviews research primarily from the 1960's.

*Eimas, Peter D.; Siqueland, Einar R.; Jusczyk, Peter; & Vigorito, James. Speech perception in infants. *Science,* 1971, *171,* 303–306. (Reprinted in Stone, Smith, & Murphy, 1973.)
The authors report evidence for categorical perception of voicing in 1- and 4-month-old infants, using synthesized speech ranging between [ba] and [pa] and a habituation-dishabituation high amplitude sucking procedure.

Moffitt, Alan R. Consonant cue perception by twenty- to twenty-four-week-old infants. *Child Development,* 1971, *42,* 717–731.
Using a habituation-dishabituation cardiac rate paradigm, 37 infants, 20–24 weeks old, were shown to discriminate between synthesized speech stimuli differing in place of articulation ("bah" and "gah").

Morse, Philip A. The discrimination of speech and non-speech stimuli in early infancy. *Journal of Experimental Child Psychology,* 1972, *14,* 477–492.
Using a procedure similar to that of Eimas et al., but adding a control group with modified, nonspeech stimuli (lacking formant transitions), Morse shows that place of articulation is discriminated in a linguistically relevant manner and that rising

vs. falling intonation is discriminated by 40- to 54-day-old infants.

Trehub, Sandra E. & Rabinovitch, M. Sam. Auditory-linguistic sensitivity in early infancy. *Developmental Psychology,* 1972, *6,* 74–77.

In a habituation-dishabituation high amplitude sucking procedure, 60 infants, 4–17 weeks old, could discriminate synthesized /b/ from /p/, natural speech /b/ from /p/, and natural speech /d/ from /t/.

Trehub, Sandra E. Infants' sensitivity to vowel and tonal contrasts. *Developmental Psychology,* 1973, *9,* 91–96.

In a habituation-dishabituation high amplitude sucking procedure, 182 infants, 4–17 weeks old, discriminated vowel contrasts, [a] vs. [i] and [i] vs. [u], but not contrasts of tone frequency, 1000 vs. 2000 Hz, 100 vs. 200 Hz, and 200 vs. 1000 Hz. Since evidence exists for tone discrimination, the results are taken to show a methodological weakness in the Eimas procedure. Reinforcement value seems to be involved as well as ability to discriminate.

*Morse, Philip A. Infant speech perception: A preliminary model and review of the literature. In Schiefelbusch & Lloyd, 1974.

Comprehensive review of methods, findings, and theories, organized by a suggested preliminary model.

Eimas, Peter D. Linguistic processing of speech by young infants. In Schiefelbusch & Lloyd, 1974(a).

Eimas briefly reviews his research method, summarizes findings on infant discrimination of voicing and place of articulation, and suggests that infants may be using linguistic feature detectors.

Eimas, Peter D. Auditory and linguistic processing of cues for place of articulation by infants. *Perception and Psychophysics,* 1974b, *16,* 513–521.

In a habituation-dishabituation high amplitude sucking paradigm, 48 infants showed categorical perception for place of articulation for synthesized speech stimuli but not for the second-formant transitions in isolation.

Fodor, Jerry A.; Garrett, M. F.; & Brill, S. L. Pi ka pu: The perception of speech sounds by prelinguistic infants. *Perception and Psychophysics,* 1975, *18,* 74–78.

Infants 14–18 weeks old were capable of grouping syllables that shared a common consonant cued by different acoustic attributes. The procedure involved head-turns to a reinforcing stimulus, with syllables as a discriminative stimulus.

Eilers, Rebecca E. & Minifie, Fred D. Fricative discrimination in early infancy. *Journal of Speech and Hearing Research*, 1975, *18*, 158–167.

Infants between 4 and 17 weeks old received controlled natural speech stimuli in a high amplitude sucking paradigm. With 24–30 infants for each comparison, they could discriminate /s/ from /v/ or /ʃ/ but not /z/.

*Lasky, Robert E.; Syrdal-Lasky, Ann; & Klein, Robert E. VOT discrimination by four to six and a half month old infants from Spanish environments. *Journal of Experimental Child Psychology*, 1975, *20*, 215–225.

In a habituation-dishabituation cardiac rate paradigm, 30 infants ages 4–6.5 months from Spanish-speaking homes showed a pattern of discrimination results suggesting the presence of three major categories along the VOT dimension. The infants did not make a discrimination that is made by Spanish-speaking adults in their environment.

*Cutting, James E. & Eimas, Peter D. Phonetic feature analyzers and the processing of speech in infants. In Kavanagh & Cutting, 1975.

Reviews evidence in support of the idea that infants may be equipped with feature detectors for analyzing phonemes.

Eimas, Peter D. Auditory and phonetic coding of the cues for speech: Discrimination of the [r-l] distinction by young infants. *Perception and Psychophysics*, 1975a, *18*, 341–347.

The distinction between [r] and [l], cued by the initial frequency of the third formant, was perceived in a nearly categorical manner by 128 two- and three-month-old infants, but the nonspeech third formant alone was not. Eimas argues that the results oppose the theory that categorical perception is attributable only to psychoacoustic phenomena rather than additional speech-specific processing.

Eimas, Peter D. Speech perception in early infancy. In L. B. Cohen & P. Salapatek (Eds.). *Infant Perception: From Sensation to Cognition*. New York: Academic Press, 1975(b), 193–228.

Summarizes research and theory, primarily based on the habituation-dishabituation studies of recent years.

Eimas, Peter D. Developmental aspects of speech perception. In R. Held, H. Leibowitz, & H. L. Teuber (Eds.), *Handbook of Sensory Physiology: Perception*. New York: Springer-Verlag, 1976.

Eisenberg, Rita B. *Auditory Competence in Early Life: The Roots of Communicative Behavior*. Baltimore: University Park Press, 1976.
  Text based largely on audiological research at the Bioacoustic Laboratory of St. Joseph Hospital, with attention to both speech and nonspeech stimuli. Discusses methodology in detail, suggests new directions for the field, and includes helpful appendices (glossary, listing of relevant studies).

Streeter, Lynn A. Language perception of 2-month-old infants shows effects of both innate mechanisms and experience. *Nature*, 1976, *259*, 39–41.
  Results with 36 Kikuyu infants in a high-amplitude sucking paradigm provide further evidence for the existence of three major categories along the VOT dimension (cf. Lasky, et al., 1975). The infants made a prevoiced/voiced distinction, as well as a voiced/voiceless distinction which was present in their language only for places of articulation other than the bilabial position used in the study.

Aslin, Richard N. & Pisoni, David B. A head-turning paradigm for research on speech perception in infants. In *Research on Speech Perception*, Progress Report No. 3, Department of Psychology, Indiana University, Bloomington, Indiana, 1976.

Leavitt, Lewis A.; Brown, James W.; Morse, Philip A.; & Graham, Frances K. Cardiac orienting and auditory discrimination in 6-week-old infants. *Developmental Psychology*, 1976, *12*, 514–523.
  Infants at 6 weeks could discriminate [ba] from [ga], based on a cardiac rate response with a critical methodological difference from experiments not finding discrimination with this response.

Trehub, Sandra E. The discrimination of foreign speech contrasts by infants and adults. *Child Development*, 1976, *47*, 466–472.
  Discusses theoretical implications of the ability of infants 5–17 weeks old to discriminate between [za]-[řa] and between [pa]-[pā], compared to adults' confusion of the first contrast.

Swoboda, Philip J.; Morse, Philip A.; & Leavitt, Lewis A. Continuous vowel discrimination in normal and at risk infants. *Child Development*, 1976, *47*, 549–565.

Presents evidence that 8-week-old infants from both populations discriminate the vowels /i/ and /ɪ/ in a continuous,
rather than categorical, manner.

Gregg, Claudette; Clifton, Rachel Keen; & Haith, Marshall. A possible explanation for the frequent failure to find cardiac orienting in
the newborn infant. *Developmental Psychology,* 1976, *12,* 75–76.

*Jusczyk, Peter W.; Rosner, Burton S.; Cutting, James E.; Foard,
Christopher F.; & Smith, Linda B. Categorical perception of
nonspeech sounds by two-month-old infants. *Perception and Psychophysics,* 1977, *21,* 50–54.

Four sawtooth-wave stimuli used by Cutting & Rosner (1974)
were perceived categorically by 18 infants of ages 5–10 weeks.

Jusczyk, Peter W. Perception of syllable-final stop consonants by two-
month old infants. *Perception and Psychophysics,* in press.

Contrary to what would be expected from Shvachkin (1948/73),
Jusczyk reports results similar to those of Eimas (1974b), but for
syllable-final rather than syllable-initial stops, using CV and
CVC syllables with 32 infants of ages 6–10 weeks.

*Pisoni, David B. Identification and discrimination of the relative
onset of two-component tones: Implications for voicing perception
in stops. *Journal of the Acoustical Society of America,* in press.
(Publication expected, 1977.)

Presents a hypothesis about VOT perception that claims to
account for the data from adults, infants, and chinchillas.

F Phonological Development in Children's Speech Production

The following publications include descriptions of the development of individual children (based on analysis of tape recordings or ongoing observations of the author's own child), theories of development, and reviews of theory and research. As noted earlier, the researchers vary in whether they aim to study observed behavior or underlying representations. Issues center on order of acquisition of phonemes and on phonological processes. Because very detailed knowledge and training in phonology and phonetics are required for this research, most of the authors are linguists. Section 12-B is most relevant for background; see also the introduction to Section 12, and, for suprasegmental phonology, Section 12-H. Of the texts cited in Section 1-A, Menyuk (1971) has the most complete coverage and Dale (1976) is the most up-to-date. Also see the reviews by McCarthy (1954), McNeill (1970b), and Braine (1971b).

GENERAL

*Jakobson, Roman. *Child Language, Aphasia and Phonological Universals.* The Hague: Mouton, 1968. (Also, New York: Humanities Press, 1969. Originally published in German, 1941.)

Jakobson divides speech development into two separate periods: babbling (in which there is phonetic freedom) and phonology (in which a much more limited range of sounds is used in words). The second period is governed by a universal hierarchy ("laws of irreversible solidarity"), progressing by the successive acquisition of new phonemic oppositions. The frequency of an opposition in the languages of the world, the relative order of its acquisition by children, and its order of loss by aphasics are highly related, the last two inversely. Very influential.

*Velten, H. V. The growth of phonemic and lexical patterns in infant language. *Language,* 1943, *19,* 281-292. (Reprinted in Bar-Adon & Leopold, 1971.)

Velten describes his daughter Joan's speech up to age 4, giving a number of details and examples. Applying Jakobson's ideas, he shows that Joan builds her own phonological system by making successively smaller differentiations. Reduplication is rare. Her slow phonemic but fast lexical growth resulted in a large number of homonyms. Some phenomena (e.g., some forms exempt from change; loan-words) are reminiscent of language change.

Irwin, Orvis C. Series of articles in the *Journal of Speech Disorders,* 1946–1948.
Description of the order in which sounds and syllabic structures are produced by infants, based on a longitudinal investigation of a large number of infants. Irwin's approach is to report findings statistically with respect to adult English phonemes, and he includes sounds from both babbling and words.

Irwin, Orvis C. & Chen, Han Piao. Development of speech during infancy. *Journal of Experimental Psychology,* 1946, *36,* 431–436.
The number of adult English phonemes present in the speech of infants at monthly intervals up to 2½ years are presented on the basis of longitudinal investigation of 95 infants.

*Leopold, Werner F. *Speech Development of a Bilingual Child: A Linguist's Record. Vol. 2, Sound-Learning in the First Two Years.* Evanston, Ill.: Northwestern University Press, 1947.
A detailed account of sounds produced, contextual constraints, and substitutions is followed by theoretical discussion of the learning sequence, learning process, and types of phonetic problems. A classic; the authors of many current theories test them against these data.

Jakobson, Roman. The sound laws of child language and their place in general phonology. In R. Jakobson, *Studies on Child Language and Aphasia.* The Hague: Mouton, 1971. (Originally published in French, 1949. Reprinted in Bar-Adon & Leopold, 1971, and in R. Jakobson, *Selected Writings,* Vol. 1, The Hague: Mouton, 1962.)
Summarizes the theory in Jakobson (1941/1968).

*Chao, Yuen Ren. The Cantian idiolect: An analysis of the Chinese spoken by a twenty-eight-month-old child. In W. J. Fischel (Ed.), *Semitic and Oriental Studies, University of California Publications in Semitic Philology,* 1951, *11,* 27–44. (Reprinted in Ferguson & Slobin, 1973.)
Structural analysis particularly of the phonology, but also the

syntax and vocabulary, of the author's Mandarin-learning granddaughter (Canta) during a 1-month period.

Leopold, Werner F. Patterning in children's language learning. *Language Learning*, 1953, *5*, 1–14. (Reprinted in Saporta, 1961, and in Bar-Adon & Leopold, 1971.)
In the first half of this article, Leopold summarizes the phonological development of his bilingual daughter, Hildegard, adopting Jakobson's feature-hierarchy approach.

Templin, Mildred C. Norms on a screening test of articulation for ages three through eight. *Journal of Speech and Hearing Disorders*, 1953, *18*, 323–331.
Articulation performance of 60 children each at ages 3, 3½, 4, 4½, 5, 6, 7, and 8 was highly related for a 50-item screening test and a 175-item diagnostic test. Medians, means and standard deviations are reported by age and sex but not by test item.

Jakobson, Roman & Halle, Morris. Phonemic patterning. In *Fundamentals of Language*. The Hague: Mouton, 1956, 37–44. (Reprinted in Kaiser, 1957; Jakobson, 1962; and Saporta, 1961.)
Further develops the feature hierarchy of Jakobson (1941/1968) and its application to phonological development.

Irwin, Orvis C. Phonetical description of speech development in childhood. In L. Kaiser (Ed.), *Manual of Phonetics*. Amsterdam: North-Holland, 1957.

Winitz, Harris & Irwin, Orvis C. Syllabic and phonetic structure of infants' early words. *Journal of Speech and Hearing Research*, 1958, *1*, 250–256. (Reprinted in Ferguson & Slobin, 1973.)
Reports statistics on the syllabic structure and the relative frequency of the phonemes produced, based on speech samples of 23 infants at 13–14 months and 35 infants each at 15–16 and 17–18 months.

Burling, Robbins. Language development of a Garo and English speaking child. *Word*, 1959, *15*, 45–68. (Reprinted in Ferguson & Slobin, 1973.)
A linguist's insightful description of the development of phonology, syllabic structure, morphology, syntax, and semantics in his child through age 2;10. Issues of bilingualism are discussed, since the child was exposed to English before 1;4 and to Garo and English thereafter. Phonological development is emphasized.

Nakazima, Sei. A comparative study of the speech development of Japanese and American English in childhood. *Studia Phonologia,* 1962, *2,* 27–46; 1966, *4,* 38–55.

*Weir, Ruth. *Language in the Crib.* The Hague: Mouton, 1962.
    Presleep monologues of one child between 28 and 30 months are analyzed primarily with respect to phonology but also with respect to syntax and discourse structure. A good deal of sound play is observed. The corpus is listed in an appendix.

Rūķe-Draviņa, Velta. The process of acquisition of apical /r/ and uvular /r/ in the speech of children. *Linguistics,* 1965, *17,* 58–68. (Reprinted in Ferguson & Slobin, 1963.)
    The author analyzes the development of /r/ and /ʀ/, based on longitudinal observations of two Czech and two Latvian children (one of whom had contact with Swedish). The results support Jakobson's hypothesis that oppositions occurring in relatively few languages are learned late by children.

Crocker, John R. A phonological model of children's articulation competence. *Journal of Speech and Hearing Disorders,* 1969, *34,* 203–213.
    Normative data on the order of emergence of phonemes (Templin, 1957) are accounted for by a model based on the theories of Chomsky and Jakobson, Fant, & Halle.

Stampe, David. The acquisition of phonetic representation. In *Papers from the Fifth Regional Meeting of the Chicago Linguistic Society.* The University of Chicago Linguistics Department, 1969.
    Stampe summarizes his theory of natural phonology. Each new phonetic opposition involves revision of an innate phonological system. Some implications: children do not have their own phonemic systems, distinct from the adult system; Jakobson's "implicational laws" are not needed. See also the paper by Kazazis.

Winitz, Harris. *Articulatory Acquisition and Behavior.* New York: Appleton-Century-Crofts, 1969.

Johnson, C. & Bush, C. N. Note on transcribing the speech of young children. In *Papers and Reports on Child Language Development,* No. 1. Committee on Linguistics, Stanford University, 1970.

*Moskowitz, Arlene I. The two-year-old stage in the acquisition of English phonology. *Language,* 1970, *46,* 426–441. (Reprinted in Ferguson & Slobin, 1973.)

The speech of each of three children at age 2 is analyzed by a different method: substitution analysis, phonological analysis, and these combined with phonetic detail. An adequate account must simultaneously deal with distinctive features, marking, individual phonemes, and phonological rules; and ways of differentiating phonetic and phonological learning must be found.

Compton, Arthur J. Generative studies of children's phonological disorders. *Journal of Speech and Hearing Disorders,* 1970, *35,* 315–339.

A phonological analysis of the speech of two children (ages 6 and 4½ years) with articulation disorders indicates that the many errors can be accounted for by a small number of phonological principles; therapy should focus on these principles.

Waterson, Natalie. Some speech forms of an English child—A phonological study. *Transactions of the Philological Society,* 1970, 1–24.

Overview of the rationale behind prosodic analysis, its application to Waterson's son at age 1½, and the development of certain forms to age 2.

Jakobson, Roman. Why "Mama" and "Papa"? In R. Jakobson, *Studies on Child Language and Aphasia.* The Hague: Mouton, 1971. (Originally published in French, 1949. Reprinted in Bar-Adon & Leopold, 1971. Also in R. Jakobson, *Selected Writings.* The Hague: Mouton, 1962.)

Jakobson accounts for phonetic similarity of the terms for mother and father in the languages of the world in terms of the infant's own speech development.

*Waterson, Natalie. Child phonology: A prosodic view. *Journal of Linguistics,* 1971a, *7,* 179–211.

Waterson proposes nonsegmental analysis to account for the speech of her son, focusing on age 1½, and to explain some of Leopold's otherwise puzzling observations.

Waterson, Natalie. Child phonology: A comparative study. *Transactions of the Philological Society,* 1971b, 34–50.

The forms produced by Waterson's son at age 1½ have regular correspondences to the adult model. These are described.

Read, C. A. Pre-school children's knowledge of English phonology. *Harvard Educational Review,* 1971, *41,* 1–34.

An analysis of preschool children's invented spellings of

English words, based on Chomsky & Halle (1968), suggests that some children "have an unconscious knowledge of aspects of the sound system of English."

Bodine, Ann M. *A Phonological Analysis of the Speech of Two Mongoloid (Down's Syndrome) Children.* Unpublished doctoral dissertation, Cornell University, 1971. (Related article in *Anthropological Linguist,* 1974, *16*(1), 1–24.)

Olmsted, D. L. *Out of the Mouth of Babes.* The Hague: Mouton, 1971. (Paperback.)

Study of the speech production of 100 children, ages 15–30 months, in the tradition of Pike's phonetics research and psychological learning theory. (Hence, questions relevant only at a phonological level of theory do not arise.)

Menn, Lise. Phonotactic rules in beginning speech. *Lingua,* 1971, *26,* 225–251.

The internal structure of the words of Menn's son is described for five stages (16–25½ months) by means of phonotactic rules.

Stampe, David. *A Dissertation on Natural Phonology.* Unpublished doctoral dissertation, The University of Chicago, 1972.

Irwin, Orvis C. *Disorders of Articulation.* Indianapolis: Bobbs-Merrill, 1972.

*Smith, Neilson V. *The Acquisition of Phonology: A Case Study.* London: Cambridge University Press, 1973. (Reviewed by Olmsted in *Journal of Child Language,* 1974, *1,* 133–138.)

Analysis of the speech of Smith's son over several months, within a generative phonology framework.

Moskowitz, Breyne Arlene. On the status of vowel shift in English. In Moore, 1973. (Author's name formerly Arlene I. Moskowitz.)

Children at ages 5, 7, and 9–12 performed a task testing their knowledge of vowel shift, an internal morphophonemic rule. This rule is learned later than external morphophonemic, allophonic, and phonotactic rules, by a process of deductive abstraction based on written English. Several theoretical points are discussed.

Ferguson, Charles A.; Peizer, David B.; & Weeks, Thelma E. Model-and-replica phonological grammar of a child's first words. *Lingua,* 1973, *31,* 35–65.

The five words produced by a child 11 months and her mother's models for them are described in terms of syllables, a set of distinctive features, and reduplication. The grammar characterizes two sets: the words usable as models, and the words which should be pronounceable; some items from both sets are "accidentally" absent.

Oller, D. Kimbrough. Simplification as the goal of phonological processes in child speech. *Language Learning,* 1974, *24,* 299–303.

Every well-documented type of phonological error in child speech is a result of simplification, i.e., it "reduces the total number of contrastive phonetic elements or strings which would otherwise occur . . ."

Braine, Martin D. S. On what might constitute a learnable phonology. *Language,* 1974b, *50,* 270–299.

Two children's single-word speech supports a theoretical framework in which phonemes are much more concrete than those of current generative phonology. Hypotheses about learning are suggested, e.g., articulatory processes impose a phonotactic filter on speech output.

*Ingram, David. Phonological rules in young children. *Journal of Child Language,* 1974b, *1,* 49–64.

Ingram surveys general phonological processes that he claims to be universal in first-language learning, putting particular emphasis on phonotactic (context sensitive) rules and general rules which affect entire classes of sounds. Data from English, French, and Czech children are cited.

Ingram, David. Fronting in child phonology. *Journal of Child Language,* 1974c, *1,* 233–241.

Diary data for an American child at 1;9 and a French child at 1;5 suggest a process of fronting, by which the successive consonants and vowels within a word move from the front towards the back of the mouth. This may be a special case of a general phonological process involving markedness conditions within syllables. (For a counterexample, see Lise Menn in *JCL,* 1975, *2,* 293–296.)

Ingram, David. Surface contrast in children's speech. *Journal of Child Language,* 1975, *2,* 287–292.

Argues against Stampe's (1969) rejection of the idea that children have their own distinct phonemic systems; he argues on the basis of surface contrasts at about 1½ that cannot be traced to aspects of the adult word.

Fry, D. B. Phonological aspects of language acquisition in the hearing and the deaf. In Lenneberg & Lenneberg, Vol. 2, 1975.

Nakazima, Sei. Phonemicization and symbolization in language development. In Lenneberg & Lenneberg, Vol. 1, 1975.

Brief, chronological overview primarily of the first 2 years, based on data from Japanese and American infants.

*Ferguson, Charles A. & Garnica, Olga K. Theories of phonological development. In Lenneberg & Lenneberg, Vol. 1, 1975.

Comparison of four theories, two well known (Mowrer's learning theory approach and modifications by Murai and Olmsted; Jakobson's structuralist theory and modifications by Moskowitz) and two recent (Stampe's natural phonology theory; Waterson's prosodic theory). There is a selected bibliography including a number of hard-to-find items not listed here. An excellent entry point to the theoretically oriented literature, especially for the reader with an elementary acquaintance with phonology.

Winitz, Harris. *From Syllable to Conversation.* Baltimore: University Park Press, 1975. (Also in paperback.)

Describes stages of training for articulation disorders.

Carterette, Edward C. & Jones, Margaret Hubbard. *Informal Speech: Alphabetic and Phonemic Texts with Statistical Analysis and Tables.* Berkeley: University of California Press, 1975.

The volume contains 380 pages of transcription of the speech of triads of first, third, and fifth graders and junior college students, 205 pages of statistical summary tables, and some discussion. Phonetic pauses, rather than word boundaries, separate phoneme sequences, making the transcripts difficult to use and affecting the statistics on sequences.

*Ferguson, Charles A. & Farwell, Carol B. Words and sounds in early language acquisition. *Language,* 1975, *51,* 419–439.

The development of initial consonants in the first 50 words provided by three children (including Leopold's Hildegard) is analyzed by *phone trees,* and theoretical implications are discussed. As in historical sound change, both lexical and phonetic parameters are involved. Also, though many of Jakobson's predictions are met, individual differences are important, and his assumption of a separation between phonetic and phonological development is questioned.

*Ingram, David. Current issues in child phonology. In Morehead & Morehead, 1976(a).

Insightful review of theory and research on children's language production and comprehension. Ingram proposes stages of development from birth to adolescence that parallel Piaget's stages of cognitive development. This probably is the best available entry point to the literature, but it assumes a very elementary knowledge of phonology.

Lorentz, James P. An analysis of some deviant phonological rules of English. In Morehead & Morehead, 1976.

Lorentz argues for the importance of phonological analysis of deviant speech, and presents such an analysis of the speech of one 4½-year-old boy.

Compton, Arthur J. Generative studies of children's phonological disorders: Clinical ramifications. In Morehead & Morehead, 1976.

Like Lorentz, Compton emphasizes the importance of phonological analysis of deviant speech, but he emphasizes clinical application. He describes the phonological system and course of therapy of one girl beginning at age 5, and summarizes the difficulties of another 20 children.

Ingram, David. *Phonological Disability in Children.* Amsterdam: North-Holland, 1976b. (Also in paperback.)

Singh, Sadanand. *Distinctive Features: Theory and Validation.* Baltimore: University Park Press, 1976b.

Introduces distinctive feature theory and applications to perception and articulation. Includes a description of a language acquisition study by Frederick F. Weiner and John Bernthal.

Branigan, George. Syllabic structure and the acquisition of consonants: The great conspiracy in word formation. *Journal of Psycholinguistic Research,* 1976, *5,* 117–133.

The syllabic structure and phonemic inventory of one child at 16–21 months suggest that particular syllabic forms play a role in phoneme acquisition. Various constraints and "conspiratorial rules" make CV the dominant production unit.

Clark, Ruth. A report on methods of longitudinal data collection. *Journal of Child Language,* 1976, *3,* 457–459.

Describes an audio recording system based on a continuously recording 30-second tape loop, the contents of which can be copied onto a permanent tape whenever an interesting utterance has occurred.

Ingram, David. Phonological analysis of a child. *Glossa,* in press.

Ferguson, Charles A. New directions in phonological theory: Language acquisition and universals research. In Cole, in press.

CONSONANT CLUSTERS

*The following papers report studies of the development of consonant clusters. The observational studies focus on children's ability to produce clusters, and the experimental studies focus on their knowledge of the **phonotactic rules** specifying constraints on segment sequences. See also Kornfeld (1971) in Section 12-G.*

Messer, S. Implicit phonology in children. *Journal of Verbal Learning and Verbal Behavior,* 1967, *6,* 609–613.

Children ages 3;1–4;5 listened to pairs of C(C)(C)VC(C) nonsense syllables, of which one satisfied and one violated English phonological restrictions on consonant clusters. The ungrammatical syllables were less often chosen as sounding like a word and were less well imitated, with errors minimizing the number of distinctive feature changes.

Menyuk, Paula. Children's learning and reproduction of grammatical and nongrammatical phonological sequences. *Child Development,* 1968b, *39,* 849–859.

Children ages 4;5–8;3 performed tasks with CCVC nonsense syllables which either satisfied or violated English phonological restrictions on initial consonant clusters. The ungrammatical syllables were more difficult in an elicited imitation task but not in a comprehension task (pointing to an associated geometric form).

Menyuk, Paula & Klatt, Mary. Voice onset time in consonant cluster production by children and adults. *Journal of Child Language,* 1975, *2,* 223–231.

Eleven children, ages 3;3–4;6, and a male and female adult imitated words with initial consonant clusters including stops, both in isolation and in sentence context. VOT duration in spectrograms and consonant identities in transcriptions were compared for different consonant types (voicing, place of articulation), ages, and the two degrees of context.

Pertz, D. L. & Bever, T. G. Sensitivity to phonological universals in children and adolescents. *Language,* 1975, *51,* 149–162.

Subjects of ages 9–11 and 16–19 years read and listened to pairs of CCVC nonsense syllables that violated English phonological restrictions on initial consonant clusters. Judging which of each pair probably occurs in more languages, they were able to reconstruct the relevant portion of the universal phonological hierarchy proposed by Greenberg (1965) and Cairns (1969).

Allerton, D. J. Early phonotactic development: Some observations on a child's acquisition of initial consonant clusters. *Journal of Child Language*, 1976, *3*, 429–433.

Outlines the development of consonant clusters in the speech of one child between ages 3;9 and 5;3.

G Speech Perception and Its Relation to Production in the Linguistic Period

The following reports are concerned with children's ability to dis-criminate and identify phonemes and with the theoretical issue of the relationship between perception and production (e.g., is production order predicted by perceptual difficulty?).

Shvachkin, N. Kh. The development of phonemic speech perception in early childhood. In Ferguson & Slobin, 1973. (Originally published in Russian, 1948.)

This is the study that Garnica (1973) attempted to replicate (see below).

Templin, Mildred C. *Certain Language Skills in Children: Their Development and Interrelationships.* Institute of Child Welfare Monograph No. 26. Minneapolis: The University of Minnesota Press, 1957.

Snow, Catherine E. A comparative study of sound substitutions used by 'normal' first grade children. *Speech Monographs,* 1964, *31,* 135–141.

Children at ages 6;5–8;7 (N = 438) were asked to label pic-tures. Most of the substitutions, reported in a confusion matrix, were consistent with the patterns found in other studies, including Miller & Nicely's (1955) study of perceptual confusions for adults.

*Olmsted, D. L. A theory of the child's learning of phonology. *Language,* 1966, *42,* 531–535. (Reprinted in Bar-Adon & Leopold, 1971.)

Olmsted presents a system of postulates, definitions, and theorems by which it is predicted that discriminability of phonemes and their input frequency predict the order in which they are produced with correct pronunciation.

Sherman, Dorothy & Geith, Annette. Speech sound discrimination and articulation skill. *Journal of Speech and Hearing Research,* 1967, *10,* 277–280.

Discrimination and articulation performance are related for kindergarteners.

Weiner, P. S. Auditory discrimination and articulation. *Journal of Speech and Hearing Disorders*, 1967, *32*, 19–28.

Tikofsky, Ronald S. & McInish, James R. Consonant discrimination by seven-year-olds: A pilot study. *Psychonomic Science*, 1968, *10*, 61–62.

Seven-year-olds making same/different judgments for initial consonants of word-word, nonsense syllable-nonsense syllable, or mixed pairs made the most errors on pairs differing by one distinctive feature. There were also differences among the distinctive features and the contexts.

Menyuk, Paula. The role of distinctive features in the child's acquisition of phonology. *Journal of Speech and Hearing Research*, 1968a, *11*, 138–146. (Reprinted in Ferguson & Slobin, 1973.)

Six distinctive features were ranked according to their proportions of correct usage in required contexts, based on existing data for American children at ages 2;6–5;0 and Japanese children from 1;0 to 2;11. The rank orders were the same, but they differed from a rank ordering on perceptual difficulty based on adult recall of CV syllables.

Menyuk, Paula & Anderson, Suzan. Children's identification and reproduction of /w/, /r/, and /l/. *Journal of Speech and Hearing Research*, 1969, *12*, 39–52.

Preschoolers and adults were asked to imitate, and identify by pointing to a picture, synthesized CVC syllables ranging among *light, white*, and *write*. Psychological boundaries between the sounds were not sharp, but they were better observed on the identification than the imitation task by children.

Graham, Louella W. & House, Arthur S. Phonological oppositions in children: A perceptual study. *Journal of the Acoustical Society of America*, 1971, *49*, 559–566.

The results of a multidimensional scaling analysis of children's discrimination errors for consonant pairs are not well predicted by Jakobson's proposed sequence of phoneme production.

Kornfeld, J. R. Theoretical issues in child phonology. *Papers from the Seventh Regional Meeting of the Chicago Linguistic Society*. The University of Chicago Linguistics Department, 1971.

Kornfeld evaluates conflicting hypotheses regarding children's perception and production of speech and analyzes initial consonant clusters in the spontaneous speech of 13 children ages $1\frac{1}{2}$–$2\frac{1}{2}$.

Locke, John L. Phoneme perception in two- and three-year-old children. *Perceptual and Motor Skills,* 1971, *32,* 215–217.

Twenty children ages 2;0–3;10 performed as well on word pairs differing in place of articulation as on other contrasts in a two-alternative picture-choice task, contrary to Miller & Nicely's (1955) adult findings on perception of speech in noise.

Liljencrants, Johan & Lindblom, Björn. Numerical simulation of vowel quality systems: The role of perceptual contrast. *Language,* 1972, *48,* 839–862.

The vowel systems of a wide range of languages can be accounted for by a principle of maximal perceptual contrast. Phonological phenomena can be predicted by the structure and optimization in use of human speech mechanisms.

*Garnica, Olga K. The development of phonemic speech perception. In Moore, 1973.

Sixteen American children ages 1;5–1;10 were required to choose one of two objects on the basis of its CVC nonsense label, where labels for each pair differed only in their initial consonant. Results only generally replicated Shvachkin (1948/73) with Russian, which supported Jakobson (1941/68); there was considerable variability that must be accounted for.

*Menyuk, Paula. Early development of receptive language: From babbling to words. In Schiefelbusch & Lloyd, 1974.

The first half of this article gives a general summary of research on perception and production of linguistic properties of speech.

Edwards, Mary L. Perception and production in child phonology: The testing of four hypotheses. *Journal of Child Language,* 1974, *1,* 205–219.

Perception data (Shvachkin-Garnica technique) and production data from 28 children ages 1;8–3;11 were used to test hypotheses on initial fricatives and glides, based on assumptions that perception precedes production and unmarked precedes marked. The hypotheses were only partly confirmed; phonemic perception develops slowly, but generally ahead of production, and there is some variation in order of acquisition both within and between tasks. (See also David Barton's criticism on statistical grounds in *JCL,* 1975, *2,* 297–298.)

Salus, Peter H. & Salus, Mary W. Developmental neurophysiology and phonological acquisition order. *Language,* 1974, *50,* 151–160.

The late production of [+strident] consonants is attributed to delays in perceptual discriminability at high frequencies, due to the low degree of myelination of the auditory nerve and associated cortical bodies in very young children.

Palermo, David S. Developmental aspects of speech perception: Problems for a motor theory. In Kavanagh & Cutting, 1975.

Zlatin, M. & Koenigsknecht, R. Development of the voicing contrast: Perception of stop consonants. *Journal of Speech and Hearing Research,* 1975, *18,* 541–553.

Identification functions for synthesized labial, apical, and velar stop consonants varying in VOT were obtained from adults and from children ages 2;6–3;0 and 6;1–6;11. The region of uncertainty was greatest for 2-year-olds; other age-related differences were found.

*Eilers, Rebecca E. & Oller, D. Kimbrough. The role of speech discrimination in developmental sound substitutions. *Journal of Child Language,* 1976, *3,* 319–329.

In a new paradigm, 14 children ages 1;10–2;2 had to choose between a familiar toy and a nonsense toy, based on which of two labels the experimenter used. The labels were the familiar toy's name and a nonsense word, forming a minimal pair. The results suggest that perceptual difficulties play a role in some production errors but not others.

H Other Topics: Suprasegmental Development and Metalinguistic Awareness

SUPRASEGMENTAL DEVELOPMENT

The first group of papers explores the relatively neglected issue of suprasegmental development. In particular, intonation and stress are often used to modify sentence meaning (e.g., the rising intonation indicating that a sentence like "You're leaving now?" is a question). It has been claimed both that intonation is the first marker of meaning used by infants and that acquisition of the many specific rules on suprasegmental usage continues past the acquisition of speech segments.

Background Publications: Linguistics

Linguistic treatments of suprasegmental phonology are not well developed, but the following publications indicate what has been done.

Crystal, David. *Prosodic Systems and Intonation in English.* London: Cambridge University Press, 1969.
> Attempts to develop a theoretical basis for the study of intonation in English within a general framework for suprasegmental phonology.

Lehiste, Ilse. *Suprasegmentals.* Cambridge, Mass.: The MIT Press, 1970.

Bolinger, Dwight (Ed.). *Intonation.* Baltimore: Penguin Books, 1972. (Paperback.)
> Collection of theoretical and descriptive papers.

Schmerling, Susan F. *Aspects of English Sentence Stress.* Austin: University of Texas Press, 1976.
> Schmerling reviews the approaches of Chomsky & Halle (1968), Bresnan, G. Lakoff, and Bolinger, and presents original proposals emphasizing the importance of pragmatic uses of stress.

Lehiste, Ilse. Suprasegmental features of speech. In Lass, 1976a.

Child Language Studies

The developmental studies follow. See also reviews like Menyuk (1974) and Section 12-D on segmental phonology.

323

Pike, Evelyn G. Controlled infant intonation. *Language Learning,* 1949, *2,* 21–24. (Reprinted in Bar-Adon & Leopold, 1971.)
Children use the rising intonation of "baby talk" because they hear it from adults. At the time Pike's daughter was using her first words, Pike deliberately exposed her to falling intonation, and the child reproduced it in her own words.

Albright, Robert W. & Albright, Joy Buck. The phonology of a two-year-old child. *Word,* 1956, *12,* 382–390. (Reprinted in Bar-Adon & Leopold, 1971.)
A phonetic transcription of 237 utterances of a child at 2;2 is presented and summarized. Of special importance is the fact that stress, intonation, and pitch are marked.

von Raffler-Engel, Walburga. The development from sound to phoneme in child language. In Ferguson & Slobin, 1973(a), 9–12. (Originally published in German, 1965.)
Reports that a contrasting intonation contour preceded appropriate segmental distinctions in the first few words of one child.

Lieberman, Philip. *Intonation, Perception, and Language.* Cambridge, Mass.: The MIT Press, 1967. (Also in paperback.)
Includes a chapter on children's acquisition of intonation.

Tonkova-Yampol'skaya, R. V. Development of speech intonation in infants during the first two years of life. *Soviet Psychology,* 1969, *7*(3), 48–54. (Originally published in Russian, 1968. Translation reprinted in Ferguson & Slobin, 1973.)
Description of intonation in Russian children's vocalizations from birth to age 2.

Kaplan, E. L. *The Role of Intonation in the Acquisition of Language.* Unpublished doctoral dissertation, Cornell University, 1969.
Includes an experiment showing that 8-month-old children can discriminate falling vs. rising intonation.

Cruttenden, Alan. A phonetic study of babbling. *British Journal of Disorders of Communication,* 1970, *5,* 110–117.

*Crystal, David. Non-segmental phonology in language acquisition: A review of the issues. *Lingua,* 1973, *32,* 1–45.
Crystal defines terms and reviews research from the late 19th century to the present. There is a need for methodological improvements and for normative descriptive data (e.g., with respect to the loosely based generalization that nonsegmental pattern, particularly intonation, is the earliest kind of linguistic structuring).

Cruttenden, Alan. An experiment involving comprehension of intonation in children from 7 to 10. *Journal of Child Language,* 1974, 221–231.

Comprehension of certain intonation patterns is still developing between ages 7;10 and 10;11 based on a study of 28 British boys.

METALINGUISTIC AWARENESS

The second group of papers considers the question of when and how children gain metalinguistic awareness regarding phonology. (See Section 4-A for the same question regarding syntax.)

Zhurova, L. Ye. The development of analysis of words into their sounds by preschool children. *Soviet Psychology and Psychiatry,* 1964, *2*(2), 11–17. (Originally published in Russian, 1963. Translation reprinted in Ferguson & Slobin, 1973.)

Russian children could resolve a word into its component sounds at about age 4–5 years if taught a method of intoning (e.g., *k-k-kozel*).

von Raffler-Engel, Walburga. An example of linguistic consciousness in the child. In Ferguson & Slobin, 1973(b). (Originally published in Italian, 1965.)

At about age 3½, the author's child made substitutions rather than correct pronunciations of Italian /r/, but the child was aware of his difficulty.

Rozin, Paul & Gleitman, Lila R. The structure and acquisition of reading II: The reading process and the acquisition of the alphabetic principle. In Reber & Scarborough, 1977.

Considers the role of metalinguistic awareness in learning to read.

Section 13
ORTHOGRAPHY
AND READING

No attempt is made here to list even the most important publications on reading, but the books that follow provide a good introduction to current trends in theory and research.

Huey, Edmund Burke. *The Psychology and Pedagogy of Reading.* Cambridge, Mass.: The MIT Press, 1968. (Also in paperback. Originally published, 1908).
A classic book, still worth reading, with a new foreword by Carroll and introduction by Kolers.

Goodman, Kenneth. *Psycholinguistic Nature of the Reading Process.* Detroit: Wayne State University Press, 1968.

Smith, Frank. *Understanding Reading.* New York: .Holt, Rinehart and Winston, 1971. (Reviewed by Legum & Cronnell in *Language,* 1973, *49,* 523–528.)
This book presents Smith's own psycholinguistically oriented theory of reading.

Kavanagh, James F. & Mattingly, Ignatius G. *Language by Ear and by Eye.* Cambridge, Mass.: The MIT Press, 1972. (Also in paperback. Reviewed by R. Söderbergh in *Journal of Child Language,* 1975, *2,* 153–168; by F. Smith in *Language,* 1974, *50,* 762–765.)
Papers from a conference, including topics on speech, writing, speech perception, levels of memory encoding, and learning to read. Most of the papers provide background information useful for the direct study of reading.

Smith, Frank. *Psycholinguistics and Reading.* New York: Holt, Rinehart and Winston, 1973.
A collection of articles that approach reading from a psycholinguistic perspective.

Gibson, Eleanor J. & Levin, Harry. *The Psychology of Reading.* Cambridge, Mass.: The MIT Press, 1975.
A fairly comprehensive application of cognitive psychology to reading. It could be used as a textbook: it is written from a particular point of view but extensively surveys the literature.

Lenneberg, Eric H. & Lenneberg, Elizabeth (Eds.). *Foundations of Language Development,* Vol. 2. New York: Academic Press, 1975.
The volume includes six papers on reading and writing.

Fox, Barbara & Routh, Donald K. Analyzing spoken language into words, syllables, and phonemes: A developmental study. *Journal of Psycholinguistic Research,* 1975, *4,* 331–342.
Children 3–7 years old were asked to repeat spoken sentences and then segment them. The skills of segmentation into words and into syllables were highly related, but both were less related to segmentation into phonemes. The results are discussed in terms of Gibson's model of reading.

Reber, Arthur S. & Scarborough, Don L. (Eds.). *Toward a Psychology of Reading.* Hillsdale, N.J.: Lawrence Erlbaum Associates, 1977.
Based on a 1974 conference at CUNY, "Basic research on the reading process."

Smith, Donald P. *A Technology of Reading and Writing* (4 vols.). New York: Academic Press, 1976 (Vol. 1); in press (Vol. 2).

Author and Publication Index

Each publication is listed with the following information—author(s), date of publication: page(s) on which there is a full entry, and (in parentheses) pages on which it is otherwise mentioned. This last category includes publications that are part of the reference for another publication, book reviews, and publications mentioned (usually by name and date) in an annotation or section introduction. For more general references to specific authors, see the subject index.

When two references are otherwise identical, a lower-case letter is appended to each date; e.g., for 1970 McNeill has 1970a (a book) and 1970c (a journal article). The letter distinguishing his remaining publication for 1970 is placed in parentheses: 1970(b). This indicates that it is a chapter of an edited book. Occasionally both the book editor and chapter author will have more than one publication in the same year, resulting in the use of two letters. For example, Lenneberg, 1964b is the listing for a book edited by Lenneberg, and Ervin, 1964(b) is the listing for Ervin's chapter in that book. Lenneberg himself has a chapter in the book, listed in Lenneberg, 1964(c). The same conventions are followed in the full bibliographic entries.

Often, chapter authors are not given a separate listing, but are mentioned in the book's annotation. In the index this is indicated by listing the author and the editor with the page(s) in parentheses. For example: Palermo, D. S., in Slobin, 1971a: (72, 215). (The "a" is associated with Slobin.) Slobin's book has two full entries that mention Palermo as a contributor.

These conventions are necessary to maintain distinct index entries, but they can usually be disregarded. In annotations and introductory remarks, a simpler system is used: if a publication with an assigned letter is cited, no parentheses or editors' letters are included.

The index is ordered alphabetically by first authors of publications; additional authors are included by name only with cross-references to first authors.

in press: 193, 207
See also Clark, H. H.; Haviland, S.
E.; Klatzky, R. L.
———— & Garnica, O. K., 1974: 192
Clark, H. H.
1969: 173, (174)
1970(a): 186, (179)
1970(b): (176)
1972: 106
1973: 176, 208
1974/76: 59
———— & Clark, E. V.
1968: 200
1977: 63
———— & Stafford, R. A., 1969:
194, (195)
Clark, R.
1974: 103, 236
1975: (135)
1976: 316
————; Hutcheson, S.; & van
Buren, P., 1974: 98
Clarke-Stewart, K. A., 1973: 259. *See
also* Glick, J.
Clay, M., 1971: 126
Clifford, J. E., 1976: 196
Clifton, R. K. *See* Gregg, C.
Cocking, R. R. & Potts, M., 1976: 113
Cofer, C. N., 1976: 62
———— & Musgrave, B. S., 1963: 71
Cohen, A. & Nooteboom, S., 1975:
293
Cohen, L. B. & Salapatek, P., 1975:
131, (305)
Cohen, L. J., 1974: 248
Cohen, M., 1971: (288)
Cohen, S. E. & Beckwith, L., 1976:
264
Coker, P. L., 1975: 202
Colby, K. M. *See* Schank, R. C.
Cole, M. *See also* Bruner, J. S.;
Sharp, D.
———— & Maltzman, I., 1969: (10)
Cole, P., in Cole & Morgan, 1975:
(248)
———— & Morgan, J., 1975: 248,
(26, 246)
Cole, R. W., in press: 24, (41, 63, 156,
250, 317)
Collier, G. A., 1973: (162)

Collins, A. M. *See also* Bobrow, D.
———— & Loftus, E. F., 1975: 163
———— & Quillian, M. R., 1969:
149, (155)
————; Warnock, E. H.; &
Passafiume, J. J., 1975: 248
Compton, A.
1970: 312
1976: 316
Comrie, B., 1976: 196
Connolly, K. J. & Bruner, J. S., 1974:
252
Conrad, R., 1971: 271
Cook, V. J., 1976: 119
Cooper, F. S. *See* Liberman, A. M.
Cooper, W. E., in Restle et al., 1975:
(293). *See also* Eimas, P. D.
Coots, J. H., 1975: (178)
Corbitt, J. D. *See* Eimas, P. D.
Corrigan, R., 1975: 99, (145)
Crelin, E. S. *See* Lieberman, P.
Cresswell, M. J.
1973: 46
1976: 237
Crocker, J. R., 1969: 311
Cromer, R. F.
1968: 197, (197)
1970: 114
1971: 197
1972a: 116
1972b: 117
1974a: 117, (117)
1974(b): 236
1974c: (12)
1975: 119
1976: 237
Croneberg, C. G. *See* Stokoe,
W. C., Jr.
Cronnell. *See* Legum
Crosby, F., 1976: 267
Cross, T., in PRCLD, No. 10, 1975:
(261)
Crowder, R. G., 1976: 62
Cruttenden, A.
1970: 324
1974: 325
Crystal, D.
1969: 323
1971: 26
1973: 324

1972: 235
1975: 47
See also Bever, T.; Fodor, Janet D.
―――――; Bever, T. G., & Garrett, M.
F., 1974: 59, (42)
―――――& Garrett, M. F., 1966: 100
―――――; Garrett, M. F.; & Brill, S.
L., 1975: 304, (299)
―――――& Katz, J. J., 1964: 22, (28,
43, 77, 100, 212)
Ford, W. & Olson, D., 1975: 279
Foss, B., 1974: (236)
Foster, G. *See* Ervin, S. M.
Fouts, R. S., 1973: 230
―――――& Fulwiler, R. L., 1974: 232
Fox, B. & Routh, D., 1975: 328
Fraisse, P., 1963: 194
Francis, H., 1969: 78
Franklin, M. B. *See* Dore, J.
Frantz, D. G., 1974: 35
Fraser, B., 1971: 39
Fraser, C.; Bellugi, U.; & Brown, R.,
1963: 96, (97, 98, 108, 113, 281)
Fraser, C. & Roberts, N., 1975: 262
Frasure, N. E. *See* Entwisle, D. R.
Freedle, R., 1976: 250. *See also*
Carroll, J.; Lewis, M.
Friedlander, B. Z., 1970: 135, 313. *See
also* Wetstone, H. S.
―――――; Jacobs, A. C.; Davis, B. B.;
& Wetstone, H. S., 1972: 258
Friedman, L. A.
1976: 90
in press: 91
Friedman, M. P. *See* Carterette, E.
Friedman, P. *See* Koenigsknecht,
R. A.
Friedman, W. J., 1973: 289
―――――& Seely, P. B., 1976: 208
Friedricks, M. *See* Schacter, F. F.
Fromberg, D., 1976: 219
Fromkin, V., 1973: 289. *See also*
Curtiss, S.
―――――; Krashen, S.; Curtiss, S.;
Rigler, D.; & Rigler, M., 1974:
227
―――――& Rodman, R., 1974: 27,
(289)
Fry, C. L. *See* Flavell, J. H.
Fry, D. B.

1975: 315
1976: 294
in Lyons, 1970a: (288)
in Smith & Miller, 1966: (288)
Fu, K.-S. *See* Zadeh, L.
Fudge, E. C., in Lyons, 1970a: (288)
Fujimura, O. *See* Miyawaki, K.
Fulwiler, R. L. *See* Fouts, R. S.
Furth, H. G.
1968: (89)
1969: 50
1974: 215
in Aaronson & Rieber, 1975: (237)
in Eliot, 1971: (4)
―――――& Youniss, J., 1976: 242

Gaer, E. P., 1969: 109, 125
Galanter, E. *See* Luce, R. D.; Miller,
G. A.
Gallagher, J. W. *See* Muma, J. R.
Gardiner, M. F., in Harnad et al.,
1976: (266)
Gardner, B. T. *See also* Gardner,
R. A.
―――――& Gardner, R. A.
1971: 229
1974: 230
1975: 230
Gardner, R. A. *See also* Gardner,
B. T.
―――――& Gardner, B. T.
1969: 228, (229)
1974a: 230
1947b: (5)
Garman, M., 1974: 118. *See also*
Crystal, D.; Wales, R.
Garmiza, C. & Anisfeld, M., 1976: 280
Garner, W. R., 1974: 149
Garnica, O.
1973: 321, (319, 321)
1975 (dissertation)/1977: (264, 288)
1976: (319)
1977: 264
See also Clark, E. V.; Ferguson,
C. A.
―――――& Edwards, M. L., 1977:
(288)
Garrett, M. F. *See* Fodor, Janet D.;
Fodor, Jerry A.

Garrod, S. & Trabasso, T., 1973: 107,
(107)
Garton, A. *See* Bruner, J. S.
Garvey, C.
1975: 274
forthc.: (54)
―――― & Hogan, R., 1973: 273
Garvin, P. L., 1970: (34)
Gay, J. & Tweney, R. D., 1976: 281
Gaynor, F., 1954: 25
Gazzaniga, M. S.
1967: (225)
1970: 225
――――; Glass, A. V.; & Premack,
D., 1973: 232
Geis, J. E., 1970: 199
Geis, M. L., 1970: 199
Geith, A. *See* Sherman, D.
Gekoski, W. L. *See* Emerson, H. F.
Geldfein, M. *See* Whitehurst, G. J.
Gelman, R.
1969: 169
1972: 170
See also Goldin-Meadow, S.;
Shatz, M.
―――― & Shatz, M., in press: 256,
(276)
Gentner, D., 1975: 160
Geodakjan, I. M., 1976: 198
Gerstel, R. *See* van der Geest, T.
Geschwind, N., 1970: 225
Gesell, A.; Halverson, H. M.,
Thompson, H.; Ilg, F. L.;
Castner, B. M.; Armes, L. B.; &
Amatruda, C. S., 1940: 7
Gesell, A. & Thompson, H., 1934: 7
Gewirtz, J. L. & Boyd, E. F., 1976:
255
Gewirtz, J. L. & Ross, H. W., in Stone
et al., 1973: (297)
Giattino, J. & Hogan, J. G., 1975: 260
Gibson, E. J., 1969: 292
―――― & Levin, H., 1975: 327,
(328)
Gill, E. *See* Rumbaugh, D. M.
Ginsberg, E. H. & Abrahamson, A.
A., 1976: 198, 203
Ginsburg, H. & Koslowski, B., 1976:
52
Ginsburg, H. & Opper, S., 1969: 49

Ginsburg, S. & Partee, B., 1969: 65
Givón, T., 1973: 191
Glass, A. L. & Holyoak, K. J., 1974/
75: 163
Glass, A. V. *See* Gazzaniga, M. S.
Gleason, H. A., 1961: 26
Gleason, J. B., 1973: 273. *See also*
Berko, J. (previous name)
―――― & Weintraub, S., in
PRCLD, No. 10, 1975: (261)
Gleitman, H. *See* Gleitman, L.;
Newport, E.
Gleitman, L. R. *See also* Newport, E.;
Rozin, P.; Shipley, E.
―――― & Gleitman, H., 1970: 100
――――; Gleitman, H.; & Shipley,
E., 1972: 102
Glick, J., 1975: 52
―――― & Clarke-Stewart, K. A.,
forthc.: (256)
Glucksberg, S., in press: 181, (182).
See also Krauss, R. M.
―――― & Danks, J. H., 1975: (55)
――――; Hay, A.; & Danks, J. H.,
1976: 182, (178)
――――; Krauss, R. M.; & Higgins,
E. T., 1975: 279
――――; Krauss, R. M.; &
Weisberg, R., 1966; 276, (273)
Goffman, E., 1976: 250
Goldfein, M. *See* Whitehurst, G. J.
Goldin-Meadow, S. & Feldman, H.,
1975: 92
Goldin-Meadow, S.; Seligman, M. E.
P.; & Gelman, R., 1976: 138
Goldman, N. M., in Schank, 1975:
(60)
Goldman, S. R., 1976: 119
Goldstein, L. *See* Harnad, S. R.
Golinkoff, R. M., 1975: 144
Goodenough, W., 1965: (183)
Goodglass, H. & Blumstein, S., 1973:
226
Goodman, K., 1968: 327
Goodman, P., (247)
Goodnow, J. J.
forthc.: (54)
in Farnham-Diggory, 1972: (51)
Gordon, D. & Lakoff, G.
1971: 246

Huttenlocher, J.
  1968: 173, (174)
  1974: 137, 217
  in Kavanagh & Cutting, 1975: (90)
  _____ & Burke, D., 1976: 237
  _____; Eisenberg, K.; & Strauss,
    S., 1968: 109, (107)
  _____ & Strauss, S., 1968: 114, 205
  _____ & Weiner, S. L., 1971: 115,
    (109)
Huxley, R., 1970: 192, 272, (125, 127)
  _____ & Ingram, E., 1971: 13, 246,
    (73, 79, 110, 216, 235, 240)
Hymes, D.
  1964: 245
  1972: 246
  1974: 247
  in Huxley & Ingram, 1971: (246)
  See also Cazden, C. B.; Gumperz,
    J. J.

Inglis, S. See Wulbert, M.
Ingram, D.
  1971: 135
  1974(a): 98
  1974b: 314
  1974c: 314
  1975: 314
  1976(a): 316
  1976b: 316
  in press: 317
  See also Morehead, D. M.
Ingram, E., 1971: 216. See also
    Huxley, R.
Inhelder, B.
  1976: 226
  in Farnham-Diggory, 1972: (51)
  See also Piaget, J.
  _____ & Piaget, J., 1959/64: 148,
    168
  _____; Sinclair, H.; & Bovet, M.,
    1974: 170
Ironsmith, M. See Whitehurst, G. J.
Irwin, O. C.
  1946–48: 309, (286)
  1957: 310
  1972: 313
  See also Brodbeck, A. J.; Winitz, H.
  _____ & Chen, H. P.

  1943: 296
  1946: 309, (296)
Ivimey, G. P., 1975: 123

Jackendoff, R. S.
  1972: 36, (77)
  1976: 45
Jacobs, A. C. See Friedlander, B. Z.
Jacobs, R. A. & Rosenbaum, P. S.
  1968: 29
  1970: 29, (34)
Jacobson, A. See Zabeeh, F.
Jacobson, M., in Lenneberg &
    Lenneberg, vol. 1, 1975: (226)
Jakobovits, L. A. See Steinberg, D. D.
  _____ & Miron, M. S., 1967: 22,
    (12, 43, 44, 212, 214)
Jakobson, R.
  1941/68: 308, (286, 297, 298, 308,
    309, 310, 311, 315, 320, 321)
  1949/71: 309
  1962: (309, 310, 312)
  1962/71: 312, (133)
  1971: (309, 312)
  _____; Fant, G.; & Halle, M.,
    1952/63: 289, (311)
  _____ & Halle, M., 1956/71: 26,
    310
James, C. T.; Thompson, J. G.; &
    Baldwin, J. M., 1973; 107
James, L. B., 1976: 269
James, S. L. & Miller, J. F., 1973: 142
Jarvella, R. J. & Sinnott, J., 1972:
    110, 142
Jarvis, P. E., 1968: 268. See also
    Flavell, J. H.
Jaynes, J. See Harnad, S.
Jeffrey, W. See Bausano, M. K.
Jenkins, J. J. See Miyawaki, K.
  _____ & Palermo, D. S., 1964: 214
Jennings, K. H. See Cicourel, A. V.
Jennings, S. H. M. See Cicourel, A. V.
Jensen, P. See Blasdell, R.
Jesperson, O.
  1922/49: 25
  1924: 194
Jobse, J. See Snow, C. E.
Johansson, B. S. & Sjölin, B., 1975:
    144

Kiparsky, P.
    1975: 290
    in Bach & Harms, 1968: (33)
Kirshner, K. *See* Schacter, F. F.
Klahr, D., 1973: 149 (51)
_____ & Wallace, J. G.
    1972: 149
    1973: 170
    1976: 53, 149
Klatt, D. H. *See* Lieberman, P.;
    Stevens, K. N.
Klatt, M. *See* Menyuk, P.
Klatzky, R. L.; Clark, E. V.; &
    Macken, M., 1973: 176
Klein, E. *See* Keenan, Elinor O.
Klein, R. E. *See* Lasky, R. E.
Klemke, E. D. *See* Zabeeh, F.
Klenbort, I. *See* Anisfeld, M.
Klima, E. S.
    1964: 77
    in Kavanagh & Cutting, 1975: (90,
        289)
    See also Bellugi, U.
_____ & Bellugi, U.
    1966: 78, (78, 80)
    1972: 92, 229
    in press: 91
Klips, B. *See* Schacter, F. F.
Knapp, M. *See* Anisfeld, M.
Knast, J. F., 1976: 233
Knobloch, H. & Pasamanick, B.,
    1974: 7
Kobashigawa, 1968: (258)
Koenigsknecht, R. A., 1975: 321. *See
    also* Zlatin. M.
_____ & Friedman, P., 1976: 128
Koff, E. *See* Kramer, P. E.
Kogan, N., 1976: 150
Kohlberg, L.; Yaeger, J.; &
    Hjertholm, E., 1968: 271, (270)
Kolers, P., in Huey, 1968: (327)
Kopchick, G. A.; Romback, D. W.; &
    Smilovitz, R., 1975: 231
Kornfeld, J. R., 1971: 320, (317)
Koslowski, B. *See* Ginsburg, H.
Kosslyn, S. M. *See* Arabie, P.; Nelson,
    Keith, E.
Kotschi, Th., 1977: (250)
Kozoil, S. M., 1970: 122
Kramer, P. E., 1973: 103

_____; Koff, E.; & Luria, Z., 1972:
    116
Krames, L. *See* Alloway, T.; Pliner, P.
Krashen, S. *See* Curtiss, S.; Fromkin,
    V.
Krauss, R. M. & Glucksberg, S.
    1969: 277, (280)
    1977: 280
    See also Glucksberg, S.
Krauthamer, G. *See* Harnad, S. R.
Kriegsmann, E. *See* Wulbert, M.
Kruppe, B. *See* Weist, R. M.
Kuczaj, S. A., II
    1975: 161, (141)
    1976: 80
_____ & Maratsos, M. P.
    1974: (98)
    1975a: 98, 124
    1975b: 206, (178)
Kuhl, P. K. & Miller, J. D., 1975: 301
Kuhn, D. & Phelps, H., 1976: 145
Kummer, I. & Kummer, W., in Van
    Dijk, 1975: (248)
Kummer, W. *See* Kummer, I.
Kuroda, S.-Y., in Van Dijk, 1975:
    (248)
Kurylowicz, J., 1972: 191
Kypriotaki, L., 1974: 123

Labov, T. *See* Labov, W.
Labov, W.
    1972: 246
    1973a: 246
    1973(b): 163
_____ & Fanshel, D., in press: 250
_____ & Labov, T., 1974: 133
Lachman. *See* Mistler-Lachman
Ladefoged, P.
    1962: 291
    1975: 290
    See also MacNeilage, P.
Lahey, M., forthc.: 15. *See also*
    Bloom, L.
Laird, C. & Gorrell, R. M., 1971: 23
Lakoff, G.
    1965/70: 33, (36, 47)
    1968: 33, (36)
    1970: 34, (77)
    1971(a): 35, (141)

346   Author and Publication Index

Lakoff, G.—*Continued*
1971b: 35, 47
1972: (162)
1973: 162
1975: 248
in Cole & Morgan, 1975: (248)
in Parret, 1974: (27)
See also Gordon, D.
_____ & Ross, J. R., 1968: 33
Lakoff, R.
1970: 195
1972: 190, 246
Lamb, in Parret, 1974: (27)
Lambert, L. *See* Richardson, K.
Lambert, W. E. *See* Hebb, D. O.
Landau, B. S.
1976: 185
1977: (185)
Lane, H., 1976: 228.
_____ ; Boyes-Braem, P.; &
Bellugi, U., 1976: 90
Langacker, R. W.
1972: (44)
1973: 26
_____ & Munro, P., 1975: 108, (82)
Lange, S. & Larsson, K., 1973: 87
Langendoen, D. T.
1969: 34
1974: 247
in Aaronson & Rieber, 1975: (100)
See also Bever, T. G.; Fillmore, C.
J.; Katz, J. J.
_____ & Savin, H. B., 1971: 246
Langer, in Mussen, 1970: (50)
Larson, T., 1971: 231
Larsson, K. *See* Lange, S.
Lashley, K. S., in Blumenthal, 1970:
(56)
Lasky, R. E.; Syrdal-Lasky, A.; &
Klein, R. E., 1975: 305, (306)
Lass, R.
1976a: 294, (294, 323)
1976b: 290
Laurendeau, M. & Pinard, A., 1970:
203, 205, (207)
Laver, J., in Lyons, 1970a: (288)
Lawson, A. E., 1976: 53
Lawson, G. *See* Baron, J.
Learned, J. *See* Ames, L. B.
Leavitt, L. A. *See* Swoboda, P. J.

_____ ; Brown, J. W.; Morse, P.
A.; & Graham, F. K., 1976: 306
Lecours, A. R., in Lenneberg &
Lenneberg, 1975, vol. 1: (226)
Leech, G. N.
1969: 44, (189)
1974: 43, (43, 156, 183)
Lee-Painter, S. *See* Lewis, M.
Legum & Cronnell, 1973: (327)
Lehiste, I.
1970: 323
1976: 323
Lehrer, A.
1971: 43
1974: 45, 157
1976: (157)
Leibowitz, H. *See* Held, R.
Leiter, K. C. W. *See* Cicourel, A. V.
Lenneberg, Eric H.
1962: 227
1964a: 224, (224)
1964b: 12, (121, 220, 224, 257)
1964(c): 224
1967a: 224
1967b: 4, 42, 225, 291, (89, 92, 224,
276)
1971: 229
1974: 226
in Eliot, 1971: (4)
in Lenneberg & Lenneberg, 1975,
vol. 1: (226)
in Smith & Miller, 1966: (288)
in Stone et al., 1973: (297)
_____ & Lenneberg, Elizabeth
1975, vol. 1: 14, 226, 293, (10, 74,
144, 215, 248, 254, 315)
1975, vol. 2: 14, 226, 328, (315)
_____ ; Rebelsky, F. G.; & Nichols,
I. A., 1965: 296
Lenneberg, Elizabeth. *See* Lenneberg,
Eric H.
Lentin, A. *See* Gross, M.
Leonard, L. B., 1975: 218
_____ & Kaplan, L., 1976: 222
Leontiev, A. A., in Lenneberg &
Lenneberg, 1975, vol. 1: (293)
_____ & Luria, A. R., in Fodor,
1972: (235)
Leopold, W. F.
1939: 84, 132, (135)

McLagen, M. *See* Stark, R. E.
McNeill, D.
1966(a): 85, (114)
1966b: 85, (114)
1966(c): 9
1970a: 4, 159, (80, 85, 87, 139, 154, 213, 242)
1970(b): 10, 30, (50, 85, 139, 141, 143, 213, 242, 308)
1970c: 235, (139, 235)
1971(a): 139, (235)
1971b: (235)
1975(a): 241, (238)
forthc.: 238, (241)
in Aaronson & Rieber, 1975(b): (100)
in Connolly & Bruner, 1974: (252)
in Slobin, 1971a(c): (72, 215)
See also Miller, G. A.
_____ & McNeill, N. B., 1968: 85
_____; Yukawa, R.; & McNeill, N. B., 1971: 116
McNeill, N. B. *See* McNeill, D.
Meadow, K. P.
1968: 91
in press: 93
See also Schlesinger, H. P.
Medow, M. L. *See* Saltz, E.
Mehan, H. *See* Cicourel, A. V.
Mehler, J., 1971: 240
_____ & Bever, T. G.
1967: 169
1968: (169)
Meissner, J. A. & Apthorp, H., 1976: 280
Melton, A. W. & Martin, E., 1972: (157, 292)
Menn, L.
1971: 313
1975: (314)
Menyuk, P.
1964: 125
1968a: 320
1968b: 317
1969: 78
1971: 4, (308)
1974: 253, 321, (296, 323)
in Aaronson & Rieber, 1975: (237)
_____ & Anderson, S., 1969: 320

_____ & Klatt, M., 1975: 317
Merleau-Ponty, 1973: 8
Mervis, C. B.; Catlin, J.; & Rosch, E. H., 1975: 165. *See also* Rosch, E. H.
Messer, S., 1967: 317
Miller, C. A., in Aaronson & Rieber, 1975: (100)
Miller, G. A.
1951: 55
1962: 106
1965: 212
1967: (148)
1969: 148
1971: 148
1972: 157
1973: 23
1974: 59
See also Smith, F.
_____ & Chomsky, N., 1963: 29, 64
_____; Galanter, E.; & Pribram, K. H., 1960: 212
_____ & Johnson-Laird, P. N., 1976: 48, 62, (195)
_____ & McNeill, D., 1969: 56
_____ & Nicely, P. E., 1955: 291, (319, 321)
Miller, J. D. *See* Kuhl, P. K.
Miller, Jon F. *See* Chapman, R. S.; James, S. L.
Miller, P. *See* Bloom, L.
Miller, R., 1973: 152
Miller, Robert T. *See* Dore, J.
Miller, S. A., 1976: 171
Miller, W. R., 1964/73: 77
_____ & Ervin, S. M., 1964: 71, (71, 100)
Mills, B. *See* Wulbert, M.
Milner, E., in Whitaker & Whitaker, 1976: (226)
Minifie, F. D. *See* Eilers, R. E.
_____; Hixon, T. J.; & Williams, F., 1973: 292
Minsky, M., 1968: 56
Miron, M. S. *See* Jakobovits, L. A.; Osgood, C. A.
Mischler, E. G., 1975: 266
Mistler-Lachman & Lachman, 1974: (230)

Newell, A., in Farnham-Diggory,
    1972: (51)
Newnham, R., 1971: 83
Newport, E. L. & Gleitman, H., 1976:
    223
Newport, E. L.; Gleitman, H.; &
    Gleitman, L., in press: 264, (220)
Newport, E. L.; Gleitman, L.; &
    Gleitman, H., in PRCLD, No. 10,
    1975: (261)
Nicely, P. E. See Miller, G. A.
Nicholich, L., 1975: 222, 241
Nichols, I. A. See Lenneberg, E. H.
Nida, E. A., 1975: 157
_____; Louw, J.; & Smith, R. B.,
    in press: 157
Nilsen, D. L. F., 1973: 40
Nooteboom, S. See Cohen, A.
Norman, D. A., 1976: 61. See also
    Bobrow, D. G.; Lindsay, P. H.
_____ & Rumelhart, D. E., 1975:
    60, (38, 60, 157, 160)
Nottebohm, F., in Lenneberg &
    Lenneberg, vol. 1, 1975: (226,
    293)
Nurss, J. R. & Day, D. E., 1971: 97
Nussbaum, N. J. & Naremore, R. C.,
    1975: 197
Nygren, C., 1972: 141

O'Brien, R., 1972: (35, 39)
O'Conner, J. D., 1974: 290
Oden, S. L. See Asher, S. R.; Austin,
    J. L.
Ogden, C. K. & Richards, I. A., 1938;
    55
O'Keefe, L. See Webb, R. A.
Oksaar, E., 1974: (13)
Oldfield, R. C. & Marshall, J. C.,
    1968: 22, (64, 85, 96, 152, 212,
    213, 268)
Oléron, P., in press: 6
Oliveri, M. See Webb, R. A.
Oller, D. K., 1974: 314. See also
    Eilers, R. E.
_____; Wieman, L. A.; Doyle, W.
    J.; & Ross, C., 1976: 298
Olmsted, D. L.
    1966: 319, (315)

1971: 313
1974: (313)
Olney, R. L. & Scholnick, E. K., 1976:
    298
Olson, C. L. See Macnamara, J.
Olson, D. R.
    1970: 50, 56, (276)
    in Eliot & Salkind, 1975: (204)
    See also Ford, W.
_____ & Filby, N., 1972: 107
Olson, G. M., 1973: 235
Olver, R. R. See Bruner, J. S.
O'Rourke, J. P., 1974: 153
Ortiz, A. & Zierer, E., 1968: 64
Osgood, C. E.
    1966: (90)
    1971: 277 (276)
    See also Snider, J. G.
_____ ; May, W. H.; & Miron,
    1975: (161)
_____; Suci, G. J.; &
    Tannenbaum, P. H., 1957: 161
Osherson, D. N.
    1974: 170, (148)
    1976: 145
_____ & Wasow, T., 1976: 231
Osser, H. See Endler, N. S.

Pachella, in Kantowitz, 1974: (58)
Palermo, D. S.
    1970: 10
    1971b: 151
    1973: 180
    1974: 181
    1975: 322
    in Slobin, 1971a(a): (72, 215)
    See also Holland, V. M.; Jenkins, J.
        J.; Weimar, W.; Wilcox, S.
_____ & Eberhart, V. L.
    1968: 121, (122)
    1971: 122, (72)
_____ & Molfese, D. L., 1972: 10
Palmer, F. R.
    1965/74: 195, (194)
    1976: 43, (43)
Palmer, H. E. & Blanford, F. G.,
    1969: 26
Papert, S., in Dalenoort, 1973: (58)
Parisi, D., 1974: 143. See also
    Antinucci, F.

Pressner, U. S. *See* Reich, P. A.
Preston, M. S. *See* Kewley-Port, D.
Pribram, K. H. *See* Miller, G. A.
Pride, J. B. & Holmes, J., 1972: (246)
Prideaux, G. D., 1976: 80
Prior, A. N.
  1957: (194)
  1967: (194)
  1968a: 194
  1968b: (194)
Průcha, J.
  1974: 87
  1976: 14, (88, 198, 260)
Pufall, P. B. & Shaw, R. E., 1973: 203
Pylyshyn, Z. W.
  1972: 100, (101)
  1973: 101

Quillian, M. R., in Minsky, 1968: (56, 163). *See also* Collins, A. M.

Rabinovitch, M. S. *See* Trehub, S. E.
Rahmy, M. *See* Droz, R.
Ramer, A. L. H., 1976: 75. *See also* Dore, J.
_____ & Rees, N. S., 1973: 122
Ramge, H., in press: 256
Rapaport, Amnon. *See* Fillenbaum, S.
Rapoport, Anatol, 1975: 47
Raphael, B., 1976: 61
Raphael, L., in Aaronson & Rieber, 1975: (237)
Rashman, S. *See* Rodgon, M. M.
Razran, G., 1973: 226
Read, C. A., 1971: 312
Rebelsky, F. G. *See also* Lenneberg, E. H.
_____ & Hanks, C., 1971: 258
_____; Starr, R. H.; & Luria, Z., 1967: 9
Reber, A. & Scarborough, D., 1977: 328
Reddy, D. R., 1975: 293
Reed, C., 1971: 12, (10, 47)
Rees, N. S., 1975: 222. *See also* Ramer, A. L. H.

Reese, H. W.
  1971-76, vols. 6-11: 50
  1971, vol. 6: (221)
  1972, vol. 7: (50, 170)
  1974, vol. 9: (215)
  1976, vol. 11: (172, 255)
  See also Lipsitt, L. P.
_____ & Lipsitt, L. P., 1970: (10)
Reibel, D. A. & Schane, S. A., 1969: 29, (78)
Reich, P. A., 1976: 134
_____; Rice, K. A.; & Pressner, U. S., 1974: 206
Reichenbach, H., 1947: 45, (189)
Reichert, D. *See* Dale, E.
Reichle, J. E.; Longhurst, T. M.; & Stepanich, L., 1976: 263
Reitman, W., in Dalenoort, 1973: (58)
Rescher, N. & Urquhart, A., 1971: 195
Restle, F.; Shiffrin, R. M.; Castellan, N. J.; Lindman, H. R.; & Pisoni, D. B., 1975: 60, 293
Rheingold, H. L., in Stone et al, 1973: (297)
Rice, K. *See* Reich, P. A.
Richards, I. A. *See* Ogden, C. K.
Richards, M. P. M.
  1974: (10, 252)
  in Connolly & Bruner, 1974: (252)
Richardson, K.; Calnan, M.; Essen, J.; & Lambert, L., 1976: 128
Richardson, T., 1975: 233
Rieber, R., 1975: 237. *See also* Aaronson, D. R.
Riegel, K. F.
  1965: (78, 84)
  1970: 125
  1972: 50
  1975: 153, 237
_____ & Rosenwald, G. C., 1975: 52, 61, (153, 237, 249, 255)
Rieger, C. J., III, in Schank, 1975: (60)
Riesbeck, C. K., in Schank, 1975: (60)
Rigler, D. *See* Curtiss, S.; Fromkin, V.
Rigler, M. *See* Curtiss, S.; Fromkin, V.

Sanders, K. *See* Schachter, F. F.
Santa, J. L. *See* Neimark, E. O.
Sapir, E., 1921: 25
Saporta, S., 1961: 22, (9, 12, 79, 121, 291, 310)
Saumjan, in Parret, 1974: (27)
Savić, S., 1975: 266
Savin, H., 1973: (45). *See also* Langendoen, D. T.
Scanlan, D. *See* van Duyne, H. J.
Scarborough, D. *See* Reber, A.
Schachter, F. F.; Kirshner, K.; Klips, B., Friedricks, M.; & Sanders, K., 1974: 273
Schaeffer, B.; Lewis, J. A.; & Van Decar, A., 1971: 154
Schaerlaekens, A. M., 1973: 87
Schane, S. A., 1973: 289, (289). *See also* Reibel, D. A.
Schank, R. C.
    1972: 158, (38)
    1975: 60
_____ & Colby, K. M., 1973: 57
Schecter, D. E.; Symonds, M.; & Bernstein, I., 1955: 196
Schiefelbusch, R. L., in press: 15. *See also* Ruder, K. F.
_____ & Lloyd, L., 1974: 14, (52, 74, 98, 136, 232, 241, 242, 253, 304, 321)
Schieffelin, B. B. *See* Keenan, Elinor O.
Schlesinger, H. S. & Meadow, K. P., 1972: 92
Schlesinger, I. M.
    1967: (215)
    1969: 89
    1971a(a): 73, (72, 72, 215)
    1971(b): 73
    1974: 74, (234)
    1975: 74, 215
Schmerling, S.
    1976: 323
    in Cole & Morgan, 1975: (248)
Schmidt, C., 1974: 163
Schnitzer, M. L., 1976: 290
Scholnick, E. K. *See also* Olney, R. L.
_____ & Adams, M. J., 1973: 111
Scholz, K. W. *See* Potts, G. R.

Schrier, A. & Stollnitz, F., 1971: (229)
Schultz, F., in Bar-Adon & Leopold, 1971: (288)
Schultz, T. P. & Pilon, R., 1973: 102
Schweller, K. G.; Brewer, W. F.; & Dahl, D. A., 1976: 249
Schwenk, M. A. & Danks, J. H., 1974: 127, 278
Scollon, R., 1976: 222, 263
Searle, J. R.
    1969: 245, (243)
    1971: 46
    1975: 248
    1976a: (248)
    1976b: 250
    in Cole & Morgan, 1975: (248)
Sebeok, T. A.
    1963-76, vols. 1-14: 26
    1966, vol. 3: (29, 44, 82)
    1974, vol. 12: (10, 46, 59, 90, 92, 110, 234, 239, 248, 293)
Seely, P. B. *See* Friedman, W. J.; Mahoney, G.
Segal, E. R., 1975: 215
Seibert, J. *See* Markman, E. M.
Seitz, S. & Stewart, C., 1975: 222, 262
Selby, S., 1972: 122
Seligman, M. E. P. *See* Goldin-Meadow, S.
Shafto, M., 1973: 40
Shankweiler, D. *See* Liberman, A. M.; Studdert-Kennedy, M.
Shannon, C. E. & Weaver, W., 1949: (55)
Shantz, C. A. *See* Griffiths, J. A.
Sharp, D. & Cole, M., 1972: 151
Shatz, M.
    1975a: 254, (256, 265)
    in PRCLD, vol. 10, 1975b: (261)
    See also Gelman, R.
_____ & Gelman, R.
    1973: 273, (276)
    in press: 276, (256)
Shaw, in Dalenoort, 1973: (58)
Sheldon, A., 1974: 118
Shepard, R. N.; Romney, A. K.; & Nerlove, S. B., 1972: 159
Sherman, D. & Geith, A., 1967: 319
Sherman, J. A., 1971: 221
Sherzer, J. *See* Bauman, R.

356   Author and Publication Index

Van Buren, P. *See* Allen, J. P.;
Clark, R.
Van Decar, A. *See* Schaeffer, B.
van der Geest, T., 1974: 217
————; Gerstel, R.; Appel, R.; &
Tervoort, B. T., 1973: 260
Van Dijk, T. A., 1975: 248, (196)
van Duyne, H. J. & Scanlan, D., 1976:
269
Vasta, R. *See* Whitehurst, G. J.
Vaughn, B. E. *See* Masangkay, Z. S.
Velten, H. V., 1943: 132, 308
Verbrugge, R. *See* Miyawaki, K.
Verschueren, J., 1976: 249
Vigorito, J. *See* Eimas, P. D.
Vinogradova, O. *See* Luria, A. R.
Voegelin, C. F. & Voegelin, F. M.,
1976: 83
Voegelin, F. M. *See* Voegelin, C. F.
Vogel, S. A., 1975: 5
Volterra, V. *See* Bates, E.
von Glasersfeld, E. C. *See* Rumbaugh,
D. M.
von Raffler-Engel, W.
1965/73(a): 324
1965/73(b): 325
1976: 6
forthc.: 15, (219)
Vorster, J. *See* Snow, C. E.
Vygotsky, L. S.
1934/62: 148, 234, 271, (235, 270,
271, 272)
in Adams, 1972: (13, 23)

Waldron, R. A., 1971: 45
Wales, R. *See* Donaldson, M.;
Lyons, J.
———— & Campbell, R., 1970: 176
————; Garman, M. A. G.; &
Griffiths, P. D., 1976: 182
———— & Walker, E., 1976: 62,
(182)
Walker, E. *See* Wales, R.
Wall, C., 1974: 80
Wall, R., 1972: 65
Wallace, A. F. C. & Atkins, J., 1960:
(183)
Wallace, J. G. *See* Klahr, D.

Walter, D. O., in Harnad et al., 1976:
(226)
Wang, W. S.-Y., in press: 290
Wanner, E., 1974: 30
Warden, D. A., 1976: 275
Warnock, E. H. *See* Collins, A.
Waryas, C. L., 1973: 127
Wasow, T. *See* Osherson, D. N.
Wasz-Hoeckert, O., et al., 1968: 296
Waters, R. S. & Wilson, W. A., Jr.,
1976: 302
Waterson, N.
1970: 312
1971a: 312, (315)
1971b: 312
Wathen-Dunn, 1967: 291, (291)
Watt, W. C., 1970: 100, (112)
Wearing, A. J., 1970: 106
Webb, P. A. & Abrahamson, A. A.,
1976: 207
Webb, R. A.; Oliveri, M. E.; &
O'Keeffe, L., 1974: 181
Weeks, T. E., in PRCLD, vol. 5, 1973:
(259). *See also* Ferguson, C. A.
Weimer, W. B. & Palermo, D. S.,
1974: 59, (59)
Weiner, F. F. & Bernthal, J., in Singh,
1976b: (316)
Weiner, P. S., 1967: 320
Weiner, S., 1974: 181
Weinreich, U.
1966/72: 44, (141)
in Greenberg, 1966b: 190, (42)
Weintraub, S. *See* Gleason, J. B.
Weir, R.
1962: 311
in Smith & Miller, 1966: (288)
Weisberg, R. *See* Glucksberg, S.
Weist, R. M. & Kruppe, B., 1977: 264
Weksel, W. *See* Bever, T. G.
Welkowitz, J.; Cariffe, G.; &
Feldstein, S., 1976: 275
Welsh, C. A. *See* Slobin, D. I.
Werner, H. & Kaplan, B., 1963: 131,
(50, 220)
Wetstone, H. S. & Friedlander, B. Z.,
1973: 103. *See also* Friedlander,
B. Z.

Serials Index

Advances in Child Development and
    Behavior
    Reese, H. W. (Ed.): 50, (50, 170,
    172, 215, 221, 255)
    Lipsitt, L. P. & Reese, H. W.
    (Eds.): (50, 221)
Anthropological Linguist: 20
Attention and Performance: 56

Brain and Language: 20

Child Development: 18
*Child Development Abstracts and
    Bibliography:* 16
Cognition: 19
Cognitive Psychology: 19
Cognitive Theory
    Restle, F.; Shiffrin, R. M.;
    Castellan, N. J.; Lindman, H. R.;
    & Pisoni, D. B. (Eds.): 60, 293
Contemporary Psychology: 16
Current Issues in Linguistic Theory: 23
Current Trends in Linguistics
    Sebeok, T. A. (Ed.): 26, (10, 29, 44,
    46, 59, 82, 90, 92, 110, 234, 239,
    248, 293)

Developing Child, The
    Bruner, J. S.; Cole, M.; & Lloyd, B.
    (Eds.): 53, (6, 54)
Developmental Psychology: 18
Dissertation Abstracts International:
    16

*ERIC Clearinghouse on Languages
    and Linguistics:* 16, (18)

Foundations of Language: 19

*Handbook of Learning and Cognitive
    Processes*
    Estes, W. K. (Ed.): 60, (294, 295)
Handbook of Perception
    Carterette, E. & Friedman, M. P.
    (Eds.): 24, 294, (11, 226)
Handbook of Social Psychology, The
    Lindzey, G. & Aronson, E. (Eds.):
    (56)
Human Development: 18

*International Journal of
    Psycholinguistics:* 19

Journal of Child Language: 18
Journal of Cognitive Science: 20
Journal of Communication: 276
*Journal of Experimental Child
    Psychology:* 18
Journal of Linguistics: 19
Journal of Phonetics: 289
Journal of Pragmatics: 250
Journal of Psycholinguistic Research:
    19
*Journal of Speech and Hearing
    Research:* 20
*Journal of Verbal Learning and Verbal
    Behavior:* 19

Language: 19
*Language and Language Behavior
    Abstracts:* 16
Language and Speech: 20
Language in Society: 20
Language, Society and the Child: 257
Lingua: 19
Linguistic Analysis: 19
Linguistic Inquiry: 19
Linguistic Reporter, The: 17

Subject Index

Scaling and similarities data. *See* Cluster analysis; Multidimensional scaling

Semantic markers, 43–45

Semantics
linguistics, 22–23, 32–48, 59, 82, 156, 157, 162, 163, 175, 189–191, 194–196, 199, 249, 250. *See also* Componential analysis; Lexical decomposition; Lexicon; Linguistics; Semantic markers; Sentence and verb form meaning
philosophy and logic, 22–23, 42, 45–48, 162, 164, 183, 184, 194–196, 202, 245, 249, 250, 265. *See also* Philosophy and logic; Presupposition and entailment
psychology (semantic or long-term memory), 22–24, 55–63, 147–149, 157–159, 161–164, 189, 213, 216, 224, 226

Sensorimotor period, 131, 239–242. *See also* Piagetian theory

Sentence and verb form meaning, 57–63, 107, 194–196, 265

Seriation, 168, 169, 171. *See also* Piagetian theory

Sign language, 13, 23, 89–92, 228, 232, 288. *See also* Chimpanzee language learning
therapeutic applications, 231–233

Situational and social context, 107, 190–192, 195, 243, 246–248, 265, 277, 280

Sociolinguistics, 4, 5, 13, 20, 23, 27, 53, 56, 97, 245, 246–248, 250, 251, 265, 281

Soviet research, 224, 226, 250

Spatial concept development (Piagetian), 203–205, 207. *See also* Piagetian theory

Spatial terms, 39, 59, 106, 189–191, 199, 208. *See also* Dimensional adjectives

Speech acts, 77, 243, 245, 248–250, 265

Speech perception, 22, 24, 55, 56, 57, 60, 63, 285–289, 291–295, 299, 300, 322–324, 327. *See also* Categorical perception of speech

Speech production, 22, 24, 55, 63, 225, 285–289, 291–294, 313, 321, 323

Strategies, 45, 151, 171, 173, 204

Stratificational grammar, 199

Strawson, P. F., 47

Subject-of relation, 83, 90, 105–108, 191

Symbolic function (Piaget), 49, 131, 234, 239–242. *See also* Piagetian theory

Symbolic or semiotic function (other), 50, 51, 54, 55, 59, 131, 238. *See also* Origin and evolution of language

Syntax, 22–41, 47, 48, 59, 64–66, 77, 82, 83, 89–91, 105, 106, 156, 194–196. *See also* Augmented transition network grammar; Linguistics; Questions; *other specific topics*

Temporal concepts and language, 44–48, 50, 189–191, 194–196, 199, 200, 202, 208

Tense and aspect. *See* Morphology; Sentence and verb form meaning; Syntax; Temporal concepts and language

Theme and focus, 35, 37–39, 41, 107

Three-term series problems, 59, 173–174

Topic and comment, 83, 90, 191

Training effects on cognitive performance, 169–172, 181

Transformational grammar. *See* Chomsky; Linguistics; *specific topics*

Transitive inference, 53, 168, 170, 171, 173, 174. *See also* Piagetian theory

Typicality (semantic). *See* Fuzzy concepts

Universals. *See* Linguistic Universals

CHILD LANGUAGE PUBLICATIONS

† Topic that has a related entry in the *Background Publications* section of the index.

† Topic that has a related entry in the *Background Publications* section of the index.

---

† Topic that has a related entry in the *Background Publications* section of the index.

† Topic that has a related entry in the *Background Publications* section of the index.

† Topic that has a related entry in the *Background Publications* section of the index.

† Topic that has a related entry in the *Background Publications* section of the index.

Play (role in language development),
54, 131, 253, 254
Plurals, 72, 96–98, 120–124, 128, 216,
219. See also Inflectional
morphology
†Polar pairs (antonyms), 161, 166,
173–182, 186, 187, 200, 203,
205–208. See also Features
(linguistic); Markedness
Polish, 86
Polite forms and honorifics, 192, 246,
255. See also Insults; Pragmatics
Polynesian languages. See Hawaiian;
Lun Bawang; Samoan
†Possessive constructions or meanings,
72, 134, 138, 156, 160. See also
Inflectional morphology
Pragmatic factor as variable. See
Predictability
†Pragmatics, 14, 81, 88, 123, 127, 145,
192, 234, 252, 255, 260, 261, 278.
See also Communicative
competence; Conversational
principles and roles; Deixis;
Discourse; Function of language;
Polite forms and honorifics;
Predictability as stimulus
variable; Speech acts; Situational
and social context;
Sociolinguistics
Precursors of language, 144, 252–255
Predicate nominative structure, 88
Predictability as stimulus variable
(pragmatic factor), 105, 106, 108,
110–113, 123
Prelinguistic period (0–12 months), 51,
52, 84, 131, 132, 135, 239–241,
251–257, 260, 264, 286, 287,
296–298, 303, 309, 315, 316, 324.
See also Periods of development
(overviews)
0–6 months, 258, 299, 300, 304–307
6–12 months (babbling period), 75,
133, 134, 137, 138, 144, 217, 222,
236, 242, 259, 308, 310, 312, 313
†Preoperational period and language.
See Communicative egocentrism;

Piagetian theory; Symbolic
function
†Prepositions, 114, 115, 128, 182, 202,
205–208. See also Case grammar;
Dative transformation; Indirect-
object-of
Preschool period (ages 3;0–6;0), 69, 74,
77–80, 84, 88, 95–97, 99, 102,
109–113, 115, 116, 118, 121–123,
125–128, 141–144, 151, 152, 154,
160, 161, 165, 169, 176–179, 181,
182, 185, 186, 192, 193, 196–198,
200–204, 206, 207, 219, 220, 236,
239–241, 252, 256, 257, 260, 261,
263, 266, 269, 271–278, 310, 312,
316–318, 320, 325, 328. See also
Periods of development
(overviews)
ages 3;0–4;0, 73, 81, 86, 92, 98, 103,
132, 187, 216, 218, 221, 255, 258,
264, 276, 308, 321
ages 4;0–6;0, 10, 52, 53, 101, 104,
108, 114, 117, 119, 120, 145, 150,
153, 155, 159, 168, 170, 171, 174,
175, 184, 205, 237, 262, 270, 271,
279, 280, 313, 319
†Presupposition and inference, 255.
See also Philosophy and logic
Private speech, 268–273
Probability as variable. See
Predictability as stimulus variable
Processes in language learning. See
Biological aspects; Competence
vs. performance; Cognition and
language relationship; Imitation;
Learning of language; Length
constraint; Mother-child linguistic
interaction; Nativism; Piagetian
theory; Pragmatics; Reduction
transformation; Rote learning;
Rule learning; Strategies;
Training studies; Transitional
phenomena
Promise, 114, 118, 119
Pronominalization, 114, 127. See also
Pronouns; Relativization

† Topic that has a related entry in the *Background Publications* section of the index.

†Pronouns, 114, 115, 127, 128, 144
  impersonal, 81, 127, 128
  personal, 79, 81, 127, 134, 160, 192,
    193, 206, 272
  relative, 116, 128
Proper nouns. *See* Names

†Quantifiers, 18
Question-answering tasks, 103, 109,
  113, 118, 141, 145, 153, 186, 196,
  200, 201
†Questions (interrogatives), 69, 77–80,
  109, 125, 252, 254, 256, 259,
  261–267, 270
  wh-questions, 72, 77–79, 200, 201,
    230, 231, 266
  yes/no questions, 77, 88. *See also*
    Tag questions

†Rationalist explanations of language
  learning, 213. *See also* Nativism;
  Rule induction; Transformational
  grammar account of syntax
  acquisition
Reaction time or latency tasks, 123,
  125, 149, 155, 177
Reading, 5, 14, 56, 58, 60, 62, 227,
  325, 327, 328
Reading skill as variable, 119, 128
Receptive language in infants. *See*
  Comprehension below age two
Reduced forms, 126, 128
Reduction in imitation, 220, 257, 264
Reduction transformation, 72, 74
Reduplication, 75, 309, 314
Referential speech, 275–281
Regulative function of speech, 268–270
Reinforcement (role in language
  learning), 215, 220–222
†Relational semantic components,
  160, 184, 185, 200–202
Relational words, 166–187, 200–208
†Relativization and relative clauses,
  77, 79, 81, 116, 118, 128. *See also*
  Embeddedness;
  Pronominalization

Repetition (role in language learning),
  222, 223, 263. *See also* Mother-
  child linguistic interaction
Requests. *See* Directives
Research before 1920, 9, 12, 17, 56,
  58, 61, 86, 132, 133, 139, 288, 324
Retardation, 14, 53, 97, 117, 153, 197,
  232, 233, 262, 313. *See also*
  Deficiency in language
†Reversibility of relations (relationship
  to language), 111, 184–186. *See
  also* Piagetian theory
Reversibility as stimulus variable, 105,
  108–113, 115, 119, 142
Rote learning, 75, 124, 215, 219, 221
Rule induction (nativist view),
  214–216, 220
Rule learning (empiricist view), 73, 75,
  217–219, 121–124
Russian, 14, 84, 86, 88, 132, 133, 324

Salience as stimulus variable, 107, 155,
  177, 178, 201
Same/different, 167, 180–182
Samoan, 75, 85, 86, 88, 126, 192, 249,
  258, 259
School-age period (ages 6;0–11;0), 10,
  52, 80, 95, 101, 102, 108–117, 119,
  121–127, 141, 142, 150–155, 160,
  165, 168, 174, 179, 184–186, 192,
  193, 196, 197, 202–205, 219, 237,
  239–241, 251, 252, 269, 270, 273,
  275, 277–281, 310, 313,
  315–317, 319, 325. *See also*
  Periods of development
  (overviews)
  ages 6;0–8;0, 53, 78, 88, 92, 97, 99,
    103, 104, 120, 128, 143–145, 161,
    167, 169, 170, 175, 177, 178, 180,
    181, 198, 200, 201, 206, 207, 216,
    223, 262, 267, 271, 272, 276, 312,
    320, 322, 328
  ages 8;0–11;0, 232, 258.
Second-language learning, 17, 223, 250
Segmentation, 72, 80, 103, 126, 236,
  237, 325, 328

† Topic that has a related entry in the *Background Publications* section of the index.

† Topic that has a related entry in the *Background Publications* section of the index.

† Topic that has a related entry in the *Background Publications* section of the index.

† Topic that has a related entry in the *Background Publications* section of the index.

† Topic that has a related entry in the *Background Publications* section of the index.